Curriculum
for Young
Children

An Introduction

Curriculum for Young Children

An Introduction

Eve-Marie Arce, EdD

with

Susan B. Ferguson, MS

WADSWORTH
CENGAGE Learning™

Africa • Australia • Canada • Denmark • Japan • Mexico • New Zealand • Philippines Puerto Rico • Singapore • Spain • United Kingdom • United States

WADSWORTH
CENGAGE Learning™

Curriculum for Young Children:
An Introduction, 2e
Eve-Marie Arce

Publisher: Linda Schreiber-Ganster

Acquisitions Editor: Mark Kerr

Development Editor: Joshua Taylor

Editorial Assistant: Greta Lindquist

Technology Project Manager: Elizabeth Momb

Marketing Manager: Kara Kindstrom

Marketing Communications Manager:
Heather Baxley

Project Manager, Editorial Production:
Matt Ballantyne

Art Director: Jennifer Wahi

Print Buyer: Becky Cross

Permissions Editor, Text: Don Schlotman

Production Service: PreMediaGlobal

Cover Designer: CMB Design Partners

Cover Image: Getty Images

Compositor: PreMediaGlobal

For product information and technology assistance, contact us at
Cengage Learning Customer & Sales Support, 1-800-354-9706

For permission to use material from this text or product,
submit all requests online at **cengage.com/permissions**
Further permissions questions can be emailed to
permissionrequest@cengage.com

Library of Congress Control Number: 2011937595

ISBN-13: 978-1-111-83799-0

ISBN-10: 1-111-83799-6

Wadsworth
20 Davis Drive
Belmont, CA 94002
USA

Cengage Learning is a leading provider of customized learning solutions with office locations around the globe, including Singapore, the United Kingdom, Australia, Mexico, Brazil, and Japan. Locate your local office at **international. cengage.com/region**

Cengage Learning products are represented in Canada by Nelson Education, Ltd.

For your course and learning solutions, visit **academic.cengage.com**

Purchase any of our products at your local college store or at our preferred online store **www.cengagebrain.com**

Printed in the United States of America
1 2 3 4 5 6 7 13 12 11

Contents

Preface

What This Book Is About

Curriculum for Young Children: An Introduction is a sensible beginning guide to early childhood curriculum planning. Simply, this book offers entry-level students and practitioners a straight-forward and useful understanding of the *how* of curriculum.

The profession of early childhood education welcomes students and teachers with a great range of academic readiness and professional preparation into the classroom. For this reason, this book was designed in a way that allows students to develop their curriculum planning skills without prerequisite coursework. Students will be able to immediately apply the information as they progress through the chapters. Each chapter builds skills with concrete strategies to understand and plan meaningful experiences that meet children's needs and interests. Useful activities illustrate the curriculum planning content. The activities are referenced with callouts embedded throughout the chapters. The Curriculum Activity Guide callouts correspond with the complete documentation in Appendix D. The figures in every chapter have been designed to summarize significant points and deliver concepts for comprehension and practical use. The textbook embraces multiple theories and methods offering strategies for planning and extending suitable experiences for young children.

New Features in the Revised Edition

Enhancements for students in this revised edition include relevant updates and up-to-date terms. The basic format and foundational knowledge about early childhood curriculum, as it was in the first edition, remains apparent. Each chapters opens with a story or situation. *Picture This . . .* invites students into the content of the chapter. New in this revised edition is the inclusion of the National Association for the Education of Young Children (NAEYC). The standards related to the chapter content are identified at the beginning of each chapter and inserted throughout book. Students will build skills to support quality and intentional planning by referencing the standards throughout the chapters and with the chapter and page correlation chart provided on the inside front and back covers.

Students will be able to link to video clips that clarify and elaborate information in the chapters. Relevant questions prepared for students relate to the specific video cases. The Curriculum Activity Guides (CAGs) have been minimally yet importantly modified. The guides now include a space for standards met and for comments. There are 50 updated Curriculum Activity Guides included with a trimmed format. The templates for the guides and additional completed CAGs are accessible at the companion website. Students will have opportunities to develop and modify the activities to meet their own program curriculum guidelines. A new appendix has been added that addresses the inclusion of standards, with examples for different states.

Acknowledgements—Eve-Marie

Any project, especially writing a textbook, is a collaboration of many: students willing to listen; program administrators supporting and using your ideas; and colleagues responding with comments and ideas. The revision of this textbook is the consequence of a professional collaboration. Susan Baron Ferguson promoted efforts to keep this book in the hands of early childhood education students. We crafted the revision, remaining dedicated to the principles of quality early learning experiences and excellence in teacher preparation. We generated a revised textbook that will continue to engage students and introduce them to what we mutually believe is essential to understanding curriculum planning for young children.

I wish to give considerable recognition to a friend and a professional colleague. Laurie Barton Koukol's ideas contributed to the earliest versions of the book. I appreciate the contributions of another long-standing colleague, Kathy Barry. Her professional insight and vivid understanding of appropriate curriculum are apparent throughout the original edition and especially in the Curriculum Activity Guides. I also remain appreciative of the professionals at the Shasta College Early Childhood Education Center. They enhanced the design of the Curriculum Activity Guides with their application and evaluation. And none the less important, my sincere gratitude goes to the students whose comments and questions continuously motivate me to contemplate more effective ways to present curriculum planning.

Finally, with love and appreciation, I recognize the influence of my family: my parents, for giving me a blend of culture and religion; my daughters, Cecily and Olivia, for continuously enlightening my perspective about child development and parenting; the memory of their father who contributed to every aspect of the first edition; my grandsons who give me more joy than ever imagined; and my husband, Henry Bose; his high regard for the professional contribution of women encouraged me to persist in my work as an early childhood educator.

Eve-Marie
La Selva Beach, California

Acknowledgements—Susan

I truly appreciate Eve-Marie's initial vision and determination to craft this textbook aimed at students and teachers needing a practical, informative guide to assist them in creating appropriate curriculum in their classrooms. My students have shared, after using the textbook, that they now feel successful and inspired, and that appropriate curriculum planning is a genuinely professional endeavor. I am so proud to have been in collaboration with her for the revised edition. It reflects our commitment to intentional practice and to high-quality early childhood education.

I wish to acknowledge and thank my husband, Steven, for his ever-constant loving support and encouragement in all that I do; my amazing daughter, Elizabeth, whose very existence has helped define me as a person; my supportive and empathizing colleagues; and my friends who always lend their kind support no matter what is happening in our busy lives.

Susan
San Diego, California

Curriculum
for Young Children

As Valuable and As Much Fun As You Make It!

© Cengage Learning 2013

Picture This . . .

You have wanted to be a teacher as long as you can remember. You are excited, a little scared, and very curious as you walk toward the children's program where you have been assigned to observe. You walk into the lobby, check in with the director, and take a seat in the observation area. You are able to see the arrangement in the main activity room that is set up for children ages three, four, and five. It is early in the morning, and children are arriving. You can see an adult, probably a teacher, greeting the children individually as they arrive. A few of the children linger with the teacher, while others move throughout the classroom stopping in various areas.

A little kitchen area is set up in one corner of the room. Sun is streaming through a window, providing natural light on the table with pretend fruits and vegetables. The furniture replicates a miniature house, complete with fresh flowers. Children are trying on clothing, sitting on blocks that look like a bed. To the right of this area, four children are pulling blocks from the shelves, which are marked with block shapes. A sign with six happy faces and the words *six friends* marks the entrance to the block area. Miniature cars and trucks, animals, and pretend people wait on the shelves.

Although families are still arriving with their preschoolers, you turn to the opposite side of the classroom and notice that children are already engaged in activities. There are four children at a table. They are busy with puzzles and locking blocks. In another area you see a child with earphones. He is turning the pages of a picture book. You look across the room and see two girls. One is dipping a brush into a cup of blue paint. Next to the art area, you notice a table covered with butcher paper. An adult is sitting at the table with three children. Each child has a small bowl. They are measuring flour. The adult is directing the children's attention to a large chart that looks like a recipe.

You look down at the notebook on your lap and then scan the classroom once more. You begin wondering who organized all of these activities. Who decided what materials would be placed on the tables? How can anyone make so many decisions? How did they know what is best for children? You look one more time at the children and adults in the activity room and again wonder if you will be able to make so many decisions about children's activities.

GUIDE TO READING CHAPTER 1

Chapter Outline

Learning Objectives

After reading this chapter, you will be able to:

1. Identify the early childhood education teacher.
2. Define the word *curriculum.*
3. Recognize the value and benefits of curriculum planning.
4. Determine the use of technology to plan curriculum.
5. Identify the general principles that shape early childhood education.
6. Compare the theories, program perspectives, and methodologies that influence curriculum for young children.
7. Recognize and begin to use the concepts of developmentally appropriate and best practices.

Key Terms

National Association for the Education of Young Children (NAEYC) Standards for Initial Early Childhood Professional Preparation Programs met by this chapter:

Standard 1: Promoting Child Development and Learning

1a: Knowing and understanding young children's characteristics and needs, from birth through age 8.

1b: Knowing and understanding the multiple influences on early development and learning.

1c: Using developmental knowledge to create healthy, respectful, supportive, and challenging learning environments for young children.

Standard 2: Building Family and Community Relationships

2a: Knowing about and understanding diverse family and community characteristics.

2b: Supporting and engaging families and communities through respectful, reciprocal relationships.

2c: Involving families and communities in young children's development and learning.

Standard 4: Using Developmentally Effective Approaches

4a: Understanding positive relationships and supportive interactions as the foundation of their work with young children.

4b: Knowing and understanding effective strategies and tools for early education, including appropriate uses of technology.

4c: Using a broad repertoire of developmentally appropriate teaching/learning approaches.

4d: Reflecting on own practice to promote positive outcomes for each child.

Standard 5: Using Content Knowledge to Build Meaningful Curriculum

5a: Understanding content knowledge and resources in academic disciplines: language and literacy; the arts – music, creative movement, dance, drama, visual arts; mathematics; science, physical activity, physical education, health and safety; and social studies.

5b: Knowing and using the central concepts, inquiry tools, and structures of content areas or academic disciplines.

5c: Using own knowledge, appropriate early learning standards, and other resources to design, implement, and evaluate developmentally meaningful and challenging curriculum for each child.

Standard 6: Becoming a Professional

6a: Identifying and involving oneself with the early childhood field.

6b: Knowing about and upholding ethical standards and other early childhood professional guidelines.

6c: Engaging in continuous, collaborative learning to inform practice; using technology effectively with young children, with peers, and as a professional resource.

6d: Integrating knowledgeable, reflective, and critical perspectives on early education.

Understanding Curriculum and Early Childhood Education

Curriculum will be about you—who you are, what you have done, and how you develop skills to plan **activities** that positively impact the lives of young children. When you step into a classroom as a teacher, you will integrate your own personal **experiences** with the knowledge you acquire about **early childhood education**. Much of what you learn will validate what you already know about children. Some ideas may change your way of thinking and modify the way you interact with young children and plan activities for them. naeyc 6a, 6d

Who Are the Early Childhood Teachers?

Teachers of young children are particularly significant because they influence children during their critical periods of growth and development. As an early childhood teacher you may work with infants, toddlers, preschoolers, kindergarteners, and primary school-age children. Early childhood education encompasses programs for children from ages zero to eight. That is why it is so important for you learn as much as you can about child development and curriculum planning.

Teachers who enjoy their careers with children do not hesitate to state that "a day in the life of

© Cengage Learning 2013

Teaching is fun, exciting, and rewarding, especially observing enthusiastic and happy children.

a teacher of young children can only be boring if you let that happen." Teaching is fun, exciting, and rewarding. Teaching young children also demands a great deal of commitment and energy. High-quality teachers generally have characteristics that include creativity, flexibility, sensitivity, and curiosity. "I enjoy young children," is the most frequent response from teachers of young children when they are asked why they chose to take early childhood education classes.

Whether you are beginning your career or returning to classes for professional development, perfecting your curriculum planning skills is essential to your development as an early childhood education teacher. Skills in curriculum planning will give you a sense of predictability, control, and confidence. These are empowering skills that contribute to your ability to provide quality programming for young children. **naeyc** 6a, 6c, 6d

---

 Video Case

Teaching as a Profession: An Early Childhood Teacher's Responsibility

Visit the Early Childhood Education Media Library, and watch the TeachSource Video Case on www.cengagebrain.com

1. List three to five teaching responsibilities that Samantha discussed in the video.

2. What did Samantha mean when she said, "…in this field you never know everything."

What Is Curriculum?

The word *curriculum* refers to a collection of ideas including such concepts as learning program, plans, school subjects, materials, and topics of study. It is not just a grab bag of fun activities to keep the children busy (NAEYC and NAECS/SDE 2003). Early childhood educators define curriculum as all the school- and program-related experiences that influence and affect the children. Curriculum involves both planned and unplanned experiences designed to help children develop skills and knowledge. The curriculum is what you will teach and how you will teach it (Frede and Ackerman 2007). The values, attitudes, and interests of early childhood teachers influence the curriculum. The curriculum is also influenced by the children, their families, and the community. Funding sources, sponsoring agencies, and state and national legislative policies impact what occurs in many early childhood programs. Additionally, the mission and goals of a school will affect the way the curriculum is planned and implemented for the young children enrolled. **naeyc** 4b, 4c, 6a, 6d

This introduction to curriculum begins your journey to develop meaningful experiences for young children. Start with an understanding of the word *curriculum* (Figure 1–1).

Educators continuously search for improved ways to guide children. Sometimes we agree, and sometimes we do not. As new ideas become familiar, they are more likely to be accepted.

Generally, when this happens the concepts are documented and become established definitions and theories about early childhood education. Some ideas emerge from previous times, often revamped or repackaged with new words. Some ideas about curriculum are improved. Some explanations of curriculum retain the basic intention about curriculum for young children from previous times. *The Platform of Beliefs,* presented by the Association for Supervision and Curriculum Development (ASCD) in 1957, listed specific words and phrases such as "equal opportunities for all children" and "individual differences" (Hanna 1972, 230). There are similarities among the words found in *The Platform of Beliefs* and in a document titled *Developmentally Appropriate Practice in Early Childhood Programs Serving Children from Birth through Age 8.* This document was initially published in 1987 by the National Association for the Education of Young Children (Bredekamp) and revised in 1997 (Bredekamp and Copple) and 2009 (Copple and

---

Figure 1–1 Use of the Word—Curriculum

curriculum	a noun	A course of study; a program of studies (Barnhart and Barnhart, 1990)
		Curriculum for young children is the topic of this textbook.
curriculums or curricula	plural	More than one course of study or program
		The teacher tried many different types of curriculums. The teacher tried many different types of curricula.
curricular	adjective	Of, having to do with, or describing curriculum
		Early childhood educators continued to develop their curricular practices.

Bredekamp). Prevalent themes in the publications emphasize the importance of each child's needs, individual differences, and helping children to achieve their fullest development possible. The 2009 NAEYC document calls attention to accountability, child-centered activities, and acknowledgment that no one teaching strategy meets all children's needs (Figure 1–2). naeyc
1a, 1b, 1c, 4b, 4c, 4d, 5a, 5b, 5c, 6a, 6c, 6d

Looking at Early Childhood Education Terminology

Early childhood students recognize right away that there are particular words, or terms, that have meaning and significance to the profession. A simple word, such as *theme*, will elicit varied reactions. Some professionals use the word *theme* to describe an approach to curriculum. You might have heard a teacher say that his program uses a theme-based curriculum. Or, you might have heard a teacher say that she includes some themes but that they offer an interest or center-based curriculum.

The differences in word definition may result from the way a word is used by teachers in a specific program. Some staff members might say that activities have a "purpose," while others indicate that activities have "goals" or "objectives." The teachers and program administrators must first agree on the definition of words commonly used every day at their school. The use of terms and words will influence curriculum planning and labeling. What do you call the area where you will find the child-size kitchen furniture and doll beds? Is it called the housekeeping corner, the doll corner, the creative dramatics center, or the dramatic play area? Early childhood programs do not have fixed rules with fixed terminology applicable to all of the different types of programs offered for young children. Environments that are print rich, for instance, might be labeled with words such as *door, table, chair, window, art,* and *dramatic play area.*

Figure 1–2 Looking Back—Looking Forward: Commonalities

Words identified in 1957 *Platform of Beliefs,* ASCD	Words identified in 2009 *Developmentally Appropriate Practice,* NAEYC
. . . needs of the learner	. . . recognizing that children are best understood in the context of family, culture, and society
. . . fullest possible development	. . . helping children and adults achieve full potential in the context of relationships that are based on trust, respect, and positive regard
. . . individual differences	. . . respecting the dignity, worth, and uniqueness of each individual
Words identified in 2009 *Developmentally Appropriate Practice*	. . . accountability through appropriate observation and assessment
	. . . intentionality with focus on child-centered activities
	. . . no one teaching strategy meets all children's needs
	. . . how children learn and what they are capable of learning

This enables staff, volunteers, parents, and students observing at the program to use the words correctly and consistently. Some programs that are bilingual and those that meet the needs of second-language learners will add words from the children's primary language and languages. Become familiar with a school's handbook of guidelines and listen to the teaching staff. Both efforts will help you to become aware of the most commonly used words, thereby enhancing your consistent communication with the children. **naeyc** 1b, 1c, 4b, 4c, 4d, 5a, 5b, 5c, 6c, 6d

Key terms are provided at the beginning of each chapter to expand your use of early childhood terminology. You can also check the glossary at the end of the book to find an alphabetized list of terminology important in early childhood education.

Activities—The Core of the Curriculum

The outcome of thoughtful curriculum planning offers a program for young children that enriches appropriate experiences for them. The experiences offered at early learning, child care, and other early childhood settings are commonly referred to as activities. The interaction between the teachers and children creates the reality of the early childhood setting, with the activities creating the only concrete part of the curriculum plan. The various activities that are planned and offered to children provide the core of your curriculum. You will hear the phrase *hands-on* used to refer to those activities in which children actively engage in some way.

"Hands-on" means that the children use their hands, arms, legs, feet, and bodies rather than just listening and observing teachers. You will also hear the word *concrete* describing activities. Concrete activities allow children to use real materials as active participants. Painting with marbles is an example of an activity that engages children in a hands-on experience **(Curriculum Activity Guide callout 43 📖)**. Sorting and cutting up a variety of apples is another example of a concrete learning experience that you and the children will enjoy **(Curriculum Activity Guide 22 📖)**.

Early childhood education students frequently talk about feeling confident when they set up what they feel are the "right activities," but they cannot explain why they chose those activities. Your ability to select appropriate concrete, hands-on activities will increase as you complete professional preparation courses and engage in implementing more practical experiences for young children. The Curriculum Activity Guides presented in Appendix C detail activities that focus on the needs and interests of young children. This activity planning format calls for you to set the stage for children to experience activities. The activities are designed to help young children become learners through exploration. The activities will help them adapt to changes within a nurturing environment. Know what children can do and what they enjoy doing. Assist them in discovering how to direct their own learning. **naeyc** 1a, 1b, 1c, 4b, 4c, 4d, 5a, 5b, 5c

Benefits of Planning and Managing Your Curriculum

Working with young children requires that teachers plan. Planning more likely will ensure that children have the best opportunities to develop in secure, stable, and interesting environments. Planning allows you to predict and to prepare for events and the actions of the children and others who participate in the program. Planning will give you an important sense of predictability, confidence, and positive control. Once you know what is best for children, you will be able to prepare the program while justifying the value of your plan. Achieving success requires that your plan is flexible and adaptable with long- and short-term goals. An unanticipated event, such as the arrival of a huge, digger tractor on the street in front of your school, becomes an exciting spontaneous adventure to the children's day. A well-established plan provides a solid base of activities that allows the inclusion of spontaneous experiences without abandoning predictability and security.

© Cengage Learning 2013

Teachers who focus on the needs and interests of young children invite them to experience the pleasure and joy of books.

Planning maximizes the use of time, and in that way, increases opportunities for quality interaction among the teachers and children. There are benefits for children when programs provide them with individualized attention. Teachers who establish flexible curriculum plans create places for effectively meeting each child's needs. A teacher who predicts the daily, weekly, and monthly flow of activities increases interaction with the children's families and the overall quality of the program. Planning brings the staff together with regularly scheduled meetings allowing time to collectively map out the curriculum to best meet the children's needs. Planning improves the quality of experiences for the children because the activities become balanced, for instance, between indoor and outdoor play and quiet and active experiences. Coordination and design of the curriculum contribute positively to the program administration, increasing utilization of resources and supporting team efforts among staff members. The consequence of curriculum planning is a design that will also educate and inform the parents about the experiences their children enjoy at school. Curriculum plans establish an accountability record for staff, parents, and the community as well (Figure 1–3). naeyc

1a, 1b, 1c, 4a, 4b, 4c, 4d, 5a, 5b, 5c

Utilizing Technology to Plan and Manage Curriculum

There are many exciting opportunities for teachers of young children to utilize technology to plan and manage curriculum for young children. Teachers are no longer limited by facts, concepts, and ideas exclusively available in books. Technology expands all limits for gathering, organizing, and applying the vast quantity of knowledge for your own education and the learning opportunities for children. The use of technology will increase the frequency and outreach communication with families, allowing them to take part in their child's learning (Mitchell et al. 2010).

The word *technology* is commonly used in educational settings to mean the application of a technical, mechanical process. This process has implied the application of the computer and related systems such as telecommunications. Businesses and schools can and do still FAX (send a facsimile of a document over a telephone line); however, scanning and e-mailing documents adds opportunities for managing information. Smart phones with numerous applications increase communication prospects and provide innovative methods to store and send information. Podcast and downlink special programs broadcast in other locations open opportunities for staff in-service learning and professional growth. More and more schools have websites for families where you will be able to share school activities and experiences with families. This also opens other options to increase communication and networking through discussion forums (Mitchell et al. 2010).

Technical applications and special social media tools, such as texting, Twitter, Facebook, LinkedIn, and specific websites, have amplified communication opportunities. Blogs and YouTube replace newspaper and television newscasts for many. Skyping keeps families connected with real-time visual and voice interaction.

Digital photography can be combined with computers to assure parents of their children's well-being, and also of the quality of learning and activities taking place in a daily, weekly, or monthly time frame. One word of caution: "Because photos on the Internet can be copied by anyone with access to the originating page, take special care to select photos for your website that do not show children's faces clearly, and do not use their names in captions" (Mitchell et al. 2010, 57).

Teachers utilize their computers and smart phones to produce digital photography of the children's activities and learning sequences. Documentation of the children's work establishes a record and improves curriculum accountability. Both adults and children can be part of this process by taking the photographs and deciding which should be used for the documentation. Management skills, that always have been important to teachers, are becoming more important as the teacher's role in overall program planning and evaluation changes. You will have long-term benefits with the ability to organize and retrieve information about the

Figure 1–3 Benefits of Exemplary Curriculum Planning

Benefits for Children	Benefits for Program
Improve quality of experiences	Empower staff
Establish stable and secure setting	Increase staff coordination
Increase child/teacher interaction	Improve resource utilization
Balance experiences	Accountability
Opportunities to develop competence	Quality experiences

enrolled children and the experiences in which they engage. You will find that computerized systems are indispensable tools in helping you to organize and manage your program. For example, **technology** augments your options for keeping records of the children's activities. A computer file established for each child maintains a running record of observed behavior and other administrative information related to enrollment as well. Printing and filing hard copies of the information entered into the computer will ensure that the data is available if technology fails or becomes inaccessible.

Access to the Internet provides limitless resources and allows teachers to connect directly with websites sponsored by organizations and institutions. Credible websites post current information about a subject directly from the professionals in that field. Teachers can also connect with other early childhood educators on a LISTSERV (online learning communities and interest forums that establish information exchanges for professionals). NAEYC hosts numerous interest forums including such groups as the Tribal and Indigenous Early Childhood Network (TIECN), Technology and Young Children, and Violence in the Lives of Young Children. Communication occurs primarily online and invites exchange of diverse ideas and opinions. Learning communities, or online communities, can connect students and teachers in early childhood education who have common and particular interests.

Program administrators and the teaching staff review the availability of technology and select appropriate computer software that the children use in school settings. School guidelines will determine the level of technology to be made available to the children and how it will be integrated into the curriculum. The National Association for the Education of Young Children's *Position Statement on Technology and Children—Ages Three through Eight,* affirms that teachers should look carefully at the potential benefits of technology for children. Preschoolers can use computers to work alone or with others. They can create art, make music, tell and record stories, hear their stories read back to them, and play educational games that can connect with classroom learning and play. Careful planning of computer use allows children to explore the opportunities in ways that fit in your schedule and teaching philosophy (Blagojevic et al. 2010). **naeyc** 1b, 1c, 2b, 2c, 4a, 4b, 4c

Fundamental Principles Shape Early Childhood Education

Activities will emerge from the curriculum you plan for the young children enrolled in your program at that current time. The selection and preparation of activities for a school is based on the program philosophy and the views administrators and teachers have about the way children develop and learn. In most situations, a set of ideas, standards, or **fundamental principles**, direct the curriculum. You will form your own ideas, adopting many from the documented statements established throughout previous years by professionals in the field. The fundamental principles in Figure 1–4,

Figure 1–4 Fundamental Principles for Early Childhood Education

Fundamental Principle	Explanation
1. Developmental practice to meet the needs of each child	Understanding that development of the child is based on interrelated physical, social, emotional, and cognitive domains and not on isolated systems and events.
2. Individual and age appropriate practice	Promoting a individualized focus with recognition of the differences between a child's developmental age and chronological age.
3. Family involvement and appreciation	Sensitively respecting the families and their languages, cultural rituals, and life patterns.
4. Authentic inclusion of children	Valuing curriculum that is sensitive to all children and avoiding separate add-on activities only for holidays.
5. Observation and assessment of the children	Using observation and assessment as the basis for curriculum planning.
6. Professional accountability	Continuing professional development to ensure that program goals support fundamental principles.

offer basic concepts for you to consider and guide many of the curriculum concepts throughout this textbook. No single underlying educational or psychological theory structures the foundation for these fundamentals. The list of fundamentals is based on what is generally accepted in the field of early childhood education and what has been found to be useful in teaching students who are learning to prepare curriculum. For instance, research confirmed the importance of quality early care with emphasis on preventive measures and early intervention (Shore 1997). Internationally noted authority on childhood trauma and crisis, Bruce Perry (2002, 82) stated, "The brain is most sensitive to experience—and therefore most easy to influence in positive and negative ways in infancy and childhood. It is during these times in life when social, emotional, cognitive and physical experiences will shape neural systems in ways that influence functioning for a lifetime."

Any list of basic ideas does not remain static. There is a presumption that those who use it will intentionally engage in a continuing review and application of current research to their teaching practices. This list of fundamental principles offers both a general guide to students who are new to child development and a conceptual framework for experienced teachers. In the course of time, students and teachers will gather ideas from a variety of sources to shape their own early childhood curriculum. The ideas are offered to help you think about what is important in the field and what you may want to consider as part of your own list of guiding principles. This framework organizes ideas about development, teaching practices, and

the importance of families. The values of diversity, balancing curriculum, and observation and assessment are listed as important ideas and ideals for quality programs during the early childhood years. Together, the organized ideas and concepts direct the core of early childhood curriculum as it is presented throughout the pages of this textbook. naeyc 1b, 1c, 2b, 2c, 4a, 4b, 4c, 5a, 5b, 5c

Theories Influencing Programs and Curricula

There are many descriptions, or theories, about how children develop as well as many varied descriptions about how children learn. Because the descriptions and explanations vary, a number of different ways to interpret children's behavior can be used. Does a child learn by observing? Does a child learn by responding? Do we know that learning has taken place by observing a child's behavior?

A theory, or particular ideology, can explain and predict the behavior. A theory is a collection of ideas, concepts, terms, and statements blended to illustrate a point or concept. A theory about children is a collection of concepts and terms that attempt to predict their development and behavior during childhood. There are numerous theories to explain and predict how children behave and learn. Some of them are complementary or have similar descriptions. Others have contradictory views. Some theories have many perspectives and are described as eclectic. Your understanding of the basic **theoretical perspectives** often used in early childhood education (Figure 1–5) will allow

Figure 1–5 Major Theoretical Perspectives

Behavioral	Maintains that environments are carefully controlled and designed to shape the child's behavior. Conditioning such as reinforcement is thought to increase a given behavior. Behavior modification and social-learning concepts are associated with this learning theory.
Cognitive	Describes mental process related to the way a child develops abilities for thinking, including logic, and problem solving. Cognitive theory refers to changes occurring in stages.
Developmental	Child's behavior and growth predicted within age-range expectations. Child learns through interaction of maturing abilities and environmental opportunities.
Ecological	Child's interaction with their family and community forms the initial environment that influences development.
Maturational	Child's growth is directed by hereditary factors. Focus on normative characteristics of children and the natural unfolding of behavior.
Psychodynamic	Childhood experiences shape behavior. Also referred to as psychoanalytic theory and focuses on personality and emotions.

you to begin to interpret research findings and apply those findings appropriately for the benefit of young children's development and learning. Major theoretical perspectives affect the planning and organization of children's activities. The level of influence is determined by the school and their program philosophy. Teachers' use of certain theoretical concepts and their application may be related to their own upbringing and formal education.

Jean Piaget, the noted Swiss psychologist, developed theories describing children's thinking. Beginning in the first half of the Twentieth Century, Piaget began writing about the mental processes of young children and gained acceptance among many early childhood educators. His theory would be classified primarily within the cognitive theoretical perspective. This stage theory also satisfies the developmental constructionist perspective. Piaget's concepts emphasize that when preschool-age children mature, their thinking connections develop bit by bit through related and repeated experiences. If you accept Piaget's theory, as a teacher of young children, you will provide materials for investigation, conversation, and opportunities for the children to repeat experiences. Children's knowledge of the world, Piaget said, lies in their actions (Piaget 1955). Teachers who follow Piaget's insight encourage children to actively engage in the activities, assisting their exploration and discovery. An activity titled "Planting Seeds" (Curriculum Activity Guide 23 📖) does just that.

Another theorist, Lev Vygotsky, is recognized as one of the researchers whose studies focused on the social interactions of children. He suggested that children learn by building, scaffolding, and layering ideas through social and cultural experiences. Vygotsky's work was influenced by his academic experiences under Marxism in Russia. A teacher would maximize learning, according to Vygotsky's theory, by offering children opportunities to learn a concept in a variety of ways, especially through communication with adults and other children. Social experience is the tool for mental activity and cooperative learning (Berk 1994). Vygotsky suggested that teachers support children's discovery with emphasis on verbal interaction between adults and children. This, Vygotsky believed, directs children toward higher levels of thinking that they might not achieve on their own (Dworetzky 1996).

Vygotsky's theory would support your guiding children to find a solution for the litter problem on the public street in front of your school. This confirms the theory of constructivism. Constructivists promote children's understanding in a context of learning that encourages children to create and discover by actively interacting with the environment. Besides Vygotsky, the constructivist perspective was integrated into the concepts that Montessori and Piaget contributed. Young children are seen as active participants in their own learning process. Debate among theorists regarding the best way children learn will continue. Research studies and reaction from those that work directly with children—the teachers— inspire renewed debate. Knowing how children learn provides you with the tools for developing appropriate curriculum.

The major theories fall into groups, yet it is rare that educational textbooks agree on the way the theories are categorized and implemented. Dr. Lillian Katz, in *Talks with Teachers* (1977), recommends continual review of learning theories because of the strong effect many theories have within the field. A widely accepted understanding, combination, or eclectic approach calls for teachers to take the best concepts from the various theories and to blend them to create an applicable ideology for the children in your program. **naeyc** 1b, 1c, 2b, 2c, 4a, 4b, 4c, 5a, 5c

Program Perspectives and Practices

The visitor described in *Picture This . . .* at the beginning of the chapter, left the observation area with several questions: Who organizes and plans the activities? Who decides what materials will be placed outside and what materials will be offered inside? How can anyone make so many decisions? The decisions about early childhood curriculum will be determined by many factors. The purpose of a school program narrows the way experiences are planned and offered to the children. The goals may be influenced by the program philosophy and theoretical perspectives that impact what experiences are planned and how the activities are offered. Staff, daily schedules, geographical location, and the features of a community determine curriculum-related choices. Some schools relate directly to specific school models and follow their methods of proposed practices. Other schools combine perspectives from various methods. Early childhood trends cycle and definitely affect the activities and experiences recommended for young children. Some perspectives and practices with different focus and functions, such as Reggio Emilia Inspired, HighScope, Waldorf Education, Montessori, and Creative Curriculum, have remained accepted and admired.

Reggio Emilia Inspired

The Reggio Emilia approach was begun in Italy after World War II by Loris Malaguzzi and parents in villages surrounding the city of Reggio Emilia. Having experienced so much destruction during the war, they sought out a new teaching approach for their children.

Curriculum inspired by the Reggio Emilia approach places the natural development of children at the center of its philosophy. Emphasis is placed on the organization of the physical environment and is often referred to as the child's "third teacher." The importance of the environment lies in the belief that children can best create meaning and make sense of their world through environments that support varied, sustained, complex, and changing relationships between people, the world of experience, ideas, and the many ways of expressing ideas (Caldwell 1997). Children are encouraged to make symbolic representations of their ideas with many different kinds of media and to revisit, reflect, and interpret their representations. This is referred to as one hundred languages of children (Fraser and Gestwicki 2002).

Parents are another vital component to the Reggio Emilia approach because they are viewed as partners, collaborators, and advocates for their children. Teachers respect parents as each child's first teacher and involve parents in every aspect of the curriculum. In the Reggio approach, the teacher is considered a co-learner and collaborator with the child, not just their instructor. Teachers are encouraged to facilitate children's learning by planning lessons based on each the child's interests, asking questions for further understanding, and actively engaging in the activities along side them. The teacher is inside the learning situation as partner to the child (Hewett 2001).

HighScope

The HighScope model was conceived by David Weikart, whose career began in special education. In the 1960s, Weikart initiated the Perry Preschool Program in the Ypsilanti Public Schools in Michigan. The study conducted at the Perry Preschool set a standard for early childhood education by confirming the importance of high-quality preschool education. The HighScope model utilized teaching techniques to help children plan, to carry out their plans, and reflect and review their own educational activities (Schweinhart 2002). Early in the development of the HighScope curriculum, the work of Piaget became influential, and the curriculum was renamed the cognitively oriented curriculum (Driscoll and Nagel 2008).

HighScope is based on the idea that children are active learners and are able to construct their own knowledge. The HighScope model recommends that teachers discontinue direct teaching and begin participating with the children in key experiences. Those experiences are organized into three categories including social and emotional development, movement and physical development, and cognitive development. The key experiences give structure to the curriculum, while at the same time allowing flexibility to accommodate new possibilities. The key experiences are linked to the assessment of the children and program (Driscoll and Nagel 2008). Teachers in HighScope programs give children a sense of control over the events of the day by planning a consistent routine. This enables children to anticipate the sequence of events. The plan-do-review sequence is an important feature to the daily routine that includes small- and large-group experiences and outside play.

Waldorf Schools

The Waldorf curriculum, or Waldorf Schools or Waldorf Education, is one that honors the child by presenting age appropriate content. The content is presented to respond to the three developmental phases of childhood: from birth to approximately six or seven years, from seven to 14 years, and from 14 to 18 years.

Waldorf Education was developed in 1919 by Rudolf Steiner, a philosopher and social thinker. In 2009 the independent school movement was reported to be active in 1600 Waldorf Kindergartens and 994 independent Waldorf or Rudolf Steiner schools internationally. Waldorf Education supports healthy self-awareness and interest and concern for all humanity (Mays and Nordwall 2004–2010). The curriculum follows the stages of child's development with integration of art, thereby educating the whole child. As the child moves through the various stages of education, the curriculum is tailored to coincide with this maturation.

The schools that use the Waldorf methods, approach learning in early childhood through the use of imitation and example. Time is allowed for guided free play in a homelike classroom environment, using simple materials drawn from natural sources. Teachers create a setting to balance the children's participation in artistic, academic, and practical work. This supports each child's physical, emotional, and intellectual growth.

Outdoor play periods at Waldorf schools are incorporated into the day, allowing time for the children to experience nature, weather, and the seasons of the year. Oral language development is addressed through songs, poems, and movement games encouraging imagination and creativity. With emphasis on imagination and creativity, Waldorf Schools generally discourage young children's exposure to the media, including television, computers, and recorded music (Mays and Nordwall 2004–10).

Montessori

Dr. Maria Montessori's perspective of children has significantly influenced the field of early childhood education. The Montessori Method has been recognized around the world since Montessori opened the first Children's House in Rome in 1907. Many early childhood strategies practiced today thread back to the methods developed by Montessori. Montessori's educational approach focuses on the needs and spontaneous interests of the individual child. She believed that a child's interest must be distinguished from those of an adult.

The Montessori approach is a philosophy of child development and for guidance of young children, ages zero to six. Dr. Montessori advised that observation of children provides important insight that enables teachers to anticipate their needs and desired choices. The Montessori Method suggests that young children absorb learning during the early, sensitive periods of their development. This should take place in environments that allow freedom to select purposeful experiences. When children are allowed to direct their own activities and proceed at their natural rate of progress in prepared settings, they learn by doing and further their potential for growth (Orem 1974).

Typically, the environments in Montessori programs meet the individual needs of young children with careful observation of children "at work" and offer experiences for children with great emphasis on learning through senses and movement. Dr. Montessori believed that we must first discover the true nature of each child, and then assist each one in his or her normal development (Montessori 1966).

Creative Curriculum

The Creative Curriculum® is an approach to early childhood education developed by Teaching Strategies, Inc. Teaching Strategies, Inc. was founded in 1988 by Diane Trister Dodge, an educator and author, who taught preschool-age and kindergarten children. Ms. Dodge was the coordinator for Head Start and child care programs in Mississippi and Washington, DC and directed projects in education and human services at the national level.

Teaching Strategies, Inc. crafted the Creative Curriculum into a comprehensive system directed to programs for infants and toddlers, preschoolers ages three to five, and children in the primary grades, kindergarten to third grade. Teaching Strategies, Inc. presents the Creative Curriculum as a method to help teachers create and implement developmentally appropriate environments and experiences with positive outcomes for children. The Creative Curriculum approach has been used widely in Head Start programs throughout the United States.

The physical space in classrooms using the Creative Curriculum is divided into interest areas that accommodate a few children at a time. These areas include block building, dramatic play, toys and games, art, library, discovery table, sand and water, music and movement, cooking, and computers.

The Creative Curriculum underlying philosophy draws from Jean Piaget's work on cognitive development, Erik Erikson's stages of socio-emotional development, and perspectives from other theorists such as Abraham Maslow and Lev Vygotsky. Research on learning, the brain, and resiliency of children also influences the viewpoint of the Creative Curriculum for Preschool. *This* offers a professional development support for teaching young children, including a checklist for implementing the approach (Dodge et al. 2002).

Types of Programs

The terms *early learning program, infant/toddler center, family child care, child development center, preschool, child care, before and afterschool child care or extended day,* and *early learning center* are references to programs or schools for young children. The title of a school may provide you with a clue to identify the purpose of a program, the type of program, and the curriculum. The title can also be misleading. Programs with similar titles may neither have the same purpose nor offer similar benefits and curricula. Some provide child care, some provide opportunities for learning, and some provide both care and early learning. Schools and facilities for young children of preschool-age accomplish their purpose in numerous ways. Some programs offer care and/or learning in homes for a specified number of children, some in center-based programs, and some on employee work sites. Some of the programs offer care and/or learning to infants and toddlers, some to preschoolers, and some to school-age children before and after school.

Opportunities in early care and learning of children result from the evolving needs of a constantly changing society. A number of programs can be readily identified offering a basis for your appreciation of the ways programs are provided for young children (Figure 1–6). naeyc 1b, 1c, 2a, 2b, 2c, 4a, 4b, 4c, 5a, 5b, 5c, 6d

Figure 1–6 Eight Types of Programs for Young Children

Child care	Operated by public agencies, community, and private for-profit businesses. Child care offered for half or full day to groups of children while parents are employed or are in training. Often called day care for children. Many center-based programs provide learning opportunities. States vary in licensing and regulation requirements. Federal government sets minimum requirements.
Cooperative	Cooperation and participation of parents create the core component of cooperatives. Some cooperatives are sponsored by school districts. A trained director-teacher is hired to facilitate the children's program and parent education. Parents also cooperate in informal play groups where the primary purpose is to have the children and adults interact.
Employer-supported	Companies support child care in a variety of ways: on-site centers, paying for child care costs, reserving spaces in community centers, hiring a professional in early childhood to refer and approve appropriate facilities for employees. Corporations have documented the benefits to employer and employees. The United States military operates the largest network of employer-supported child care.
Enrichment/compensatory	Head Start, the icon in enrichment programs, was established in 1965 by the federal government to provide opportunities for children with low-economic resources. Head Start also was established to offer compensatory opportunities to children whose circumstances limited their experiences. There are other enrichment programs. Some focus on language development, for instance when English is the second language for children.
Extended – before and after school	Extended care is provided, often year-round, for school-age children. Programs are offered by private schools, community agencies such the YMCA, and some public school districts. The care meets the needs of parents who are employed, attending school themselves, or participating in training.
Faith-based	Religions support private sector programs for young children in various ways. Some faith-based programs introduce children early to their religious doctrines. Churches, mosques, temples, and synagogues may provide programs including day nurseries for children whose parents either work or are unable to care for the children during the day. Day-of-worship child care has been traditionally offered by many religions.
Family child care	More children in the United States receive child care in private homes other than their own than any other form of child care arrangement. The setting can replicate a child's own home and provide individual attention. There are great variations in state licensing and regulation requirements.
Infant-toddler	Center-based programs specifically designed for infants and toddlers who had been cared for primarily in family child care homes. Early Head Start is a prime example of a funded program for infants and toddlers from low-resource communities.
Pre-kindergarten	The majority of children in the United States spend some time in organized group programs before they enter kindergarten. Schools, or programs for children prior to enrollment in kindergarten, is pre-kindergarten (pre-K). Many states have initiated publically funded pre-kindergarten programs.
Preschool/nursery	Accommodates preschoolers ages two-and-a-half to kindergarten age. The preschool program was traditionally referred to as the nursery school. Preschools offer a half-day program concentrating on young children's social development. Activities and experiences may be offered during open blocks of time for free play with choices of child-initiated and teacher-directed activities.
Training/lab	College or campus child care/training facilities have multiplied with the increase for child care needs and increased enrollment of parents in college coursework. Many of the early nursery schools were initiated at universities. Some of the programs and practices provided for children today were developed on campuses. Today colleges and universities offer various forms of teacher training laboratories. Some of the programs meet the child care needs of the college student-parent and support observation and practicum coursework in child development and early childhood education.

Best Practices for Quality Programs Are Developmentally Appropriate Practice

When we look at what is valuable for young children, we find that programs of quality meet the needs of the children who are enrolled in the schools. Best practices describes programs that follow standards of quality with teachers who appreciate the diversity of the children, their families, and the communities.

The standards for quality and the well-being of children have been defined within a framework, specially referred to as best and developmentally appropriate practice. Education encounters changes like any other discipline or profession in society. Nonetheless, the core understanding of how children learn and develop remains consistent for early childhood educators. Our fundamental commitment to excellence and equity for all children remains strong. We celebrate the knowledge gained from research that has been importantly focused on young children. That knowledge deepens our understanding and refines our ideas, enabling us to promote every child's optimal development and learning. Three important points have endured the changing educational climate for early childhood educators. The three positions provide the framework for the fundamental principles that were introduced to you earlier in this chapter and are threaded throughout this textbook. The points that remain consistent include the need to understand young children's developmental stages, how to best meet their individual needs, and the significance of their social-emotional context.

Developmentally Appropriate Practice in Early Childhood Programs Serving Children from Birth through Age 8 (NAEYC) summarized pertinent issues in the 2009 revision. The issues, as topics regarding young children, elaborate the basic beliefs of the National Association for the Education of Young Children. The issues set a framework for critical decisions that teachers make regarding the experiences they offer in their programs for young children. Contemplate the following issues as you evaluate the focus of early education and the needs of young children:

- Establish accountability through appropriate observation and assessment.
- Understand how children learn and what they are capable of learning.

- Appreciate that no one teaching strategy meets all children's needs.
- Adopt intentionality towards the best possible outcomes for young children.
- Focus on child-centered activities rather than curriculum-oriented activities (Copple and Bredekamp 2009).

The movement for developmentally appropriate curriculum, **developmentally appropriate practice** (DAP), and **best practices** was initiated in the 1970s in reaction to demands for earlier academic achievement. With school-age work increasingly thrust upon preschoolers, the "pushed down curriculum" required young children to work at their desks, completing endless dittoed assignments. In response, NAEYC advanced DAP that supported child development and relations between the home and program, appropriate hands-on activities, and choice and flexibility to accommodate each child's developmental level (Bredekamp 1987; Copple and Bredekamp 2009).

Early childhood educators can confidently say that children are born meaning-makers. This informs us that they are constantly trying to make meaning of their experiences. Teachers need to respond by providing children with the opportunities and experiences to achieve optimal development; this essentially includes social and emotional growth to sustain children's natural joy of learning. Early childhood is and should be a special time of laughter, love, and great fun through playful learning. This focus is especially important because early childhood educators are continually challenged to disregard their beliefs about how children develop in favor of academic skill concentration. We just need to be resilient about our intentions for young children and what we understand to be in their best and long-term interests.

Developmentally appropriate curriculum planning will support high-quality play experiences while, at the same time, reinforce children's optimal skill development and educational success. You will successfully guide children's development by intentionally and judiciously using a variety of strategies with carefully planned developmentally appropriate curriculum (DAP) (Copple and Bredekamp 2009). This asks that you actively interact with children encouraging warm and caring relationships, understand the developmental areas of growth, vary methods of instruction, and assure long periods of sustainable time for play.

naeyc 1a, 1b, 1c, 4a, 4b, 4c, 4d, 5a, 5b, 5c, 6b, 6d

Strengthening Connections: Harmony, Equity, Respect in Children's Programs

Quality programs for young children demonstrate best practices with strong connections between the children and teachers. One of the most important ways teachers create connections is to caringly and actively interact with the children. Sincere and meaningful relationships will contribute to forming an essential foundation for assuring developmentally appropriate practice.

Each child arrives for what might be their first experience away from home with behaviors strongly influenced by their family, culture, and community. Families influence the way a child approaches new experiences, the other children, and the adults in the program. Family expectations and values further direct perceptions of what is considered to be appropriate child behavior. Variation will exist between parents and staff regarding expectations and child-rearing practices (Bhavnagri and Gonzalez-Mena 1997). Issues of cultural differences and the need for cultural sensitivity prevail throughout early childhood education (Gonzalez-Mena 2005).

Teachers need to be able to prepare curriculum that is responsive to the great diversity of homes and communities. These call for teachers to support harmony, equity, and respect in their early childhood programs. Educators who remain sensitive to behavioral similarities and differences will best create harmonious settings. Sensitive behaviors and actions support the relationships that strengthen harmony among the adults and the children and establish more equitable opportunities. Teachers can model perceptive interactions by respecting one another's customs and traditions. Children and families will benefit from a program where they respect, listen to, and learn about each other's languages and religions, and where appreciation for diversity is anticipated. There are binding commonalities among families and their goals for their children. Find the threads of similarities as you offer curriculum that is relevant to the specific children in your school and in the school's community.

One way you will be able to establish appropriate curriculum is to represent and include all children realistically and appropriately. The words *all children* translates to typical and nontypical developing children, children with abilities, children with disabilities, children from families of one ethnicity, and those from families of multi-ethnicities, children from low resource families and those who are privileged. You will show regard for each

© Cengage Learning 2013

Best practices in early childhood settings encourage meaningful relationships among the children.

child by understanding that children's identities are formed by their gender, capabilities, individuality, the social circumstances of their families, their communities, and the patterns of their family life. It is **authentic inclusion** that will build an anti-bias and multicultural curriculum to achieve culturally affirming programs for children and families. Authentic inclusion integrates anti-bias experiences into the whole curriculum rather than adding on "holiday" activities.

The Network of Educators of the Americas is a nonprofit organization which promotes peace, justice, and human rights. This nonprofit group promotes equitable relationships among children, families, staff, and community (Boyd 1998). Recognition, representation, and inclusion of children must closely and consistently represent American cultures within this diverse American society (Gollnick and Chinn 2006). Teachers need to fully appreciate the identity of each child and each adult participating in their programs by recognizing commonalities and welcoming differences. **naeyc** 1a, 1b, 1c, 2a, 2b, 2c, 4a, 4b, 4c, 4d, 6a, 6b, 6d

Thinking About What You Have Learned

✓ Collect two brochures from early childhood programs. Read each brochure to identify the curriculum program offered at each school. List two features of the curriculum described that you would consider using in your own program and explain why.

✔ Review the fundamentals for early childhood programs in Figure 1–4. Select one of the six fundamental principles. Think about the statement you selected and write a response, including the way you would incorporate the concept into your own teaching strategy. Document your written statement with two references from other books, research studies, or websites.

✔ Select a program from the list in Figure 1–5. Call to arrange a visit and an interview with the director or one of the teachers. Develop a list of six questions about the program's educational philosophy and curriculum to ask during the interview. Prepare a written response summarizing the interview. Be prepared to discuss your questions and the interview responses with other students during class or in an online forum.

✔ Access one of the following websites. Describe the information available and how you might use the information to encourage authentic inclusion in a program for young children:

Adoptive Families of America
http://www.adoptivefam.org/
Children's Book Press—Many Voices, One World
http://www.childrensbookpress.org/
Native American Resources on the Internet
http://hanksville.org/NAresources
March of Dimes
http://www.modimes.org/

Chapter References

Barnhart, Clarence L., and Robert K. Barnhart. eds. 1990. *The world book dictionary* (1). Chicago: World Book.

Berk, Laura. E. 1994. Vygotsky's theory: The importance of make-believe play. *Young Children* 50(1): 30–38.

Bhavnagri, Navaz . P., and Janet Gonzalez-Mena, 1997. The cultural context of infant caregiving. *Childhood Education* 74: 2–8.

Blagojevic, Bonnie, Sue Chevalier, Anneke MacIsaac, Linda Hitchcock, and Bobbi Frechette. 2010. Young children and computers: Storytelling and learning in a digital age. *Teaching Young Children* 3(5): 18–21.

Bloom, Benjamin S. 1981. *All our children learning.* New York: McGraw-Hill.

Boyd, Barbara. F. 1998. A guide to multicultural education. *Childhood Education* 75(1): 33.

Bredekamp, Sue. ed. 1987. *Developmentally appropriate practice in early childhood programs serving children from birth through age 8.* Washington, DC: National Association for the Education of Young Children.

Bredekamp, Sue, and Carol Copple. eds. 1997. *Developmentally appropriate practice in early childhood programs serving children from birth through age 8.* rev. ed. Washington, DC: National Association for the Education of Young Children.

Cohen, Dorothy H. 1972. *The learning child: Guidelines for parents and teachers.* New York: Pantheon.

Copple, Carol, and Sue Bredekamp. eds. 2009. *Developmentally appropriate practice in early childhood programs serving children from birth through age 8.* 3rd ed. Washington, DC: National Association for the Education of Young Children.

Dodge, Diane T., Laura J. Colker, and Cate Heroman. 2002. *The creative curriculum for preschool.* 4th ed. Washington, DC: Teaching Strategies, Inc.

Driscoll, Amy, and Nancy G. Nagel. 2008. *Early childhood education: Birth– 8: the world of children, families, and educators.* Upper Saddle River, NJ: Merrill.

Dworetzky, John P. 1996. *Introduction to child development.* 6th ed. St. Paul, MN: West.

Fraser, Susan, and Carol Gestwicki. 2002. *Authentic childhood: Exploring Reggio Emilia in the classroom.* Albany, NY: Delmar–Thomson Learning.

Frede, Ellen, and Debra J. Ackerman. 2007. Policy Brief-Preschool curriculum decision-making: Dimensions to consider. *National Institute for Early Education Research* (12): 1–16. http://nieer.org/docs/index.php?DocID=

Gollnick Donna. M., and Philip C. Chinn, P. C. 2006. *Multicultural education in a pluralistic society* 7th ed. New York: Merrill.

Gonzalez-Mena, Janet. 2005. *Foundations of early childhood education: Teaching children in a diverse society.* New York: McGraw Hill.

Hanna, L. 1972. Meeting the challenge. In B. C. Mills. ed. *Understanding the young child and his curriculum.* New York: Macmillan.

Hewett, Valarie. 2001. Examining the Reggio Emilia approach to early childhood education. *Early Childhood Education Journal* 29, 95–100.

Hymes, James L. 1969. *Early childhood education.* Washington, DC: National Association for the Education of Young Children.

Katz, Lillian G. 1977. *Talks with teachers: Reflections on early childhood education.* Washington, DC: National Association for the Education of Young Children.

Lindsey, Gail. 1998/99. Brain research and implications. *Childhood Education* 75(2), 97.

Mays, Robert, and Sune Nordwall. 2004–2010. What is a Waldorf education? http://www.waldorfanswers.org/waldorf.htm

Mitchell, Sascha, Teresa S. Foulger, and Keith Wetzel. 2010. Ten tips for involving families through Internet-based communication. In *Teaching Preschoolers:*

Supporting Children, Families, and Yourself 2: 56–59. Derry Koralek. ed. Washington, DC: National Association for the Education of Young Children.

Montessori, Maria. 1966. *The secret of childhood.* New York: Fides.

National Association for the Education of Young Children and the National Association of Early Childhood Specialists in State Departments of Education (NAEYC and NAECS/SDE). 2003. *Joint position statement on early childhood curriculum, assessment, and program evaluation building an effective, accountable system in programs for children birth through age 8.* Washington, DC: National Association for the Education of Young Children.

National Institute of Child Health and Human Development. 1997. *Results of NICHD study of early child care reported at society for research in child development meeting, 1–6.* http://www.hih.gov/nichd/html/news/rel4top.htm

Orem, Reginald C. ed. 1974. *Montessori: Her method and the movement—What you need to know.* New York: Capricorn Books, Putnam's Sons.

Perry, Bruce. 2002. Childhood experience and the expression of genetic potential: What childhood neglect tells us about nature and nurture. *Brain and Mind* 3: 79–100.

Piaget, Jean. 1955. *The language and thought of the child.* New York: Meridian Books.

Shore, Rima. 1997. *Rethinking the brain: New insights into early development.* New York: Families and Work Institute.

Schweinhart, Lawrence J. How the highscope Perry preschool study grew: A researcher's tale. Phi Delta Kappa Center for Evaluation, Development, and Research June, 32. http://www.highscope.org/content.asp?contentId=232

Understanding and Facilitating the Development of Young Children

© Cengage Learning 2013

Picture This . . .

Whether you are looking through photo albums, digital photo frames, or your smart phones, photographs of children invite you to reminisce. The photos and the reminiscing nudge you into realizing how quickly children grow. You learned about growth and development in your college child development class. Children develop rapidly, especially infants during their first year.

The moments and memories you have captured in photographs also illustrate how children become increasingly more capable. Within a few months, an infant rolls over. In a few more months, most infants begin to crawl, or creep, then sit up, and before their first birthday, many begin walking. Toddlers move quickly through their second year, accomplishing more and more through activity and movement. By the end of the third year, young children's imagination allows them to fantasize, for example, about transforming the hillside they have just climbed into a castle.

You have known toddlers who have grown into busy and active preschoolers. Just last week you overheard someone talking about the children they saw crawling through a tunnel in a carpeted area at an airport terminal. One child, who looked about two years old, turned plastic knobs and tugged on an oversized head phone. The two-year-old tried to spin a metal steering wheel. A boy and a girl, who might have been three or four years old, peeked through small portholes of the wooden structure replicating an airplane. The girl, who looked older than the boy, climbed to the top of the structure and then jumped down. The boy backed out of the opening. The children's busy activity stopped when they heard the loud announcement. Although the children played in the same area and waited for the same airline flight, each child used the structure and equipment differently. The differences in children's abilities are not always apparent in photographs. The differences, though, become more fascinating as you become increasingly interested in the developing skills of young children.

GUIDE TO READING CHAPTER 2

Chapter Outline

What You Need to Know About Meeting the
  Needs of Young Children
  Influences on Young Children's Growth and
    Development
      Temperament
      Maturation
      Family Experiences
      Positive Interaction
      Movement and Activity
  The Significance of Early Experiences to Brain
    Development
  Each Child Is an Individual
  The Concept of the Whole Child
Supporting the Young Child's Development
  Developing Skills: A Process
  Reasonable Expectations
  Becoming Acquainted with Developmental
    Focus Areas
      Physical Development
      Affective (Social-Emotional Understanding)
        and Aesthetic Development
      Cognitive Development
Suitable Experiences and Expectations to Meet
  Children's Needs
  Developmentally Appropriate
  Culturally Appropriate
  Linguistically Appropriate
Thinking About What You Have Learned

Learning Objectives

After reading this chapter, you will be able to:

1. Determine influences on the growth and development of young children.
2. Discuss the significance of early experiences to brain development.
3. Identify the developmental focus areas: physical, affective and aesthetic, and cognitive.
4. Recognize suitable experiences and expectations that are developmentally, culturally, and linguistically appropriate.

Key Terms

National Association for the Education of Young Children (NAEYC) Standards for Initial Early Childhood Professional Preparation Programs met by this chapter:

Standard 1: Promoting Child Development and Learning

1a: Knowing and understanding young children's characteristics and needs, from birth through age 8.

1b: Knowing and understanding the multiple influences on early development and learning.

1c: Using developmental knowledge to create healthy, respectful, supportive, and challenging learning environments for young children.

Standard 5: Using Content Knowledge to Build Meaningful Curriculum

5a: Understanding content knowledge and resources in academic disciplines: language and literacy; the arts – music, creative movement, dance, drama, visual arts; mathematics; science; physical activity, physical education, health and safety; and social studies.

5b: Knowing and using the central concepts, inquiry tools, and structures of content areas or academic disciplines.

Standard 6: Becoming a Professional

6c: Engaging in continuous, collaborative learning to inform practice; using technology effectively with young children, with peers, and as a professional resource.

6d: Integrating knowledgeable, reflective, and critical perspectives on early education.

What You Need to Know About Meeting the Needs of Young Children

Children of all ages move about and behave in their own unique ways. As you focus on the behavior of young children, you will become aware of their reactions, expressions, and activity levels. You will also notice their personality and characteristics. Even though the birthdates of the children enrolled in a particular preschool classroom are only a few months apart, their sizes and behaviors will illustrate differences in growth and development.

A preschooler's **chronological age** identifies his or her date of birth. Chronological age will also inform us about that child's stage of development and the expectations for that developmental stage. A chronological age, however, does not correlate with specific measurements and abilities. Two preschoolers, both with a chronological age of 4.2 (four years and two months) will likely exhibit differences in their weight, height, and abilities. Each preschooler will behave individually and distinctively. This same concept of **development** applies to children who are twins. When you watch them closely, you will become aware of their separate and unique behaviors. Each twin is an individual even though they may physically, in many cases, resemble one another (Arce 2010).

© Cengage Learning 2013

Meeting the needs of young children invites teachers to recognize the varied stages of growth and development during the preschool years.

Most young children grow physically and rapidly during the early childhood years. Children actively explore whatever is available in their environment. As they explore, they develop **skills** and learn about their world. They continue to acquire basic skills throughout the preschool years. Their acquisition of skills follows a distinct pattern, one that is unique for each child.

Influences on Young Children's Growth and Development

Growth and development are about change. Understanding growth and development is comprehending how children change over time in their **physical**, behavioral, and thinking characteristics. "To teach young children well you must study children" (Hymes 1969, 71).

Teachers ensure children's healthy development by creating nurturing environments for them. A nurturing environment for young children offers them relationships with caregivers and teachers who are responsive to their developing needs. You have already begun supporting nurturing environments by beginning your coursework to become an early childhood teacher. Research has confirmed your efforts. For example, the Family and Work Institute documented that children will more securely attach to a child care provider who has completed effective training (Shore 1977). The quality of relationships between teachers and young children directly affect the children's behavioral and early school adjustment (Ewing and Taylor 2009).

Understanding the development of young children has many advantages. Teachers benefit because the knowledge about children increases their abilities to guide their growth and development. As your knowledge about child growth and development increases, you will become more proficient in planning appropriate experiences for young children. Knowing what children are like, what they do, and how they behave becomes the key consideration for curriculum planning (Cohen 1972). There are many factors that influence the development of a child. **Influencing factors** include the child's temperament, maturation, **family experiences**, interaction with others in their environment, and opportunities for **movement and activity.** naeyc 1a, 1b, 1c

Temperament

Most psychologists believe that infants are born with tendencies for certain behaviors. This is also referred to as temperament. The innate temperament creates individual differences in such characteristics as activity level, attitudes, and emotions. Individual temperament is our natural way of behaving, how we act and interact with others and the environment. Your temperament unfolded as you matured. It was affected by environmental conditions, especially family members and other caregivers. They reacted to your behaviors and influenced how your temperament was expressed. Your family's cultural values and the individual traits and preferences of your parent(s) strongly affected your temperament and modified your behavior (Cook and Cook 2010).

One of the most famous and classic studies about temperament was initiated in 1956 by the New York Longitudinal Study. The study identified three types of temperament. The lead researchers, Alexander Thomas and Stella Chess, demonstrated that almost half of the infants in the study were documented as having an easy temperament. Easy babies are primarily positive with a flexible approach to new situations. Fifteen percent of infants were slow to warm up. We can use the findings from this famous study to anticipate that some babies will take a little time to settle into new experiences. They may react mildly negatively to new experiences, but with repeated exposure gradually develop a quiet, positive interest. Ten percent of children were found to have more difficult **temperaments**. They are easily frustrated, frequently negative, and slow to adapt to change. The dispositions of approximately 35 percent of children were and can be identified with one or more of the three categories (Thomas et al. 1970).

Children are more likely to have positive developmental outcomes when there is a "goodness of fit" between their innate temperaments and their environments (Thomas et al. 1970). The responsibility for providing "goodness of fit" lies with the adults in the child's life. Teachers of young children will contribute to positive developmental outcomes by recognizing and responding to the individual temperaments of the children enrolled in their programs.

Maturation

The natural process of growth promotes abilities in all areas of development. The rate of growth, or **maturation**, especially of preschoolers, young children between the ages of three and five, varies considerably. Children are individuals; therefore their rate of growth, or their unfolding of development, will be their own. Variation within the individual stages of a child's development can also be noted. There are predictable stages. Infants become toddlers. Toddlers become preschoolers. However, development does not proceed in an absolute, predictable manner. Babies who are beginning to express their first words may suddenly become disinterested in walking and may even regress in that ability.

As preschoolers mature, they accomplish more skills. For instance, they will be able to balance, jump, and hop. They might enjoy the challenges of an activity such as an obstacle course. Young children will best enjoy movement experiences that do not mandate rules and competition (Copple and Bredekamp 2009).

Young children will achieve certain skills when they are given opportunities to explore and work with specific materials. Skills in drawing, painting, cutting, and writing with precision will be acquired in environments that are comforting and encouraging. Unstructured activities that honor children's readiness and allow them time to explore will give preschoolers the necessary opportunities to grow physically (Copple and Bredekamp 2009). Early childhood educators and the environments they provide influence the ongoing unfolding of young children's maturation.

Family Experiences

The family is the cultural base for children. "To be tender, loving, and caring, human beings must be tenderly loved and cared for in their earliest years, from the moment they are born" (Montagu 1971). In almost all human cultures, the family plays a fundamental role in their children's development. Families, including the family experiences, create the system for care, protection, and relationships. Children acquire cultural nuances such as traditions and rituals with their families. It is in a family that children gain a sense of group identity and belonging.

The developmental outcomes of children are influenced by family members, primarily their parents. Parents and other members of the family, such as siblings and grandparents, establish behavioral guidelines including boundaries and expectations. Within the family, the most important features are parenting styles, particularly in guiding children's innate temperament (Galinsky 2010).

In our families, we learn to become a social being. The family is the place where we begin to develop emotionally and socially. We acquire attitudes, beliefs, and social mores. We adopt certain ways of behaving. We learn the family language and languages. We may practice the religion or faith of our family. The family establishes our first group experience, manifesting tremendous influence on the growth and development of young children. The well-being of a child, including the positive development of competencies in life skills, depends on the quality of relationships and communication experienced in the family.

Positive Interaction

The relationships that children experience within their families establish a foundation for their emotional and social interaction with others. **Positive interactions**, first experienced with caring and responsive family members, are the building blocks of healthy development. Children thrive in the context of close and dependable relationships. These relationships provide love, nurturance, security, and encouragement for exploration. Such positive behaviors prepare the children for interaction at school with teachers and peers and with members of the community (Shonkoff 2000).

Interaction in the community may present different experiences for children. A sense of belonging and ethnic identity becomes more challenging for children whose families may have immigrated. Many families, whose roots are well established in a community, may face lingering issues regarding their bicultural identity and acceptance. Schools and community centers have opportunities to establish events and experiences that celebrate and respect multicultural families. Intentional practices designed to encourage respect for all cultures will positively influence the development of young children.

Movement and Activity

Preschoolers are physical in response to their environment. They respond physically with movement and activity. They began responding during infancy to sights, sounds, scents, touch, and especially to the people in their environment. They were carried, rocked, and swung. They learned playfulness and, perhaps, rhythm. They watched others, practiced moving themselves, and learned to inhibit some of their actions and activity.

Children, as they mature from infancy to toddlerhood and into the preschool stage, are in constant motion. They are able to sit, crawl, walk, run, and jump; many react joyfully to opportunities for dancing, creative movement, and dramatic play. Children react positively to activity and being outdoors where they can move freely (Copple and Bredekamp 2009).

There is a strong connection between physical activity and healthy lifestyles (Copple and Bredekamp 2009). Teachers of young children substantially influence the quality of physical activity available for preschoolers in programs designed to meet their needs. Movement and activity contribute to the quality of the program. Teachers who establish programs that promote health and well-being are enhancing the healthy growth and development of young children. **naeyc** 1a, 1b, 1c

The Significance of Early Experiences to Brain Development

Research studies have focused more and more on the developing brains of infants. The research findings have revealed how babies learn. The brains of infants seem to be wired so that they can begin

Everyday experiences offered to toddlers help build the connections that guide their brain development.

to understand the world in certain ways. We have known for some time that babies are fascinated by almost every new sight and sound. In fact, this is one way researchers show us that the babies have actually learned. When the babies become more familiar with a person or object they begin to lose interest, or become bored with it. New, or novel, sights and sounds can often reengage a baby's interest.

Researchers have also illustrated that before babies reach their first birthdays, they have what Ellen Galinsky of the Family and Work Institute calls a language sense, a numbers sense, and a people sense (2010).

A number of factors influence brain development of babies. The development of a baby's brain is influenced by their genetic makeup, their prenatal experience, and the care they receive during infancy. These important influences during infancy take account of the responsiveness of the parents and other primary caregivers, daily experiences, and physical activity. In particular, parents and caregivers should be aware of the importance of creating loving, nurturing relationships; furnishing healthy, nutritious diets; providing interesting,

varied everyday experiences; and giving infants and young children positive, sensitive feedback that meets their developmental and **individual needs**.

Early experiences have a decisive impact on the actual structure of the infant's brain. The experiences each infant receives will affect the specific ways in which the circuits (or pathways) of their brain become "wired." The outside world shapes the brain's development through the experiences that infants and children take in, or assimilate, through their senses. Those experiences help build the connections that guide **brain development**. Everyday sensory experiences reinforce the connections between brain cells and further affect brain development (Shonkoff and Phillips 2000).

The functioning core of the brain is made up of neurons. A neuron has branches or dendrites emerging from the cell body. The dendrites pick up chemical signals across a synapse, and the impulse travels the length of the axon. Each axon branch has a sac containing neurotransmitters at its tip. The electrical impulse causes the release of the neurotransmitters, which, in turn, stimulates or inhibits neighboring dendrites, like an on-off switch. A single cell can connect with as many as 15,000 other cells. With appropriate care and experiences, a remarkable increase in synapses may occur during an infant's first year of life. This incredibly complex network of connections becomes the circuitry or wiring of the infant's brain (Brotherson 2005).

Practically, from the perspective of parents, caregivers, and teachers, a baby's brain is strengthened through repeated experiences. This is the way learning takes place. Connection and pathways are formed, and these structure the way an infant and child learns. If a pathway is not used, it is eliminated. When a connection is used repeatedly, it becomes permanent. For example, when adults repeat words and phrases as they talk to babies, babies learn to understand speech and strengthen the language connections in the brain.

The cortex is the top layer of the brain and is about the depth of two dimes placed on top of each other. The cortex is the executive branch of the brain that regulates decision making and controls thinking, reasoning, and language. The cerebral cortex contains 80 percent of the neurons in the brain. Because it is the least developed part of the brain at birth and keeps developing until adolescence and even beyond, the cortex is more sensitive to experiences than other parts of the brain.

Brain development proceeds in waves, with different sections of the brain becoming active construction sites at different times. The brain's ability to respond presents exciting opportunities for a child's development (Gopnik et al. 1999). The prime times or windows of opportunity for learning exist when the brain absorbs new information more easily. Research has demonstrated the significance of opportunities occurring during the early years of childhood.

Each Child Is an Individual

Have you ever wondered why some children look and act so differently from their parents or their siblings? Four-year-old Joshua has blond hair and blue eyes. He holds his younger sister Emily's hand as they walk into the preschool. You notice that Emily's big, dark brown eyes stand out against her black hair and olive complexion skin. Researchers continue to investigate hereditary influences, searching for answers about appearances of children, such as Joshua and Emily. Why do some children in families look very much alike while others look very different? Social scientists combine efforts with genetic scientists to unravel the factors in families and environments that affect the development of children.

Teachers who understand the development of young children will marvel at each child, that is each child as an individual. You will appreciate that each child's development—the sequence of changes and patterns of his growth—is his own. A child's temperament, responses and reaction, as well as their level of curiosity contribute to their own way of participating. A child's rate of maturity or growth is another factor that influences their individuality. Children who are within the same age range follow similar developmental sequences. The timing of specific achievements, such as crawling, walking, and reading, is highly individual (Cohen 1972). For instance, Hector walked at nine months and Marc took his first solo steps when he was 16 months. The norm for walking for the majority of children is 12 months. Hector and Marc are within the normal range for walking, yet they demonstrated individualized sequence of development. The development of abilities can occur within a span of two years, from one year proceeding the age to one year beyond. Variation is the rule, even though children go through the same stages of growth we cannot expect them to do so on the same timetable (Gesell et al. 1974).

The Concept of the Whole Child

Early childhood educators consider each child to be an individual and value their unique individuality. Early childhood educators also view each child as an individual who is developing as a whole individual. The concept of the **whole child** supports the development of the child in all areas of growth. Looking at growth and development in areas or domain, allows us to organize the information and to examine research studies related to that particular aspect of development. Information throughout this book is organized into three major areas of development: physical, **affective (social and emotional understanding)**, and aesthetic, and **cognitive**. The cognitive area includes language and literacy.

Supporting the Young Child's Development

You have learned that each child is an individual. You also learned that the study of child development is categorized into areas. This facilitates our understanding of the information while retaining focus on the concept of the whole child. You will appreciate watching three-year-old preschooler Chole as she progresses along a path of development that is her own. She will acquire skills and build on those, becoming increasingly more capable. You will expand your understanding of development as you observe children like Chole mature in physical, affective (social-emotional) and aesthetic, and cognitive developmental areas.

The teachers who appreciate young children's healthy development will value the time they spend observing and gathering information about them. When you know a child's capabilities, you will be able to plan balanced experiences for that specific child. Balanced experiences encourage children to explore and discover the activities and experiences that are appropriately planned for them. Children will progress developmentally when the balanced experiences are offered in nurturing settings that are satisfying, safe, and interesting.

Developing Skills: A Process

Children are born with innate, natural biological capabilities. Their capabilities continue to progress as they mature. Children's capabilities will progress into particular skills as they interact with people and objects in an environment. They are able to accomplish increasingly more complex tasks through continuing maturation. The development of a child's skills is dependent on both their maturation and their environment (Figure 2–1). You were born with the ability to speak a language.

Figure 2–1 An Ability Becomes a Skill	
Ability	**Skill**
Innate/biological	Develops
Occurs with maturation	Influenced by environment
Progresses as a child matures	You developed the skill to speak Farsi, Mandarin, Spanish, English, or another language
You were born with the ability to speak a language	

Figure 2–2 Developing Skills
A skill can be a developed ability in movement. For example, a child develops the skill to walk.
A skill can be a developed ability in social-emotional understanding and behavior.
A skill can be a developed ability in thinking, creativity, and problem solving.

You developed the skill to speak English, Spanish, French, Mandarin, or another specific language. Some of you learned two languages during childhood, a critical time for language development, and therefore retained the skill in speaking both languages.

Most children are born with the ability to walk, to push, and to grasp an object. Walking, pushing, and grasping are some of the abilities needed to ride a tricycle. As children mature they may be able to combine the abilities to develop the skill for riding a tricycle. However, developing this skill is dependent on the availability of a trike in the child's environment. Developing skills is a process.

Skills are developed abilities in body movement, thinking, and social and emotional behaviors (Figure 2–2). As children mature, they acquire physical skills, affective (social-emotional understanding) and aesthetic skills, and cognitive skills. In doing so, children become more independent. They begin to unbutton their own sweaters, recognize their name in print, and develop self-confidence. When Charlotte is able to pedal a two-wheel bike, she begins riding with her friends around the path. Her skill in sociability increases along with the motor achievement of pedaling the bike.

Children attain new and diversified abilities as they grow and change. Their brains mature and their bodies change, causing development of movement, sociability, and thinking. There is great variability among children. Maturational progress takes place, and changes occur in the ability to control the head, torso, legs, feet, arms, hands, and fingers. A healthy body allows a child to participate and interact. Participation, interaction, and practice increase opportunities to develop added proficiency in the development of skills. **naeyc**
1a, 1b, 1c

Your role, as a teacher, will be to focus on the children's developing abilities, the innate capacities of children, so that you can enhance their **developing skills**. The acquisition of skills illustrates a sequence of behaviors. The child has opportunities to master a skill that will open up new options for acquiring additional skills. For example, three-year-old Nate begins to jump after watching other children for several days on the small, round trampoline. He moves his feet up and down throughout the week—at the snack table, while sitting and standing, even while he watches the fish swim in their glass bowl. Nate begins to jump to music while playing in the outside music/movement area. The next week, the teachers observe Nate jumping while he hangs his jacket in the activity room and then again when he approaches the snack table. Nate may be ready to enjoy jumping on an obstacle course. **(Curriculum Activity Guide 38 📖).**

Reasonable Expectations

A child pushes the pedal down on the tricycle with great determination. Another child, Elena, walks around and around the blanket in the dramatic play area trying to smooth each corner, while a third child, Rickie, stacks the blocks repeatedly to balance the geometric shapes. The longer you observe children, the more you see how common, basic characteristics of childhood are revealed. Healthy children are determined to master the challenges in their environment. Their determination encourages them to explore and strive for independent action. Children reach developmental milestones in the early childhood stage. For example, Trisha balances on the walking beam; Gilbert pedals the two-wheel bike; LeBron unzips his jacket. Your familiarity with capabilities and patterns of growth that normally occur in certain stages helps you predict and anticipate certain behavior. Your reasonable expectation of children's behaviors will guide your appropriate curriculum planning.

Many of the early descriptions of children's behaviors are available as a result of the systematic research efforts of the Gesell Institute of Child Development. Arnold Gesell's early work was continued by medical and educational experts including Frances L. Ilg and Louise Bates Ames. The Gesell Institute produced books and research findings about infant and child behavior and the nursery school. Dr. Gesell's research continued until he retired from the Clinic of Child Development of the School of Medicine at Yale University in 1950. Gesell focused on the genetically determined developmental sequences of growth noting that "environmental factors modulate and inflect but do not determine behavior" (Gesell et al. 1974, 31). The behavior of children, according to Gesell, develops and unfolds in predictable and patterned schedules. Many of the developmental profile charts that identify motor, language, and personal-social behaviors considered to be in the normal range for certain ages and stages are based on the findings of the Gesell Institute of Child Development. naeyc 1a, 1b, 1c

Becoming Acquainted with Developmental Focus Areas

Look at the photographs from your own childhood. You can see how rapidly you developed. You were able to roll over and crawl; before or shortly after your first birthday, you walked. You recognized your family members, and within a few years you could point to your printed name. You developed your feelings, attitudes, social skills, and thinking abilities.

Early childhood teachers, child development specialists, and developmental psychologists find that it is easier to understand the behavior of children when the areas of development are categorized into major groups or areas. When we study development within the designated areas of development, we are able to focus more precisely on one aspect of growth. Generally, the physical development is discussed first. The reason the physical area is covered first is because we are most familiar with the concepts. We can see the rapid changes that occur in the infant, toddler, and the preschooler. **Affective development**, also and often referred to as social-emotional development or understanding, and **aesthetic development** are reviewed next. The cognitive area includes language and literacy yet it is often just called the cognitive developmental area.

The identification of **developmental focus areas** helps us to organize and study the large and increasing volume of knowledge about young children.

Knowledge about child growth and development continuously changes reflecting the changes in our lives, societal events, and revealing research findings. Research findings from many disciplines, or professions, modify the traditional and accepted practices. Research findings can change childrearing practices, family dynamics, and certainly educational methods. Although practices may be adopted and applied in education, we should remain cautious about the source of information and its applicability for the specific group of children. Not all study findings apply to all children in all early childhood programs. We cannot assume that there is universal acceptance and applicability of child development theory (Bhavnagri and Gonzalez-Mena 1997).

Categorizing the areas of child development helps teachers and child development specialists more effectively focus on specific behaviors and needs of children. When a teacher focuses on a developmental area and then on all the developmental areas, the needs of the whole child will be conscientiously included. Development does not occur in one area. Children develop physically. Children develop affectively (social and emotional understanding) and aesthetically. As well, children develop cognitively, with predictable sequences of development within each area or domain (Figure 2–3).

Physical Development

Physical development is the area of growth that relates to basic physiological changes. The developmental changes of physical development include height, weight, and motor capabilities. A child's genetic makeup and their environment affect their physical development.

Young children generally are in motion. That is what makes them so observable. They develop rapidly throughout their preschool years, although more slowly than the growth they experienced in the first two years of their lives. Young children are increasingly more capable of physical activities. Children mature and develop their large motor skills, also referred to as gross motor skills. They use their large muscles for walking, running, climbing, rolling, pedaling, and throwing. They develop dexterity by participating in both group and solitary play. Young children's coordination, balance, and control mature as they develop.

Figure 2–3 Developmental Focus Areas

Area	Description	Also referred to as
physical	Basic physiological changes such as height, weight, and motor skills.	Biosocial
affective (social-emotional understanding) and aesthetic	Affective (social-emotional understanding): changes in social-emotional abilities; psychological and personality related interactions; and relationships. Aesthetic: artistic, creative, and expressive characteristics, including sensorial awareness.	social-emotional psychological creative artistic
cognitive	Thinking and mental abilities, including language, critical thinking, and problem solving. *Cognitive* is derived from a Latin word meaning "to know."	Mental Intellectual Thinking

This maturity increases children's movement and their participation in movement activities. When a teacher of young children invites them to pour, dig, hold, stack, reach, and assemble objects, they develop their small muscles and improve their motor abilities. When young children improve their motor abilities, their self-confidence increases and they gain mastery of movement and physical development.

▶❚❚ **Video Case**

2–5 Years: Gross Motor Development for Early Childhood

Visit the Early Childhood Education Media Library, and watch the TeachSource Video Case on www.cengagebrain.com

1. Gross motor skills are also referred to as large motor development. There are rapid gains in gross motor skills during early childhood and these vary among children. What can most four-year-olds do that they were unable to do when they were three years old?

2. Describe the gross motor performance of girls and boys during the preschool years.

Fine motor development follows a sequence leading to expected tasks. At a preschool you will see children learn to hang their jacket on a hook, hold the drinking faucet long enough to get a drink of water; stretch out their hand for the guinea pig to nibble the feed.

▶❚❚ **Video Case**

2–5 Years: Fine Motor Development for Early Childhood

Visit the Early Childhood Education Media Library, and watch the TeachSource Video Case on www.cengagebrain.com

1. What changes occur during two to five years that enables the fine motor skills of children to improve?

2. How could you support the mastery of young children's developing fine motor skills?

Healthy children develop positive attitudes about physical activity when they enjoy positive experiences. Teachers who are patient and encouraging facilitate children's confidence for approaching physical tasks. Teachers create inclusive settings when they modify materials and experiences or offer alternative activities to allow the most participation possible.

Children benefit from frequent opportunities to engage their large and small movement muscles. Experiences that encourage balance, spatial relations, and directions match well with children's needs. Opportunities to engage the senses, particularly hearing, seeing, and touching, promote perceptual-motor development. For example, when a teacher traces a child's body and names the parts of the body, the child hears the teacher's words, feels her hand, and perceives her own body in a different way.

Early care and learning professionals support physical health and safety by arranging activities for children to experience self-help skills. These skills that encourage physical well-being include washing, toileting, dressing, and eating. Lessons regarding personal and public safety extend the learning about physical capabilities. **naeyc** 1a, 1b, 1c

Affective (Social-Emotional Understanding) and Aesthetic Development

Affective (social-emotional understanding) development of young children includes their social and emotional growth as well as the changes in their social and emotional behaviors. Aesthetic development refers to awareness and sensorial responsiveness to their our surroundings, especially the natural and artistic beauty in our environments. Although there is overlap among the characteristics of affective and aesthetic development, each area benefits children's development in unique ways.

Affective development is related to the dimensions of feelings, emotions, and sociability. Affective (social-emotional understanding) development includes discussion about innate behaviors, or temperament, and learned traits such as personality. Children's feelings, emotions, social behaviors, and attitudes become apparent as they mature. Children's behavioral outcomes within the affective developmental area are strongly influenced by their environment. Characteristics such as temperament and personality, attachment and autonomy, trust, self-esteem, and self-confidence are discussed in the affective area of development. Other behavioral aspects include interactions and reactions, prosocial abilities, and gender and role identity.

Children's emotions and reactions to circumstances provide an indication of their feelings, their likes and dislikes, and their attitudes. Some children readily adjust to new situations and people. Other children may have difficulty separating from their parents or primary caregivers. Contextual experiences—influenced by family, siblings, community, religion and faith, economic level, ethnicity, and gender role expectations—contribute to the child's social and emotional identity. During early childhood, the socialization process expands beyond the home to child care and educational settings, where children encounter adults other than their parents and family members. Participation in group settings exposes children to different expectations, values, and languages. As they spend more time with other children, they may acquire social skills that will help them to become a group participant. You will guide the development of children's skills such as listening, waiting, sharing,

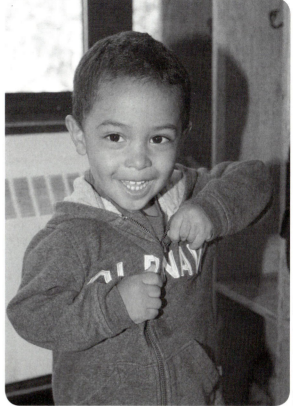

Some children readily adjust to new situations, such as preschool.

© Cengage Learning 2013

and problem solving. At the same time you will be nurturing the children's interaction in group settings. This will encourage the development of their social and emotional behaviors.

The basic elements of aesthetic development are sensitivity and responsiveness to the beauty in our surroundings. Aesthetic development is essentially responsiveness and sensitivity to nature and art. The development of aesthetic awareness emerges when children feel pleasure in their expressions, find new ways to enjoy tasks, use their imaginations, and explore novel objects. The potential for creative appreciation and expression is greatest for children in programs that offer them activities to express themselves. The word *aesthetics* actually has to do with responding to our environment through our senses. Through contact with the environment there are possibilities for children to enjoy and wonder (Haskell 1979). Using all or some of the senses allows children to develop preferences for color, form, shape, and sound. When young children are encouraged to be curious they will explore and discover. This is how they will enhance their senses. They will become more capable of discriminating the features in their surroundings.

The school guidelines and program philosophy provide direction to the staff and influence the curriculum. Activities that help children feel secure and welcomed enable them to separate, adjust, and expand their social interactions. This is affective (social-emotional) development. Giving children opportunities to make independent choices increases their feelings of trust, confidence, identification, and understanding of inclusion. Self-directed activities promote competence and pleasure in self-expression. Using some or all of the senses to enjoy art and art media allows children to be explorative and creative. This is how they develop aesthetic skills. For example, an activity about the colors found naturally in the outdoors increases awareness of colors in nature **(Curriculum Activity Guide 29 📖)**. Curriculum that encourages non-bias experiences promotes experiences that are authentically inclusive. naeyc 1a, 1b, 1c

Cognitive Development

Cognitive development relates to knowledge and how it is acquired. This category of development includes a child's growing thinking abilities and

© Cengage Learning 2013

When teachers listen and respond to the language of young children, it provides a glimpse of their understanding and feelings.

language acquisition. Other descriptive phases of the cognitive developmental focus area include thinking and mental abilities, memory and logic, intellectual growth, conceptualizing, language, problem solving, creativity and divergent thinking, language, literacy, and communication.

All children are born ready to learn. What happens from birth to five years of age is important because it sets either a sturdy or fragile stage for what follows. Young children develop capabilities during their early childhood years on which subsequent development builds (Shonkoff 2000). As we begin to think about the fragile first stage, it is important to understand that infants are born actively seeking information. Inquisitive behavior and innate reflexes allow babies to interact with their environment. Babies sense the sights, tastes, sounds, and smells in their environment. This gives them information (sensation) that they then process (perception), acquiring beginning knowledge (cognition). Very young children understand objects in terms of their own action on objects. There is a cumulative advantage to learning and gaining knowledge that is associated with well-planned activities that permit the children to go on to something else, sustaining their intrinsic motive for learning (Bruner 1960). Appropriate settings should be filled with experiences that have relevance to the children's lives and are related to their capabilities. Healthy preschool children are curious and motivated to investigate new experiences.

Focused language skills, a critical part of cognitive development, point out the importance of activities that emphasize listening abilities. Focused language skills also encourage expression and verbal communication. Language and communication skills are valuable for social interaction. The language of the home and community is the way that children express knowledge about their reality, their communities, and their families (Elkin and Handel 1989). When we listen and respond to the language of young children, it provides us with a glimpse of their understanding and feelings.

Suitable Experiences and Expectations to Meet Children's Needs

Teachers who understand the development of young children will plan **age-appropriate** and **developmentally appropriate** experiences for them. The word *appropriate* implies that an activity is suitable for the currently enrolled children. The suitability of a particular activity is dependent on many factors. Early childhood educators understand the development of children, including the variations that occur during these early years (Copple and Bredekamp 2009).

Each child is an individual with abilities and skills. Each has a temperament, history of interaction, and movement that is his or her own. We build activities that are suitable for early childhood when we consider the child as an individual with many characteristics.

Developmentally Appropriate

Each young child is an individual. Some are active, some quiet. You see differences among them in their size, appearance, activity level, and maturity.

The emphasis on age is significant in our society and is an important part of everyone's identity. "How old are you?" is a frequent inquiry filled with anticipation of expected behaviors. The expectations for specific behaviors are age-related. A child's chronological age is the numerical indicator that marks the child's number of years since birth. The chronological age provides a hint to a broad range of behaviors and skills that may occur during a particular age. However, each child follows a sequential direction of growth that is distinct. Children follow a pattern of growth that is sequential and appropriate for their age. Norms are established as standards to assess individual children. Norms, such as the developmental milestones charts, provide a general guide by age. Behavioral differences in the rate of growth place children into their own individualized and natural pattern of growth.

Developmental age is influenced by the child's individuality. This reflects a child's unique hereditary and life experiences. The developmental age takes shape as it is influenced by temperament, rate of growth, emotional responses, activity level, abilities, interests, family, and environment. Children's patterns and pace of development contribute to the developmental age (Figure 2–4). Different children, even those who are in the same age range, will approach the same learning opportunity in different ways. The behavioral outcomes will most likely vary because of their individual behavioral differences and characteristics.

Knowing a child's age and, more importantly, focusing on his developmental age, provides careful clues to matching appropriate curriculum experiences to individual needs. The developmental age describes the abilities, capabilities, skills, and

Figure 2–4 Factors Influencing Developmental Age	
temperament	abilities
rate of growth	interests
emotional responses	family
activity level	environment

readiness for new challenges. Knowing the general capabilities of three- and four-year-olds will help you select a book to read during small-group time. Knowing the specific listening and attention capabilities of the children expected to participate in the small group helps you to more precisely match the book selection to the developmental level of the children (**Curriculum Activity Guide 19**).

Appropriate practice for early education is a curriculum that will assist children in gaining and improving their skills. naeyc 1a, 1b, 1c, 5a, 5b

Culturally Appropriate

A child's family culture and language are intricately woven into the development of identity. This is one reason it is important for children to acquire positive views about our multicultural and multilingual society during their early years of schooling. Children need to appreciate that we live in a world where people come from different places and backgrounds and that we are more alike than we are different (Fillmore 1993).

Activities and experiences during early years of schooling are suitable when they respond to the child's cultural and linguistic diversity. Experiences are responsive when they are **culturally appropriate** (Copple and Bredekamp 2009). Appropriate practices provide opportunities for children to learn more about their own family culture, other family cultures, and communities. Experiences are valuable when they use non-stereotyping portrayal of families and cultural traditions. Sensitively presenting historical information to young children will help them appreciate the diversity in our communities and contribute to their growth of positive identities.

Cultural and linguistic relevance extends to all areas of the curriculum. Curricula for children's programs are most appropriate when they offer experiences to satisfy curiosity, build confidence, and challenge the young learners in nurturing environments. Responding to the children's activities and observations with accepting comments promotes their tolerance for differences and new ideas: *Are you looking at the hat that Tuan is wearing today? It is very colorful, isn't it? His grandmother knitted it for him. You piled the sand in an interesting way, and quite different from Noel's pile.* Ongoing and supportive interactions encourage developmentally and culturally appropriate experiences.

Linguistically Appropriate

Since America is ethnically diverse with many cultures and languages, children enter early childhood programs from homes and communities where English is not the primary language of their family. The terms *linguistically* and *culturally diverse* are defined by the U.S. Department of Education as the children who might not be proficient in English or are limited in their English speaking abilities (NAEYC 1995).

Language is tied to our family existence and our culture. Linguistically diverse children will benefit from programs where teachers are responsive to their home language and offer **linguistically appropriate** opportunities. Teachers will be most responsive by first acknowledging the importance of the home language. Secondly, teachers who respect and value the culture of home enable children to become more cognitively and socially competent. Lastly, the National Association for the Education of Young Children position statement about linguistic and cultural diversity recommends that teachers promote and encourage families to be actively involved (1995).

There are many opportunities to enhance children's language and linguistic development. An increasing number of teachers create classrooms in which meaningful talk and relationship building can take place. The teachers who advance language and literacy are those who are most likely to demonstrate higher responsiveness to children's questions by, for instance, interacting affectionately during storytelling (Soundy and Stout 2002).

You will observe in early childhood programs that teachers significantly influence the development of children's social competencies. To assure positive outcomes, educators are compelled to examine their own beliefs and family cultural values. Examining our own beliefs and values will help us to give more thoughtful consideration to the many different ways children learn and the many different perceptions their families may have about learning. This is particularly important because teachers generally view competence through their own culture rather than through a perspective more consistent with the cultural patterns of the children's families. This is significant because the ethnicity of most teachers does not reflect the ethnicity, culture, and language of their students (Harlin 2010).

Cultural continuity between home and school is important. The interaction among multiethnic, interracial, and multicultural families and staff is advantageous for the children in early care and learning settings. If teachers are sensitive to their own cultural bias and show good modeling examples, children can learn early to respond in positive ways to diversity (Gonzalez-Mena 2009). **naeyc** 1a, 1b, 1c, 5a, 5b, 6c, 6d

---

Thinking About What You Have Learned

✔ The director of your center has asked you to prepare a five-minute presentation for the monthly parent meeting. The purpose of this meeting is to help the family members of the enrolled children to understand that each child develops as an individual. Prepare an outline for this presentation. Include discussion about developmental age and the developmental focus areas. Document your outline with at least six current references from journal articles and textbooks. You may cite one website from a professional organization, school, or agency.

✔ If you are a parent, review the photographs and records of your child or children. What age did your child or children roll over, walk, talk, and attend a birthday party? If you are not a parent, call your own parent and ask when you and your siblings accomplished certain skills, or developmental milestones. Write a summary describing the similarities and differences among your children or you and your siblings. Note the age with year and month of each milestone. For example, 2.3 would be two years and three months.

✔ Explain how the organizations such as the Children's Defense Fund and the National Center for Child in Poverty support authentic inclusion for young children. You can access the Children's Defense Fund (CDF) at http://www.childrensdefense.org/ and the National Center for Children in Poverty (NCCP) at http://www.nccp.org/publications/pdf/text_949.pdf.

Chapter References

Arce, Eve-Marie. 2010. *Twins and supertwins: A handbook for early childhood professionals.* St. Paul, MN: Redleaf Press.

Bhavnagri, Navaz P., and Janet Gonzalez-Mena. 1997. The cultural context of infant caregiving. *Childhood Education* 74: 2–8.

Brotherson, Sean. 2005. *Understanding brain development in young children.* Bright Beginnings. #4 NDSU FS-60.

Bruner, Jerome S. 1960. *The process of education.* New York: Vintage.

Cohen, Dorothy. H. 1972. *The learning child.* New York: Pantheon.

Cook, Greg, and Joan Littlefield. 2010. *The world of children.* 2nd ed. Boston: Allyn and Bacon.

Copple, Carol, and Sue Bredekamp. 2009. *Developmentally appropriate practice in early childhood programs serving children from birth through age 8.* 3rd ed. Washington, DC: National Association for the Education of Young Children.

Elkin, Frederick, and Gerald Handel. 1989. *The child and society.* 5th ed. New York: Random House.

Ewing, Allison R., and Angela R. Taylor. 2009. The role of child gender and ethnicity in teacher–child relationship quality and children's behavioral adjustment in preschool. *Early Childhood Research Quarterly* 24(1): 92–105.

Fillmore, Lilly Wong. 1993. Educating citizens for a multicultural 21st century. *Multicultural Education* 1(1): 10–12.

Galinsky, Ellen. 2010. *Mind in the making: The seven essential life skills every child needs.* New York: Harper and Washington, DC: National Association for the Education of Young Children.

Gesell, Arnold, Frances L. Ilg, Louise Bates Ames, and Janet Learned Rodell. 1974. *Infant and child in the culture of today: The guidance of development in home and nursery school.* New York: Harper & Row, Publishers.

Gonzalez-Mena, Janet. 2009. *Child, family and community: Family-centered early care and education.* 5th ed. Upper Saddle River, NJ: Merrill.

Gopnik, Alison, Andrew N. Meltzoff, and Patricia K. Kuhl. 1999. *The scientist in the crib: Minds, brains, and how children learn.* New York: William Morrow & Co. Inc.

Harlin, Rebecca. 2010. Summary of sociocultural influence on children's social competence: A close look at kindergarten teachers' beliefs, by Heejeong Sophia Han. *Journal of Research in Childhood Education* 24(1):80–96. http://acei.org/knowledge/online-resource-center/research-reound-up/j

Haskell, Lendall. L. 1979. *Art in the early childhood years.* Columbus, OH: Charles E. Merrill.

Hymes, James. L. 1969. *Early childhood education.* Washington, DC: National Association for the Education of Young Children.

Montagu, Ashley. 1971. *Touching: The human significance of the skin.* New York: Columbia University Press.

National Association for the Education of Young Children. 1995. *Responding to linguistic and cultural diversity recommendations for effective early childhood education.* A Position Statement of the National Association for the Education of Young Children. Washington, DC: National Association for the Education of Young Children.

Shonkoff, Jack P., and Deborah A. Phillips, eds. 2000. *From neurons to neighborhoods: The science of early childhood development.* National Research Council Institute of Medicine. Washington, DC: National Academies Press.

Soundy, Cathleen S., and Nancy L. Stout. 2002. Pillow talk: Fostering the emotional and language needs of young learners. *Young Children* 57(2): 20–24.

Thomas, Alexander, Stella Chess and Herbert G. Birch. (1970). The Origin of Personality. *Scientific American* 102–109. http://www.acamedia.info/sciences/sciliterature/origin_of_personality.htm#authors

Linking Curriculum to Child Development and Observation

© Cengage Learning 2013

Picture This . . .

Your first assignment to observe preschool-age children required that you visit the campus child development center. Or you may have been instructed to observe children in a non-school program. Regardless of the setting, you were prepared with specific rubrics, or guidelines and criteria, for observing and recording the actions of the three-, four-, and five-year-olds. You might remember an assignment that required you to record the behavior and language of three children, all the same exact age and who were busy in the same activity. You were required to write down as much observed information as you could for one minute. You might have recorded information quite similar to the example describing the actions of Lee, Martin, and Justin provided in the example below.

Lee	Martin	Justin
Runs to climbing structure. Leaps up the ladder using every other rung. Pounds his hands on chest and yells, "I'm here, I'm great." Runs to opposite slide with hands in air. Lands backward. Stands up, walks backward to end of sanded area surrounding the structure. Falls backward, legs raised, laughs. Looks around, fixes on teacher hanging butcher paper on fence. Calls out, "I want to, I want to . . ."	Slides down climbing structure slide holding hands on side. Lands on sand with bottom hitting first. Leans over, pushes himself up with both hands. Rubs hands together, trying to remove sand. Wipes hands on pants. Walks quickly to just abandoned tricycle. Looks at child who just got off. Mounts tricycle, pushes pedals. Moves rapidly down path to cardboard box that has been decorated to look like a gas station fuel tank.	Standing by climbing structure watching Lee. Leans on slide. Holds hands over sand before pressing them into sand. Raises eyebrows and watches when Lee shouts. Looks up at Lee and then slowly walks along the side of the tricycle path. Stops and watches Lee moving toward fence.

GUIDE TO READING CHAPTER 3

Chapter Outline

Observation and Assessment: The Value of Documenting What Children Do and Say
    Ongoing Observation and Assessment
    Program Accountability
    Achieving Accountability with
        Accreditation
Observation and Assessment: Collecting Information and Record Keeping
    Objectivity
    Confidentiality and Privacy
    Informal Assessment
        Daily Informal Notes
        Anecdotal Records
        Logs and Notebooks
        Running Records
        Checklists
        Interviews and Conversations
        Portfolios
        Documentation and Work Sampling
    Formal Assessment
        Standardized Tests
        Individual Education Plan (IEP)
        IEP: A Teacher's Role
        Becoming Part of an IEP Team
    Assessment to Inform Educators
    Assessment to Inform Families
Observation and Assessment: Using the Cues from Children for Curriculum Planning
    Documenting the Work of Young Children
    Allowing Time for Child-Teacher Talks

Supporting the Cycle of Documentation, Planning, and Evaluation
Thinking About What You Have Learned

Learning Objectives

As you read this chapter, you will be able to:

1. Recognize the value of observation and assessment of children's development.
2. Use current professional standards to observe and document young children.
3. Discuss and use the cycle of observation, assessment, and curriculum planning.
4. Maintain confidentiality and privacy regarding all observation and assessment processes.
5. Define informal methods for collecting and record keeping.
6. Identify formal assessment of young children.
7. Compare assessment to inform educators and assessment to inform families.
8. Use the cues gathered through the documentation of children's work to plan curriculum.

Key Terms

accountability, *p 39*
anecdotal records, *p 43*
assessment, *p 37*
confidentiality, *p 42*
documentation, *p 38*
formal observation, *p 41*

Individual Education Plan (IEP), *p 46*
informal observation, *p 41*
objectivity, *p 42*
observation, *p 37*
portfolios, *p 39*

National Association for the Education of Young Children (NAEYC) Standards for Initial Early Childhood Professional Preparation Programs met by this chapter:

Standard 1: Promoting Child Development and Learning

1a: Knowing and understanding young children's characteristics and needs, from birth through age 8.

1b: Knowing and understanding the multiple influences on development and learning.

1c: Using developmental knowledge to create healthy, respectful, supportive, and challenging learning environments for young children.

Standard 2: Building Family and Community Relationships

2c: Involving families and communities in their children's development and learning.

Standard 3: Observing, Documenting, and Assessing to Support Young Children and Families

3a: Understanding the goals, benefits, and uses of assessment—including its use in development of appropriate goals, curriculum, and teaching strategies for young children.

3b: Knowing about and using observation, documentation, and other appropriate assessment tools and approaches, including the use of *technology* in documentation, assessment and data collection.

3c: Understanding and practicing responsible assessment to promote positive outcomes for each child, including the use of assistive *technology* for children with disabilities.

3d: Knowing about assessment partnerships with families and professional colleagues to build effective learning environments.

Standard 4: Using Developmentally Effective Approaches

4b: Knowing and understanding effective strategies and tools for early education, including appropriate uses of technology.

4c: Using a broad repertoire of developmentally appropriate teaching/learning approaches.

4d: Reflecting on own practice to promote positive outcomes for each child.

Standard 5: Using Content Knowledge to Build Meaningful Curriculum

5c: Using own knowledge, appropriate early learning standards, and other resources to design, implement, and evaluate meaningful and challenging curriculam for each child.

Standard 6: Becoming a Professional

6b: Knowing about and upholding ethical standards and other professional guidelines.

6c: Engaging in continuous, collaborative learning to inform practice; using technology effectively with young children, with peers, and as a professional resource.

6d: Integrating knowledgeable, reflective, and critical perspectives on early education.

Observation and Assessment: The Value of Documenting What Children Do and Say

Knowing as much as you can about the children in your program will guide your planning of meaningful and beneficial curriculum. The more you know about the children, the better prepared you will be to make important and appropriate curriculum planning decisions for them. When you have insight into their growth, development, skills, strengths, and needs, you will become increasingly competent in creating an environment that further enhances their growth and development. By combining the information gathered through **observation** and **assessment** with your expanding knowledge about best practices and development, you will achieve valuable outcomes for young children in your program.

You read the example of a one-minute observation of three children: Lee, Martin, and Justin in the chapter opening *Picture This . . .* All three of the preschool boys are 3 years and 11 months (3.11) old. Although the boys are the same ages in years and months, you probably noticed observable differences in their activity levels, language expressions, and physical behaviors. The individual actions of each boy were recorded in their regular play setting. When you observe children in their usual play settings, outdoors or indoors, you will record their natural and spontaneous behaviors. When you do, you more likely will identify each child's strengths and needs, particularly if you have a set of criteria guiding your observations (Beaty 2010). naeyc 1a, 1b, 1c

Ongoing Observation and Assessment

Ongoing observation and assessment of young children help teachers make good decisions about curriculum for them. Observation in an educational setting is a practice that helps teachers gather information about children. Initially, you may identify the purpose for the observation. Secondly, you will follow a procedure related to the purpose of the observation that may include viewing, monitoring, studying, and surveying the actions and behaviors of children. The purpose of an observation may be to identify a child's specific ability at a task, such as riding a tricycle. You may want to inquire if a child is competent at joining a small group of children in the sand area. The purpose of an observation identifies the reason you are observing and the focus of observation. Will you observe a child's physical activity, perhaps how he participates in an obstacle course? Or, will you observe a child's social interaction, for instance how she participates with other children in the sand area. The observation you complete will identify children's abilities, needs, and interests in a specific developmental area, physical, social-emotional, or cognitive. Some observations may focus on behavior in more than one developmental area.

Assessment is the practice of observing and documenting what children do and say. Assessment is valuable because it provides specific information about the children and helps teachers make important daily decisions about curriculum planning. Assessment establishes essential information by engaging both practices: observation and **documentation**. The information you collect through assessment will help you to effectively plan curriculum that best matches the children's development, needs, and interests. You will collect information about the children's development by carefully watching what they do in the early childhood setting. In this way, you are evaluating their progress to help you support their development.

Assessment will provide information about a child's capabilities, particular learning style, interaction with other children, and how that child approaches activities and uses the material and equipment. Assessment will guide your curriculum planning and also offer a way to meet your program requirements. When you collect information about children while they participate in what they do routinely at school, you avoid the stigma of evaluation for exclusion from the program or for unrealistic grading. Assessment can describe what is really important, a child's progress in different areas of development. Importantly, assessment that reflects the philosophy of your program will be authentic. You will find that authentic assessment realistically connects each child to the curriculum.

There are numerous descriptive words related to assessment. One example, performance assessment is used to describe the observations of children in their natural settings. This is one reason it is considered to be an authentic assessment. Performance assessment is authentic, and in this format, you will collect data about children's developmental progress. If you decided to assess the children authentically, and chose to refer to the review as performance assessment, you would identify in advance what behavior or ability you would observe. Some teachers set up particular situations or activities so they can focus on a particular action or behavior (Mindes 2011).

Formative assessment is another descriptive example of authentic assessment. Like performance assessment, formative assessment mirrors the philosophy of each program (Sluss 2005). For instance, HighScope programs, those which use the Creative Curriculum method, and Reggio Emilia inspired programs have their own approach and assessment methods that reflect their program's goal and objectives. Observation is the focal point of the authentic assessment of young children. Formative assessment includes feedback to the children, and in this way supports high-quality learning opportunities (Mindes 2011). Observing a child during play will present you with many different views on that particular child's behavior and skill sets. If you engage this child to reflect on what they did and plan what they will do, you will be practicing formative assessment.

Formative assessment occurs throughout the year on an ongoing basis. Your observations will be more focused by utilizing various observation methods. Some of the methods available and those that provide feedback to guide curriculum include daily notes, anecdotal records, logs, notebooks, running records, checklists, photographs, and **portfolios** with work samples. This kind of documentation provides an overall picture of the child's social-emotional, cognitive, language, and physical growth and development. As well, this kind of documentation should be based upon appropriate expectations for learning and development of the children. Teachers can provide information back to children in ways that can help them improve their learning. A teacher can design a review activity using different strategies if a child does not understand a concept. The purpose of this assessment is to support high-quality learning (Sluss 2005).

There are different strategies for storing assessment data. Many programs use computer software data collection folders where the teachers post the information they gather from work samples, checklists, photographs, parent input, anecdotal records and daily notes. Teachers in state-funded early childhood programs and in many Head Start programs in California appraise the children with the use of an assessment tool called the Desired Results Developmental Profile (DRDP) ©. The data is compiled within the first 45 calendar days of a child's enrollment. Teachers all over the United States, including those working in military child care programs and Head Start utilize software data collection folders that are specific to their curriculum model such as the Creative Curriculum. naeyc 3a, 3b, 3c, 3d

Program Accountability

Many, but not all programs for young children have a built-in system for **accountability**. Accountability builds your school's credibility and enhances the worth of your curriculum. Accountability is a way of acknowledging your efforts to provide quality curriculum for young children. You will find that programs that receive federal or state funding will have specific requirements for accountability. The requirements vary by program and often include mandated forms and documentation for every classroom and every child. Programs that are not required to be accountable still strive to achieve effective programs and quality curriculum by using assessment data to improve early childhood programs. In 2007 quality rating systems were implemented in 42 states to assess agencies with layers of program standards. At the same time different views among professionals become apparent with strong concerns

about possible "standard-based assessment and the misuse of assessment data." Realistically, accountability needs to begin within a design that includes criteria for quality program services and the desired outcomes for the children participating in a program (National Early Childhood Accountability Task Force).

Head Start is an example of a program that receives federal funding support and complies with specific guidelines of accountability. Head Start has a mandated system through which the grantee agencies are required to evaluate their performance in relation to Performance Standards. These Performance Standards, yearly self-assessments, are conducted by staff, parents, and community representatives. They define the objectives and features of a quality Head Start program in concrete terms; they articulate a vision of service delivery to young children and families; and they provide a regulatory structure for the monitoring and enforcement of quality standards. (US Department of Health and Human Services 2002). Time frames vary as well; however, each is put into place to mark the children's progress in skill development, and track the quality of the program. They serve as common reference points for teachers, aides, directors, and administrators (Caruso 2007).

The Waldorf Education method for assessing children takes in the full context of their circumstances. The teachers in a Waldorf School would avoid testing performance against a standardized norm. Observations of children give rise in a teacher to what the Waldorf method would describe as *intuitive insights*. Intuitive insights can be used for the design of activities. When the teacher observes the children, she activates her own imagination that allows her to bring assistance and attention to the children. An awareness of multiple intelligences, as described by Howard Gardner, also guides a teacher's educational methods and assessment process.

Lessons in a Waldorf School would consist of visual, auditory, and experiential components. Assessment would be based on multiple ways that children learn. Assessment would track the children's strengths and weaknesses within differing learning styles, such as visual, auditory, and kinesthetic. Observation of the activities allows a team of teachers to inspire and guide the children. In the Waldorf Schools, assessment furthers each child's progress with the full engagement of the teacher or team of teachers. naeyc 3a, 3b, 3c, 3d, 6b

Achieving Accountability with Accreditation

The practice of accreditation arose in the United States as a means of conducting nongovernmental, peer evaluation of educational institutions and programs. Private educational associations of regional or national scope have adopted criteria reflecting the qualities of a sound educational program and have adopted procedures for evaluating institutions or programs to determine whether or not they are operating at basic levels of quality (www.ed.gov 2000).

Accreditation is both a status and a process. As a status, accreditation provides public notification that an institution or program meets standards of quality set forth by an accrediting agency. As a process, accreditation reflects the fact that in achieving recognition by the accrediting agency, the institution or program is committed to self-study and external review by one's peers in seeking not only to meet standards but also to continuously seek ways in which to enhance the quality of the services provided.

The accreditation process is continually evolving. The trend has been from quantitative to qualitative criteria, from the early days of simple checklists to an increasing interest and emphasis on measuring the outcomes of educational experiences. The NAEYC has offered a national, voluntary accreditation system to set professional standards for early childhood education programs, and to help families identify high-quality programs since 1985. The NAEYC program standards and accreditation criteria were updated in 2006 to include (1) setting explicit program standards for early childhood programs serving children birth through kindergarten and (2) making the standards more evidence-based and aligned with the profession's knowledge of best practice. There are ten program standards, with specific criteria attached to each one that programs must meet in order to achieve NAEYC Accreditation. The framework of the standards and criteria focuses on best practices in the field and the benefits to stakeholders in early childhood education. There are four groups of early childhood education stakeholders: children, teachers, family and community partners, and the program administration. These ten standards cover the areas of relationships, curriculum, teaching, assessment of child progress, health, the qualifications of teaching staff, families, community relationships, physical environment, and leadership and management. Over 7,000 child care programs, preschools, early learning centers, and other center- or school-based early childhood education programs are currently NAEYC-accredited. These programs provide high-quality care and education to nearly one million young children in the United States, its territories, and programs affiliated with the US Department of Defense (naeyc.org, 2010). The National Association for Family Child Care (NAFCC) sponsors the only nationally recognized accreditation system designed specifically for family child care providers. This system was designed by hundreds of providers, parents, and early care and education experts in an effort to create a quality indicator for family child care programs across the country. NAFCC accreditation is awarded to family child care providers who meet the eligibility requirements and the quality standards for NAFCC accreditation. Accreditation reflects a level of quality through a process that examines all aspects of the family child care program; that is, relationships, the environment, developmental learning activities, safety and health, and professional and business practices. Once family child care providers become accredited, they agree to abide by the standards set forth and to be measured against those standards, with periodic integrity and compliance reviews. There are over 2100 NAFCC accredited providers throughout the United States and in other locations worldwide where military family child care professionals operate.

The National Private School Accreditation Program and the NPSAA Accreditation Alliance has an accreditation process that requires private schools to examine their goals, activities, and achievements. Since accreditation status is reviewed on a periodic basis, recognized schools are encouraged to maintain continuous self-study and improvement mechanisms.

The process begins with the private school "self-study." A comprehensive effort is made to measure progress according to previously accepted objectives. The self-study considers the interests of a broad cross section of constituencies, students, faculty, administrators, alumni, trustees, and, in some circumstances, the local community. **naeyc** 3a, 3b, 3c, 3d, 6b, 6c, 6d

Observation and Assessment: Collecting Information and Record Keeping

The observations of children's behavior and actions and the records you keep will illustrate their capabilities. The observations will also inform you about their needs and interests. You will notice the children's strengths and the areas of development that might need particular attention. Over time, observations and the records you keep will reveal how the children's growth and development progresses and transforms.

Information about children is collected **informally** and **formally**. Information is also gathered individually by teachers and collaboratively by the staff. Continuing to take cues from the children will help you learn more about them and prepare you for the more formalized process of assessment. Assessment may take many forms, including listening to what children say, observing what they do, and appraising and predicting their behavior. Children change, and so must the curriculum. Collected data, fundamental principles of child development, and your program guidelines will come together to create a curriculum with appropriate expectations for children.

Casual conversations with families during routine arrival and pickup will balance the pre-planned sessions such as interviews and conference meetings. Jotting down notes during the day is a convenient and popular way for teachers to keep records of what children say and do. More elaborate strategies include checklists, journals or logs, running records, and time samples.

Assessment tools provide a more focused view about a particular child, a group, or the interaction between a child and the group. Review of data will help you to make more meaningful decisions to sustain the children's activities. For example, a closer look at the log or notebook in the block interest center might reveal that the children who left the block area in tears did so at 11:45 AM. Teachers need to review the daily schedule and the log and consider whether an earlier lunchtime might be more beneficial for the children. Or, adding a calming, teacher-directed activity, such as body tracing, would offer a needed transition from an active experience. **(Curriculum Activity Guide 44 📖)**.

A record of a child's progress in different areas of development is referred to as a *developmental profile*. This is a record of a child's physical,

© Cengage Learning 2013

Teachers who continually take cues from the children make more meaningful decisions to sustain the children's activities and meet their needs.

cognitive, social, and emotional development. Some programs that contract with funding agencies must complete a developmental profile of each child on enrollment and at least once every 12 months thereafter. This application connects the needs of children to the curriculum. The intent of the developmental profile is that it be used to plan and implement age and developmentally appropriate activities. In California, the Department of Education directs state-funded child development programs to utilize the Desired Results Developmental Profile—Preschool (DRDP-PS©) (2010).

Assessment and review contribute to more appropriate planning and also help parents understand whether their children are developing well. Parents want to know if their children are behaving and learning normally. Does the child need extra support and possible intervention? Parents' insight into the daily behavior of their children may contribute significant data for teachers (Wolfendale 1998). Parents can gather information about behavior to pinpoint periods when their children's actions may be out of adjustment with their emerging needs (Katz 1994, EDO-PS-94-15).

Documentation of the experiences in which children participate regularly places assessment within the domain of the teacher. The work sampling assessment method can be used to observe and record the actions of children in different educational areas and at different times. The Work Sampling System was developed by Samuel Meisels to "assess and document skills, knowledge, behavior, and accomplishments" of children. This performance assessment system reviews the children's work completed in the different areas of the curriculum with checklists, portfolios, and summary reports (Meisels 1993, 36). The actions of children are observed and recorded in different education areas and at different times, causing work sampling to be a curriculum-embedded assessment (Meisels 1996/1997, 60). **naeyc** 3a, 3b, 3c, 3d

Objectivity

Objective assessments describe behavior without the observer's personal opinions or inferences. Teachers can reflect on the gathered information and observations as an appraisal of children's strengths and needs. Professionally reliable interpretation rests primarily on objective data. Your **objectivity** is important when you prepare a written observation about a child. Observations made over time allow teachers to see patterns of behavior that will drive curriculum modification.

Confidentiality and Privacy

Confidentiality is an ethical issue concerning the right to privacy. As a professional, you are obligated to carry out certain ethical and legal responsibilities regarding confidentiality and privacy of information about the children and their families. At the most basic level, the information and records a school collects should not be shared or casually disclosed to others. This implies that information about a child and family should not be divulged to other families in the program. The Family Educational Rights to Privacy Act (FERPA) is a federal law. This law applies to all schools and obligates teachers and program administrators to protect the privacy of student education records. Records maintained by the school can be inspected by parents. Parents also have the right to ask that the program administrator modify records that they consider to be inaccurate or misleading (U.S. Department of Education 2011).

The NAEYC Code of Ethical Conduct and Statement of Commitment (2005) offers guidelines for professionally responsible behavior. The code sets forth a basis for resolving ethical dilemmas commonly encountered in early childhood education programs. For example, one principle underlines the urgency of developing written policies covering confidentiality and children's records. Program administrators and staff shall respect the right to privacy of all families, refrain from disclosing confidential information about them, and avoid intrusion into their family life. However, when staff members are concerned about a child's welfare, it is permissible to reveal confidential information to agencies and individuals who may be able to act in the child's interest. In cases where family members are in conflict with one another, staff members shall work openly to help all parties involved make informed decisions (NAEYC 2005).

Hard copy and electronic records of children, including observation notes and details of parent conferencing, must be protected and stored appropriately. Program guidelines provide a method for clarifying the conditions for sharing and release of records.

Confidentiality and privacy also involves the images of children. A parent or guardian's permission is needed for photographing and displaying images of a child. You should obtain signed authorization from parents and guardians providing permission to photograph and record children's images. Include in your school's authorization form the various media devices to be used to record the children's images and the potential uses of the images. For example, the children's images may be taken with digital cameras, smart phones, and webcams as appropriate for educational purposes. The images may be shared with the parents and utilized for bulletin boards, the school website, teacher training, newsletters, and for the children's portfolios. Current permission forms signed by the children's parents or guardians should be maintained for all photographs that will be used. Images of the children should not be displayed or released in any way without the written consent of the children's parents or guardians. **naeyc** 3a, 3b, 3c, 3d, 6b

Informal Assessment

Learning and continuing to take cues from children will prepare you for the more formalized process of assessment. Assessment may take many forms, including listening to what children say, observing what they do, and appraising and predicting their behavior. Children change and so must the curriculum. That is the reason you need to gather information about each child in some way. You will combine the data you collect about the children with what you learn about best practices. You will also consider your program vision and goals to create curriculum with appropriate expectations for young children. Your expectations

Figure 3–1 Three Assessment Methods Used Most Often

Anecdotal Record	A short narrative record usually written down by the teacher after the child has been observed. The anecdotal record reports what the child did in a factual manner.
Log and Notebook	Available for teachers throughout the indoor and outdoor environment to offer convenient opportunities to record the behavior and actions of children as it happens. The information can be used for parent conferences, to complete checklists, and to help write anecdotal records.
Running Record	A written narrative recording all of a child's behavior as it occurs during a specified period of time. Observer remains apart from the child and activity in order to observe and record detailed accounts of a child's body movements, facial expressions, and interaction with others.

will be appropriate because your assessment will be conducted on the children in their own school settings, the spaces that are familiar and comfortable. This is considered naturalistic observation.

Early childhood educators have several options available for informally assessing the children in their programs. You can collect information about the children on a daily basis. A useful and common way to record what children are doing is to write down casual, informal notes. Additionally, three observation methods used most often are **anecdotal records**, logs and notebooks, and running records (Mindes 2011) (Figure 3–1). There are numerous additional techniques for assessing children and as many or more ways to describe and categorize the methods. Some of the additional techniques for collecting data about children include checklists, interviews and conversations, portfolios, and documentation.

Daily Informal Notes

Brief records are written throughout the day on small tablets kept in the pockets of the teachers' aprons or smocks. Clipboards are placed in accessible locations throughout the indoor and outdoor areas. Notes may include words to help you remember to record more detailed observations at the end of the day. A casual, informal note may include language samples, children's participation in activities, and information about their interests.

Anecdotal Records

An anecdotal record is a popular way to collect information because teachers can capture what they see a child doing and saying. Anecdotal observations are short and usually written down after the event. Recording a selected event requires a teacher to remember what the child did. A teacher may choose to focus on a particular behavior. Teachers need to be mindful about describing an incident as factually as possible. Opinions about what a teacher thinks a child did should be recorded in a separate commentary or part of an anecdotal record (Beaty 2010).

Logs and Notebooks

Teachers are busy and may not have release time to observe the children in their group. This is the reason that logs, sometimes referred to as notebooks, are popular. Logs and notebooks available for teachers throughout the indoor and outdoor environment offer a way to record the behavior and actions of children. Having these items conveniently located in interest centers and areas gives teachers the chance to capture in writing the action of a child as it happens. The information can be used for parent conferences, to complete checklists, and to help write anecdotal records.

Running Records

Running records require uninterrupted time. Teachers who may have extra assistance with their group or release time may be able to focus on data collection utilizing the running record format. This observation method records in a written narrative all of a child's behavior as it occurs during a specified period of time. The teacher remains apart from the child and activity in order to observe and record all actions. The narrative recorded by the teacher includes as much as possible of the child's body movements, facial expressions, and interaction with others. The records generally provide a detailed narrative of the observed action, language, and behaviors of a child (Beaty 2010).

Checklists

A checklist offers teachers a convenient system for assessing skills, abilities, and behaviors through observation. For example, when a child is observed pulling another child in a wagon for the first time, you can indicate the date on a checklist next to the skill. A checklist may be based on a rubric (a way to measure) the action or ability. A checklist provides prescribed skills generally organized in developmental categories or areas. A teacher can check if a child is able to accomplish a particular skill or displays an ability, or if that skill, ability, or behavior is absent. Generally, an action that is repeated can also be noted on a checklist. A child may be observed periodically to assess his or her progress.

The *Child Development Checklist* developed by Janice J. Beaty is an example of a practical and useful tool for teachers of young children. The checklist is organized into six areas with each including child behaviors in the sequence in which they occur. Particularly valuable is the focus on identifying what the child is able to do. Hints are provided for teachers to use a child's strengths in continued program and curriculum planning that meets his or her needs (2010) (Figure 3–2).

Interviews and Conversations

Your informal and formal interviews with families and children will provide rich and valuable information. The interviews with the family during the initial enrollment meeting establish needed background information. The interviews and conversations, both spontaneous and planned, establish the ideal assessment technique.

The ongoing, and often daily, conversations you have with family members will keep you updated regarding changes in the child's life. Questions from parents and children reveal their concerns, needs, and interests. The conversations you have with children build a warm, accepting environment. Setting aside specific time and enjoying every opportunity to talk with the children create meaningful relationships. The conversations will give you immense insight to their true understanding, needs, and interests.

Portfolios

The methods by which teachers gather information about children has changed and so have the materials used to document behavior and actions. The conventional cumulative folder, with records and testing results, has been replaced with portfolios. Samples of the children's work placed in a portfolio are valuable documentation of learning and progress. Portfolios, added at all educational levels, document progress of an individual child. Portfolios can identify a child's competency, information that is valuable in guiding her or his participation in school activities. Portfolios, to be considered a method of assessment, must be more than an expandable folder holding random observations and examples of a child's work (Epstein et al. 2004). Staff need to identify the reasons and methods for collecting portfolio materials

---

Figure 3–2 Sample Checklist Assessing Emotional Development

Child Development Checklist

The sample below provides the second section of the eleven areas of development included in the complete Child Development Checklist developed by Janice J. Beaty and presented in her book *Observing Development of the Young Child* (2010).

Name_____   Observer_____

Program_____   Dates_____

Directions:

Put an **X** for items you see the child perform regularly. Put an **N** for items where there is no opportunity to observe. Leave all other items blank. Item_____

Dates_____   Evidence_____

2. Emotional Development

_____Releases stressful feelings in appropriate manner

_____Expresses anger in words rather than negative actions

_____Remains calm in difficult or dangerous situations

and data. A portfolio provides a systematic and appropriate method for assessment of young children. Portfolios include samples of the children's work, tape recordings, checklists, videos, observations, photographs, records of parent conferences and interviews, parent evaluations, developmental profiles, and health evaluations. These items can show children's learning styles, interests, and unique talents of each individual child (Helm and Katz 2010). The portfolio is an authentic record of a child during his or her participation at your school.

Portfolios encourage two- and three-way collaboration among students, teachers, and parents; promote ownership and motivation; integrate assessment with instruction and learning; and establish a quantitative and qualitative record of progress over time. They can provide credible, meaningful evidence of students' learning and development to parents, teachers, and others that can be used to inform practice and policy in the preschool classroom. Portfolios document and share the children's progress with families and administrators. For portfolios to be used for program accountability, as well as student learning and reflection, the evaluated outcomes must be aligned with curriculum and instruction. Children must have some choice about what to include if they are to feel ownership and pride in their work and participation in the program (Epstein et al. 2004).

Documentation and Work Sampling

Documentation is another way for you to collect and record information about children and in this way it becomes a form of record keeping. The information or evidence you gather includes photographs, video recordings, audiotapes, and work samples. These illustrate the children's progress, including what and how the children are learning through the program experiences and activities offered (Seitz 2009).

Meisels Work Sampling System supports assessment of children's skills, knowledge, behavior, and accomplishments. The performance assessment system allows teachers to use checklists, portfolios, and summary reports to review children's work. You will be able to observe the children's actions and collect samples of their work throughout the regularly scheduled program (1995).

The Work Sampling System, an example of a curriculum-embedded assessment, provides reliable data about a child's participation at school. The data can be used to enhance instruction because it is based on teachers' perceptions of the participating children in actual classroom situations. It simultaneously informs, expands, and structures those perceptions while involving children and parents in the learning process. The guidelines and checklists provide detailed, observation-based information about the child's skills, accomplishments, knowledge, and behavior. The summary reports help record, summarize, and aggregate information on children's overall educational progress (Meisels 1996/1997).

Documentation is a method of assessment utilized in the Reggio Emilia inspired schools. A more thorough discussion of documentation is provided in the last section of this chapter, *Observation and Assessment: Using the Cues from Children for Curriculum.*

Formal Assessment

Standardized Tests

Standardized tests are designed to provide objective accounts or reports. These tests encompass an increasing list of instruments and procedures. Some of the instruments rate behavior of children with scales or test visual perception. Other instruments screen self-concept or evaluate social competence. The developmental schedules originally developed by Arnold Gesell have been revised and are research based. The Gesell Developmental Observation-Revised (GDO-R)© is an assessment system that focuses on direct observation of children to measure their neuro-motor, language, cognitive, social-emotional, and adaptive development (Guddemi 2011) (Figure 3–3).

State offices and departments of education have required programs to complete developmental profiles of the children enrolled in their publically funded programs. Other schools utilize pictorial intelligence tests, developmental screening tests, video and audio recordings (Beaty 2006). Funding sources that mandate programs to justify the progress of the participating children generally select the standardized test or instrument to be administered. Standardized tests are based on numbers or numerical scores that theoretically provide comparable score results. The intent of standardized tests is to measure all the children in the same way. This strategy, assessing children with standardized tests, has critics. Teachers know that every child's growth and development fluctuates. Fluctuating development and changes in daily routines can cause test scores to fluctuate. Teachers express concerns about the pressures to prepare children for these tests and that preparation for standardized tests replaces the early childhood curriculum that is good for young children. Regardless, many funding agencies continue to

Figure 3–3

Gesell Developmental Schedules Today

A set of developmental schedules was published in 1925 by Dr. Arnold Gesell. *The Mental Growth of the Preschool Child: Developmental Tests for Children 4 weeks through 5 years of age*, brought Dr. Gesell into worldwide acclaim. He is also recognized as the first school psychologist. Still popular today, the developmental schedules are the basis of the 2010 publication of the Gesell assessment, known as the Gesell Developmental Observation-Revised (GDO-R)©. The new GDO-R is based on current and scientifically sound normative data collected on over 1300 children nationwide ages 3–6. This much needed study took place over three years and was supervised by the Mid-Continent Research for Education and Learning. *Harvard Education Letter* online was the first to announce the results of the study saying, "Oldest voice in America weighs in with new data . . . children haven't changed, but Kindergarten has."

The Gesell Institute of Human Development celebrated its 60th anniversary in 2010. As a preeminent research institute, always an educational resource for both parents and teachers, and a national voice for children; today the institute continues its lifelong history of advocacy. The institute advocates for understanding and using child development knowledge to nurture and support the optimal growth and learning of all children. Today's institute provides resources in the form of printed/media materials, professional development, and direct service programs to children and families. To give examples of the popularity of Gesell Institute at one time, 25% of all children were screened using the GDO to determine readiness for school. The series is still quite popular. Gesell was known as the "Voice of Reason."

Today, the institute is alive and thriving. Participating in the national conversation on the importance of quality early childhood, ages birth to age 8 years. The updated Gesell Developmental Observation-Revised (GDO-R) © 2010, is a multidimensional developmental assessment system along with its shorter version, the Gesell Early Screener (GES). With a carefully researched Parent Guardian Questionnaire and Teacher Questionnaire, the criterion referenced, performance assessment assists parents, educators, and other professionals in understanding characteristics of a child's behavior and development in relation to typical growth patterns based on sequential, normative stages of development. The GDO assessments focus on direct observation to measure a child's neuro-motor, language, cognitive, social-emotional, and adaptive development.

The Institute carries on the legacy of Dr. Arnold Gesell by providing professional development surrounding the administration and interpretation of scores with the GDO and other child development topics.

Marcy Guddemi, PhD, MBA
Executive Director
Gesell Institute of Human Development
New Haven, Connecticut

require standardized tests in early childhood programs for program accountability.

Standardized tests are often commercially prepared and marketed. Early childhood educators seeking appropriate assessment tools can turn to the guidelines issued by professional organizations. Recognizing the benefits of child assessments, the NAEYC and the National Association of Early Childhood Specialists in State Departments of Education (2003) published a joint position statement that emphasized critical recommendations regarding assessment including, "Policymakers, the early childhood profession, and other stakeholders in young children's lives have a shared responsibility to make ethical, appropriate, valid and reliable assessment a central part of all early programs."

A variety of assessments to choose from as well as information about them is available online.

Some of the tools and systems available are designed to measure overall development. Others assess literacy or social-emotional development. A few of the assessments were identified by Amy Shillady in "Choosing an Appropriate Assessment System" (Figure 3–4). **naeyc** 3a, 3b, 3c, 3d, 6b

Individual Education Plan (IEP)

The Education for All Handicapped Children Act, passed in 1975, was later amended and renamed the Individuals with Disabilities Education Act. This is the most significant law affecting the testing and measurement of children in the United States. The act guarantees all children with disabilities the right to an appropriate education in a free public school and placement in the least restrictive learning environment. The use of nondiscriminatory testing and evaluation is required with this

---

Figure 3–4 Choosing an Appropriate Assessment

Five Assessment Methods

Identified by Amy Shillady in "Choosing an Appropriate Assessment System"

The Developmental Continuum Assessment Toolkit for Ages 3–5
Diane Trister Dodge, Laura J. Colker, and Cate Heromann (2002)
Teaching Strategies, Inc., Washington, D.C

The Devereux Early Childhood Assessment (DECA)
Paul LeBuffe and Jack Naglieri (1998)
Devereux Early Childhood Initiative
Devereux Foundation, Villanova, PA

High Scope Preschool Child Observational Record: For Ages 21/2–6 (COR)
HighScope Staff (1992)
HighScope Press, Ypsilanti, MI

Social Competence and Behavior Evaluation (SCBE), Preschool Edition
Peter J. LaFreniere and Jean E. Dumas (1995)
Western Psychological Services, Los Angeles, CA

Preschool Individual Growth and Development Indicators (IGDIs)
Early Childhood Research Institute on Measuring Growth and Development (1998)
Author, Minneapolis, MN

---

law. Amendments to the act were passed in 1991. The amended act requires that the individual educational needs of all young children with disabilities must be met in all early childhood programs.

One of the features of the law requires that the educational needs of all young children with disabilities are reviewed by a team. The law mandates that the team is made up of teachers, parents, diagnosticians, school psychologists, medical personnel, social workers, or representatives of government agencies or institutions. The team is required to consider the child's placement in a specific program or find appropriate therapy methods. The team maintains oversight for the screening, testing, and development of an IEP for each child. The IEP will be based on the findings from the screening and testing (Wortham 2005).

IEP: A Teacher's Role

Teachers of young children become keen observers of actions, behaviors, and the development of children in their groups, classrooms, and programs. You will become increasingly more skilled at recognizing the

stages of children's development and will be able to determine if a certain child's behavior and development is within the expected range for children of that age. Appropriate assessment can help you form a concrete picture of a child's development. Documentation over time is important. This allows colleagues, directors, and support staff to be able to determine whether or not there is a legitimate concern. Each program has its own policies regarding contacting parents to discuss these kinds of concerns.

The assessments conducted by classroom teachers are not formal evaluations. However, you will, along with other teachers, need to become aware of the guidelines for early intervention services. These services are designed to meet the developmental needs of each eligible infant, toddler, or preschool child, and the needs of the family related to the child's development.

State and federal guidelines will outline early intervention services including referral procedures. The prompt and appropriate identification of risk factors and delays is important to establish the necessary and proper assistance for young

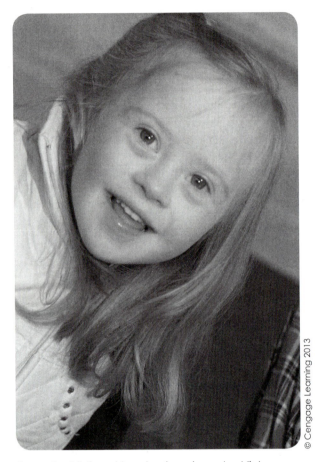

© Cengage Learning 2013

An early childhood teacher is an important link with parents of a child with special needs ensuring that the educational needs of the preschooler are appropriately considered and met.

children and their families. Early intervention services may eliminate or minimize the need for special services later in life.

Becoming Part of an IEP Team

Teachers who have children with special needs in their classrooms play an important role in their observation and assessment. You may also play a key role in the implementation of their IEP. As a teacher of young children you may be asked to provide documentation, for instance your observation records of a child. Your observation may indicate that a child needs formal evaluation. In some communities, teachers of special needs infants, toddlers, and preschoolers are invited to participate in meetings. Most often kindergarten teachers will be asked to serve on the interdisciplinary team that creates the IEP. When an IEP is in place, you may be asked to assist in the process; for example, you may coordinate the scheduling of specialists such as speech therapists and occupational therapists. You will be an important link

with parents of the child with special needs ensuring that they receive clear communication from the specialists. Importantly, you will comfort and guide the child with the process. naeyc 3a, 3b, 3c, 3d, 6b, 6c, 6d

Assessment to Inform Educators

Assessing a child's behavior will contribute to your ability to identify age-appropriate activities, which match the range of competence and readiness of the children in your program. The intended use of assessments should be identified because that will determine how you will conduct the assessment. The timing of data collection will be most helpful if the collection occurs regularly as children acquire skills and learn content (Shepard et al. 1998).

Parents' insight into the daily behavior of their children may contribute significant data for you and the other teachers in your program. Assessment takes time. Some types, like the casual notes and checklists, may require the least time, yet even those place demands on teachers because they need to be entered into some form of file for permanent documentation. Teachers value observation and documentation; therefore they dedicate extra efforts to maintain records. "Teachers often comment that there is little time in the daily schedule for observation and record keeping," explains Lorraine Haas, Shasta College Early Childhood Education Instructor. Lorraine, who also directs college students at the campus child development center, cautions students that many teachers often use their own personal time to complete observations and assessment records (2011).

▶ ‖ **Video Case**

2–5 Years: Observation Module for Early Childhood

Visit the Early Childhood Education Media Library, and watch the TeachSource Video Case on www.cengagebrain.com

1. What informal assessment would you use to collect data about the children in the first two segments of the video?

2. In the third and fourth segments, a teacher asked two preschool girls questions. What did the teacher learn about the girls during his questioning interviews?

Assessment to Inform Families

Families want to know about their children. Now more than ever, they are concerned about their children's education and the process of learning (National Early Childhood Accountability Task Force 2007). You will be accountable to families by keeping them informed about their children's early learning and development. Assessment of the children and the systematic records you share with families help them understand their children's development. The observations and samples of their work give families insight into their children's participation at the school. Specific observations will illustrate a child's behavior and facilitate your discussions with a family member. Assessment of individual children may reveal the need for extra support and possible intervention. Parents can gather information about behavior to pinpoint periods when their children's actions may be out of adjustment with their emerging needs (Katz 1994).

Assessments of children become particularly valuable ways to inform families during conferences. Conferences between family members and teachers are important. At the preschool level, all conferences offer beneficial time for teachers to sincerely collaborate with families. The fifth guideline in NAEYC's position statement on developmentally appropriate practice, *Establishing Reciprocal Relationships with Families*, underlines this point, ". . . teachers and parents share their knowledge of the child and understanding of children's development and learning as part of the day-to-day communication and planned conferences. Teachers support families in ways that maximally promote family decision-making capabilities and competence (Copple and Bredekamp 2009, 182).

Teachers and other child caregivers as well as family members will support a child's development by sharing information. The exchange of information, including preschool and home experiences, observations, goals, and beliefs, nurture the teacher-family relationship and contribute to the child's well-being. The conferences present opportunities for parents and other family members, as appropriate, to ensure that their child is receiving a fitting foundation for developmental growth. Conferences establish welcoming occasions for the parents to share knowledge about their child, including their hopes for their child's future (Robertson 2010).

Conferences in the early childhood settings may provide opportunities for teachers to engage family members in the educational progress of their children. A well-planned conference may be the first positive experience with the educational system for a family member. A positive experience results when teachers project accepting and sincere attitudes. Parents will respond optimistically when you begin conference sessions with encouraging informational updates about their child or children. Informational updates can share observations about the child's physical progress, social interaction, emotional maturation, and acquisition of skills in listening, communicating, and literacy.

Conferences will also offer you opportunities to increase parents' awareness of their children's classroom experiences and how their children relate to the adults and other children within the school environment. Discussion of a child's need for early intervention may be the reason for a specifically scheduled parent conference.

Regular conferences with families should be scheduled at least two times during the school

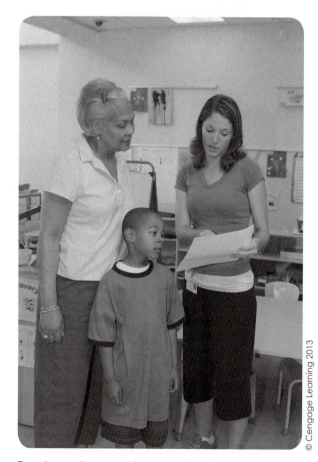

Teachers, other caregivers, and family members support a child's development by sharing information.

© Cengage Learning 2013

year. In early childhood programs, teachers and child care providers can be available to meet with parents at various times when necessary (Snuggs 2008) and enjoy the advantage of daily contact with a family member when a child is signed in and out of the program.

Preparation before a conference requires you to examine a child's folder and portfolio. Familiarize yourself with the checklists and anecdotal records. Organize the work samples, notes regarding the child's peer and adult interactions, skills in the developmental areas, and general participation in activities. In this way, you will be prepared to share the child's strengths and abilities in several developmental areas with the family member (Seplocha 2007). An anecdote about the child playing with a particular child, sharing materials, exhibiting enthusiasm during cleanup, or other information that adds interest and will bring the family member into the child's life at school is encouraged. naeyc 3a, 3b, 3c, 3d

Children's natural curiosity is a powerful motivator that will further engage their interest in specific activities.

© Cengage Learning 2013

Observation and Assessment: Using the Cues from Children for Curriculum Planning

As you further consider assessment and its relationship to curriculum planning, you might have noticed that children engage in activities that have relevance for them. Relevant experiences have connection to their families and engage the children in movements and actions that are familiar to them. Children's natural curiosity is a powerful motivator that will further engage their interest in specific activities. Their interest in their environment should contribute to the design of activities and curriculum (Espinosa 2002). Children, particularly the youngest preschoolers, need to experience activities that satisfy their curiosity and engage their senses. What can they see? What can they hear? What can they touch? What can they smell and even taste?

Although children are naturally curious and ready to explore, their interest on a particular day may relate to their own activity level and well-being. For instance, a hungry child may be more interested in the cooking activity with inviting aromas of pancakes and syrup than the materials provided on a manipulative table. Another child may walk away from the firefighter hats and boots in the dramatic play area because he remembers the loud fire engine sirens during his morning drive to school.

Documenting the Work of Young Children

Documentation is another way to collect and record information about children. Documentation can become an important means of learning for children and their parents and for teachers. Observation and interpretation of experiences create a deep learning process that supports both the teacher and child as researcher and investigator (Khokha and Heimann 2010).

Documentation is a key feature of the Reggio Emilia approach. The practice of documentation, utilizing large photo-journal-like panels, makes learning visible. The large panels cover the Reggio classroom walls and tell stories about the projects in a photojournalistic style. Children are captured at key moments in projects. The boards allow the child to recall the activities and seeing what they did prompts them to continue developing concepts and gain competence about their idea. The displays offer insight into the school's life and gives families and the community a glimpse into the program successes. Because the display boards document the program and reveal children's thinking, they are a way of assessing the children's progress (Lewin-Benham 2008).

Methods that can be used to document the work of children include checklists, rating scales, digital cameras, videos and tape recordings. These can capture dialogue, portfolios with samples of the children's work, and anecdotal records. Sketches or diagrams can also help illustrate what is going on in the classroom (Mathivet 2008). This kind of documentation provides an overall picture of the child's social-emotional, cognitive, language, and physical growth and development. It gives a picture that is both visual and written, provides feedback that can be shared and discussed by all in a team approach, and can be used to guide curriculum. All through this process, conversations can take place with children, with parents and other adults, providing teachers with a perspective to help form a rounded, balanced picture of the child.

Documentation is a significant way for children to represent their own learning. You have read about the importance of assessment, including the documentation of children's work to plan appropriate curriculum. You also understand that children learn best when the activities are connected to their own experiences. As an intentional teacher, you will value the opportunities to engage the children individually. When you do, you will be able to ask them questions and discover ways for them to represent their interests, their needs and, their own learning.

When you review a documentation panel with children, you might hear them tell you more about what they did or what they want to do. It might be the time to write down the story or information a child is dictating. You and Vincent could be looking at a photograph of a walk taken months earlier and while you listen to him, you learn that he had really wanted to collect tree pods that have fallen on the ground. You can immediately begin extending Vincent's learning and the curriculum by planning a walk to collect the pods. When you do, you identify that the pods fell off a eucalyptus tree. The experience will be further extended when you provide Vincent with an opportunity to watch you write down his ideas about the eucalyptus pods. Children may respond to specific inquiries from you and talk about their families, perhaps their pets, or trips to

visit relatives during the holidays. Some children might want an idea written down or label the items they finger painted, or painted on the easel, or drew on construction paper.

Digital photography has become an accessible and practical way for you and the children to document activities and experiences. You might take photographs of the children engaged in various activities. The children may also take photographs of their project and the other children busy in different activities. When teachers document children's work with photographs it creates an authentic assessment of what they do and have done. Photography can document the experiences you offer to the children and the activities they select in the classroom. Giving children opportunities to look at and take classroom photographs will give you insight into their interests, such as seashells, and their view of the classroom setting (**Curriculum Activity Guide 29**).

Children who use a camera to take their own pictures will be able to label the content in their pictures and identify the objects, events, and feelings about the photographs (Byrnes and Wasik 2009). For instance, a child might want to photograph an elaborate canal created in the sand or a bridge structured in the block area. You will optimize children's learning experiences with cameras by encouraging them to take photographs of the activities that are meaningful to them (Byrnes and Wasik 2009).

Another beneficial aspect of documentation and photography will be documentation of the day's happenings and events. Parents will appreciate viewing photographs throughout your classroom especially because it fosters communication between staff and parents and between parents and children (Good 2010). **naeyc** 1a, 1b, 1c, 2c, 3a, 3b, 3c, 3d, 4b, 4c, 4d, 5c

Allowing Time for Child-Teacher Talks

The teachers who listen to questions and comments gain an essential understanding about the children. As an intentional teacher, you will present meaningful questions to children. Your questions may stimulate their thinking, engage them in a conversation, and encourage soothing communication. Providing time for meaningful talks will allow children to give you feedback (Epstein 2007). Perhaps you will comment about the tunnels in the sand area or the seeds that sprouted in the planting trays. Teacher Marisa provided a flannel board activity about apple trees. The children

Teachers who listen to questions and comments gain an essential understanding about the children.

© Cengage Learning 2013

in her group, all three- and four-year-olds enjoyed varied curriculum activities throughout the week that related to the concept—*an apple can be different colors.* Two of the four-year-olds, Christina and Jake, joined the cooking experience table where apples were organized by their color into small, plastic containers. Jake pointed to the golden delicious apple and said, "That's a pear, that's a pear, it's yellow." Teacher Marisa responded, "Some apples are yellow, Jake, and that fruit is an apple, not a pear." Teacher Marisa made a note about Jake's comment and thought that she might continue offering experiences to enrich the children's knowledge about apples; she thought that she would expand their knowledge about the concept: *an apple can be different colors.* Even though the concept would be expanded, Teacher Marisa planned to keep the initial activities simple. Children may be accustomed only to one or two apple types, even though there are hundreds of varieties. Young children learn about the apples they see, touch, and smell and these are generally the varieties that grow regionally.

When you listen and communicate with young children as they participate in the activities, as teacher Marisa did, you will gain important insight into their understanding and thinking. When teachers pay attention to what the children say and do, it can lead to an emergent curriculum that builds on their interests and needs. This approach

is different from a preplanned, "canned" thematic curriculum model (Seitz 2006). When you are familiar with the process of listening, observing, and talking to young children, you will increasingly be able to modify curriculum plans to more effectively meet the children's developmental needs. The specific curriculum plans and activities will be based on your observations and assessments of them. Effective teachers also take cues from the children to gauge whether an activity is not working, and they make adjustments accordingly (Heroman and Copple 2006).

Supporting the Cycle of Documentation, Planning, and Evaluation

Teaching young children is a multifaceted task. Teaching requires you to closely observe and study children's unfolding activities. You will take the time to notice, document, and reflect on the children's activities. You will listen to their ideas and record their progress. All these tasks allow you to make effective and meaningful decisions about curriculum that responds to children. You can keep the joy of being with children at the heart of your teaching.

Documentation, planning, and evaluation of the children's participation in the activities help early childhood education teachers focus on the developmental needs, emerging skills, and interests of individual children. Your assessments and documentation of the children's reactions to and use of materials support authentic assessment.

Documentation, then, becomes the process for "making learning visible" so that together with others you can study the evidence of children's efforts and their learning (Edwards et al. 2004). You will learn to collect and organize concrete evidence in many forms, including audio/video recordings, digital photos, text, observational field notes, and samples of children's work. The documentation process is more than gathering observations; it also includes reflecting, collaborating, planning, and communicating. The documentation process is part of a *cycle of inquiry* (Edwards et al. 2007).

Children will respond to the materials and activities planned with their needs and interests in mind. When these are highly compelling, appealing, and engaging, children work at tasks longer and try harder than they might with materials or activities they find less interesting. naeyc 1a, 1b, 1c, 2c, 3a, 3b, 3c, 3d, 4b, 4c, 4d, 5c

Thinking About What You Have Learned

✔ Ask three teachers of young children how they observe and document the children in their programs. Find out if their schools have required observation and documentation procedures. Inquire about the amount of time dedicated to observation and record keeping. Write a summary about your findings, including a comparison of the responses from the three teachers.

✔ Return to the chapter opener and review the notes about Lee, Justin, and Martin. Describe how you would use these observations.

✔ Outline your plan for a conference you have scheduled with a parent who has expressed concerns about the observations completed and photographs taken of her son Max.

✔ Choose one of the assessment tools designed to measure overall development, literacy, or social and emotional development discussed in this chapter. Review the tool you select and discuss the ways this tool will be helpful to you as a classroom teacher.

✔ What activities would you add to enhance the children's learning about apples and apple trees? Refer to the description of Teacher Marisa and the children in the section titled "Allowing Time for Child-Teacher Talks."

Chapter References

Beaty, Janice J. 2010 *Observing development of the young child.* 7th ed. Upper Saddle River, NJ: Merrill.

Bredekamp, Sue, and Carol E. Copple, eds. 2009. *Developmentally appropriate practice in early childhood programs serving children from birth through age 8.* 3rd ed. Washington, DC: National Association for the Education of Young Children.

Buell, Martha Jane, and Tara M. Sutton. 2008. Weaving a web with children at the center. A new approach to emergent curriculum planning for young preschoolers. *Young Children.* http://www.naeyc.org/files/tyc/file/YCBuell.pdf

Byrnes, Julia, and Barbara A. Wasik. 2009. Picture this: Using photography as a learning tool in early childhood classrooms. *Childhood Education* 85.4 (6): 243. http://findarticles.com/p/articles/mi_qa3614/is_200907/ai_n32127447/

California State Department of Education, Child Development Programs. 2010. Desired Results Developmental Profile–Preschool©. Sacramento, CA.

Caruso, Joseph, with M. Temple Fawcett. 2007. *Supervision in early childhood education: A developmental perspective.* New York: Teachers College Press.

Edwards, Carolyn Pope, Susan Churchill, Mary Gabriel, Ruth Heaton, Julie Jones-Branch, Christine Marvin, and Michelle Rupiper. 2007. Students learn about documentation throughout their teacher education program. *Early Childhood Research and Practice* 10:2. http://ecrp.uiuc.edu/v9n2/edwards.html

Epstein, Ann S., Lawrence J. Schweinhart, Andrea DeBruin-Parecki, and Kenneth B. Robin. 2004. Preschool assessment: A guide to developing a balanced approach. *National Institute for Early Education Research* 7. http://nieer.org/resources/policybriefs/7.pdf

Espinosa, Linda M. 2002. High-quality preschool: Why we need it and what it looks like. *Preschool Policy Matters: National Institute for Early Education Research* 1. http://nieer.org/resources/policybriefs/1.pdf

Good, Linda. 2005. Snap it up! Using digital photography in early childhood. *Childhood Education* 82.2. http://find.galegroup.com/gtx/infomark.do?&contentSet=IAC-Documents&type=retrieve&tabID=T002&prodId=AONE&docId=A140921765&source=gale&srcprod=AONE&userGroupName=nu_main&version=1.0

Guddemi, Marcy, "Gesell Developmental Scheduels Today," e-mail message to author, March 22, 2011.

Haas, Lorraine (early childhood education instructor) in discussion with the author, August 2011.

Helm, Judy Harris, and Lillian Katz. 2010. *Young Investigators: The project approach in the early years.* New York: Teachers College Press.

Heroman, Cate, and Carol Copple. 2006. Teaching and learning in the kindergarten year. Dominic F. Gullo. ed. National Association for the Education of Young Children. http://www.naeyc.org/files/naeyc/file/Play/Ktodayplay.pdf

Lewin-Benham, Ann. 2008. *Powerful children: Understand how to teach and learn using the Reggio approach.* New York: Teachers College Press.

Katz, Lillian. G. 1994. Assessing the development of preschoolers. Urbana, IL: ERIC Clearinghouse on Elementary and Early Childhood Education.

Khokha, Ellen, and Roleen Heimann. 2010. Exploring the role of socio-constructivism in college instruction and child development center planning. Paper presented at Monterey, CA. November 19, 2010.

Mathivet, Stephanie. 2008. Observing, recording and planning young children's learning. *Early Years Update.* http://www.teachingexpertise.com/articles/observing-recording-and-planning-young-childrens-learning-3352

Meisels, Samuel J. 1996/97. Using work sampling in authentic assessments. *Educational Leadership* 54(4), 60–65.

Meisels, Samuel J., J.R. Jablon, D.B. Marsden, M.L. Dichtelmiller, A.B. Dorfman, and D.M. Steele. 1995. *The work sampling system: An overview.* Ann Arbor: Rebus Planning Associates, Inc.

Mindes, Gayle. 2011. *Assessing young children.* 4th ed. Boston: Pearson.

National Association for the Education of Young Children. http://www.naeyc.org/academy/primary/standardsintro

_____. 2005. Code of ethical conduct and statement of commitment: A position statement of the National Association for the Education of Young Children. Washington, DC: National Association for the Education of Young Children.

National Association for the Education of Young Children (NAEYC) and National Association of Early Childhood Specialists in State Departments of Education (NAECS/SDE). 2003. Early childhood curriculum, assessment, and program evaluation: Building an effective, accountable system in programs for children birth through age 8. Joint Position Statement. Washington, DC: National Association for the Education of Young Children.

National Association for Family Child Care. http://www.nafcc.org/accreditation/about_accreditation.asp

National Private Schools Accreditation Alliance. http://www.npsag.com/accreditation.htm

Robertson, Anne S. 2010. The importance of the parent-teacher conference. *Parent News.* http://library.adoption.com/articles/the-importance-of-the-parent-teacher-conference.html

Seplocha, Holly. 2007. Partnerships for learning: Conferencing with families. *Spotlight on Children and Families.* Washington, DC: National Association for the Education of Young Children.

Schwartz, Eugene. 2009. Discover Waldorf education: Assessing without testing. *Discover Waldorf Education* 9. http://knol.google.com/k/eugene-schwartz/discover-waldorf-education-assessing/110mw7eus832b/4

Seitz, Hilary Jo. 2006. The plan building on children's interests. *Beyond the Journal Young Children* 1–5. http://www.naeyc.org/files/yc/file/200603/SeitzBTJ.pdf

Shillady, Amy. 2004 . Choosing an appropriate assessment system. *Young Children.* National Association for the Education of Young Children. http://journal.naeyc.org/btj/200401/shillady.pdf

Sluss, Dorothy J. 2005. Supporting play: Birth through age eight. Clifton Park, NY: Thomson Delmar Learning.

Snuggs, Carla. 2008. Prepare for preschool conferences: The parent-teacher conference for preschoolers. http://www.suite101.com/content/preschool-conferences-a48642#ixzz15aspM8AN

State Regulation of Private Schools US Department of Education Office of Non-Public Education. June 2000. www.ed.gov/pubs/RegPrivSchl/title.html

U.S. Department of Education. 2010. Family educational rights and privacy acts (*PERPA*). http://www2.ed.gov/policy/gen/guid/fpco/ferpa/index.html

U.S. Department of Health and Human Services. 2002. *Head Start 101 tool kit.* http://eclkc.ohs.acf.hhs.gov/hslc/resources/ECLKC_Bookstore/PDFs/HeadStart10 1.pdf

Wortham, Sue C. 2005. *Assessment in early childhood education.* Upper Saddle River, NJ: Prentice Hall.

Creating Meaningful Places in Your Program to Support

Children and Families

© Cengage Learning 2013

Picture This . . .

What do you remember about your school experiences? Did you attend a preschool or a child care program? What happened in kindergarten? What do you remember that made you feel happy or sad? Responses to these questions from students enrolled in Early Childhood Education classes were collected over an eight-year period. There were many similarities among the students' comments and their responses logically organized into positive and negative remarks about their school experiences. The positive remarks are helpful reminders for teachers who intend to create meaningful places and experiences for children.

Level	Most Positive Remarks	Most Negative Remarks
Preschool	Playing	Napping (most mentioned)
	Painting	Leaving mother
	Liking teacher	Missing mother
	Stacking blocks	Having a mean teacher
	Singing and music	Not allowed to use bathroom
Kindergarten	Liking the teacher	Taking naps
	Loving recess	Having different teachers
	Making friends	Spanking
	Cutting and pasting	Feeling bad/not recognizing name

GUIDE TO READING CHAPTER 4

Chapter Outline

Places for Children
    Environments for Meaningful Program Experiences
    Benchmarks for Quality Environments
    Creating Indoor Space
    Creating Outdoor Space
    Interest Centers and Activity Areas
        What to Call the Interest Center?
        How to Set Up Interest Centers
Authentic Curriculum: Environments and
  Learning for All
    Modeling Multicultural Understanding and
      Encouraging Non-Bias Behaviors
    Accommodating Children with Special Needs
    Acknowledging Multiple-Birth Children
Places for Families
    Partnering with Families for Meaningful Program
      Experiences
    Sharing Helpful and Healthful Information
    Conferencing
    Families as Resources and Participants
    Communities as Resources and Participants
    Trips in the Neighborhood
Thinking About What You Have Learned

Learning Objectives

After reading this chapter, you will be able to

1. Support meaningful environments and quality experiences for young children.
2. Organize and arrange indoor and outdoor settings that strengthen curriculum for young children.
3. Demonstrate the function and design of interest centers and activity areas that respond to children's needs.
4. Create curriculum to meet the needs for enriching multicultural experiences.
5. Support settings and curriculum that meet the needs of children with special needs.
6. Encourage partnerships with families and strategies to support their participation.
7. Identify community resources for cultural connections and curriculum enhancement.

Key Terms

National Association for the Education of Young Children (NAEYC) Standards for Initial Early Childhood Professional Preparation Programs met by this chapter:

Standard 1: Promoting Child Development and Learning

  1a: Knowing and understanding young children's characteristics and needs.

  1b: Knowing and understanding the multiple influences on development and learning.

  1c: Using developmental knowledge to create healthy, respectful, supportive, and challenging learning environments for young children.

Standard 2: Building Family and Community Relationships

  2a: Knowing about and understanding diverse family and community characteristics.

2b: Supporting and engaging families and communities through respectful, reciprocal relationships.

2c: Involving families and communities in their children's development and learning.

Standard 4: Using Developmentally Effective Approaches

4a: Understanding positive relationships and supportive interactions as the foundation of their work with young children.

4b: Knowing and understanding effective strategies and tools for early education, including appropriate uses of technology.

4c: Using a broad repertoire of developmentally appropriate teaching/learning approaches.

4d: Reflecting on own practice to promote positive outcomes for each child.

Standard 5: Using Content Knowledge to Build Meaningful Curriculum

5a: Understanding content knowledge and resources in academic disciplines: language and literacy; the arts – music, creative movement, dance, drama, visual arts; mathematics; science; physical activity, physical education, health and safety; and social studies.

5b: Knowing and using the central concepts, inquiry tools, and structures of content areas or academic disciplines.

5c: Using own knowledge, appropriate early learning standards, and other resources to design, implement, and evaluate meaningful and challenging curricula for each child.

5d: Integrating knowledgeable, reflective, and critical perspectives on early education.

Places for Children

In Early Childhood Education we use the word **environment** to describe the surroundings, the conditions, and the locations where care and learning opportunities are offered for young children. Environment also describes the inside space and outside space. The environment influences the growth and development of children participating in your program. It is in the environment that children interact with one another, with their teachers, other adults, and their families. The space, including the furnishings and materials provided, affect the relationships and determine how children and adults interact. In places designed for quality early care and learning, environments can support relationships and promote interaction. By surveying the environment, you may discover the program type and curriculum approach. The way in which an environment is arranged may illustrate program guidelines and goals. Programs that are arranged with age-appropriate furniture for young children indicate that the needs of preschoolers are the priority. Classrooms that are filled only with tables and chairs indicate an expectation for children to spend time at desks working. When the shelves are arranged and filled with materials for children to choose, they become more actively involved. They will show initiative in using the materials and gain more independence. Providing choices for young children in a developmentally planned environment more closely fits the needs of preschoolers.

Environments for Meaningful Program Experiences

Young children see, hear, and fit into spaces differently than adults do. This is why renowned early childhood educator Jim Greenman advocated for caring places for young children in 1988. Greenman indicated that the environment has the power to influence people. Spaces do more than speak—they load our bodies and minds with sensory information. The learning setting should be attractive, interesting, and enjoyable for children and adults, and it should be organized in a way to maximize the teacher's time when providing care (Greenman 2005).

The spaces we arrange for young children must be safe. The spaces should also offer sufficient number and variety of age-appropriate materials and equipment to create a stimulating learning environment (Copple and Bredekamp 2009). Child-size furniture and equipment create nurturing and homelike settings. The addition of soft and cozy items, such as sofas and pillows helps to establish comfortable environments. Flowers, plants, and other natural items encourage an appreciation of the outdoors. Teachers will maintain flexibility in the environment by providing permanent and movable equipment and furniture. Flexible furnishings make it easier to accommodate the changing needs of young children. Flexible environments are particularly important for children who use adaptive equipment, such as a wheelchair.

The classroom environment supports movement and the children's independence when they are able to make decisions about their actions and manage some of their own materials (Cook et al. 2000). Young children need space to try out new activities and experiences, and that space needs to be divided in such a way that the children feel secure and are able to explore (Caples 1996). When there are limited or no distinctions between the outdoor spaces and the indoor spaces, children enjoy ideal flexibility and participate most effectively in the program.

The organization of the school and classroom space will affect the behavior of children, regardless of the curriculum approach offered. The environment determines how children respond to other children and the adults. The environment determines how children play. The building design, including the ceiling height, door placement, and lighting within the facility, influences the curriculum and often the daily schedule. For instance, the layout and space in a room can determine the type of experiences offered, the length of time allowed for the experiences, and the follow-up opportunities for the children. Materials that give children choices will facilitate their creativity and decision making abilities (Gestwicki 1999). Wooden unit blocks that are placed into well-organized and accessible storage shelves allow children to make decisions and thereby build their cognitive skills. A music area or a reading corner needs to be well defined. Partial partitions and bookcases can be used to define the areas and should improve the spatial and

Partitions and bookcases define areas and improve spatial and acoustical conditions for particular activities.

Courtesy of Cecily Mendell Courtesy of Cecily Mendell

acoustical conditions for particular activities. The subdivided space, or activity pockets, will allow the children's activities to proceed without crossover interference into other areas (Moore 1997).

Accessibility to the buildings, classrooms, restrooms, and exits should be given high priority when decisions about the environment are reviewed. The ages and needs of the children enrolled in the program, the size of the children's groups, and the number of adults who will participate are important considerations. In addition, you will want to balance the areas dedicated for active play and those dedicated for quiet play when designing and arranging the environment for young children.

The placement of **activity areas** and the movement of children and adults around the center and classrooms will determine the pattern of traffic or pathways used by the children and adults in the program. The traffic patterns are factors you and the staff will continuously review because they affect the children's behavior and functionality of the environment. naeyc 1a, 1b, 1c, 4a, 4b, 4c, 4d, 5a, 5b, 5c

The weather is another consideration for you to think about when you and your teaching colleagues are determining how the indoor and outdoor spaces are to be used. You may work in a community that enjoys specific seasons that directly affect curriculum opportunities and how those are scheduled. Extremely hot temperatures in some regions will limit outdoor activities just as cold winters do in other areas. Pollution levels will determine whether or not the children can safely enjoy participating in outdoor activity. In areas where agricultural burning or crop spraying are routine, staff members will need to review environmental hazards before allowing outdoor curriculum activities for young children.

Sharing facility space with another early childhood program or community group may present challenges for the administrative and teaching staff. Some programs are required to dismantle components of their program at the end of each week so that a weekend program for children can be offered. Examples of shared spaces are facilities used by faith-based schools for weekend services or religious school.

When teachers of young children are asked to indicate what they really need most in their centers and classrooms, a usual response is that they need storage. Adequate storage is necessary for indoor space and for outdoor space to ensure that materials can be organized, retrieved, maintained, and safeguarded. Storage is indispensable for materials frequently used in outdoor interest centers and activity areas. The materials requiring storage include art easels and paint, sand toys, dramatic play items, manipulatives, such as puzzles, and, gardening, and construction tools. Wheel toys need to be stored daily to be protected from weather and vandalism (Sciarra and Dorsey 1998).

Long-term storage is needed for supplies purchased in quantities, items used for seasonal events and celebrations, and prop boxes that relate to thematic and project curriculum activities and materials.

Benchmarks for Quality Environments

Early childhood education programs are governed by licensing regulations established within each state. Most state regulations address only the safety of the children. Program standards improve as increasing numbers of programs participate in voluntary accreditation programs. Ten years after a voluntary accreditation process by the National Academy of Early Childhood Programs, a division of the National Association for the Education of Young Children (NAEYC), the accredited programs were found to be six times more likely to be considered high in quality than those programs that were not accredited (Bredekamp 1999). The characteristics of high-quality facilities are based on the criteria developed by the Academy and include staff–child and staff–parent interaction, administration, staffing and staff qualifications, physical environments, curricula, health and safety, nutrition and food service, and program evaluation. Criteria call for developmentally appropriate practices with suitable expectations, activities, and materials (National Association for the Education of Young Children 2005).

The National Association for Family Child Care (NAFCC) offers a process for accreditation for child care that is home based. The standards were initially developed in collaboration with Boston's Wheelock College Family Child Care Project. Another organization, the National Afterschool Association (NAA) offers their members an improvement process with features that focus on children ages 5 to 14. In meeting school-age children's needs, the organization recommended guidelines of evaluation particularly important for afterschool programs. Issues covered included topics such as sharing space with other agencies, programs, and schools.

Preparation and training programs also commit to standards and quality. The Child Development Associate Credential (CDA), sponsored by

© Cengage Learning 2013

Accredited programs have been found to be six times more likely to be considered high in quality, especially where children have ample time for large motor activities.

the Council for Early Childhood Professional Recognition endorses candidates working with young children, infants, toddlers, and preschoolers, in center-based care, family child care, and as a home visitor. Competency goals include the ability to establish and maintain a safe, healthy learning environment (Puckett and Diffily 1999).

Centers that earn high scores when evaluated with the Early Childhood Environment Rating Scale-Revised (ECERS-R) excel in features such as safety, organization, and variety of equipment and materials in the activity areas. The ECERS-R assesses process quality in programs with the use of rating scales, as an indicator of the rating scale (Harms et al. 2005) (Figure 4–1). **naeyc** 1a, 1b, 1c, 4b, 6d

Creating Indoor Space

Indoor space enhances the positive growth and development of young children. You will meet your program's guidelines by creating and maintaining an environment that offers a quality curriculum and best practice for Early Childhood Education.

Jim Greenman, in his book *Caring Spaces, Learning Places: Children's Environments That Work,* suggested ten innovative ideas for designing a quality setting. He requested that teachers offer and include comfort and security, softness, safety and health, privacy and social space, order, autonomy, and mobility in their school environments (1988).

The child-centered learning environment, including the space and equipment, is age appropriate

Figure 4–1 The Early Childhood Environmental Rating Scale-Revised

Space and Furnishings is one of the seven subscales in the revised Early Childhood Environment Rating Scale (ECERS-R). The Space and Furnishing subscale includes eight items of the 43 included in the ECERS-R. An additional reference for teachers and directors includes a two-page Playground Information handout to use with the ECERS-R.

SPACE AND FURNISHINGS

1. Indoor space
2. Furniture for routine care, play and learning
3. Furnishings for relaxation and comfort
4. Room arrangement for play
5. Space for privacy
6. Child-related display
7. Space for gross motor play
8. Gross motor equipment

(Harms, et. al 2005)

when it is kept simple for the youngest learners. The spatial organization of materials in **indoor places** will need to be inviting and accessible to the children and adults in the program. "The key is *access*—access to a range of working spaces, access to materials, access to other children and other adults; in short, the ability to access their own creative process" (Hubbard 1998).

Creative and efficient use of the available space in your school requires you to keep in mind your program guidelines. Focus on the needs of the children you are serving. "Children and adults tell us how the room should be by their behavior" (Greenman 2005). John Sorenson, director of the Bøernehaven Kløvermarken in Skagen, Denmark, identifies space to be the place where children have as much freedom to be a child as possible (Mecham 2010).

Appropriately designed features in the school environment will help you facilitate a curriculum that fits the children's development and interests. Cooking activities proceed smoothly when children are able to conveniently wash their hands at an accessible sink that is within suitable proximity to the cooking project. The location of bathrooms affects the daily schedule and the flow of children's activities. Bathrooms that allow easy access reduce interruptions to the children's activities and their interaction and exploration of materials.

Teachers can adapt the space in indoor and outdoor spaces by enhancing the physical design with varied lighting. Room dividers, lower shelving, fabric safely draped to lower ceilings, and

clear pathways for flow of movement and activity enhance the physical design of spaces. The flow of traffic is important for all children. The flow throughout the environment is especially important for children with special needs because clearly defined wider spaces encourage mobility. The floor space needs to be free of islands and equipment that are fixed permanently (Caples 1996). Renovating buildings to accommodate all children may require that walls are removed to provide large activity areas, improve traffic flow, and enhance supervision.

The use of movable shelving in early childhood programs allows the greatest flexibility for room arrangement. The child-size, sturdy shelves create zones for interest areas and activity centers. Organized shelves encourage children to select materials themselves and return these materials to the same places. Labeling the shelves with pictures and words to identify the places where the items are to be returned will add to each child's independent participation in the environment. Organized shelves and cabinets should be height-appropriate for young children and large enough to store containers. Materials and supplies stored in mesh baskets, woven baskets with natural materials, plastic tubs with handles, and trays need to be attractively arranged on shelves to invite a child to experience the activity fully. Materials placed on a shelf can be stored in containers made of different tactile materials to assist visually impaired children to select a particular manipulative or material. naeyc 1a, 1b, 1c, 4a, 4b, 4c

Creating Outdoor Space

Young children develop responsibility and respect for the natural surroundings when teachers invest as much time planning learning experiences in outdoor places as they do for indoor places. Outdoor play is essential for children's health and well-being. The outdoor space gives children a sense of peace and pleasure as they experience fresh air, the warmth of the sun, birds, butterflies, and insects. Movement, such as running, jumping, and climbing, are preferred exercise activities for most young children. These activities are more easily accommodated in outdoor places.

The time children spend enjoying the outdoors every day is as essential to their learning as the time they spend in the inside space. Places created in the outdoors nurture children's learning about the environment. Environmental education promotes literacy and supports exploration. When children are outdoors they can observe, experiment, collect, predict, analyze, and report their discoveries—all part of the investigation process (Torquati et al. 2010).

Activities offered to children in **outdoor places** contribute to their well-being in ways that are not addressed by academic learning. Children acquire a sense of wonder about nature when they are outside. Outdoor play benefits young children physically and, in some unexpected ways, psychologically. Outdoor play time reduces their stress, increases their creativity, and encourages their concentration (Noventy 2008). Children form an appreciation of nature that can stay with them throughout their lifetime. Free and unstructured play outdoors provides children with a sense of wonder and deeper understanding about the responsibility to take care of the earth (Louve 2005).

Too often in today's society nature is the last place children are found. Taking the time to appreciate nature, animals, and plants, in the outdoors has been replaced with the television, computer, and assorted technological devices. Electronics, primarily available indoors, lure children away from the activities that allow them to discover the outdoors. The focus on academic achievement in the classroom and increased reliance on standardized tests to measure children's success are expanding the time children spend indoors. Indoor academic work replaces outdoor play time (Klein 2008). The sacrifice of outside time is thought to be counterproductive because the time children spend outdoors has been found to improve academic learning. Accordingly, the developmentally

Children acquire a sense of wonder about nature in outdoor spaces.

© Cengage Learning 2013

appropriate practices outlined by the National Association for the Education of Young Children (NAEYC) specifies that outdoor play spaces should foster the development of gross motor skills, provide opportunities for children to play freely and loudly, and help children learn about the natural environment (Bredekamp and Copple 1997).

Physical development has long been considered the primary purpose of the playground. Too often outside time is disvalued as play time without the type of learning that takes place in the classroom. In actuality, getting children outside helps to stretch their thinking and challenge them intellectually. The outdoors will offer you many ways to enrich the curriculum for children's development and learning. There are many ways to connect with, add to, and extend teaching and learning while outdoors. There is a greater variety of experiences for children outside. The variety gives you more chances to offer meaningful and creative experiences that will better satisfy varied learning styles presented by the children. Outside is a place that should include the learning activities that we traditionally set up to take place inside the classroom (Klein 2008). Have you thought of offering rest and nap time outside? When children are in outside places they can find objects in the play yard to match colors. They can collect items during a neighborhood walk. Children can watch the wind in trees. They can collect leaves and match them to trees and branches or insects **(Curriculum Activity Guide #25 📖)**.

Outdoor places are safe for children when they have fencing and ground cover under climbing

© Cengage Learning 2013

Outdoor spaces and activities are beneficial for school age children especially when their school day schedules provide minimum recess and breaks.

structures that meet maximum safety codes. Outdoor places become spaces for quality development when they offer sand areas, paths for wheel toys, climbing structures, and gardens. Outdoor places that also offer opportunities in all curriculum content areas, including dramatic play, art, science, math, and reading provide the best opportunities for the children's growth and development. The outdoor environment should also feature innovative activity areas. Maintenance and security of these areas may require additional consideration. Tables might need to be permanently secured to the ground and hard-surfaced areas, sandboxes or areas should be covered. Wheel toys and other materials will most likely need to be stored inside a storage shed or inside the building each night.

The outdoor equipment should be scaled to the different physical abilities and activity levels of the children enrolled in your program. The outdoor areas also need to be sheltered to create shade during sunny weather and protection from rain and snow. Permanent sites provide outdoor garden areas supplied with running water. An outdoor area adjacent to the indoor area encourages a free-flow program, allowing children to move between the indoor and outdoor interest centers and activity areas. Planning and tending a garden help children to appreciate the natural process of growing; gardens with raised beds are easiest to tend (Clemens 1996). Arranging movable equipment to create an obstacle course can challenge the children's skills and imagination. Obstacle courses extend the available outdoor equipment and provide large motor activity. Popular materials for imaginative and safely constructed obstacle courses

include tires, boxes, hoops, pillows, plastic stepping tiles, and tunnels (Griffin and Rinn 1998).

Outdoor activities are beneficial for children who attend extended day times, especially if their school schedules have minimum breaks for recess and lunch. Children who spend the full day in school need programs that schedule outside time for longer periods, even in extreme temperatures. Outdoor experiences can include walks with appropriate winter clothing, gardening, winter picnicking, spring snack and walks, and bird and wildflower watching (Hosfield 1998).

Studies have shown that children who engage in positive outdoor experiences with nature during early childhood develop trustful perspectives about nature. Positive exposure to the outdoors also helps children develop respect for the environment (Wilson et al. 1996). naeyc 1a, 1b, 1c, 4a, 4b, 4c

Interest Centers and Activity Areas

When you observe programs for young children, you will notice that environments are arranged into areas. The indoor space is defined by areas that are dedicated to specific activities. You might notice an area for blocks, another for dramatic play, and others that offer opportunities for the children to experience art, literacy, mathematics, and science. Some programs will enjoy ample space for indoor water or sand tables and stationary snack and lunch tables. Each space can be identified as an **interest center**. These centers are the core of the curriculum because the curriculum activities are organized around them. They allow children to learn from the environment. Your role as the teacher is to craft spaces that invite young children to observe, to be active, to make choices, and to experiment (Dodge and Colker 2002).

Interest centers are also called activity areas, centers of learning, discovery stations, learning areas, and learning stations. The delineated areas within the program environment invite children to participate in different types of activities. Specialized areas also allow teachers to plan activities for children to engage in small groups and in individualized experiences. Interest centers support a flexible curriculum to match the needs of young children. Teachers plan experiences within the interest centers and activity areas to meet the current needs of the specific children attending the program. The program curriculum approach and school guidelines determine how the interest centers are arranged and what materials are provided in the spaces. The way a center is arranged and the nature of the materials provided in the center or area influences the children's play and their exploration of the materials.

Each interest center is best implemented with a clear purpose and description. Nevertheless, both of these can change with the differing needs and interests of the children. Your review and modification of curriculum plans will naturally bring about changes in the interest centers. A dramatic play center may change with the seasons or, based on the interests of children, become a post office, grocery store, restaurant, or medical clinic. A description of each interest center delineates the activities to be offered and informs the staff and families about the expected participation and possible learning outcomes.

What to Call the Interest Center?

Program administrators and teachers will have some flexibility in labeling the interest centers at their schools. You may or may not be required to standardize the names of these centers. However, it is advisable for staff members to agree on a name for each. This establishes consistency for the children and all the adults who participate in the program. An art interest center may be called the creative activity area, the art activity area, or the arts and crafts area. The area offering the children science experiences area may be called the science center, or the discovery zone. The block area may be referred to as the building area. An area that displays indoor plants, a fish aquarium, and a rabbit cage may be referred to as the center for living things. When new ideas and concepts emerge, related items and props are incorporated into the interest centers. The technology areas, or computer centers, where children use microcomputers alone and in small groups, have become integrated into early childhood programs (Figure 4–2).

Temporary interest centers may be set up following special events and field trips. A trip to the neighborhood bakery may stimulate an interest center about baking. A visit to the hair salon or barber shop may encourage you to create an interest center about the healthy care of hair. Follow-up activities can also relate to projects about farmers, firefighters, or airline pilots, and fill an interest center with sociodramatic play.

Interest centers can be further categorized as indoor and outdoor areas to help the teacher in planning. Centers with a wide variety of names (Figure 4–3) meet program requirements when they evolve from the needs of the children and keep program guidelines in clear focus. Replicating similar and related spaces outdoors improves chances that children will participate in situations within each of the developmental domains. There may be more opportunities for small muscle

Figure 4–3 Areas for Interest Centers

Indoor	Outdoor
Manipulatives	Sand and Water
Sensory	Sensory
Dramatic Play	Dramatic Play
Block	Construction
Music	Music and Movement
Quiet Reading Loft	Quiet Reading Pillows
Discovery	Discovery
Art	Art
Technology	Trike Path-Climbing
Science	Science
Cooking/Nutrition	Gardening
Pets	Pets

Figure 4–2 What to Call the Interest Center?

Art	Exploratory	Creative	Media
Literacy	Language	Library	Quiet
Music	Listening	Rhythm	Movement
Dramatic	Housekeeping	Social Play	Imaginary
Science	Experiment	Cooking	Exploration
Block	Building	Construction	Unit Block
Gardening	Living Things	Pets	Plants
Computer	Technology	Telecommunications	

development indoors and large movement outdoors. Therefore, manipulation will more likely be found indoors, and a wooden bridge for wheel toys and dramatic play outdoors.

How to Set Up Interest Centers

You will be able to set up interest centers to facilitate activities that provide either child-directed experiences or teacher-guided experiences. The arrangement of materials in the interest center should offer multiple ways for children to use the supplies. The children's ages and abilities should determine the degree of teacher supervision necessary for the interest center. For example, a center equipped with magnifying glasses and seeds placed on trays may encourage children to view the seeds independently with little teacher supervision. A tracing of the magnifying glass, taped on the table or on a tray, signals that the lens is to be placed back on the tray. This same interest center might also include photographs of seeds in different stages of growth. A drawing of seeds is another way to encourage children to match seeds and the growing plant. Magnifying glasses with increased strengths can be added later in the same week or in future weeks. A sign hung or placed near the interest center, indicating the number of children that the activity will accommodate at one time, positively directs the children's participation.

There are no specific early childhood Education mandates defining the setup of interest centers.

Block play builds friendships and enhances self-esteem as children share, communicate, and problem solve.

© Cengage Learning 2013

Figure 4–4 Interest Centers Benefit Children	
Help achieve program goals	Engage individual children
Encourage exploration	Engage small groups of children
Introduce concepts	Initiate child-directed experiences
Expand projects	Create follow-up neighborhood trips
Expand themes	Organize space for discovery and play

You will find similarities among programs that individualize curriculum for child-initiated play. For example, the manipulative center generally offers opportunities for children to develop their fine motor skills. Children use their small muscles to place and manipulate small pieces of puzzles, matching boxes, and sequenced shapes. Activities in the manipulative center might offer children experiences to match, organize, fit, cut, place, and move objects. Besides development of small motor skills, there are opportunities to develop skills in mathematical concepts such as classifying, critical thinking, verbalization, and problem solving.

A block center or area, with unit blocks and related objects such as community helpers, animals, and transportation vehicles, provides opportunities for the children to use their large muscles while exploring mathematical concepts and social understanding. The organization of blocks is important because the arrangement enhances children's exploration and discovery. Block play builds friendships and enhances self-esteem as children share, communicate, and problem solve. Children who are building with blocks often role play events and work through their feelings (Mayesky 1998). Interest centers offer benefits for the entire program (Figure 4–4). **naeyc** 1a, 1b, 1c, 4a, 4b, 4c, 5c

Authentic Curriculum: Environments and Learning for All

Early childhood professionals are positioned to create authentic curricula in **inclusive settings**. An authentic curriculum is one that values and respects all families, cultures, abilities and limited abilities, and faiths. An authentic curriculum supports environments that are culturally and linguistically relevant. An authentic curriculum champions human rights and recognizes economic dissimilarities. An authentic curriculum is inclusive. You will achieve this type of curriculum by supporting multicultural understanding and encouraging non-bias behaviors among your staff, the children, and their families. You will achieve an authentic curriculum by accommodating children with dissimilar abilities (Derman-Sparks and Olsen-Edwards 2009) and by acknowledging children who represent a small percentage of the population, such as multiple-birth children.

Modeling Multicultural Understanding and Encouraging Non-Bias Behaviors

Environments will best meet children's needs in places where authentic curriculum is offered. An authentic curriculum supports environments that are culturally and linguistically relevant to the children enrolled. This curriculum is inclusive because the activities model multicultural understanding of other communities, families, individuals with abilities and limited disabilities, and faiths. Families and children are represented respectfully and regularly. This requires that you to display photographs, drawings, and artifacts representative of all children, their families, and communities. We are a multicultural, multiracial, multiethnic, multilingual, multieconomic, and multireligious society.

You will profoundly influence multicultural understanding and non-bias behaviors by incorporating literature that is representative of our culturally diverse society. An outstanding resource is the *Children's Book Press* (2008-09). The catalogue organizes children's books by cultural communities identifying ethnicities by country of origin or identity. Some books are in Spanish, and some have teacher guides. For example, in the Latino communities category, the 15th anniversary edition of *Family Pictures* is presented. The paintings and stories by Carmen Lomas Garza capture her childhood growing up in Kingsville, Texas. Listed among the books about Asian American communities, *Sachiko Means Happiness* is introduced. The book is a story about a Japanese American girl's relationship with her grandmother who has Alzheimer's disease (Children's Book Press 2008-09). Another way to encourage multicultural understanding is to routinely include families and guests. Their perspectives are important for promoting non-bias views. For instance, as you expand your outdoor learning environment be aware that various cultures view nature differently, and their perspectives are valuable to your authentic and inclusive curriculum.

As you facilitate meaningful places for children and their families, check that your spaces foster positive racial identity, build on the cultures of the families and promote cross-cultural respect, preserve the children's home languages and encourage all children to learn a second language, allow reflection about race, language, and culture (Chang et al. 1996), and provide for children who are new to the community. Children move with their families because of employment transfers, seasonal and agricultural work, military placement, homelessness, and changes in the structure of the family unit. Curriculum is meaningful when it offers opportunities to welcome all the children and respectfully acknowledge their transitions.

Teachers are encouraged to meet children where they are by making programs effective, inclusive, and culturally relevant. You can do this by using materials that show what children already know from their daily life and local culture. You can blend traditional practices with aspects of current, more contemporary society. Programs show respect for children's linguistic and ethnic diversity by using local languages and culturally relevant references. Whenever possible, use bilingual teachers and teacher assistants, and initiate storytelling and reading in multiple languages (Modica 2010). naeyc 1a, 1b, 1c, 2a, 2b, 2c, 4a, 4b, 4c, 4d, 5c

Accommodating Children with Special Needs

The inclusion of **children with special needs** in programs offering care and learning opportunities for preschoolers has become expected and more widespread. Parents, teachers, and researchers have found that children benefit in many ways from integrated programs where they participate in classrooms with children who are typically developing. Appropriate programs developed and provided for infants and young children with special needs in their early years are also appropriate for children without special needs (Kolucki 2000). The physical setting and environmental arrangements that are effective for all preschoolers are also suitable for children with varying abilities and children from culturally and ethnically diverse families. A flexible setting accomplishing best practices can be modified to help children with special needs. Flexibility and modifications will contribute to children with disabilities functioning more comfortably once their individual needs have been identified (Loughlin and Suina 1982).

Inclusion of children with special needs requires that they participate as fully as possible in all activities. Universal design is the concept that materials and environments need to be usable by everyone, including those with disabilities to the greatest extent possible. An example of universal design is the use of curbside ramps that are essential for people in wheelchairs, but they also benefit skateboarders, cyclists, and parents with children in strollers. In a preschool environment, puzzles that have bright colors and interesting textures draw all the children in, but can also be supportive to a child who is visually impaired or legally blind. Large knobs on a puzzle could support a child with cerebral palsy who needs assistance in developing coordination skills. Wide spaces between shelves and tables enable a child using a wheelchair to maneuver independently (Bredekamp 2011).

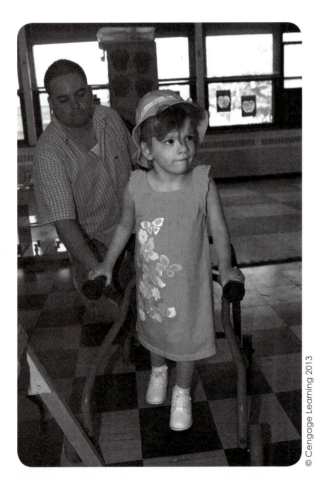

© Cengage Learning 2013

Movable equipment in open areas provides the greatest opportunity to create meaningful spaces for children with special and individualized needs.

Movable equipment in open areas provides the greatest opportunity to modify the environment and create meaningful spaces for children with special and individualized needs. Inclusive environments adapt the spaces with modifications to welcome children with disabilities. The environment should remain culturally and linguistically sensitive through each day, week, and month with respect for the children and their families to achieve an authentically inclusive program. Generally, the physical space and arrangement that are effective overall for young children are also suitable for children with varying abilities.

Program facilities will need to comply with the **Americans with Disabilities Act** (ADA). Public Law 94–142 became effective in 1975, authorizing children with special needs to be mainstreamed as early as possible into the regular setting. Removal of barriers opens the environment to include children with disabilities; thus all children are allowed to explore materials, to experiment, and create (Udell et al. 1998). Teachers will meet needs of children with special needs by adapting the environment to the needs of children as the necessity arises. One way would be to clearly display materials. For example a teacher ensures that paste and paper are within a student's reach and that other jars are not in the path of her arm movement. Clear placement and display of materials help children with perceptual problems to focus on the meaningful components. Children with limited mobility can be aided by placing collections of materials in varied locations in the indoor and outdoor classroom environment. Multiple accessible art shelves with paper, crayons, markers, and scissors facilitate more immediate and active participation for all children (Cook et al. 1996).

Utilizing varied shelf levels provides adaptable access to children with limitations of reach. Modification of carriers, with flexible handles and straps, assists young learners with limited balance or mobility (Loughlin and Suina 1982).

Children with visual limitations benefit from classroom arrangements that are consistent and that have direct pathways free of obstacles. Auditory and tactile cues enhance the environment as a means of designating specific areas. The use of both carpeted and uncarpeted zones encourages independence because the change in floor surface physically tells the child that she is in a specific activity area. Modified easels, magnetic boards, tables with rims, easily grasped objects, and portable work spaces increase accessibility and help children to participate in activities applying their capabilities (Loughlin and Suina 1982).

Technology is transforming education, increasing opportunities for children with special needs. Technological tools such as computers modified with larger screens and voice-activated modifications open up successful school experiences for children with disabilities. Boundaries are reduced when the world becomes accessible on screen. Teacher-guided, online communication through Internet links introduces young children to interaction previously inaccessible to them. "By giving students access to and training in the Internet, we empower them to become active learners" (Doyle 1999).

Teachers who make thoughtful use of computers in the classroom can enable children to seek information, solve problems, understand concepts, and move at their own pace (Copple and Bredekamp 2009). naeyc 1a, 1b, 1c, 4a, 4b, 4c, 4d, 5c

Acknowledging Multiple-Birth Children

Multiple-birth children—twins, triplets, quadruplets, and more—are enrolling in preschools more frequently. There is an escalating need for teachers to understand the particular developmental and program needs of multiple-birth children. Multiple-birth children are referred to as twins and supertwins, the latter being a reference to groups that exceed two children who are born on the same day to the same parents (Arce 2010).

Twins and supertwins comprise about three percent of the population, yet little information about their unique needs has been available to early childhood educators. Multiple-birth children and their families have unique needs and circumstances related to being a twin or supertwin. Early childhood programs can expand inclusive practices and environments by acknowledging the unique needs of twins and supertwins—each an individual child as well as a member of a pair or group.

Practical and research-based information about the circumstances of twins and supertwins will be useful for guiding them and interacting with their families. Twins and supertwins experience patterns of growth and development similarly to singleborn children and in many ways experience life differently. For instance, a twin enters and experiences preschool with a same-age sibling. Some twins are quite familiar with clarifying their identity for others, including teachers. Knowing about twins and supertwins will help you make informed decisions to guide interaction with multiple-birth children and their families

© Cengage Learning 2013

Twins, especially those who look similar, are quite familiar with clarifying their identity for others, including teachers.

and dispel the misconceptions that surround their identity and development (Arce 2010).

Places for Families

"To serve children well, we must work with their families," states Linda Garris Christian. As a professor of education at Adams State College in Colorado, Dr. Christian communicates that inclusion of families is vital. Our role is to first understand the families and their diversities (2007). To understand families it is valuable to know that families arrive with their own beliefs that have been influenced by their cultures, faiths, and neighborhoods. Their beliefs and perceptions about learning began with their own successes and failures with school. Differences in beliefs and childrearing approaches are additionally apparent with the enrollment of children whose families are grandparents or guardians (Ball 2010).

Engaging families in the daily activities at your school will have a positive outcome for the children. Families who are involved early in their children's schooling are more likely to continue participating when their children attend elementary school. Purposefully including families also enhances the quality of your program (Stark 2010). You will be able to establish meaningful places for families by encouraging partnerships, sharing helpful and healthful information, and bringing them into the program as resources and participants.

Partnering with Families for Meaningful Program Experiences

Families are most important for children's well-being and development. Social and academic success of children can additionally be expected when their families participate in their learning (Powell et al. 2010). That is why **partnering with families** should be present in all aspects of your program. Teachers who take a comprehensive approach will integrate the perspectives of families into their children's experiences, including decision making about the curriculum (Stark 2010). The school that promotes partnerships with families will determine how parents become involved in their children's education (Epstein and Sanders 1998). This message directs us to build trust and open communication with families. Educators need to assure families that they do make a difference in their children's lives.

Five elements of effective family engagement in early childhood education were summarized from the research and reported by The PEW Center for the States (Stark 2010):

- Early learning programs expect, welcome and support family participation in decision making related to their child's education.

- Families and early learning programs engage in consistent, two-way, linguistically and culturally appropriate communication.

- Families' knowledge, skills and backgrounds are integrated into the learning experience.

- Programs help families foster a home environment that enhances learning.

- Early learning programs create an ongoing and comprehensive system for promoting family engagement.

One of the most sincere and simplest ways to build trustful relationships and communication is to establish actions that welcome families every day. Teachers who are extra supportive during the daily transitions from home to school will enhance the home-school relationships (Ball 2010). You understand that families are most important for children's well-being and successful development. Remember to assure family members that they make a difference in their children's lives. The more teachers and families work together, the more likely there will be consistency between what goes on at home and what happens in the center and classroom. Taking a partnership approach benefits parents and other family members by giving them a greater understanding of how early childhood education works in general, and in their children's program specifically (Gonzalez-Mena 2010).

Sharing Helpful and Healthful Information

Early childhood educators will build links between the school and the child and their families because children become competent when the links are strong (Garbarino 1992). For this to happen, family members will rely on you, as the early childhood professional, for information. They will need to know about development, behavior, and, often, about learning that relates to their child or children. The relationship and welcoming contact you have with families will be enhanced by sharing helpful and healthful information with them. You may be eager to share what you consider to be important educational and social practices, yet studies indicate that parents decide on child care differently from early childhood professionals. When they are able to select the program, they tend to choose programs where staff has cultural values and beliefs similar to their own (Daniel 1998). Once a family chooses your program, respond initially by providing them with information that will help facilitate the transition from home to school for themselves and their child or children. Encourage family members to spend time in the classroom and become familiar with the staff, classroom, and materials. Review the school guidelines and policies with them, inviting their input and suggestions. Support picture taking of the indoor and outdoor places and questioning.

You will be able to further guide family members by helping them to establish positive goodbye routines. Create a welcoming setting by placing meaningful photographs and relevant books through the school to honor cultural identities; for instance, *On My Block Stories: Paintings by Fifteen Artists* (Goldberg 2007). Suggest that both the parent and child sign in, greet the teacher who is welcoming the children, and then together check out the new objects on the discovery table in the science area before saying goodbye.

The initial contact and communication with families offer an opportunity for you to gather insightful information about their child or children. This crucial perspective about the family and a child's needs and abilities will facilitate your delivery of appropriate feedback and information to the family. The family perspective and details relating to a child's strengths and needs allow you and the family members to more effectively support his or her experiences and activities at school and at home.

Communicate frequently with families. Informal contact and communication will occur daily by making yourself available when families arrive and sign in. More formal or scheduled contact takes on many different forms, including phone calls, e-mails, and written notes sent home with a child. The most contact happens when you or the families schedule special meetings and conferences. You may maintain some record of the informal encounters and definite documentation of the formal meetings and conferences.

Another strategy for sharing information with families is to help them understand the role of questioning. When we formulate better questions, there are benefits for children, especially in children's language and literacy development. Emphasizing the role of questioning in learning can include posting the question of the week or month. That can also include the questions children have asked at school in the newsletter, sending home ideas about outings and activities and questions that could be asked during these outings and routines at home. Parents can be asked to record children's questions at home (Birbili and Karagiorgou 2010).

Teachers of young children find that they are a resource for parents in most areas that affect the development of their children, and a link between parents and technology. Providing information about technology creates another connection between the school and home. Computers, software questions, and especially Internet-access concerns face teachers and parents alike. Teachers need to apply the same principles recognized to ensure healthy growth and development of young children when commenting on the selection of appropriate software programs and access to the Internet.

Another way families can contribute is to participate in policy setting meetings. This will include, for instance, technology use and practices at the school. Experienced parents will contribute to the teachers' knowledge, and parents just arriving into the computer age will benefit from the discussion and decisions.

Ongoing contact and communication are important for all families and more so for families with children who have disabilities. Similarly, informing all families about resources in the communities is essential and may be imperative for parents with special needs children. Communicating frequently is the key (Ray et al. 2010).

Programs can now encourage active participation and partnerships by involving families through Internet-based communication. You can use technology most effectively by initiating a school or classroom website. You can post information about classroom activities, create a family response link, and encourage communication through a discussion forum. Communicate easily and often by sending individual e-mails to families. Provide positive feedback about their child's participation. Post photo stories about the children on the website (with security protocal in place) and deliver individual photographs of a child or children's participation to families. Post activities and follow-up experiences to curriculum activities for the children to enjoy at home. The success that families will have with Internet-based communication will be determined by their access to technology and the opportunities they receive to increase their technology skills (Mitchell et al. 2010).

Conferencing

Conferencing with parents and other family members is one of the most frequently used methods for communication with families. Conferencing offers a favorable way for teachers to gather information about the children and share information about the curriculum (Barbour et al. 2011). Conferences with families will give you the opportunity to build sincere relationships with them. The time you dedicate for conferencing with parents or other family members lets them know you value them and respect their views. Face-to-face meetings establish a chance to ask them what they want the school to provide for their child. During follow-up conferencing, you will be able to inquire whether the school is meeting their expectations.

You will create collaborative conferencing experiences by inviting families to request and set up informal sessions. An open-door policy reduces the stress that some families might feel for the more formal, teacher-scheduled conferences. Let families know what they can expect at a conference. Remain positive and prepared with samples of a child's work, photographs of his or her participation, and handouts that might clarify questions about development and learning. Create opportunities for children to be included in conferencing. The first conference you schedule might be the most beneficial. You would guide the children in sharing their work and experiences with their parents.

Share your own family, culture, and interests with the children and their families. This will further engage families in your school and assure more positive interaction with them. It is also valuable for you to ask the families about their preferred method of communication and language. You may need to invite translators for assistance; nonetheless, families will appreciate your sincere efforts to keep them informed and include them in decision making about their child or children (Teaching Young Children 2010).

Video Case

Communicating with Families: Best Practices in an Early Childhood Setting

Visit the Early Childhood Education Media Library, and watch the TeachSource Video Case on www.cengagebrain.com

1. Explain how the preschool teacher, Mona Sanon, used the parent notebook.

2. How did the father respond to the parent conference with Teacher Mona?

Families as Resources and Participants

Parents turn to early childhood professionals, who provide the care and education for their children, for answers about how their children learn, behave, and progress. Education for families offers information to help them with parenting. Parents may not have all the information about child development and curriculum, but they have plenty of information about their own child that the teacher does not have. They know their child's history and interests as well as their hopes and plans for their child's future. A partnership relationship with their child's teacher will encourage families to share that knowledge and important current information as situations arise. A key to working with all families is to be sensitive, understanding, and empathetic, and to remember that each family has its own strengths (Gonzalez-Mena 2010).

Partnering with families suggests that we include them as resources and participants in the programs. Encourage parents and other members of the family to participate in the classroom as volunteers, offer their perceptions and skills, participate in early learning activities at school and home, and advocate for their children. Parents can be instrumental in preparing their children for school when they are involved in the school. They will be able to encourage literacy-related activities, and

these are associated with better school readiness. Furthermore, children's social and relationships skills are primary basics for school readiness. You can help parents become proactive in modifying their home environment. In this way they will be able to utilize the resources that exist in the home practically to enhance learning of their children (Farver et al. 2006). Involving parents will enable them to regularly provide input that can lead to curriculum improvement.

Families have knowledge and skills that will significantly add to the school program and curriculum. Welcoming and providing opportunities for parents to volunteer will contribute valuable knowledge. The familial cultural and historical knowledge will be relevant and valuable, adding depth and enrichment to your program curriculum.

Staff members recognize the benefit of family involvement to children and the program because the family expands learning opportunities to the children in the school. These expanded opportunities occur particularly when the children's program provides ongoing communication with the family through, for example, a newsletter (Figure 4–5).

It has been demonstrated that, at all income and education levels, parents become partners in their children's education when schools reach out (Epstein and Sanders 1998).

Curriculum for children expands when families and guests participate in the program. You will learn about curriculum resources, and you will find that the family members, including grandparents and siblings of the children, offer the best resources for your curriculum. What occupations, careers, interests, and hobbies relate to the overall curriculum plan? Families are the first level of resources and also the most valuable.

Receptive teachers enhance family partnership opportunities by surveying the interests and talents of families of the children participating in their programs. Follow up the informal surveys with calls to welcome and encourage family members to share their time and abilities in their children's classrooms.

Family members will also benefit from participating in program activities and events. Children especially enjoy experiences with their families, including their grandparents and other extended family members such as aunts, uncles, and older siblings. Classroom participation, both indoor and outdoor, creates many shared experiences for the child to discuss with family members at a later time. Parent-child interactions can be observed by teaching staff, who gather additional insight into

Figure 4–5 Newsletter for Children and Families

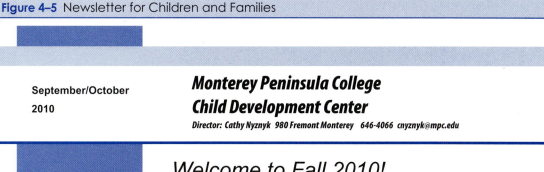

September/October 2010

Monterey Peninsula College
Child Development Center
Director: Cathy Nyznyk 980 Fremont Monterey 646-4066 cnyznyk@mpc.edu

Welcome to Fall 2010!

Help your Children Love Reading

Reading is the foundation for all future learning. Reading also enriches a child's life. All parents can help children with reading. Above all, they can make reading interesting and enjoyable and show that it is important. Children who enjoy reading are likely to read frequently.

Some Ways to Interest Children in Books

- *Start reading aloud to your child at an early age.*

Use simple picture books.

- *Read to your child every day.*

A family reading routine stresses the importance and value of reading. Find a quiet, cozy place to read together.

- *Make Story time special*

Treat this time together as a bonus, not an alternative to other activities. Add interest by reading poems, and riddles, singing songs, and sharing

Try this cooking project with your child

- Put a few graham crackers in a zip lock bag. Let your child crush with a rolling pin.

- Place 2 tsp. of apple sauce in the bottom of a cup and sprinkle the graham cracker crumbs on top
- Apple Delight!

Torn Paper Collage

*Old magazines

*Construction Paper

*Glue

Have your child tear pictures from magazines and glue to paper.

Are you ready for an Emergency?

The Children's Center Staff are responsible for the safety of all the children enrolled at the Center. We practice monthly earthquake and fire drills. Our teachers are current with CPR and First Aid Cards. We have prepared emergency snack bags for the children. We discuss and fix possible hazards on going. Are you prepared for an emergency? Here's some questions to ponder & a few suggestions…

✓ Do you have a disaster and evacuation plan?

✓ Who is responsible for turning off the electricity, gas, and water if necessary?

✓ Is the water heater secured to the wall?

✓ Is all heavy furniture, like bookcases and shelves secured to the wall?

✓ Do you have safety latches on kitchen cabinets?

✓ Is there a clear path in your home for safe exiting?

✓ Have you moved your bed away from the window?

✓ Have you gotten down to your child's level and looked around to see what might fall on them?

the child's individual characteristics. (**Curriculum Activity Guide 5**).

Family participation in their child's program might seem to be related to a parent's perception of his or her own parenting role and whether there will be a positive effect on the child's education. Consistent participation in meetings is often related to basic support such as child care (Powell 2010).

Figure 4–6 Families as Resources for the Curriculum

Family Activities	→	Resources for Curriculum
Family collects pine cones and river rocks during day trip to the mountains		Pine cones and rocks for display
Parent works in the medical field		Surgical uniforms, safe copies of x-rays, extra bandages
Parent works in construction		Demonstrate tool use
		Donate wood pieces
		Minor repairs
Family gardening and produce farming		Donate extra produce
		Present planting activity
		Field trip to produce stand

Another way to increase partnerships is to help families to create settings for learning in the home. Encouraging children to bring books and manipulatives home and initiatives such as "care for a pet for the weekend" contribute to the home-school partnership. Parents' contribution to the school comfortably begins when common items from home add to the curriculum needs. This exchange can expand the families' and children's concept of family pride. Although it may be difficult for one teacher to obtain enough empty paper towel rolls or plastic containers for the entire group, families that bring in requested items feel good about contributing needed supplies. The parent and child who drag in the walnut branch that broke from their backyard

tree contribute to the curriculum. A teacher's appreciation is magnified when children begin to explore the tree branch and ask questions such as: "Who brought the tree branch? What are those round things on the tree? I have a tree that has nuts, too." The children's questions and responses suggest ideas for new curriculum planning. Their interest may lead to a classroom filled with tree branches from many homes and places. Continued questions and interest lead to a project about fruit trees. These are all initiated by the supportive involvement of a family. Supporting families, the most important resource in a program, will contribute ongoing benefits to the curriculum (Figure 4–6). **naeyc** 1a, 1b, 1c, 2a, 2b, 2c, 4a, 4b, 4c, 4d, 5a, 5b, 5c

Trips throughout the neighborhood allow children to experience real situations and community services firsthand.

© Cengage Learning 2013

Communities as Resources and Participants

Parent education and family-centered programs join together in schools and communities. The efforts can change families in ways that improve parenting quality. Plus, community relationships positively affect the well-being of young children. Schools and communities can join efforts in effective and culturally relevant ways by using and adapting the resources found in their communities. Using school buildings for community events creates trust and acceptance of your program. Involving family and community members as aides and volunteers supports literacy development and staffing needs. Acquiring supplies and materials locally involves the community as stakeholders in the education of young children and integrates local resources (Modica 2010).

Family member visits to the school will contribute to meaningful experiences for all the children. Family visits will also add to their sense of confidence and satisfaction. When Tanya's mother, a telephone company representative, visits, she brings equipment and a known relationship with the children— Tanya is her daughter.

Guests whose occupation relates to the curriculum theme or project will stimulate more involvement because the children are introduced to information about the jobs featured in thematic activities. Uniforms, products, and other types of work-related items encourage more active participation from the children. There are many hands-on items a baker or a florist can bring to the program to share with the children in the surroundings of their familiar facility.

Businesses that adopt a school or early care program connect with the children on a continuing basis and provide them with another link to the community and to jobs.

Trips in the Neighborhood

There will be opportunities for planned and spontaneous walks within the neighborhood of your center. Walks with the children need to occur as often as possible, with the same degree of preparation about safety and consideration for routine scheduling needs. Trips in the neighborhood allow children to experience real-life situations firsthand. Visits to places and with people in their community may help the children to understand and clarify what they see in books and what they hear about in group times.

All trips and visits should be suitable developmentally for the children enrolled in your program. Consider the length of the visit, including the time to travel and/or walk there and back. What will the children actually see, hear, and feel? Will the experience be meaningful to them?

Trips require preparation and follow-up. Your visit to the location prior to taking the children will allow you to check for safety, evaluate the value of the visit, determine the needed time, and speak to the person or persons responsible for the location. This preparation will help to ensure that the presentation is suitable for young children. The children need to be acquainted with the trip location and the people they will meet. Children can be introduced to these concepts over several days and weeks prior to the trip. Follow-up promotes good relations with the community. A greeting from the children, a thank-you note from the director and a photo of the children taken on the visit all contribute to positive and cordial follow-up practices. Follow-up activities can also be integrated into the curriculum plan. Trips to the neighborhood may be done in stages. The first walk to the post office might be to pick up the mail. The next few walks might be to mail letters and buy postage. After several brief visits, the children may be ready to go inside the post office. The same guidelines for quality curriculum apply to the neighborhood trips you plan for your group. Children can begin learning about buses and rapid transit systems by first walking to the bus stop or the station. On a later trip the children could climb into the bus or train, allowing them to acquire information about public transportation in steps **(Curriculum Activity Guide 8 and 2** \\). naeyc 1a, 1b, 1c, 2a, 2b, 2c, 4a, 4b, 4c, 4d, 5a, 5b, 5c

---

Thinking about What You Have Learned

✔ Consider the interest centers you would create for an early childhood program. Label or decide on the name for each center. Sketch a layout of a floor plan for the indoor space and one for the outdoor space.

✔ Participate in an outdoor adventure with at least two children, either with a school program or as a personal experience. You can walk in a park, picnic in the snow, or visit a garden or nursery. Observe the children's reactions during the adventure. Write a one-page summary about the benefits to the children.

✔ Connect with a website about outdoor learning for young children. Identify the website and list five ideas, activities, or recommendations provided at the site.

✔ Visit a center where children without special needs attend along with children with special needs. Observe how the environment promotes inclusion of children with special needs. List five modifications to the outdoor space and five to the indoor space that allow children with varying capabilities to participate in the curriculum.

Chapter References

Ball, Ruth Ann Halacka. 2007. Supporting and involving families in meaningful ways. In *Spotlight on Young Children and Families*. Washington, DC: National Association for the Education of Young Children.

Barbour, Chandler, Nita H. Barbour, and Patricia A. Scully. 2011. *Families, schools, and communities*. 5th ed. Boston: Pearson.

Birbili, Maria, and Ioanna Karagiorgou. 2010. Helping children and their parents ask better questions: An intervention study. *Journal of Research in Childhood Education* 24(1): 18–31.

Bredekamp, Sue. 1999. When new solutions create new problems: Lessons learned from NAEYC accreditation. *Young Children* 54(1): 58–63.

Bredekamp, Sue, and Carol Copple. eds. 1997. *Developmentally appropriate practices in early childhood programs* (rev.). Washington, DC: National Association for the Education of Young Children.

Caples, Sara. E. 1996. Some guidelines for preschool designs. *Young Children* 51(4): 14–21.

Chang, H. N. L., A. Muckelroy, and D. Pulido-Tobiassen. 1996. *Looking in, looking out: Redefining child care and early education in a diverse society.* San Francisco: California Tomorrow.

Children's Book Press. *2008-09 award-winning multicultural literature for children.* San Francisco, CA.

Christian, Linda Garris. 2007. Understanding families: Applying family systems theory to early childhood practice. In *Spotlight on young children.* Washington, DC: National Association for the Education of Young Children.

Clemens, J. B. (1996). Gardening with children. *Young Children* 51(4): 22–27.

Cook, Ruth. E., Annette Tessier, M. Diane Klein, . D. 2000. *Adapting early childhood curriculum for children in inclusive settings.* 5th ed. Englewood Cliffs, NJ: Merrill.

Copple, Carol, and Sue Bredekamp. 2009. *Developmentally appropriate practice in early childhood programs serving children from birth through age 8.* 3rd ed. Washington, DC: National Association for the Education of Young Children.

Daniel, J. E. 1998. A modern mother's place is wherever her children are: Facilitating infant and toddler mother's transitions in child care. *Young Children* 53(6): 4–12.

Derman-Sparks, Louise and Julie Olsen Edwards. 2009. *Anti-bias education for young children and ourselves.* Washington, DC: National Association for the Education of Young Children.

Dodge, Diane. T. and L. J. Colker. 2002. *The creative curriculum.* 4th ed. Washington, DC: Teaching Strategies.

Doyle, Al. 1999. A practitioner's guide to snaring the net. *Educational Leadership* 56(5): 12–15.

Epstein, Joyce L. and Mavis G. Sanders.1998. What we learn from international studies of school-family-community partnerships. *Childhood Education* 74(6): 392–394.

Farver, Jo Ann M., Yiyuan Xu, Stefanie Eppe, Christopher J. Lonigan. 2006. Home environments and young Latino children's school readiness. *Early Childhood Research Quarterly* 21(2): 196–212.

Garbarino, James. 1992. *Children and families in the social environment.* 2nd ed. New York: Walter de Gruyter.

Gestwicki, C. 1999. *Developmentally appropriate practice: Curriculum and development in early education.* 2nd ed. Albany, NY: Delmar.

Goldberg, Dana. ed. 2007. *On my block: Stories and paintings by fifteen artists.* San Francisco: Children's Book Press.

Gonzalez-Mena, Janet. 2010. *50 Early childhood strategies for working and communicating with diverse families.* Upper Saddle River, NJ: Prentice Hall.

Greenman, Jim. 2005. *Caring spaces, learning places.* 2nd. ed. Redmond, WA: Exchange Press.

Griffin, C., and B. Rinn. 1998. Enhancing outdoor play with an obstacle course. *Young Children* 53(3):18–23.

Harms, Thelma, Richard M. Clifford, and Debby Cryer. 2005. *Early childhood environment rating scale-revised.* New York: Teachers College Press.

Hildebrand, Vera, and Patricia F. Hearron. 1997. *Management of child development centers.* 4th ed. Upper Saddle River, NJ: Merrill.

Hosfield, D. 1998. A long day in care need not seem long. *Young Children* 53(3): 24–28.

Hubbard, R. S. 1998. Creating a classroom where children can think. *Young Children,* 53(5): 26–31.

Klein, Amy Susana. 2008. Children are born to be outside and wild—Not stuck inside and mild. *Early Childhood News.* Excelligence Learning Corporation. http://www.earlychildhoodnews.com/earlychildhood/articleview.aspx?ArticleID=479

Kolucki, Barbara. 2000. Children and youth: A historic perspective: Inclusion for infants and young children with disabilities. *Disability World* 2 April-May 2000. http://www.disabilityworld.org/April-May2000/Children/Historic.htm

Loughlin, C. E., and Suina, J. H. 1982. *The learning environment: An instructional strategy.* New York: Teachers College Press.

Louve, Richard. 2005. *Last child in the woods: Saving our children from nature deficit-disorder.* Chapel Hill, NC: Algonquin Books.

Mecham, Neil A. 2010. Denmark's Bøernehavens: A place to grow. *Young Children* 65(6): 38–40.

Mayesky, Mary. 1998. *Creative activities for young children* 6th ed. Albany, NY: Delmar.

Mitchell, Sascha, Teresa S. Foulger, and Keith Wetzel. 2010. Ten tips for involving families through Internet-based communication. In *Spotlight on Teaching Preschoolers—Supporting Children, Families, and Yourself.* Derry Koralek. ed. Washington, DC: National Association for the Education of Young Children.

Modica, Sarah, Maya Ajmera, and Victoria Dunning. 2010. Meeting children where they are: Culturally adapted models of early childhood education. *Young Children* 65(6): 20–26.

Moore, G. T. 1997. Houses and their resource-rich activity pockets. *Child Care Information Exchange* 113:15–20.

National Association for the Education of Young Children. 2005. *Introduction to the NAEYC accreditation standards and criteria.* http://www.naeyc.org/academy/primary/standardsintro

Novotney, Amy. 2008. Getting back to the great outdoors. In *Monitor on Psychology.* Junn, Ellen and Chris Boyatzis, eds. Annual Editions: Child Growth and Development. 2011/2012. NY: McGraw Hill.

Powell, Douglas R., Seung-Hee Son, Nancy File and Robert R. San Juan. 2010. Parent–school relationships and children's academic and social outcomes in public school pre-kindergarten. *Journal of School Psychology* 48(4): 269–292.

Puckett, Margaret B. and Deborah Diffily. 1999. *Teaching young children: An introduction to the early childhood profession.* Orlando, FL: Harcourt Brace.

Ray, Julie A., Julia Pewitt Kinder, and Suzanne George. 2010. Partnering with families of children with special needs. In *Spotlight on Teaching Preschoolers- Supporting Children, Families, and Yourself.* Derry Koralek, ed. Washington, D.C: National Association for the Education of Young Children.

Sciarra, Dorothy Anne D. J. and A.G. Dorsey, 1998. *Developing and administering a child care center* 4th ed. Albany, NY: Delmar.

Teaching Young Children/Preschool. 2010. Engaging families in preschool programs. *Teaching Young Children* 4(1): 6–7. Washington, DC: National Association for the Education of Young Children.

Torquati, Julia, Mary M. Gabriel, Julie Jones-Branch, and Jennifer Leeper-Miller. 2010. Environmental education—A natural way to nurture children's development and learning. *Young Children* 65(6): 98–104.

Udell, T., J. Peters, and T.P. Templeman. 1998. From philosophy to practice in inclusive early childhood programs. *Teaching Exceptional Children* 30(3): 44–49.

Wilson, R. A., S. J. Kilmer and V. Knauerhase. 1996. Developing an environmental outdoor play space. *Young Children* 51(1): 56–61.

Managing Ideas with Intention, Purposeful Goals, Standards and Fundamental Principles

© Cengage Learning 2013

Picture This . . .

What do you want to know about early childhood curriculum? Both entry level students and experienced teachers have responded to this question in brainstorming sessions. Review their responses. Do their responses answer the questions you have about early childhood curriculum?

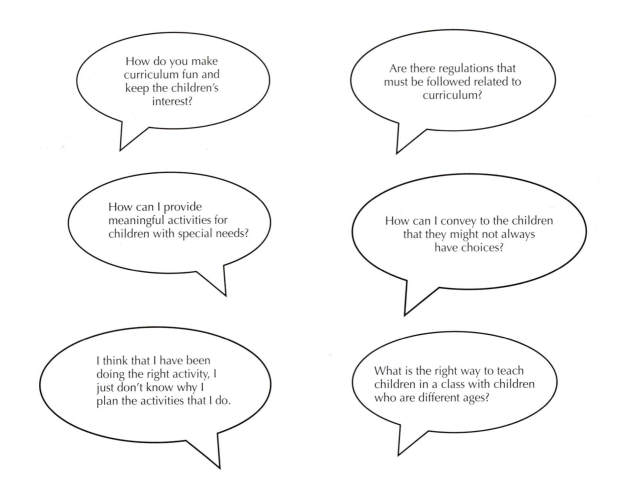

GUIDE TO READING CHAPTER 5

Chapter Outline

Vision for Managing Curriculum That Is Good
for Early Learners
    Intention
    Goals
    Guidelines and Standards
    Fundamental Principles
Creating Emergent and Integrated Curriculum
Individualizing Curriculum Experiences
    Observe/Review/Plan
    Child-Initiated Activities
    Inclusive and Sensitive
    Multi-Age Grouping
    Teacher-Guided Experiences and Group Time
Approaches to Planning
    Developmental Focus Areas
        Physical
        Affective (Social-Emotional Understanding)
          and Aesthetic
        Cognitive
    Curriculum Areas
        Art

        Creative Dramatics
        Social-Emotional Understanding
        Health, Safety, Nutrition
        Communication and Literacy
        Mathematics
        Movement
        Music and Rhythm
        Science
Documentation and Blending Concepts
    Themes
    Project Approach
Balancing Curriculum with Emergent
    and Integrated Experiences
Thinking About What You Have Learned

Learning Objectives

After reading this chapter, you will be able to

   1. Explain how early childhood educators manage curriculum for early learners with intention and goals.

   2. Recognize appropriate applications of standards and guidelines in curriculum for early learners.

3. Describe emergent and integrated curriculum.

4. Use observe/review/plan for individualizing curriculum experiences.

5. Define child-initiated and teacher-guided activities.

6. Discuss inclusive and multicultural learning.

7. Examine and compare the approaches to planning curriculum for young children including the developmental focus curriculum areas.

8. Review the thematic and the project approach.

9. Describe the curriculum content areas.

10. Identify appropriate themes that can be included in curriculum plans.

Key Terms

National Association for the Education of Young Children (NAEYC) Standards for Initial Early Childhood Professional Preparation Programs met by this chapter:

Standard 1: Promoting Child Development and Learning

1a: Knowing and understanding young children's characteristics and needs.

1b: Knowing and understanding the multiple influences on development and learning.

1c: Using developmental knowledge to create healthy, respectful, supportive, and challenging learning environments, for young children.

Standard 3: Observing, Documenting, and Assessing to Support Young Children and Families

3a: Understanding the goals, benefits, and uses of assessment including its use in development of appropriate goals, curriculum, and teaching strategies for young children.

3b: Knowing about and using observation, documentation, and other appropriate assessment tools and approaches, including the use of *technology* in documentation, assessment and data collection.

Standard 4: Using Developmentally Effective Approaches

4a: Understanding positive relationships and supportive interactions as the foundation of their work with young children

4b: Knowing and understanding effective strategies and tools for early education, including appropriate uses of technology.

4c: Using a broad repertoire of developmentally appropriate teaching/learning approaches.

4d: Reflecting on own practice to promote positive outcomes for each child.

Standard 5: Using Content Knowledge to Build Meaningful Curriculum

5a: Understanding content knowledge and resources in academic disciplines: language and literacy; the arts – music, creative movement, dance, drama, visual arts; mathematics; science; physical activity, physical education, health and safety; and social studies.

5b: Knowing and using the central concepts, inquiry tools, and structures of content areas or academic disciplines.

5c: Using own knowledge, appropriate early learning standards, and other resources to design, implement, and evaluate developmentally meaningful and challenging curriculum for each child.

Standard 6: Becoming a Professional

6d: Integrating knowledgeable, reflective, and critical perspectives on early education.

Vision for Managing Curriculum That Is Good for Early Learners

Intention

Teachers are being asked to be **intentional** about teaching young children. Intentional teaching solicits you to be purposeful about what skills and knowledge you seek to foster in children. While most of us claim to act with "intention" in our interaction with young children, it is worth pausing to reflect on what this term really means. "Intentional teaching means teachers act with specific outcomes or goals in mind for children's development and learning," explains Ann Epstein, author of *The Intentional Teacher* (2007, 1). You will be an intentional teacher whenever you determine how the children in your group are moving toward specific goals and when you assess the developmental learning outcomes of the children (Epstein 2007).

There is no single formula for good teaching; however, the main attribute that seems to be characteristic of outstanding teachers is *intentionality*, doing things on purpose, according to Robert Slavin, Co-Director of the Center for Research on the Education of Students Placed at Risk, Johns Hopkins University, who affirms that intentional teachers meet children's individual needs. Slavin asserts that teachers with intentionality (2000):

- maintain a working knowledge of relevant research
- remain purposeful and think about *why* they do what they do
- combine knowledge of research with professional common sense
- establish the habit of informed reflection on their teaching.

As an intentional teacher you will apply child development and learning theories to your everyday work with preschool children. You will also draw from widely accepted research and theories of child development and learning.

With an understanding of content and how children learn it, teachers can expand the opportunities they offer children to acquire knowledge and understand concepts. When the content of the curriculum is taught with children's development in mind, children are more likely to be successful learners who feel excited about, and challenged by, what they are learning. naeyc 1a, 1b, 1c, 4a, 4b, 4c, 4d, 5a, 5b, 5c, 6d

Goals

The **goals** of your early childhood program affect the curriculum choices you make. Many publically funded programs such as federal, state, or local school district departments of education have goals for the entire network of centers. Some private programs and faith-based schools may have goals adopted by the school owners or the board of directors (Sciarra and Dorsey 2010). The educational beliefs and philosophy held by the school administration and teaching staff will also influence the school's goals.

Guidelines and Standards

The **guidelines** for a school or program can be an idea or a plan that defines intended directions and preferred goals. Perceptions and beliefs about children—how they develop, behave, and learn, vary. The varied views and attitudes affect the design of program guidelines. Guidelines become part of what we need to accomplish, what opportunities we want to offer children, what skills we want them to develop, and what content we want for the curriculum.

Stemming from the desire to improve child outcomes in early care and education programs, most states have developed documents known as early learning **standards**. Early learning standards are also called "early learning guidelines." These documents outline expectations for what preschool-age children should know or be able to do. As well, the guidelines detail standards and expectations for children's knowledge and abilities that should be attained before kindergarten. The documents come in a variety of formats. They outline measures of quality, and are being required in most programs that receive state funding. Not only are standards viewed as a starting point and a resource to promote high-quality programming, curriculum planning, accountability, and assessment processes in early childhood classrooms, but they also offer a connection or alignment to each state's K-12 standards (Scott-Little et al. 2007).

One overarching reason for adopting standards is the expectation that documents that define what children should learn can help teachers to be more intentional about what they teach and, in turn, help improve child outcomes (Scott-Little et al. 2006).

NAEYC and NAECS—SDE affirmed, in a position statement dated April 2010, that "standards—challenging and achievable, appropriate to children's development, and addressing each area of children's inter-related development and learning—are an important component of teaching and learning success for every child." The joint position statement, *Early Learning Standards: Creating the Conditions for Success*, was based on research of child development and learning and the input of numerous experts and practitioners. The statement proposes that standards can be a valuable part of a comprehensive, high-quality system of services for young children.

Implementing standards-based education in a child-centered and developmentally appropriate manner requires that teachers recognize three important ideas. First, you need to recognize where individual children are in relation to indicators specified in the standards. Second, you need to understand what skills and abilities individual children need to develop in order to make progress. Third, you need to be able to implement activities that help children make progress in a way that is sensitive to each child's individual interests and current cognitive and developmental levels (Scott-Little et al. 2006).

The Curriculum Activity Guides throughout this book provide an area for you to identify the *standards met*. Because standards vary from state to state, you will be able to insert the standard that matches your own program guidelines and in a way that provides rationale for an activity. Appendix A also provides additional information about standards with reference to a website so that you may access your own state's standards. Sample Curriculum Activity Guides include selected standards to illustrate how you will be able to utilize the format, and they include relevant standards. **naeyc** 1a, 1b, 1c, 4a, 4b, 4c, 4d, 5a, 5b, 5c, 6d

> **▶‖ Video Case**
>
> The Quality Child Care
>
> Visit the Early Childhood Education Media Library, and watch the TeachSource Video Case on www.cengagebrain.com
>
> 1. Discuss the signs of good child care presented in the video by Ellen Galinsky and the moderator.
>
> 2. What does curriculum planning have to do with quality in childcare environments?

Fundamental Principles

Fundamental principles in early childhood education are based on practices for young children accepted by professionals in the field. The practices that frame fundamental principles value the development of young children and the importance of their families. Diverse and balanced curricular experiences based on observation and assessment are considered to be important for quality programs during the early childhood years (Morrison 2011).

Your curriculum activities should evolve from assessments of the children and from your beliefs about children and how they learn. Fundamental principles, or a set of ideas, guide the development of curriculum. Prominent fundamental principles for early childhood education were provided in Chapter 1, Figure 1–4. **naeyc** 1a, 1b, 1c, 3a, 3b, 4a, 4b, 4c, 4d, 5a, 5b, 5c, 6d

Creating Emergent and Integrated Curriculum

Experiences that invite children to choose activities form the basis for curriculum that offers them emergent and integrated experiences. Experiences and activities that flow from the children's interests are considered to be emergent. **Emergent experiences** focus on teaching strategies that follow the child. Following the child invites teachers to plan experiences after watching and listening to the children. Following the child's lead was documented by John Dewey and Maria Montessori. The use of the word *emergent* in relation to early childhood curriculum gained additional recognition early in the 1970s with Betty Jones's article *Curriculum Is What Happens* (Taylor 1999).

Curriculum is emergent when teachers identify general directions for the activities and remain open to the children's needs and interests. In Reggio Emilia inspired schools, curriculum emerges with each activity or project. Teachers adjust to the reactions and needs of children but do not establish the curriculum in advance. Children's ideas are given respect and held in high regard. The end result cannot be predicted at the beginning because ideas emerge throughout the children's activities (Wurm 2005).

Activities that expose children to concepts in more than one subject area offer **integrated experiences**. For instance, an integrated curriculum might offer children activities with opportunities to experience mathematics, literacy, and, perhaps, art. A balanced, integrated curriculum covers different developmental focus areas. It ensures that activities present chances for children to develop physically, socially, emotionally, and cognitively. Experiences are integrated across the curriculum areas when the children have opportunities to enjoy activities in art, math, movement, science, and other curriculum content areas.

Curriculum can be described and organized in many ways. Children's growth and development in all the domains are continuous, as is the need to meet their changing developmental needs. You will facilitate meaningful choices for children throughout the day. You can ensure meaningful choices with careful observation of what the children are doing. Observing children will allow you to balance the developmental focus areas and curriculum areas.

When four-year-old Matthew shows enthusiasm for the obstacle course, incorporate another

© Cengage Learning 2013

Most of the information teachers gather about children will be collected as they interact with them during daily activities.

area of the curriculum that is interesting and purposeful for him. When Matthew questions, "What is square?" respond to his interest and enthusiasm by adding square boxes and shapes to the obstacle course. The course challenges his large muscles, and the square boxes add mathematical concepts to an activity individualized for this child.

Individualizing Curriculum Experiences

Chapter Three detailed the importance and value of documenting what children do and say. You learned that ongoing assessments of the enrolled children help teachers make curriculum planning decisions. As you observe and listen to children, you will gather important data about their needs, interests, and skills. Most of the information will be collected as you interact with the children during the daily schedule. You or other staff may also record what you hear and see using the various strategies, and likely the three most frequently used assessment methods discussed in Chapter Three (Figure 3–1). Observation and assessment provide you with documentation, including language samples, that reveals children's feelings, understanding, interests, and needs (Figure 5–1). **naeyc** 1a, 1b, 1c, 3a, 3b, 4a, 4b, 4c, 4d, 5a, 5b, 5c, 6d

Observe/Review/Plan

Children change rapidly. The curriculum, essentially, should change as well. Events and relationships affect the behavior of the children at home and at school. That is why it is important for you to continually adjust schedules and planned experiences to accommodate them. Changes at school, such as the absence of a teacher or arrival of a new staff member, will impact the children. Children act out their feelings of stress, anxiety, or discomfort, yet may not be able to relate the causes. You will have assessments of the children to help you understand causes of their behavioral changes. You will effectively link curriculum to assessment when you observe the children, review observations of them to identify behavioral changes, and plan or (**observe/review/plan**) adjust the curriculum experiences accordingly.

The observation of Bradley (Figure 5–1) provides a language sample: "I can't get those to work" and a glimpse of his behavior. An observation of Laila (Figure 5–2), reveals another language sample. Look again at Laila's comment to determine if the curriculum plan could be modified to better meet Laila's needs (Figure 5–2). The teacher's comments, or review, indicated that Laila was

---

Figure 5–1 Assessment Can Reveal Child's Feelings and Understanding

Anecdotal Assessment

Child's Name *Bradley*	**Age** *4.2*	**Date** *0/0/00*	**Time** *9:05AM*
Observer *Teacher Saul*	**Location** *Outside Manipulative Table*		

Observation of Behavior

Bradley throws scissors down on table. "I can't get that to work." Picks up piece of paper and tears it into pieces. Lifts scissors with his left hand, places it in his right hand, then throws it down again.

Comments

Bradley is interested in the scissors. He is not successful but tries again. Plan specific small motor activities for him.

Figure 5–2 Review an Assessment to Clarify Child's Needs

Anecdotal Assessment

Child's Name *Laila*   **Age** *3.8*   **Date** *0/0/00*   **Time** *3:20PM*

Observer *Teacher Brett*   **Location** *Block Interest Center*

Observation of Behavior   **Comments**

Laila returns the last blocks she was using to the shelf. She walks to the window, looks out, turns and looks at the clock. She comments as she walks away from the window, glancing back, "My mama's never gonna pick me up."

Laila's careful watch of clock and window shows that she is anxious for her mother's arrival. Laila has been sucking her thumb and watching the clock. She was delivered to school by her grandmother.

---

delivered to school by her grandmother because Laila's mother is out of town for two weeks. If you respond to Laila's immediate needs, you might invite her to join a small group of children who are waiting in the comfortable book area for a story to be read. Laila may need individual attention and direction until her grandmother arrives to pick her up. At the end of the day, you would collaborate with other teachers and assistants to individualize the curriculum plans for the next week. Individualizing the curriculum, simple review, and modification of plans (Figure 5–3) takes a little time, but the potential benefit for Laila is great. naeyc 1a, 1b, 1c, 3a, 3b, 4a, 4b, 4c, 4d, 5a, 5b, 5c

Child-Initiated Activities

As you look more closely at the methods for organizing children's activities, pause and appreciate the ways programs meet the needs of children with child-initiated activities that can be set up in indoor and outdoor spaces. **Child-initiated activities** encourage and support children to select the projects they prefer for the amount of time they wish. These activities are most effective during free time and open blocks of uninterrupted time in the daily schedule.

The early childhood profession offers considerable validation for including child-initiated experiences with planned activities. One of America's early noted educators, John Dewey, validated this type of activity. He recommended that you remain in harmony with principles of growth and development and that you promote quality experiences that are worthwhile and meaningful to the children (Frost 1973).

Benjamin Bloom, another noted educator, provided justification for child-initiated activities. He spoke about allowing children to discover pleasure in learning (1981). In the Montessori environments

Figure 5–3 Assessment: Observe/Review/Plan

Anecdotal Assessment

Child's Name *Laila*   **Age** *3.8*   **Date** *0/0/00*   **Time** *3:20PM*

Observer *Teacher Brett*   **Location** *Block Interest Center*

Observation of Behavior   **Comments**

Laila returns the last blocks she was using to the shelf. She walks to the window, looks out, turns and looks at the clock. She comments as she walks away from the window, glancing back, "My mama's never gonna pick me up."

Laila's careful watch of clock and window shows that she is anxious for her mother's arrival. Laila has been sucking her thumb and watching the clock. She was delivered to school by her grandmother.

1. Request grandmother to arrive earlier if possible and join afternoon snack time.
2. Add book about parent taking trips.
3. Add suitcases to dramatic play area.
4. Place lotto game about departing and returning in manipulative area.
5. Encourage Laila to talk about and draw pictures for her mother and her grandmother.

Children become active learners when teachers encourage them to choose their own experiences from the materials set out in the environment.

children choose to work individually, with another child, or in small groups (Humphryes 1998). Children who are encouraged to choose their own experiences from materials set out in the environment are considered to be active learners (Weikart 1988) who make meaningful choices through active involvement (Copple and Bredekamp 2009). The curriculum activities *Let's Look it Up!* and *What Kind of Muffin?* allow children to make choices with child-initiated activities. **(Curriculum Activity Guide 33 and 34 \ \ ).**

You will discover best practices for the children in your program when you offer them meaningful choices within boundaries (Copple and Bredekamp 2009). Your growing knowledge about child development and cultural sensitivity to your school's community contribute to establishing the best practices for young children. Remain sensitive to the children's varied and extreme differences in choices. However, be aware that some communities prefer that children adapt the values and practices as they exist in their community. The community may not value giving choices to children (Gonzalez-Mena 2005).

Inclusive and Sensitive

Inclusive and sensitive curricula respond to the diversity of families and communities. Modeling

positive interactions and values for children will prepare them for an increasingly diverse and international world. Authentic inclusion encourages programs to provide experiences that meet all of the children's needs with respect for their identities. Identities are formed by our family, our culture, our language, our race, our religion, our social circumstances, our gender, and our capabilities. You can offer non-biased experiences with sensitive communication, bulletin boards, materials, books, and activities that validate respectful representation of children and their families. Have clear program guidelines to share cultures, holidays, foods, and traditions throughout the year. Inclusive and sensitive programs also support creating curriculum experiences for children with special needs to learn "what they can do."

Inclusive and sensitive curriculum can be supported by placing dolls that represent different races and ethnicities in the dramatic play center. Attempt to represent biracial and multiracial children. Include dolls with walkers, braces, eyeglasses, and hearing aids. Place cushions from different cultures displaying traditional patterns, colors, and designs in both the dramatic play area and the reading area. Provide food containers from a variety of cultures with labels in different languages. Add culturally relevant clothing, eating utensils, bedding, and infant carriers (Wardle 2008). **(Curriculum Activity Guide 4 \ \ ).** naeyc 1a, 1b, 1c, 4a, 4b, 4c, 4d, 5a, 5b, 5c, 6d

Multi-Age Grouping

When you visit an early childhood care and learning center, you might notice the children participating in same-age groups or in multi-age groups. **Multi-age groups** would include children of different ages; for instance, a classroom would have children who are three, four, and five years old. Programs for young children tend to cluster children into same-age groups. Their placement is determined by the developmental needs of the children, program guidelines, licensing and funding regulations, availability of staff, and facility resources. Placing children into small groups throughout the early childhood years has been consistently justified (Bloom 1981). Two to four children ages three and four years old would comprise a group that is considered to be small. A group of six children who are older four- and five-year-olds would be defined

© Cengage Learning 2013

as a small group as well. Children's ages and their developmental stages affect group formation and functioning. This tends to be consistent, whether children group themselves or the group is directed by the teacher.

Single-age grouping includes children who are about the same chronological age. Chronological age identifies the number of years since a child was born. Single-age grouping provides opportunities that are arranged to accommodate children who are within a specific age range. Multi-age grouping places children of different ages in settings where they participate together in the program for partial or full-day scheduling.

Studies indicate that teachers more likely attend to differences among the children in multi-age grouping than to children enrolled in single-age clusters. When there is a wider age span among the children within a group, a broader range of behavior and abilities exists. These wider ranges of behaviors and performances of the children in multi-age groups are more likely to be accepted

and tolerated by the supervising adults (Katz 1995). **naeyc** 1a, 1b, 1c, 4a, 4b, 4c, 4d, 5a, 5b, 5c, 6c, 6d

Teacher-Guided Experiences and Group Time

Your commitment to early childhood education incorporates ideas you have about the way children learn. You will guide the children's experiences in the way you set up the environment, plan activities, and watch for cues from children. While you strive to provide child-initiated experiences, you will also set up teacher-guided experiences. These experiences are most appropriate when materials for an activity are complex and unknown to the children. Activities that you direct for a child or children give ample opportunities for you to pose interactive questioning. Interactive and open-ended questioning stimulates children's thinking and will help you clarify children's participation in activities. Children benefit from your supervision and guidance in cooking activities. Guidance is also valuable for many science and art projects. Teacher guidance does not need to restrict children's exploration, discovery, and creativity. **Teacher-guided experiences** include group time, which is also referred to as circle time or meeting time. Whether or not to require all children to participate in a group time is up to each teacher. Group times that include all of the children are useful for establishing feelings of community within the group. Information and stories can be shared with the whole group and then revisited with activities in smaller groups. Ideas and information can be explored in more detail.

Whether or not you require all children to participate in a group time, the experience is more suitable for young children when the group is small. When groups are small the children can see and touch the materials you are introducing and see the book you are reading. Group time can be offered in various formats. In an open schedule, children spontaneously gather around the teacher to read a book, to meet a visitor, or to sing and enjoy fingerplays. Group time can be scheduled for different times throughout the day. Some teachers offer group time during the morning and afternoon, allowing children to choose the time they will join in. Group times provide chances for teachers to introduce new ideas and materials and enjoy guiding the planning and reviewing the day with the children (Figure 5–4). **naeyc** 1a, 1b, 1c, 4a, 4b, 4c, 4d, 5a, 5b, 5c, 6d

© Cengage Learning 2013

Activities teachers guide in small groups give opportunities to pose interactive questioning which stimulates children's thinking.

Figure 5–4 Mentoring Early Childhood Students for Successful Group Times

New Early Childhood Education students are frequently intimidated by the prospect of leading group time, yet veteran teachers often view it as one of their favorite daily activities. The journey from anxiety to enjoyment can be facilitated by adherence to the motto, "Planning is the key."

Successful group time planning is based on a logical sequence of components, regardless of the topic or focus. Ideally, all group time elements should be related to the topic or theme for optimum continuity.

I. *Arrival to Group Time/Settle Down*

Familiar songs with large motor movement to "get the wiggles out." (Depending on the children's readiness to settle down, additional large motor songs can be added.)

II. *Focusing/Fingerplay*

From large motor actions, the teacher now focuses the children's attention with a fine motor fingerplay or two.

III. *Main Focus/Body of Group Time*

Now that the children are settled down and attentive, you can read a story, enact a flannelboard story, or introduce a "surprise bag." While this component is typically teacher-directed, it should also be interactive to engage the children and sustain their interest. (Beginning group times limit this component, and increase over time and as children develop their attention spans.)

IV. *Dismissal*

Children are usually dismissed individually to the next activity with a song or departing activity. Anxious students are always advised to "Relax and Enjoy." Young children are not as critical as college students are on themselves.

—Kathy Barry, MA

Principal, Shasta County Office of Education

Approaches to Planning

You have read about curriculum that is good for young children. You may have considered goals for meaningful experiences and how you will intentionally integrate standards and guidelines into the environment and activities. It is time for you to begin planning the activities to match curricular guidelines and standards. It may be adapting your vision to the curriculum that exists at a school where you are employed. Or, your ideas might influence the school's program administrator and staff to revise their goals. There are many strategies for planning and managing curriculum. Some approaches for organizing experiences for young children are complementary. This allows you to utilize ideas from curricular approaches and programs.

Some programs for young children follow a particular curriculum. For instance, many Head Start programs use HighScope emphasizing children's key experiences (Gestwicki 1997). You may relate to a particular curriculum because it is similar to the type of practices utilized where you work. You might be familiar with other curricular approaches because you learned about them in college courses or by attending workshops.

A curriculum plan designates a specific method or approach to organizing the experiences in an early care and learning program for young children. A plan can combine one or more curriculum approaches. Even though a school or program's curriculum plan is set, there are ample opportunities for unexpected and spontaneous learning. Four approaches to planning the curriculum for young children will be reviewed:

- developmental focus area approach
- curriculum area approach
- thematic approach
- project approach

Ideally, each approach focuses on the needs of young children, their individual differences, and the relevancy of activities to the children's cultures and languages. naeyc 1a, 1b, 1c, 4a, 4b, 4c, 4d, 5a, 5b, 5c, 6d

Developmental Focus Areas

The **developmental focus area** approach emphasizes growth and developing skills of young children. This approach organizes experiences and activities to help children become competent in the different areas of development. The experiences that are planned and offered are compatible with young children's developing abilities. The developmental focus areas encourage opportunities for children to explore, to discover, and to build on their own interests.

The developmental approach offers a framework that encourages teachers to provide challenging, yet age-appropriate experiences. An activity in one developmental area may influence the children's development in another area. This is one of the reasons this approach is considered to be holistic. It meets the needs of the "whole child." Visualize three- and four-year-olds painting on a large stretch of butcher paper hung across an outdoor fence. The children use big brushes and make large strokes. Their large movements contribute to their physical development. Once the paint dries, the children and teachers decide to hang the colorfully painted butcher paper to create a shaded shelter. They are developing social skills as they work together. Some of the children bring picture books to this outside shaded area, further developing skills. Reading books contributes to their language acquisition and literacy and cognitive development.

The developmental focus areas used throughout this textbook are physical, affective (social-emotional understanding) and aesthetic, and cognitive.

Physical

The physical developmental focus area relates to the children's physiological growth and changes. This focus area is important for early childhood programs. Children need to move their bodies (within their capabilities), engage their senses, and challenge their growing muscles. As you consider offering experiences for children, expand the physical developmental focus area to include sensory experiences. These experiences invite the children to use their senses, including their eyes, ears, nose, hands, taste, and other parts of their body. Sensory education, a major aspect of the Montessori Method, introduces materials sequentially, with emphasis on sensory growth. Qualities of color, form, dimension, sound, and texture are presented with concrete experiences to educate

the children's senses (Orem 1974) **(Curriculum Activity Guide 26).**

Affective (Social-Emotional Understanding) and Aesthetic

The affective (social-emotional understanding) and aesthetic developmental focus area encompasses growth and change in social and emotional behaviors as well as a growing sensitivity to beauty in nature and art. The affective domain looks at children's sociability, feelings, personality, reactions, and interactions. The aesthetic aspect of this developmental focus area covers creativity and expressiveness **(Curriculum Activity Guide 45).**

Cognitive

The cognitive developmental focus area is the category that includes mental and thinking abilities. The acquisition of language, communication, and literacy is considered an area of development included in the cognitive domain.

Children's behaviors and changes within each developmental focus area can be related to appropriate and meaningful experiences that support their developing abilities (Figure 5–5).

Curriculum Areas

Teachers of young children can manage experiences by organizing the children's activities through curriculum areas, also referred to as subjects or subject areas. The term **curriculum area** is used throughout this textbook. The curriculum area approach is organized by the content or subject. Content and subject areas may include disciplines such as art, language, mathematics, music, physical education, science, and social studies. Educational practice has favored dividing curriculum into subjects.

During the beginning stages of the early childhood movement in the late 1960s, the experiences planned for pre-kindergarten children were influenced by the elementary school format. Generally, schools divide curriculum into subjects. The early childhood education curriculum evolved with that foundation in subject areas (Hymes 1981). Today, most school levels, including elementary, middle, and high schools continue to support this approach. You may work in an early care and learning program that uses different terms. Remember, there is a great variability in early childhood terminology (Figure 5–6).

The curriculum content areas generally include recognizable categories. Curriculum areas will reflect the preferences of the program

Figure 5–5 Developmental Focus Areas Support Children's Developing Abilities

Areas of Development	Children's Related Developing Abilities	
Physical	physiological changes	
	growth, height, and weight	
	large muscle movement	
	small muscle movement	
	motor abilities	
	perceptual/motor abilities	
	health/safety/nutrition/wellness awareness	
	movement responses to music and rhythm	
Affective (Social-Emotional Understanding) and Aesthetic	sociability	prosocial
	emotions and feelings	gender role identity
	temperament and personality	creative expression
	self-awareness	discovery
	trust	making choices
	self-confidence	artistic expression
	interactions and reactions	dramatic expression
Cognitive	thinking and mental abilities	literacy
	memory and logic	listening
	intellectual growth	comprehension
	conceptualizing	inquiry
	grouping, matching, ordering	intuition
	creativity	imagination
	communication	verbal fluency
	language	problem-solving
	seeing cause/effect	

Figure 5–6 Familiar Curriculum Areas

What Curriculum Areas Are Commonly Called	What Curriculum Areas Are Often Included
Curriculum areas,	Art
Subject areas,	Language and Literacy
Content areas	Health, Safety, Nutrition
	Mathematics
	Music and Rhythm
	Movement
	Physical Education
	Science
	Social Studies

learning. Consider the subject categories you might select using the curriculum content area approach. Would you use the term *science* or *science and nutrition?* Would you have a separate curriculum area for nutrition or health? What would you call the art area—*art* or *arts and creativity?* Related subjects and topics can be categorized within curriculum areas. You will likely have many options for organizing experiences to meet school and program guidelines. You will find that you can meet children's needs and interests with practical management of ideas. For instance, you may find it convenient to organize activities by categorizing the subjects and topics within curriculum areas (Figure 5–7). naeyc
1a, 1b, 1c, 3a, 3b, 4a, 4b, 4c, 4d, 5a, 5b, 5c, 6d

Art

Art provides opportunities for children to explore and create in a natural setting. Activities in the content area of art encourage children to experience creative and spontaneous pleasure with the materials. Basic art expression materials include clay, crayons, chalk, pencils, markers, glue, paint, paper, collage materials, magazines, prints, modeling dough, and scissors.

administrators, boards of directors, and teaching staff. Preferences change as research documents new information about development and learning. Trends and societal needs also affect the focus of early education. Literacy and technology are included with social-emotional understanding, which have gained attention as categories of early

Figure 5–7 Subjects and Topics Categorized within Curriculum Areas

Art	**Communication and Literacy**	**Science**
art media	literature	sciencing
artistic experiences	communication	physical science
arts and crafts	literacy	biological science
creative activities	reading	science
shape and form	linguistics	discovery
	reading readiness	plants
	language arts	animals
		technology
Mathematics	**Social-Emotional Understanding**	**Music and Rhythm**
math and technology	social world	music and rhythm
time, space, numbers	community helpers	music experiences
size and shape	people in the world	songs and fingerplays
math experiences	sociodramatics	musical sounds
pre math	learning culture	
Movement	**Creative Dramatics**	**Health, Safety, Nutrition**
movement	dramatic expression	health
perceptual motor	puppetry	safety
sensorimotor	sociodramatics	nutrition
sensorial		cooking
health and safety		well-being

Creative Dramatics
Creative dramatics is the curriculum content area that gives young children opportunities to express themselves through movement, gestures, language, and nonverbal communication. Creative dramatics encourages children to improvise drama when teachers provide suggestions, stories, or point out events. **(Curriculum Activity Guide 6)** Children will respond naturally with your support to use their own actions and verbal responses. Masks, puppets, flannel board figures, scarves, and hats are examples of materials that can be used to stimulate children's imaginations and expressions (Edwards 1990).

Social-Emotional Understanding
The curriculum area of social-emotional understanding contributes to young children's self-awareness. Social-emotional understanding experiences help them to accept feelings, comfort themselves and others, express their needs, and initiate new actions. Children's emotional well-being will develop as they interact with adults and other children during activities specifically planned to promote social-emotional understanding.

Social-emotional understanding activities expose children to their community and the people who work and participate in it. The curriculum area of social-emotional understanding will expand opportunities for children to learn about cultures and elaborates on the multicultural experiences immersed through all content curriculum areas. **(Curriculum Activity Guide 7)**

Health, Safety, Nutrition
The curriculum area of health, safety, and nutrition will introduce concepts about healthy living habits to the children. Through meaningful experiences and activities related to health, safety, and nutrition, children will develop lifelong healthy habits to understand their own development and safety and wellness behaviors. Particular emphasis on nutrition and healthy eating patterns has gained nationwide support.

Communication and Literacy
Experiences that develop children's communication skills will also increase their listening and verbal abilities. Literacy opportunities will occur every day in an early care and learning program

that is print rich. A print-rich environment is filled with books, bulletin boards at the children's level, and word labels. Nurturing teachers who listen to the children and respond to their questions create environments that support communication and literacy. They also ask many open-ended questions throughout the day to encourage children's thinking and verbal skills.

Mathematics

The curriculum area of mathematics supports children's exploration and discovery of materials and ideas. Children will discover mathematical concepts in everyday environments that provide real materials for them to manipulate. Mathematics can be integrated throughout the program curriculum giving children opportunities to analyze, arrange, compare, graph, measure, order, pair, pattern, and reverse.

Movement

Children develop motor skills through physical movement. The curriculum area of movement offers them chances to feel their bodies move and begin to understand the changes in body movements. Children develop their large motor skills and small motor skills in environments that allow them to participate in active movement experiences. Coordination, balance, and control are skills that mature as children participate in appropriate movement activities.

Music and Rhythm

The curriculum content area of music and rhythm provides opportunities for children to hum, repeat

Movement and rhythm activities provide a wide variety of movement opportunities for young children.

© Cengage Learning 2013

parts of songs, listen to music, move to the rhythm of music, participate in fingerplays, and enjoy musical instruments. You will guide children in music and rhythm activities by encouraging both large and small group participation, providing adequate space for movement, offering a wide choice of types of music and rhythms and appropriately responding to young children's attention span and interests.

Science

Activities and experiences in the curriculum area of science will expand the children's awareness of their surroundings and the world. Both biological and physical science concepts are included within most science curricula for young children. Science allows children to discover, explore, and examine objects. Discovery can occur through cooking activities, caring for classroom pets, exploring items from nature and gardening. Science activities give children chances to observe cause and effect of matter, life cycles, energy, and space.

The activities you organize for young children within the curriculum area approach will often integrate more than one curriculum area. For example, when children prepare cream cheese, celery, and raisins to make "bumps on a log" for a snack, they interact. While interacting, they gain skills in the curriculum area of *social understanding*. When they wash their hands to prepare for preparation of the snack, they validate learning in the curriculum area of *health*. When you listen to the children and answer their questions about "bumps on a log," they develop abilities in the curriculum area of *communication and literacy*. When the children carefully cut the celery into three pieces, they begin to gain concepts in the curriculum area of *mathematics*. **(Curriculum Activity Guide 35)**

Documentation and Blending Concepts

Teachers and program directors often incorporate the concepts from different theorist and curriculum approaches. Professionals who incorporate different concepts recognize common threads leading to quality experiences for young children. They embrace observation, assessment, and documentation of children. They plan experiences accordingly.

You may decide to remain true to the Montessori Method and encourage self-development within a prepared environment. Montessori strongly urged teachers to first discover the true nature of children, then to proceed to assist them in their normal development (Orem 1974). You may use the Reggio inspired practices with emphasis on constructivist theory, encouraging the children to explore and problem solve. You may find that the Project Approach provides the exact model for your program. Intentions to meet the children's needs can be achieved in different ways.

Themes

The thematic approach in early childhood organizes the curriculum around a topic or theme. A theme sets a broad, general framework that allows children to construct their own learning. This approach allows children to explore a topic in depth as they participate in a collection of related activities. The activities should not be over-programmed with unrealistic expectations for children to acquire concepts from preplanned activities (Katz 1994). Instead, the activities should maximize the potential of themes with support for children's activity, curiosity, and creativity (Kamii 1973).

You will be integrating curriculum for young children when you use the **themes** approach. You will be developmentally appropriate by utilizing your observations of the children to adjust and modify the themes to match their needs and interests. A theme can connect activities from different curriculum areas. The activities become particularly important when the children contribute to, and participate in, the curriculum planning.

The thematic approach allows you to arrange activities that respond to the children's interests and extend their ideas and thinking. The thematic approach can introduce new ideas and develop the children's skills within several of the curriculum areas. *Unit* and *resource unit* are words that are used interchangeably with *theme*. A unit connects several themes. Regardless of the word used to describe your curriculum approach, you will be able to plan in a way that reinforces your curricular goals and maintains flexibility in your daily, weekly, and monthly plans.

Using themes to plan the curriculum continues to be popular in early childhood programs. Program administrators and teachers establish long-term goals while continuing to adjust plans to meet the needs and interests of the children. Themes guide and organize activities and provide numerous ways to balance activities among the curriculum areas.

© Cengage Learning 2013

Children construct their own learning when teachers organize experiences around the interests and experiences of the children in the group.

If you intend to use themes, collaborate with the other teachers to select themes that are most familiar to the children in your program. Avoid emphasis on prepared holiday units because these tend to interfere with a developmentally relevant curriculum (Derman-Sparks and ABC Task Force 1989). **naeyc** 1a, 1b, 1c, 4a, 4b, 4c, 4d, 5a, 5b, 5c, 6d

Frequently scheduled themes include those that relate directly to the child, such as This is Me and This is My Family. You will be able to expand to topics such as outdoor plants, pets, friends, music from around the world, and neighbors. The themes or thematic approach supports emergent and developmentally appropriate practices when activities are integrated and related to a theme. Themes will vary by regional locations, communities, and events in the children's lives. The transportation theme has relevancy to many children, especially those living near an interstate highway. Remain responsive to the children and adapt to their different developmental stages with familiar themes that have become popular and well liked by teachers. Add new themes as special events and circumstances in the children's lives suggest (Figure 5–8).

Another way to present themes is to arrange them to focus on the children. The Self-Concept Curriculum Model (Essa and Rogers 1992) is divided to include the child, home and family, friends and school, and community and community helpers. Your program's enrollment

Figure 5–8 Clarification of Themes

This is Me My Body—I Am Growing	Baby Animals
My Senses	Pets
Family Celebrations	Animals on Farms
I Am Special	Animals in Zoos
Trucks	Animals in the Ocean
Trains	Animals Live in Different Places
This is My Family	Life Cycle of Birds
Firefighters	Life Cycle of Reptiles
Many Families at Our School	Life Cycle of Amphibians
Friends	Life Cycle of Insects and Spiders
The Sun, Stars, and Planets	Dirt, Water, Soil, Rocks
Tools and Machines	Shells, Sand, Seaweed
Our Neighborhood	Transportation
Museums and Libraries	Medical Workers
Camping Outdoors	Community Service Workers: Postal, Sanitation Police
Changing Seasons Growing our Food	
Gardening for Landscape	Many Types of Sports: Soccer Basketball Football Swimming Gymnastics Rodeos
Changing Weather Food Production	

pattern and schedule may influence the themes you select and how you choose them. Children's enrollment may replicate their parents' work or training schedules. Some children may attend only Tuesday and Thursday, some only afternoons. The variation in enrollment patterns will challenge you to offer themes that overlap and extend over weeks and even months. Even if a list of possible or recommended themes exists for a school, it is not essential that you implement all of them each year. The emphasis of curriculum should remain on the developing abilities of the children, the life experiences of their families, and events and circumstances in the communities.

Teachers who use themes to organize their curriculum will plan and prepare activities that interest the children in their group. Long-term planning will provide you with time to gather information about the theme and to collect the related materials to implement the activities. The related materials are called props. Teachers, volunteers, and parents collect and replenish props over time. Some of the props and small equipment that are difficult to locate quickly can be stored in labeled boxes called "prop boxes." Prop boxes are ready when a theme calls for specific materials (Figure 5–9).

Project Approach

The **Project Approach** organizes and integrates curriculum activities. A project, by definition, is an in-depth investigation of a real-world topic worthy of children's attention and effort. The study may be carried out with an entire class or with small groups of students. Teachers select a topic of study based on students' interests, the curriculum, and the availability of local resources. They help the children brainstorm (and represent) their own experiences, knowledge, and ideas about the topic in a web. This web becomes a central part of the project process where both children and adults contribute. Children thoroughly explore an idea about real topics by working together, or in small groups. The Project Approach

Figure 5–9 Prop Boxes Related to Themes

Theme: Picnic	**Theme: Market**
picnic basket	cash register
paper plates	play money and debit cards
napkins	reusable bags
table cloth	signs
backpack	coupons

Theme: Gas Station	**Theme: Emergency Room**
gas hose	clip boards
window cleaner	uniforms
tire pump	stethoscopes
credit card register	scale
signs	X-ray images
maps	medical supplies

builds on their natural curiosity, enabling children to interact, question, connect, problem-solve, communicate reflect and more. This is authentic learning because it connects children to the real world (Chard 2010). Children explore creatively and meaningfully by drawing, writing, designing charts, constructing, and engaging in dramatic play. This type of critical thinking, collaboration, and creativity builds on the individual needs, interests, and strengths of all the children and allows them to progress at their own pace. Project work is complementary to the elementary level curriculum and to the more informal aspects of the curriculum for young children (Katz 1994).

Children can explore a project within a theme or unit for an extended time depending on their ages, interests, and skills. Organizing the curriculum activities around a project avoids curriculum that only offers activities in subject areas. The project approach will allow you to expand topics related to the children's interests and everyday experiences. The project approach depends on the availability of local resources, and the personal experiences and knowledge about the project topic (Katz 1994). As children help plan activities, they become more experienced in planning activities.

The Project Approach uses a webbing structure to record children's ideas, interests, and responses about a topic (Figure 5–10). Webbing is the creating and recording of the ideas suggested by children during "brainstorming" sessions. The teacher encourages participation by asking the children questions and recording their ideas. The procedure works well with older preschoolers and primary-age children because they have a greater foundation of knowledge and experiences. The webbing process graphs ideas for activities that emerge from the children's knowledge and interests with guidance and input from the teachers. Younger children may simply indicate what they know about a topic, which can provide the basis for planning.

Balancing Curriculum with Emergent and Integrated Experiences

Whichever technique you utilize, curriculum areas, themes, or a project approach, you can balance the experiences for children in a way that supports their development. Their interest in trucks, for example, opens many opportunities for you to enhance their understanding and build their skills in the developmental and curriculum areas (Figure 5–11). naeyc 1a, 1b, 1c, 3b, 4a, 4b, 4c, 4d, 5a, 5b, 5c, 6d

Figure 5–10 The Project Approach: Beginning with the Children's Ideas

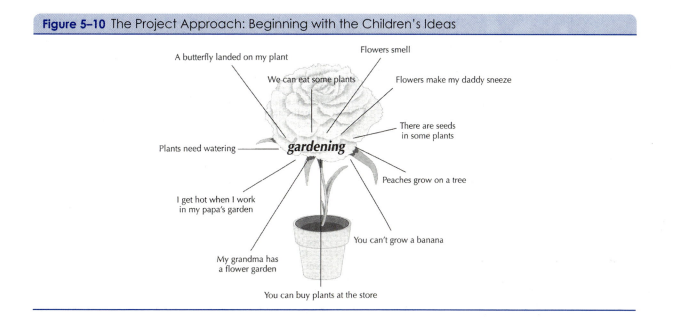

- A butterfly landed on my plant
- Flowers smell
- We can eat some plants
- Flowers make my daddy sneeze
- There are seeds in some plants
- Plants need watering
- *gardening*
- Peaches grow on a tree
- I get hot when I work in my papa's garden
- You can't grow a banana
- My grandma has a flower garden
- You can buy plants at the store

Figure 5–11 Balancing Curriculum with Focus on Transportation

Art	small toy tire track art fence painting with toy vehicles color rubbing, transportation vehicle	**Social Studies**	vehicles in block area, roadway in sand table, travel props
Language	color assessment of vehicle, vehicle guessing game, word choices: *car, bike, train*	**Movement**	red/green light, trike path, wheels on the bus, follow directions
Science	tools/machines magnet activities. auto parts	**Group time**	truck sizes, what trucks do. safety signs. public transportation
Mathematics	size sequence/vehicles cars/garages—counting vehicle sorting size progression cards (dump truck)	**Visitor**	parking officer bus driver bike repair service
Health and Safety	safety, street signs, cross street safely, safety lotto game	**Bulletin Boards**	"Be safe, buckle up" safety signs trucks and cars

Resource: Shasta College Early Childhood Education Center (1996), Redding, California.

© Cengage Learning 2013

Children will explore a topic, such as transportation, with props and experiences that meet their needs and expand their learning opportunities.

Thinking About What You Have Learned

✔ Identify three curricular guidelines for young children. Review these with another teacher or classmate. Write three additional guidelines that include your vision and commitment to children.

✔ Research some of the standards that have been implemented in your state. How has your program modified curriculum planning to meet the requirements of the standards?

✔ What approach to curriculum planning best matches the curricular guidelines you would plan for young children? Explain the reason for the selection, and describe how you will document the curriculum approach.

✔ Become familiar with two early childhood programs in your community. Review the school brochure and/or speak to the program administrator or center director about the curriculum. Which curriculum approach discussed in this chapter best matches the curriculum at each program?

✔ Access one of the websites listed below, and provide two curriculum ideas found at the sites.

Using Ideas from Reggio Emilia in America
http://ericeece.org/reggio/nlspr95a.html
National 4-H Council
http://www.fourhcouncil.edu/
Project Approach
http://www.projectapproach.org
HighScope Educational Research Foundation
http://www.highscope.org/

Chapter References

Bloom, Benjamin. S. 1981. *All our children learning: A primer for parents, teachers, and other educators.* New York: McGraw-Hill.

Chard, Sylvia 2010. *The project approach. http://www. projectapproach.org/about-this-site-m1*

Copple, Carole and Sue Bredekamp. eds. 2009. *Developmentally appropriate practice in early childhood programs serving children from birth through age 8.* 3rd ed. Washington, DC: National Association for the Education of Young Children.

Derman-Sparks, Louise., and A.B.C. Task Force. 1989. *Anti-bias curriculum: Tools for empowering young children.* Washington, DC: National Association for the Education of Young Children.

Edwards, Linda. C. 1990. *Affective development and the creative arts.* Columbus, OH: Merrill.

Epstein, Ann S. 2007. *The Intentional teacher: Choosing the best strategies for young children's learning.* Washington DC: National Association for the Education of Young Children.

Essa, Eva. L., and Penelope R. Rogers. 1992. *An early childhood curriculum: From developmental model to application.* Albany, NY: Delmar.

Frost, Joe. L. ed. 1973. *Revisiting early childhood education: Readings.* New York: Holt, Rinehart & Winston.

Gestwicki, Carol. 1997. *The essentials of early education.* Albany, NY: Delmar.

Gonzalez-Mena, Janet. 2005. *Foundations of early childhood education: Teaching children in a diverse society.* New York: McGraw Hill.

Hendricks, Joanne. 1980. *Total learning for the whole child: Holistic curriculum for children ages 2 to 5.* St. Louis, MO: Mosby.

Humphryes, Janet. 1998. The developmental appropriateness of high-quality Montessori programs. *Young Children,* 53(4): 4–16.

Hymes, James. L. 1981. *Teaching the child under six.* 3rd ed. Columbus, OH: Merrill.

Jackman, Hilda. L. 1997. *Early childhood education curriculum: A child's connection to the world.* Albany, NY: Delmar.

Kamii, Constance. 1973. A sketch of the Piaget-derived preschool curriculum developed by the Ypsilanti early education program. In Frost, J. L. ed., *Revisiting early childhood education.* New York: Holt, Rinehart & Winston.

Katz, Lillian. G. 1994. The project approach. *ERIC DIGEST* (EDO-PS-94-6). Urbana, IL: ERIC Clearinghouse on Elementary and Early Childhood Education.

_____. 1995. The benefits of mixed-age grouping. *ERIC DIGEST* (EDO-PS-95-8). Urbana, IL: ERIC Clearinghouse on Elementary and Early Childhood Education.

Montessori, Maria. 1966. *The secret of childhood.* New York: Fides.

Morrison, George S. 2011. *Fundamentals of Early Childhood Education.* 6th ed. Columbus, OH: Merrill.

National Association for the Education of Young Children and the National Association of Early Childhood Specialists in State Departments of Education. (April 2010). Joint statement on the common core standards initiative related to kindergarten through third grade, 46(3): 21–38.

Orem, Reginald. C. 1974. *Montessori: Her method and the movement, what you need to know.* New York: Capricorn.

Sciarra, Dorothy J. and Ann G. Dorsey. 1998. *Developing and administering a child care and education program.* 7th ed. Belmont, CA: Wadsworth/Cengage.

Scott-Little, Catherine, Jim Lesko, Jana Martella, and Penny Milburn. 2007. Early learning standards: Results from a national survey to document trends in state-level policies and practices. *Early Childhood Research and Practice* 9(1): 1–22.

Scott-Little, Catherine, Sharon Lynn Kagan, and Victoria Stebbins Frelow. 2006. Conceptualization of readiness and the content of early learning standards: The intersection of policy and research? *Early Childhood Research Quarterly* 21(3): 153–173.

Slavin, Robert. 2000. *Educational psychology: Theory and practice. 6th ed.* Englewood Cliffs, NJ: Allyn and Bacon.

Taylor, Barbara. J. 1999. *A child goes forth: A curriculum guide for preschool children.* 9th ed. Upper Saddle River, NJ: Merrill.

Wardle, Francis 2008. Meeting the needs of multiracial and multiethnic children. *Early Children Childhood News,* http://www.earlychildhoodnews.com/earlychildhood/article_view.aspx?ArticleID=124

Weikart, David P. 1988. Quality in early childhood education. In C. Warger, ed. *A resource guide to public school early childhood programs.* Alexandria, VA: Association for Supervision and Curriculum Development.

Wortham, Sue C. 1996. *The integrated classroom: The assessment-curriculum link in early childhood education.* Englewood Cliffs, NJ: Merrill.

Wurm, Julianne P. 2005. *Working in the Reggio way: A beginner's guide for American teachers.* St. Paul, MN: Redleaf Press.

Designing Developmental Curriculum for Play, Discovery, and Learning

© Cengage Learning 2013

Picture This . . .

The exhibit halls at conferences for professionals in early care and education attract attendees, whether the meeting is scheduled for one day, two days, or three days. It is no wonder: the exhibitors display new and interesting materials, equipment, and "freebies." Conference participants leave with at least one new bag, badges, stickers, bubble wands, and ideas for new activities. The conference workshops and sessions additionally fill our bags with handouts and ideas for activities. We are quite visible as we board buses, load our vehicles, and manage bulging bags filled with extra new manipulatives. We cram our overstuffed carry-ons into the overhead compartments on airplanes. We have new puppets, new samples of markers and stamps, and lots and lots of books with ideas for new activities. Songs, conversations, and displays for new activities repeat in our heads. We look forward to returning to school to share ideas for new activities with our teaching team and, of course, the children. However, the demands of daily teaching schedules too often hinder our intentions to organize the new songs and the recipes we learned at the conference. What happened to that creative, new recipe for modeling dough? What book described harvest celebrations? Where is the handout about literacy? And, where is the activity about taking care of our world? Early care and education professionals need an efficient way to store and access the ideas for new activities. We need a way to convert the ideas as the children's needs and interests appear. What you need is a practical and efficient way to manage your activity ideas.

GUIDE TO READING CHAPTER 6

Chapter Outline

Learning Objectives

After reading this chapter, you will be able to:

1. Define the value and significance of play in the lives of young children.
2. Understand how to support creativity.
3. Examine the ways children think and learn.
4. Identify active questioning methods.
5. Discuss how children's questions generate curriculum ideas.
6. Understand that activities need to be planned to introduce ideas, encourage exploration, stimulate questioning, and ensure spontaneous learning.
7. Identify the curriculum elements: activity title, goal, materials, approach, outcomes, and teaching strategies.
8. Use the Curriculum Activity Guide as a tool for documenting the curriculum experience in writing.
9. Recognize how activities can be sequenced to support child-centered learning.
10. Consider ongoing assessment as a vital step for revising activities.
11. Recognize that curriculum plans and Curriculum Activity Guides assist teachers in setting up activities.

Key Terms

National Association for the Education of Young Children (NAEYC) Standards for Initial Early Childhood Professional Preparation Programs met by this chapter:

Standard 1: Promoting Child Development and Learning

1a: Knowing and understanding young children's characteristics and needs, from birth through age 8.

1b: Knowing and understanding the multiple influences on development and learning.

1c: Using developmental knowledge to create healthy, respectful, supportive, and challenging learning environments, for young children.

Standard 2: Building Family and Community Relationships

2c: Involving families and communities in their children's development and learning.

Standard 3: Observing, Documenting, and Assessing to Support Young Children and Families

3a: Understanding the goals, benefits, and uses of assessment including its use in development of appropriate goals, curriculum, and teaching strategies for young children.

3b: Knowing about and using observation, documentation, and other appropriate assessment tools and approaches, including the use of *technology* in documentation, assessment and data collection.

3c: Understanding and practicing responsible assessment to promote positive outcomes for each child, including the use of assistive technology for children with disabilities.

Standard 4: Using Developmentally Effective Approaches

4a: Understanding positive relationships and supportive interactions as the foundation of their work with young children

4b: Knowing and understanding effective strategies and tools for early education, including appropriate uses of technology.

4c: Using a broad repertoire of developmentally appropriate teaching/learning approaches.

4d: Reflecting on own practice to promote positive outcomes for each child.

Standard 5: Using Content Knowledge to Build Meaningful Curriculum

5a: Understanding content knowledge and resources in academic disciplines: language and literacy; the arts – music, creative movement, dance, drama, visual arts; mathematics; science; physical activity, physical education, health and safety; and social studies.

5b: Knowing and using the central concepts, inquiry tools, and structures of content areas or academic disciplines.

5c: Using own knowledge, appropriate early learning standards, and other resources to design, implement, and evaluate developmentally meaningful and challenging curriculum for each child.

Standard 6: Becoming a Professional

6c: Engaging in continuous, collaborative learning to inform practice; using technology effectively with young children, with peers, and as a professional resource.

6d: Integrating knowledgeable, reflective, and critical perspectives on early education.

Promoting Playful Experiences during Early Childhood

Play is a child's spontaneous, unrestricted, and joyful response. Children are playing when they react positively to the events and people and circumstances in their environment. Child's play can appear random to some adults. Some adults even see play as undisciplined, unproductive, and even something to hold in check. In contrast, early childhood professionals believe that children must be able to play, and it is play that will guide their socialization. Children's instinct to play is natural and is a positive tool for them to develop.

Play is a word that we use often in early care and education. Nevertheless, play too often generates negative responses from individuals outside our profession, despite the quantity of data substantiating the benefit and value of play for young children.

We know that play helps children learn about their world. We know that play helps children acquire the competencies they will need for the rest of their lives. Children resolve challenges and conflicts in all developmental areas (Cohen 1972). The baby plays with a rattle, the toddler plays with a ball, and the preschooler plays with a tricycle. The babies', toddlers', and preschoolers' play are important for their developing skills. Playing peek-a-boo, pointing to people and saying their names, and sitting with friends at preschool while a story is read are activities that help children develop their skills. naeyc
1a, 1b, 1c, 2c, 3a, 3b, 3c, 4a, 4b ,4c, 4d, 5a, 5b, 5c, 6c, 6d

Activity time for play in early childhood programs provides opportunities for children to gain confidence. Activity time also helps them develop skills in running and jumping, and gain knowledge through varied experiences. Play offers children occasions to observe, to discover, and to understand their world. When activities are self-chosen, playing can be therapeutic, satisfying, and fun.

During play children interact with others, adults and children, to acquire socially acceptable skills, try out social roles, test behaviors, and begin to understand their surroundings. When children play, their activity is real to them. When three- and-a-half-year-old Kirk announces he is the bus driver, he is playing and learning more about what he can do and what a bus driver does. When Vivienne brings books from the community library, she tells you that she wants to live in the library. She is learning about the role of a librarian.

When children engage in dramatic play they learn about people while developing their own social skills and imagination.

© Cengage Learning 2013

Children imitate the adult world, trying to recreate behaviors of their parents and other adults that they observe. This happens especially when the setting allows them to engage in what is called dramatic and sociodramatic play. Children naturally progress through play stages. As an intentional teacher, you will encourage playful interaction by setting up group activities to encourage collaboration (Epstein 2007) among the children as they progress through the stages of play. Children learn to play with other children by trying out behaviors, by watching others, and by imitating their behaviors (Epstein 2007).

There are various theories about play, ideas and concepts defined from the adult perspective. The theories developed by Mildred B. Parten and Sara Smilansky seem to have retained visibility in the early childhood reference literature. Parten classified social participation among preschool children in free-choice play into different categories (Figure 6–1). Sara Smilansky described the stages of play development in *The Effects of Sociodramatic Play on Disadvantaged Preschool Children* (1968). Dramatic play is valuable in developing children's social skills and imagination. It occurs when children voluntarily engage in social activity using imaginary objects and imitating people and surroundings. Sociodramatic play, as Smilansky presented, is the most developed form of play because children engage in play related to a theme and in cooperation with at least one other child. naeyc 1a, 1b, 1c, 4a, 4b, 4c **(Curriculum Activity Guide 1**)

The Value of Imaginative Play

Our world's rapid pace is a challenge to early childhood teachers who believe that play is essential for young children. Supportive statements and validation for play have been made by researchers, philosophers, and educators (Figure 6–2). Yet, we consistently must defend children's right to play. We defend the right and choice because we understand that play is the way a child learns.

When the environment supports play, children become totally involved and focused when they play. Play is the way they learn and understand. In play, children practice, pretend, and participate, and, in doing so, they acquire skills. Play engages children actively so that they learn by doing, manipulating, and moving. As children develop their abilities, they begin to master their world because play allows them to gain control of their bodies, experience the objects in their surroundings, and become aware of their emotions. Play is truly

Figure 6–1 Categories of Social Participation

Unoccupied behavior	The child is watching anything that is happening, glancing at others or following the teacher, generally remaining in one place.
Onlooker	The child watches certain children play, perhaps talking to other children. Remains close to the group of children but does not enter into their play situation.
Solitary independent	The child plays independently, or alone, making no effort to contact or get close to other children.
Parallel activity	The child selects an activity near other children but not with them; plays independently with toys similar to those used by the group in close proximity.
Associative	The child engages in conversation and plays in activity with other children. Each child follows their own direction of player. Children in associative play situations do not organize their play and do not assign roles and assignments to one another.
Cooperative	Children play in an organized group activity, constructing a product, achieving a goal, dramatizing, or playing formal games. One or two of the children in the group control the play activity.

Parten, Mildred. B. (1996). Social participation among pre-school children. In K. M. Paciorek and J. H. Munro (eds.). *Notable selections in early childhood education*. Guildford, CT: Dushkin. (pp. 116–118).

Figure 6–2 The Importance of Play— Lawrence K. Frank

Play is a child's response to life—almost where life begins, play begins. Play—is the way the child learns what no one can teach him.

play whenever children choose the activities from available selections in an appropriately prepared environment where choices are available.

Play fosters a child's physical development and, in the process, their deliberate behaviors. Play affects a child's sense of self and his or her motivation. Play supports cognitive development, including decentering that allows a child to take the perspectives of others. Play advances a child's ability to mentally represent objects and symbols (Bodrova and Leong 2004). The values gained through play translate to courage, curiosity, commitment without reserve, self-acceptance, optimism, gaiety, cooperation, and emotional maturity (Hartley 1973).

You will value the support for play provided by significant voices of early childhood education. Their statements provide the rationale you will share with families, communities, and some educators who do not embrace play as a significant and necessary facet in early childhood development and education. Play allows children to learn naturally about the world. "As a child begins to move around and develop motor coordination, his play—which is really his work throughout his childhood—enables him to exercise his muscles as well as his imagination" (Salk

Figure 6–3 The Importance of Play—Maria Montessori

It is important for us to know the nature of a child's work. When a child works, he does not do so to attain some further goal. His objective in working is the work itself, and when he has repeated an exercise and brought his own activities to an end, this end is independent of external factors. As far as the child's personal reactions are concerned, his cessation from work is not connected with weariness since it is characteristic of a child to leave his work completely refreshed and full of energy.

Montessori, Maria. (1966). *The secret of childhood*. New York: Fides.

1983, 152). Dr. Maria Montessori exemplified play in *The Secret of Childhood* (1966, 196). She wrote about the child's work (Figure 6–3), emphasizing the fundamental differences between the work of children and that of adults. **naeyc** 1a, 1b, 1c, 4a, 4b, 4c, 4d

Author-educator John Holt documented that the child "wants to make sense of things, find out how things work, gain competence and control over himself and his environment, do what he can see other people doing" (1969, 184). Yet, as psychologist and author David Elkind warns, a fear could exist if we consider a child's play to be work. That could place children at risk to be miseducated if work is interpreted as conventional elementary school lesson plans for preschool children. This, he believes, will discourage the sense of competence and creativity that play should generate during the early childhood years (Elkind 1992). Dr. Elkind wants early educators to be mindful about play and to consider play as basic and meaningful, as loving and working (2004).

Your attitude about play will likely influence the acceptance of play by the families you work with in your school. This rationale provides ample reason for you to understand and appreciate the benefits that play generates for children. Your attitude and commitment to support play in your program will affect the families' acceptance. Teachers need to understand the **value of play** and the relationship of play to the skills and concepts that children gain. It is also essential that you respect and value the opinions about play held by parents. Your encouraging introduction of quality play opportunities and the intentionality of your curriculum will offer families opportunities to gain insight into the value of play. **naeyc** 1a, 1b, 1c, 2c, 4a, 4b, 4c, 4d

Programs that honor play for young children are obliged to make time available for the children to play. Children need uninterrupted time to become absorbed in an activity. Children stay with an activity longer when they are interested, curious, and have some connection to the object and situation. When longer play segments are allowed, preschoolers participate in more group play, constructive play, and group-dramatic play (Christie and Wardle 1992). Early childhood programs generally allow time for what is called free play. This time affords children the opportunities to be able to choose what they do, how they do it, how long they do it, and with whom they play. During free play children are allowed to choose activities of interest and to enjoy those interests at their own ability levels. Teachers must be ready to develop the educational content of any activity in a way that does not deny a child the chance for discovery during free play (Landreth 1972). There are ample chances for children to think creatively and respond to unexpected outcomes during free play. The skills gained actually contribute to a child's lifelong success because the rapidly changing world depends on quick and creative responses. Play gives children time for them to practice choosing, doing, and problem solving (Jones 2004).

"Free play is 'play' because the activity strikes so deep a chord of pleasure within them. But free play is learning" (Hymes 1981, 92) and considered to be educationally productive as the hallmark of early childhood. Some professionals believe that teachers of young children will promote playful experiences by setting the stage for play. Setting the stage requires that we allow ample time, provide appropriate materials, and encourage choices. We can promote playful experiences by guiding with play-coaching strategies, by modeling actions, and by reinforcing verbal interactions. As teachers, we can also promote playful experiences by observing children to better understand their development, interest in the play activities, and their level of participation (Nourot and Van Hoorn 1991).

Even as we support play, we best remind ourselves of the joyful experiences of childhood play. We need to allow ourselves to be playful and embrace the joy of working with young children by making it as much fun as we can. A college student enrolled in an introductory early childhood course shared her exceptional insight. She used an example from the movie *Hook* to emphasize the importance of "getting inside the child, remembering what it was like to pretend and to play." She explained that "the Lost Boys were trying to tell Peter Pan that to be like them, he needed to believe in what they did. He needed to believe in pretending. He needed to be able to play." **naeyc** 1a, 1b, 1c, 4a, 4b, 4c, 4d, 5b, 5c **(Curriculum Activity Guide 3 📖)**

Using Questioning as a Teaching Strategy

You understand the importance of involving children in their curriculum. By engaging them in conversation, you will be able to expand their

Time for play gives children many opportunities to practice choosing, doing, and problem solving.

© Cengage Learning 2013

interests and provide information for their curiosity. Questions are common basic instructional tools in early childhood classrooms. The kinds of questions you ask make a difference in the types of responses and learning that happens (Kostelnik et al. 2011). Closed-ended or low-level questions lead to single word answers and do not stimulate higher levels of thinking. Open-ended questions encourage thinking, enrich conversations, and extend children's imaginations (Bredekamp 2011). Teachers can ask open-ended questions providing many opportunities for practice that fosters the ability to make connections between ideas. This can provide links with their past and current events in their lives. Asking open-ended questions can also help children identify patterns or sequences (Bosse et al. 2009).

Invite children into a positive communication experience by showing an interest in what they say, listening to them, and observing their activities. You can accomplish this by smiling, nodding, and reflecting back the comments, words, and phrases of the children. Use indirect questions, and statements: *What makes it do that? I was wondering if the bird would jump down.* Once you observe that the children are ready, ask open-ended, or interactive, questions, such as: *Can you tell me why? Would you show me how? What do you think about the end of the story?* Help children discuss and describe by saying: *Tell me what is happening in the sand. What do you think will happen next? Let's think about what will change when you put the juice in the gelatin* (Charlesworth 1987). You will be able to enhance children's language, problem solving, and critical thinking skills by giving them space and time, and by avoiding over-questioning and talking over them. Children need several seconds to think about what has been said and to come up with their answers.

One way to engage them in curriculum planning and acquire more information about them is through **interactive questioning**. Children will become alert to, and interested in, your communication with them. They will respond to your language, and the words. You will be able to communicate through meaningful activities and in playful ways. Interactive questioning adds an important aspect to teachers' questioning skills.

Interactive and open-ended questioning goes beyond giving instructions, describing, and giving examples. Help children become aware of their own thinking by asking questions such as

What are you trying to do now? Do you have a long enough hose to reach? Assist children in developing reflective attitudes so that they can learn to ask themselves questions: *Which brush should I use to create that pattern? What button should I click on to close the screen?* (Antonietti 1997).

When you use interactive questioning purposefully, you respect children's linguistic abilities, including the language or languages of the children's homes. Interactive questioning allows us to become familiar with children's facial expressions. Children who are acquiring English as their second language may communicate differently from the majority culture. For instance, a child might respond to your questions with raised eyebrows (Greenberg 1998). Teachers should encourage and exchange language, in a way that maintains cultural and linguistic respect.

Conversations and discussions with individual children after storytime are beneficial for the children and you. Have them make predictions before the story is read, and then discuss whether their predictions were correct afterwards (Kostelnik et al. 2011). Personalize your questions and responses to their ages and interests; for example, ask: *What would you say goodnight to in your bedroom?* (Howard et al. 1998).

naeyc 1a, 1b, 1c, 4a, 4b, 4c, 4d, 5a, 5b, 5c, 6d

© Cengage Learning 2013

Interactive questioning allows teachers to respect each child's children's linguistic ability and to become more familiar with characteristics, skills, and needs.

Many Ways to Think and Learn

In all probability, you hear the word **creativity** if you spend any time in a program for preschoolers. This word holds a certain status. Creativity actually means the quality and ability to create. Creative is defined as inventive, productive, and having the ability to make a thing that has not been made before (Barnhart 1990). In early childhood settings, creativity can refer to the planned activities for the children. The children who are identified as creative or demonstrate creative abilities may be the ones who notice differences, see the unusual, want to complete tasks by themselves, are confident, and are able to solve problems (Todd and Heffernan 1977).

Behaviors related to creativity involve thinking, acting, solving a problem or making something new (Mayesky 2009). Other behaviors attached to the concept of creativity allow children to be original, explore the new, and find their own creative ways to problem solve. You can apply the concepts about creativity for young children by highlighting the process of experiencing creative expression. The prime years for creative development are between the ages of three and five years (Pica 2004). Creativity can develop in all areas of a child's development, including physical, affective (social-emotional understanding) and aesthetic, and cognitive. When you observe children, you quickly notice how they react to materials that are new to them in novel ways. Watch children on a sandy beach for the first time and observe what they do with the seashells and seaweed.

There are many different ways to think about the sand from the beach or a seashell. Objects take on meaning with use and vary within families, cultures, regions, and countries. How we think and what we think about is affected by our availability to information. The Internet and other technological advances have radically changed what we can think about and how we think. Premises about thinking and, in fact, multiple ways of thinking qualify the need for children's play and opportunities for discovery. Howard Gardner's model of the multiple intelligences theory outlines different capacities of intelligence, combining several independent abilities. The theory of multiple intelligences (MI) initially outlined seven distinct categories of intelligence, including: linguistic, musical, logical-mathematical, spatial, kinesthetic, interpersonal, and intrapersonal (Craig 1996). An eighth intelligence focusing on nature has been added to the initial list of seven.

Gardner's concept of multiple intelligences is valuable for educators. The view of multiple intelligences supports learning, thinking, and creativity in a variety of ways. Multiple intelligences may be particularly important because schools too often place intense focus on the linguistic and logical-mathematical intelligences. Early educators know that adults and children display different strengths of intelligences, with unique talents and skills (Feeney et al. 2006). One may have strength in language ability and another in interpersonal ability. It is not necessary for you to determine how many intelligences a child may display. Rather, you will further children's competence in learning and social-emotional development by planning and offering a curriculum that responds to multiple modes of thinking and doing.

Supporting Creativity

Teachers who remain true to the meaning of creativity allow children to explore materials and discover solutions. You will enhance creativity and satisfy multiple intelligences by allowing children to make choices and to try out new and different materials. Children learn by figuring, themselves, how objects work and what materials will do. That is how they make sense of their world. Early childhood teachers can unlock creativity by using materials from real life and by appreciating the different ways that children approach the materials (Antonietti 1997). The theories of Jean Piaget, Maria Montessori, and Lev Vygotsky validate creativity and learning. Children are naturally curious about their surroundings. Curiosity during the early years of development is displayed by the children's active manipulation of objects. As children mature, curiosity becomes apparent in their questions. The early education program will help to gratify children's curiosity by providing activities matching their developmental level. Children and adults who use their abilities to produce a new idea or product are exhibiting creativity. The natural spontaneity of the creative mind may develop when the attributes are valued by supportive adults. Development of creativity can actually be blocked when adults impose their expectations and standards on children's work and efforts (Elkind 1976).

You will encourage creativity by offering opportunities for children to come up with new questions, solutions, and novel ideas. Listen to the children's questions. Enjoy all the "why teacher" questions. Allow time to respond with interactive questioning as appropriate. Be mindful that creativity is a higher mental process because it causes learning to be exciting and playful (Bloom 1981). naeyc 1a, 1b, 1c, 4a, 4b, 4c, 4d, 5a, 5b, 5c, 6d

Curriculum Activities—What to Consider

Experiences, particularly activities are the core of the curriculum for young children, including the ones you plan and those that occur spontaneously. They are a consequence of the environment you create. The way you plan and organize activities is influenced by what you know about children and your approach to organizing the curriculum. Your understanding of the importance of the early years, developmentally suitable experiences, authentically inclusive programs, and family participation will enhance your curriculum.

You are not expected to instantly present activities that perfectly match the needs of all of the children in your program. It takes time to accumulate activities that are relevant to their changing needs. Instead, you and your teaching team will blend, adapt, and modify your ideas for appropriate experiences and activities.

Ideas and Goals Become Activities

"Teacher, look." "Teacher, see my rock." "Teacher, watch, I can reach the clouds." "I brought my special book." "I have a Band-Aid on my knee today." "That's not a cat; I know it's a rabbit!"

Children's questions and statements are wonderful to hear. Their questions and statements generate curriculum ideas. The experiences you plan will stimulate responses and ideas, giving you opportunities to enhance and reinforce their learning. Your responses to questions, particularly interactive questioning, may prompt you to add opportunities for spontaneous learning. When Trevor asks you why the sand is heavy today, you might reply with a question, asking him what he thinks. Trevor may provide a few responses. You might suggest that he feel the sand again and ask if the sand is wet or dry. Together you and Trevor will explore ideas about the sand, and he may say with excitement, "The sand is wet and heavy." You will note in the interest center log to plan additional activities related to dry

and wet materials including sand, soil, sponges, rocks and shells. You will encourage creativity by introducing new ideas to allow exploration and discovery.

Utilizing the various assessment methods will help you identify ideas and topics that interest the children. In this way, you will ensure that the experiences present fundamental knowledge in terms of the child's way of viewing yet are challenging in a way that will hold their curiosity (Bruner 1960). naeyc 1a, 1b, 1c, 3a, 3b, 4a, 4b, 4c, 4d, 5a, 5b, 5c, 6d

Defining an Activity

An activity is generally defined as an action using movement or mental activity (Barnhart and Barnhart 1990). In early childhood, an **activity** is an experience planned for young children. Activities, intentionally planned, will be developmentally appropriate and meet your school's goals for children and curricular guidelines. An activity is an experience that provides opportunities for children to actively participate. Activities are learning opportunities that actively engage children. The experiences include large and small movement activities as well as social and solitary time. The experiences allow children to work alone or in small groups, in child-initiated and teacher-directed activities. Experiences also promote development in physical, cognitive, affective (social-emotional understanding), and aesthetic areas.

Planning activities that are appropriate for young children will require you to shape inviting activities. You will encourage children to participate by encouraging them to question and to respond (Figure 6–4).

Figure 6–4 What to Consider When Planning an Activity

Meet curriculum guidelines.

Children's assessed needs.

The individual child.

Children with special needs.

Small groups of children.

Introducing new ideas.

Encouraging exploration.

Stimulating interactive questioning.

Ensuring spontaneous learning.

What It Takes to Create an Activity

A starting point when you begin to shape curriculum activities for young children is to become familiar with procedures related to activity planning. Just as with every other aspect of early childhood education, activity planning and organization vary. Some programs require that teachers simply identify, in writing, the title and purpose of each activity. Other programs require teachers to write down the goals and materials for the activities (Figure 6–5). Understanding methods for planning curriculum activities will allow you to adapt your skills in a variety of school settings. naeyc 4a, 4b, 4c, 4d

Activity Goals

The **Curriculum Activity Guide**, which is used as a template to document activities throughout the text, is designed to guide the direction of the experiences you plan for young children. Emphasis is placed on your role in creating experiences that will invite children to participate in ways that best suit their interests and stages of development. When you use the Curriculum Activity Guide format, you will facilitate children's growth and development because the activities you plan will

clarify, stimulate, and verify their ideas and developing skills.

You will observe and listen to the children. Your observation will provide insight into the children's development. The experiences you offer in your program will allow children to contemplate, discover, and solve problems in an inviting environment. Professionals support possibilities for children with open-ended questions to expand their play, reinforce their language, and help them see relationships among people, objects, and ideas. For example, Teacher Marquez responds to five-year-old Jasmine, who pushes forward her potted, wilted plant: "What do you think the plant needs, Jasmine?" Later in the day he asks, knowing that she already watered the plant, "Jasmine, how is your plant doing now?"

Activities will identify goals to allow children to shape their own experiences. The process for designing the curriculum generally, and activities specifically, begins with a framework based on our knowledge about child development. The process also respects children's uniqueness (Burts and Buchanan 1998).

A goal is a general statement that defines an aim or a purpose. Generally, the statement of purpose has an outcome in mind that indicates what you are trying to achieve (Ornstein and Hunkins 2009). Goals are written in sentences or phrases. Goals can be stated in a single word. A goal statement can begin with the word *to* (infinitive verb), indicating that there is an expectation (Ornstein and Hunkins 1998). Objectives differ from goals because objectives must clearly identify an end product or the intended skill or behavior outcome (Arends 1991). Behavioral objectives require that the student's behavior, situation, and performance criteria are stated. A behavioral objective, as defined by behavioral theorists, would be stated in this way: the child, given a variety of ten pictures, will be able to identify four of the five flowers correctly in 29 percent of the opportunities. Others argue that objectives can be written more generally and that an objective might specify that a child will understand and appreciate the diversity of the flowers presented in pictures (Arends 1991).

Activities designed around specific behavioral objectives would require you to identify the expected behavior change that will result from the planned experience. For example, a statement that the child will be able to point to the blue block is a behavioral objective. The observable behavior following the learning experience indicates that the objective has been met. You would also need

---

Figure 6–5 Listing Title, Purpose, Goals and Materials

Some Schools Require Teachers to Write the Title and Purpose of an Activity

Title: *Wet Sand and Dry Sand*

Purpose: *Children will feel the difference of sand wet with water and sand that is dry.*

Some Schools Require Teachers to Write the Title, Purpose, Goals, and Materials

Title: *Wet Sand and Dry Sand*

Purpose: *Children will feel the difference of sand wet with water and sand that is dry.*

Goals: *To offer children opportunities to feel wet and dry sand.*

To help children identify that wet sand is heavier.

Materials: *Sensory table with divider separating the wet and dry sand, sand shovels, measuring cups, additional water as needed to keep wet sand damp, paper towels to wipe hand.*

to indicate the conditions under which the child is expected to achieve the objective. Controversy remains regarding the use of objectives because they predetermine the child's actions, place unrealistic performance standards on the children, and cause teachers to design curricula with specific achievement outcomes. It is more appropriate for teachers of young children to identify the goals for planned activities. When precise evaluation of a child's behaviors is required, a professional reference would be recommended. For example, requirements for specific objectives may be specified for a child with disabilities in an individual educational plan. **naeyc** 1a, 1b, 1c, 3a, 3b, 4a, 4b, 4c, 4d, 5a, 5b, 5c, 6d

Children will enjoy the freedom to wonder and explore when you allow spontaneous and meaningful activities. Goals for activities can define what you offer to the children without conditions of measurable outcomes. A predetermined measurable outcome could interfere with the children's engagement in the experience. Children should be permitted to approach each activity in

Teachers who take the time to document an activity understand that the process increases their time to directly interact with the children.

their own way. This requires that you allow children enough latitude to bring their own understanding and reality to the experience. Stating a behavioral objective would control the experiences with unrealistic and fixed expectations. Your responsibility is to provide the appropriate opportunities, materials, and guidance. We can anticipate and encourage children to engage in activities in their unique ways by allowing choices, by reinforcing the divergent use of materials, and by supporting their emerging actions.

Activity Elements

What will you need to shape an activity for the children? What do you have available? Questions like these will help you to formulate the pieces, or elements, that create meaningful activities for young children.

When you plan activities after considering the important elements, you will confirm your curricular guidelines. You will know if you are balancing appropriate experiences in the **developmental focus** and curriculum areas to stimulate optimal growth and learning.

Remembering the focus on sand, and considering a child's understanding of wet and dry sand, what would you need to plan a responsive activity about wet sand? Does your school have an organizing theme? Will the activity be offered in specific interest centers? Will you list the activity within a content area?

Managing curriculum activities effectively involves your time for planning. Planning requires that a proposed activity be thoroughly examined. The outcome of your planning is a **written documentation**. Documenting an activity may minimally explain the purpose of the experience or list numerous defining elements.

You may naturally feel some resistance to changing the way your school has presented activities. Not all teachers, especially experienced teachers, welcome the revision of their curriculum. "We always do our lesson plans a certain way." "Filling out a long form for each activity seems time consuming." "Why should we spend so much time writing out all that information, I know what I need to do!" "This looks like a lot of work, is it worth it?" Remarks like these are typical comments from teachers. Even those who enthusiastically welcome new ideas may lack time for curriculum revision.

Efficient organization of curriculum will create additional time in your busy schedule. Teachers interact with the children, with other staff members,

© Cengage Learning 2013

with families, and with volunteers. The adults who participate in the program require different levels of guidance and supervision. A teacher may spend five to ten minutes explaining how to set up and how to facilitate an activity. Think about how many activities need to be arranged and how many times that same activity is reviewed with different staff members, family participants, and volunteers. If you provide all needed information about an activity in writing, the directions are also thoroughly explained in the written documentation. Appropriately completed written forms will document the basic information about the activities. The documentation will actually increase the time you are able to interact with the children and generate free time for you to guide the implementation of the activities. **naeyc** 3b, 4a, 4b, 4c, 4d, 5a, 5b, 5c, 6d

Understanding the Elements of an Activity

Each activity you plan and offer to children has several features. When you have an idea for an activity, perhaps from observations and assessment of the children, begin developing the activity by considering the many features. Think about the features of an activity as parts or elements describing what you need to prepare and how you might implement the experience. Activity **elements** describe the parts of an activity, such as the title, the goal or goals, and the materials. Your curriculum activities will be more thoroughly documented with additional elements. A thorough documentation of an activity will guide you, other teachers, and adult participants in offering appropriate and relevant activities for young children. Documenting each activity completely will also provide accountability and illustrate intentional teaching strategies. Sixteen elements are suggested for activity documentation. The elements, listed in Figure 6–6, provide a starting point for you to begin planning and managing your own curriculum.

The way you use the elements in planning will depend on your school guidelines and program administration. When you know what is required, decide how to best utilize the suggested elements for planning activities for your program. Documenting only the activity title and the materials may satisfy your program guidelines. Nevertheless, you will come to appreciate the **value of documenting** each activity more comprehensively. Documentation that includes all the suggested elements will validate your intentional preparation.

Documentation of activities is also beneficial for families. Listing details about activities will guide family members, and other volunteers may experience their participation with the children's activities more positively. When you, parents, and volunteers know what is expected and what to do, anxieties are lowered. Knowing what to do may increase parent involvement. Parents are interested in the way your program contributes to their children's growth and development. Parents who become familiar with the concepts, vocabulary, songs, and materials for the activities will more likely enjoy and want to extend their participation.

The first step in documenting an activity is to identify an **activity title**. The title describes the experience that you are planning. A suitable title can be as creative as the activity or simply define the experience to be offered. The title of the experience documented in Curriculum Activity Guide #3 is Body Tracing. This title defines the activity. An activity title for another experience, Valentine Friends, suggests an anticipated outcome of the activity. This title does not specify what will happen as precisely but nevertheless is an effective and suitable title.

The **activity goal** is a statement that describes the purpose of the experience. The goal relates to what you will offer for children to experience. Goal statements usually begin with the word *to*. A typical goal statement that allows the children to direct their own behavior for the activity about wet sand might be, "to experience touching and talking about the differences between wet sand and dry sand." The goal for an activity entitled Hole Punching might be, "to safely use a hole puncher." The goal for the activity entitled Valentine Friends could be, "to become aware of the association of Valentine's Day and friendship."

The identification of the **theme**, although not listed as an element, may be important if your school uses a thematic approach to planning and organizing the curriculum. You might indicate a project topic on a Curriculum Activity Guide if your school primarily follows the project approach for curriculum planning. An activity may relate to more than one theme. Often, an activity relates to all the themes. An activity that invites children to scoop out seeds from a pumpkin relates specifically to a harvest theme. The activity Valentine Friends could relate to a theme about friendship or the February holiday. An activity entitled Hole Punching would fit with almost any theme because the experience supports the development of small motor skills.

Figure 6–6 Elements of an Activity

Activity Title	The name of the activity, describes the experience.
Activity Goal	A statement that describes the purpose of the activity. The goal relates what the teachers would like the children to experience and perhaps, achieve.
Curriculum Area	A curriculum area is a discipline or area of study. Curriculum areas can include art, health–safety–nutrition, literacy, mathematics, music and rhythm, science, physical movement, social studies, and technology.
Developmental Focus Area	Developmental focus indicates the primary focus of an activity. The activity will be within a developmental area, or domain, such as physical, affective (social-emotional understanding) and aesthetic, or cognitive.
Location/Interest Center	The location/interest center identifies the recommended location for the activity. The location may include circle, outside, inside, art, dramatic play and other areas in the school environment.
Participants	Participants identifies the recommended number of child participants that would be appropriate for the activity.
Time	Time identifies the estimated length of time that may be needed for the activity.
Age Range	Age range identifies that the activity would be suitable for children in certain age ranges, such as children 3–4 years, or 4–5 years.
Materials	Materials identifies the recommended materials and supplies needed for the activity.
Preparation/Set Up	Preparation of materials identifies the recommended procedures to be followed for facilitating the activity.
Teaching Strategies	Teaching strategies identifies the recommended actions to be taken by the teacher who is guiding the activity. Teaching strategies also may suggest the sequence to follow in guiding a child's participation in the activity.
Possible Outcomes	Possible outcomes is the description of the behavior that a child may be expected to achieve with their participation in the activity. Includes concepts, skills, and vocabulary.
	Concepts—A single idea written clearly and simply at a young child's level of understanding.
	Skills—The skills are the developing abilities that may be affected by the children's participation in the activity. Skills relate to a developmental focus area.
	Vocabulary—Vocabulary are the words related to the activity and to be used appropriately in conversation with the children participating in the activity.
Date	Notation of the date when the Activity Guide was completed.
Standards Met	**Standard** is an element that can be used to establish program accountability. The standards referenced in this textbook are from the National Association for the Education of Young Children (NAEYC). Standards from other accrediting organizations or agency requirements may be included.
Comments and Reflection	The **comments** section is for a brief review. Note the children's reactions, list children who participated, indicate what supplies might enhance the children's experiences. As a lead teacher you would add comments recording whether the children responded to the teaching strategies and if the possible outcomes were suitable for the activity.

The listing of a **curriculum area** indicates that the activity relates primarily to a specific curriculum category. Does the activity offer a specific experience in areas such as mathematics, art, or movement? The curriculum area you list for an activity should complement the areas your school uses. The curriculum areas may be identified in your school's curricular guidelines, the mission statement, or in the school brochure. The curriculum areas generally include art, literacy, mathematics, music, physical movement, science, and social studies. More often programs include other areas such as technology, nutrition and health, and ecology. Review the section on curriculum areas in Chapter 5 (see Figure 5–6). If you are not currently teaching, which curriculum areas would you select for your school? The developmental focus is another element that describes how an activity might benefit children within a developmental area. The developmental focus lists three areas: physical, affective (social-emotional understanding) and aesthetic, and cognitive. Your school may identify alternative terms and labels. You might use terms such as literacy and motor development. When you identify the developmental focus for an activity, it indicates that the experience may enhance development in that area. Does the activity you are documenting offer the children opportunities to develop large motor skills? If so, the activity's developmental focus area is physical. Many of the activities that you are planning will relate to more than one developmental focus area. A mural-painting activity, using large house-painting brushes, could be set up to engage children in a social interaction. Therefore, the developmental focus area of that mural painting activity might be listed as affective (social-emotional understanding) and aesthetic. This activity also offers children opportunities to develop their large motor skills. Consequently, you may decide to offer this activity as a physical developmental focus. You either decide yourself which areas would be identified or in collaboration with the other teachers. You will learn that you can take significant liberty in deciding how an experience satisfies the needs of an individual child or group of children.

Knowing in advance the location where an activity will be presented is important. If all activities are documented with the **location/interest center**, program administrators and teachers can check for efficient utilization of space, indoors and outdoors. Identifying the location/interest center on the Curriculum Activity guide will assist you in facilitation of family members and other volunteers. An activity planned for each activity area can be communicated verbally to the staff, volunteers, and family members. A documented form acts as a visual backup to reinforce verbal explanations.

You can document the number of child participants recommended for an activity with the element called **participants**. The number of children recommended for an activity provides guidance for the setup of the activity and for maintaining appropriate supervision during the implementation of it.

Another element, **time**, identifies the length of time for the proposed activity. Even though a Curriculum Activity Guide has a time listed, you will need to remain flexible and responsive to the needs of the children. The intent of indicating a time is to allow appropriate blocks of time for participation.

When you identify **age range** on a Curriculum Activity Guide, it refers to the chronological ages of the children who may participate in the activity. Children, even though they are the same chronological age, are achieving different skills. They will have different needs and interests. Chronological age provides a general idea about the broad range of behaviors and skills that may occur during a particular age. Plan some activities that are suitable for three-, four-, and five-year-olds. Young children approach and engage in experiences at their own ability level. Suggested age range categories for you to use in planning activities include:

18 months to three years
three-year-olds
three- and four-year-olds
four-year-olds
four- and five-year-olds
six-, seven-, and eight-year-olds
okay for all ages.

Identifying the age range will also depend on the organization of the program and grouping of the children. Activities with the most flexibility welcome the participation of children with different interests and skills.

Another element in the planning process for activities is the definition of **materials.** Listing the materials for an activity can determine the success of that experience and the effectiveness of curriculum plans. Knowing in advance what recommended materials and supplies will be required will help you and the program administrator manage and prepare the needed items. The activity entitled Hole Punch will need the following materials: three to four hole punchers, three to four bowls, and small pieces of construction paper. When teachers plan curricula in advance and know which materials are required, it leads to successful management and to successful experiences for the children.

Preparation/setup is the element that defines the suggested sequence of procedures. The procedures, or steps, define what and how to prepare for the activity. The preparation/setup will also indicate the advance preparation time needed to arrange the experience.

Another element to document in the Curriculum Activity Guide is **teaching strategies**. Teaching strategies recommend the behaviors and actions to be taken by the teacher or another adult who will be guiding the activity. The teaching strategies element describes the suggested teaching methods and procedures in facilitating the children's participation in the activity. This element is particularly important for teachers in training, volunteers, and family members participating in your school. The step-by-step procedures provide a flexible guide for inviting children to participate, engaging their involvement and supporting their self-initiated learning. Teaching strategies that enhance interaction with the children could include: sit with children; listen to questions; ask and answer questions; engage in interactive questioning; encourage touching; support children's interaction; facilitate discussion; introduce new equipment; invite new children to join; offer to write down the child's name and comments; and place materials for children's easy access.

Possible outcomes is the element used to document the concepts, skills, and vocabulary that an activity will introduce. Possible outcomes might also describe the concepts, skills, and vocabulary that an activity will reinforce during the activity.

Concepts are general ideas related to an activity. Concepts are abstract ideas about objects or events. The actions and concrete materials suggested for an activity offer visible and hands-on opportunities for the children to begin to comprehend the abstract concepts. This is why it is important for you to consider what information and concepts are necessary to carry out an activity. Then, you need to decide how you can clarify the concept in simple, concrete terms. Identifying concepts helps children place objects into groups or classes. For example, the word *family* is used to define a group that includes separate, individual members (father, mother, grandma, grandpa, sister, brother, aunt, uncle, and cousins). The word *color* describes a group of objects that includes

different shades of color such as red, blue, and green. You will expand the children's learning by providing additional words, for example: "A car is also called an automobile." "A tractor can be a digger or an excavator." "Transportation gets us from one place to another." "An airplane is one form of transportation."

Concept development is more than just naming an object. Children will acquire abilities to think about objects belonging to classes or categories (Vance 1973), such as "My bedroom is part of my home." Children also learn to generalize, for example, "Kittens and puppies are pets." In addition, children will develop skills in discriminating: "Calves are usually farm animals, not house pets." Relationships among concepts will become apparent; for instance, "The key unlocks the wheel toy shed" (Figure 6–7).

Concepts must be introduced with concrete, hands-on objects. Children, as much as they are able, need to smell, see, touch, and handle an object to begin to grasp its abstract idea. Documenting a concept for an activity will assist you in helping children to recognize the many dimensions of one object. Expanding their awareness of the relationships among ideas and objects will also increase their critical thinking, problem solving, and communication skills. Familiar concepts about cats for young children would be characteristics they can recognize through their senses: a cat is furry; a cat purrs; a cat can be a family pet; and a cat has whiskers. **naeyc** 1a, 1b, 1c, 3a, 3b, 4a, 4b, 4c, 4d, 5a, 5b, 5c, 6d

Another element to document on the Curriculum Activity Guide is **skills**. Skills are developing abilities in body movement, thinking and language, or in social and emotional behavior. An activity inviting children to participate in Let's Pretend to be a Cat offers them chances to develop physical skills when they pounce like a cat. Meowing like a cat gives them chances to develop communication skills by listening and repeating sounds. Imitating a cat purring allows children to imitate the expression of good feelings. The value of an activity may be identified by the skill you document. Think about the abilities and skills that a particular activity might enhance. A list of skills categorized by developmental focus areas will be useful as you begin to document skills for activities (Figure 6–8). **Vocabulary** is another element to include in the Curriculum Activity Guide. Vocabulary identifies words related to an activity and can be used appropriately during the conversations you have with the children participating in the activity.

Figure 6–7 Documenting Concepts

Examples of concepts to give children opportunities to categorize and classify:

My bedroom is part of my home.

We use forks and spoons for eating.

Forks and spoons are also call utensils.

Examples of concepts to give children opportunities to discriminate:

Kittens and puppies are pets.

A potato is a vegetable, not a fruit.

The oven timer rings differently than the my mommy's cell phone.

Examples of concepts to illustrate relationships among concepts:

Keys unlock the wheel toy shed at my preschool.

When I blow through a straw I can make bubbles in the water.

Paste makes some items stick to a piece of paper.

The magnifying glass makes objects look bigger.

Figure 6–8 Skills Categorized by Developmental Focus Area

Physical	Affective (social-emotional understanding) and Aesthetic	Cognitive
Sensory discrimination	Empathy, compassion, understanding, decision making	Classifying
Eye/hand coordination	Cooperation	Comparing
Following directions	Self-expression	Discriminating
Fine motor control	Creative expression	Observing change
Sensory awareness	Independence	Exploring
Visual tracking	Understanding	Seriation
Coordination	Social play	Concept awareness
Nutritional awareness	Nurturing	Sequencing
Balance	Interaction	Expanding
Strength	Role-playing	Listening
Left/right movement	Making choices	Experimenting
Body awareness	Initiating	Print recognition

Standards met is an element added to the Curriculum Activity Guide form. Standards can be identified to meet accountability requirements and guidelines. Identifying standards is one way for programs to rationalize their intentional teaching strategies. An important element on the form is the **date**.

The last element is **comments and reflection**. This section provides teachers and others who may have facilitated an activity to write a brief review and reflection of their experience with the children. The review might note the children's reactions or list the names of the children who participated. You could also use the *comments* section to indicate what supplies might enhance the children's experiences. You would also record whether the children responded to the teaching strategies and indicate if the *possible outcomes* were suitable for the activity. This is the place for you to reflect on your own experiences with the particular activity and indicate what

worked and what might be modified. naeyc
1a, 1b, 1c, 4a, 4b, 4c, 4d, 5a, 5b, 5c, 6d

Advantages of Using a Guide to Document Activities

Documentation of activities frees you to enjoy the interaction with the children during the experiences. Written plans substantiate your program goals. Advance preparation allows you to continue offering meaningful and flexible activities with the spontaneity needed to meet the children's needs. Written documentation of activities increases your efficiency and elevates your management skills. Preparing Curriculum Activity Guides gives you more time with the children, more time to inform their families about curriculum, and more time to provide inservice guidance for volunteers.

Curriculum Activity Guides

Curriculum Activity Guides (CAGs) are useful to you and other members of your staff and teaching team. The CAGs inform about the planned experience with a visual. A CAG is like a map; it tells us where we are going. It clarifies expectations. The Curriculum Activity Guide arranges ideas and our intentions for the experiences we want to offer to children. You have been reviewing the Curriculum Activity Guides related to information in each chapter. The CAG callout directs you to a specific CAG in Appendices C and D. Appendix C list activities by developmental focus areas. Appendix B provides a template for the CAG. There are 50 complete CAGs in Appendix D.

As you review the Curriculum Activity Guides, you will begin to recognize how simply these can be adapted to meet your own programs' guidelines and the needs of the children in your program. You will select and use certain CAGs based on observation and assessment of the children. The CAGs will indicate whether the curriculum is balanced and if your planned activities are in the appropriate sequence for the children's developing needs. Basic information detailing the activity is practical and applicable when the emphasis is on flexibility. Your program may have adopted a form. That could be called an activity sheet, an activity record, or lesson plan forms. The activities available to you in this textbook will reference written documentation of an activity as a Curriculum Activity Guide (CAG).

Once you have assembled a collection of CAGs, you can modify them easily as you acquire new ideas from the children's assessments. You will find that you do not have to create CAGs every time; for example, you plan to offer an activity in art appreciation or sociodramatic play for a domestic scene. Routinely, you will be able to modify sections of the CAGs. For instance, you might only need to modify the materials, or the location, or the vocabulary. Because CAGs are reusable, you will reduce the time-consuming task of writing and rewriting activity plans. The Curriculum Activity Guide template, including 18 elements of an activity, is provided as one design for documenting an activity. The activities displayed throughout the textbook and on the accompanying website use this form (Figure 6–9). A full-size, reproducible version of this template is in Appendix B. naeyc
1a, 1b, 1c, 2c, 3a, 3b, 4a, 4b, 4c, 4d, 5a, 5b, 5c, 6d

Reusing and Displaying Curriculum Activity Guides (CAGs)

Curriculum Activity Guides are also reusable. They can be used again because you can reprocess most of the information or elements completed on the activity form. Access the template of the CAG on your computer. File completed CAGs in folders. For example, if you use an edition of Microsoft Word©, you may choose to file the CAGs by developmental focus area or curriculum area. Use any organizational system that fits your curriculum needs. If a computer is not your choice for managing your curriculum, file the CAGs in a binder. Make copies of the CAG template as needed when you are ready to plan and document another activity.

You will appreciate your commitment to documentation when you begin reusing or reprocessing the Curriculum Activity Guides (CAGs). Initially, you will need to invest time to build a collection of CAGs. When you adapt an existing CAG for an individual child or the changing needs of a group, your task will be simpler. Your work will be reduced because you will have already conceptualized the activity. Most of the elements will remain the same, especially the concepts and skills that tend to take more time to document. Another way to document an activity is to write or print the information on index cards. Index cards can be laminated and filed in a box. The cards can be categorized by curriculum area, developmental area, theme, or project. Index cards are easy to handle and can be readily available to teachers, family members, and volunteers for quick reference during the activity.

Figure 6–9 Curriculum Activity Guide

Title

Goal

Curriculum Area   **Developmental Focus Area:**   **Location/Interest Center:**

Participants   **Time:**   **Age Range:**

Materials

Preparation/Set up

Teaching Strategies

Possible Outcomes

   Concepts

   Skills

   Vocabulary

Date

Standards Met

Comments and Reflections

Curriculum Activity Guides will become a visual record of your curriculum. Display the CAGs you anticipate offering for the week on bulletin boards that are for the teaching team, the families, and volunteers. A large visual of the curriculum plan clarifies intended experiences for the children in the program. naeyc 4a, 4b, 4c

Checking: Is the Activity Meaningful and Suitable?

As you continue observation and assessments of the children, you will gain additional insight into their capabilities. This insight will guide your decisions about the curriculum and, in particular, the selected activities. Be sure to maintain realistic expectations for the children's development. In this way, you will provide the continuity and sequence of learning essentially needed for children (Bloom 1981). How will you know when an activity is suitable for a child? How will you know when an activity is suitable for a group of children?

By following the development of children over time, you will naturally begin offering activities to meet their developing needs. The more confident you become in applying child development knowledge and assessment findings, the easier it will be to arrange activities to match the children's progress. Catherine Landreth tells us, "What a

young learner wants to do is what he feels ready and eager to master and what is just a little different from what he can do already" (1972). According to Vygotsky, children need to experience challenging curriculum and content that moves them ahead in thinking and problem solving. Once children master the assembly of certain puzzles, provide them with other, more complex, puzzles having more pieces (Bredekamp 2011).

Plan activities to help children understand their capabilities and support their own learning. Give your curriculum credibility by considering the sequence of activities (Landreth 1972). As you observe the children you will recognize their new behaviors, skills, and interests.

As you continue to observe and assess the children, you will recognize the children who are ready for new experiences. Plan some activities in sequence because the foundation for new learning is grounded on old learning (Essa and Rogers 1992). Help children understand concepts by presenting simple ideas first. Then move toward more complex ideas and skills (Gestwicki 2002). naeyc 1a, 1b, 1c, 3a, 3b, 4a, 4b, 4c, 4d, 5a, 5b, 5c, 6d

Clustering Activities

When you think of a cluster you probably envision a group of people or objects that are in close proximity. They may be related in some way.

Think about **clustering**; you may find this concept useful for organizing your curriculum. Clustering implies that activities are related but not in any rigid order. You may introduce an idea or concept and return to it at a later time. Clustering activities allows you to group experiences to match the children's needs while maintaining a child-centered and intentional curriculum. Several interest centers may be set up to explore the same concept. Clustering encourages rotation of activities and reinforcement of the children's experiences in different developmental areas.

You will support integrated curriculum by clustering activities. Clustering allows you to implement experiences sequentially with appropriate expectations for progression of the children's skills. Children benefit from repeated exposure to an experience that develops a skill or concept. Even after a skill is learned, children benefit from opportunities to reinforce it.

Some activities naturally flow from one to another. For example, expose children to basic concepts about the post office before their visit. Reading stories, trying on uniforms, and mailing letters prepare the children for their trip.

Clustering activities will oblige you to sequence some of the activities. The process of sequencing requires that activities offer opportunities to develop skills and ideas, progressing from concrete, simple tasks to more abstract and complex ones. Fingerpainting with primary colors on day one and two may be followed with options to mix food coloring and water. The children will discover secondary colors. On the fifth day you might introduce modeling dough in primary colors (Figure 6–10). Clustering will remind you to incorporate the children's past experiences with their developmental level. Clustering will also remind you to begin with concrete experiences and to set up the experiences to progress from simple to complex. naeyc 4a, 4b, 4c

Three-year-old David is able to distinguish the differences among textures after participating in several activities with rough and smooth

Activities that are clustered reinforces the children's experiences in different developmental areas.

Figure 6–11 Clustering Activities for Concept of Rough and Smooth

Concept: Rough
Activity Ideas:

Touching different sandpaper textures

Sorting dried beans

Stacking tree bark

Concept: Smooth
Activity Ideas:

Fingerpainting

Washing river rocks

Feeling lotions

Clustering Activities by Combining Concepts:
Rough and Smooth

Activity Ideas: Fingerpaint on corrugated paper
Wash sea shells and river rocks
Rub ice cubes on pebble textured sidewalk

---

materials. David's understanding was enhanced when both types of materials were provided. Concepts become more apparent to children when the activities cluster over time without increasing the complexity. The more of David's senses that are active during the activity, the more he will retain ideas and develop skills (Figure 6–11).

Clustering activities also allows you to pattern experiences to progress from the simple to the more complex. Joe, four years and three months, is observed recognizing the three primary colors: red, yellow, and blue. The next day, he is seen at the outdoors discovery center mixing drops of primary colors into containers of water. Additional experiences related to color mixing would benefit Joe. You might introduce secondary colors during group time.

Figure 6–10 Considerations for Clustering Activities

Child's past experiences

Child's developmental level

Beginning with concrete activities

Progressing from simple to complex

Containers of modeling dough in green, orange, and purple are added to the art shelf. Joe pulls the purple modeling dough from the container, telling Angela, "I need the roller for my purple modeling dough." Additional activities to further reinforce the color purple would likely interest Joe and Angela. Listening to the book *Little Blue and Little Yellow* (Lionni 1994) adds to their expanding awareness of color. [naeyc] 1a, 1b, 1c, 4b, 4c, 4d, 5c

Revising and Updating Activities

A curriculum is successful when it is reviewed regularly. Informal reviews should occur ideally each day. The teachers and program administrators review to determine what activities worked, what activities did not work, and what needs to be modified. Informal, daily reviews improve the quality of interactions between the teachers and children. Frequent reviews contribute to the quality of the curriculum and direct necessary modifications. Staff interaction and regular meetings provide occasions for discussion about the children's use of materials and participation in the activities. Additional collaboration among the teachers will lead to plans that, for example, add props to the dramatic play area or the trike path. Your continuing observations determine what props are not needed and what equipment and materials should be rearranged or removed.

More formal evaluation may involve video recording of the children participating in the activities. Teachers who listen and observe the children's responses will gain insight into their understanding. Check the children's progress to determine whether they would benefit from keeping certain activities or adding new ones. The last element, Comments and Reflections on the Curriculum Activity Guide (CAG), invites teachers to write notes about the activity. The section offers you a chance to write down your insight for future planning and activity modification.

Listen to children and watch them participate. Review their participation, recognize their interest, and note their readiness. Modify curriculum plans to more effectively present activities that are suitable for the children enrolled in your program. [naeyc] 3a, 3b, 3c, 4b, 4c, 4d, 5c

Activity Setup—What Will You Need?

The **curriculum plan** outlines the essentials. This is a guide that allows you to access or plan activities that help you to accomplish the curricular guidelines anticipated for the week, for weeks, or for a month. The plan establishes a guide for the activities that you anticipate will best meet the children's interests and needs for the week. You have based the selection of activities on observations and assessments. A plan will also alert the program administrator about the materials and supplies needed. The use of facilities and scheduling extra staff and volunteers might be also noted in a curriculum plan.

As a component of the overall curriculum plan, the CAGs provide specific activities with the materials needed and the locations and participation of the teachers who will be needed to implement the experiences. Staff meetings give teachers time to review the plans and CAGs that create the map guiding your successful and meaningful curriculum. This is achievable most likely when planning and preparation time for teachers are supported by the school administration and program guidelines (Figure 6–12). [naeyc] 3a, 3b, 3c, 4b, 4c, 4d, 5c, 6c

Adapting Curriculum Plans to the Day and Moment

Curriculum plans provide you with a map that will guide your decisions and changes. The curriculum plan establishes credibility for you as a professional and for the accountability of your program. As an early childhood professional, you will continue to respond to children by listening, observing, and understanding their growth and development.

Your desire to facilitate an accountable program should not lessen your need to adapt the curriculum plan changes that will occur every day. You will need to adapt your plan to the moment and day and be able to substantiate accountability by also documenting the change. Children change, teachers change, and circumstances of the families change. Adapting curriculum plans will not compromise the integrity of your teaching. Adapting

Figure 6–12 Essentials for Setting Up an Activity
Curriculum plan
Activity Guides (CAGs)
Teacher collaboration
Preparation time

curriculum plans will instead place you among the remarkable early childhood teachers who suitably support children's growth and development in all developmental areas. naeyc 1a, 1b, 1c, 4b, 4c, 4d, 5c

Responsively Utilizing Resources: Label, Maintain, Store

Busy teachers need efficient methods to implement their plans. Teachers require sufficient and accessible storage for the curriculum supplies, materials, and equipment. Efficient storage also positively affects the children because it models organizational skills (Greenman 1988). Labeling curriculum materials and supplies encourages children to return items to the designated places. "Classrooms that are cluttered with material, walls completely covered with displays, and overflowing storage bins contribute to chaos, making it difficult for children to select activities" (Dodge, Jablon, and Bickart 1994, 95).

If you are trying to maximize your storage, you will want to carefully select your materials. Roger Neugebauer, publisher of the *Child Care Information Exchange,* suggests that if you are considering purchasing equipment, question whether the vendors are capable of providing support and if the product can be tried out before purchase (1998).

In a quality child care and education setting, the environment is scaled to, and accessible for, the children. However, your environment "must have some inaccessible storage areas like closets and high book shelves for securely stowing supplies, nap mats and folding cots, teachers' belongings, medical kits, and cleaning supplies" (Caples, 1996). Appropriate storage helps organize similar materials together. The location of materials, whether the storage is fixed or movable, affects the flow of movement in a classroom. Do your storage areas allow supplies to be really accessible? Are the materials and supplies stored in a way that there is little disruption to the children (Loughlin and Suina 1982)? A hinged cabinet unit on wheel casters stores woodworking equipment well. It can be wheeled out to an interest area as needed, indoors or outdoors. Whether storage is for multiple or specialized items, it is important to create efficient space. Space is efficient when it is aesthetically pleasing, creative, and in close proximity to the area in which items are needed (Greenman 1988). Effective storage will improve the management and implementation of curriculum ideas. naeyc 1c, 4b, 4c

Establishing a Curriculum Schedule

Collaboration among the teachers, program administrators, and participating families will establish program consistency for the children. A schedule can facilitate a natural flow of activities and routines. Planning and implementing a balanced program, consistent with a responsive schedule, promotes security and safety for the children (Read 1976). Continuity, consistency, security, and safety are critical considerations in the establishment of curriculum plans and schedules for early childhood care and learning programs.

Plans Based on Children's Needs and Interests: What's Happening Now?

How do you do your planning for the day when children's needs change rapidly? How can you avoid mistakes in the schedule you project for the activities? Staff who collaborate in planning for their program have the maximum chances to make the day happen as you would wish. Teachers and program administrators who collaborate are informed. They have assessed children. They avoid preplanned, structured curriculum developed from industry far removed from the children who are enrolled in their program. Collaborative teachers who practice intentionality avoid watered-down elementary school lesson plans. Intentional teachers avoid forcing inappropriate experiences on the children in their programs. You will avoid setting up casual, unrelated activities by staying away from the ones randomly based on, "What shall we do with the children today?" or "They seem to be interested in bugs this week." Children's needs are met when their interests and perspectives are integrated into purposeful curriculum planning.

Start by looking at your program. What experiences do you offer now? Which of these experiences seem interesting to the children? Do you know what activities they enjoy? Review the assessments of the children. How does the teaching team react? Which activities and experiences do they believe work, and which would they modify? How does the environment, indoor and outdoor spaces, function? Does the existing curriculum meet your school's curricular guidelines? Are you in line with required standards? Is your curriculum accountable? Create a complete analysis describing the curriculum as it exists. With all members of the staff, review the resulting analysis.

Invite input about the curriculum from parents and volunteers. This review of your existing curriculum prepares you for the next step, identifying a framework for your curriculum. naeyc 1a, 1b, 1c, 2c, 4a, 4b ,4c, 4d, 5a, 5b, 5c, 6c, 6d

Flexibility within a Framework

The most effective way to construct a meaningful framework for your curriculum is to remain flexible. Stay flexible as you establish plans and carry out activities, both planned and spontaneous. Regularly examine the children's experiences to confirm that they are balanced. Are their opportunities for the children to enjoy individual activities? Are there opportunities for them to enjoy small-group activities? Are their opportunities for larger group interaction?

As you examine your overall curriculum, check that the experiences support child-directed activities that encourage children to make choices. Teacher-guided activities encourage children to work together in small groups. They also teach children to follow directions and develop their abilities to wait and take turns.

Remaining flexible will allow you to offer children the greatest degree of experience choices. Yet, the materials are determined by the teaching team and program administrator. Besides flexibility, you will find variability in curriculum planning among schools. Even with flexibility and variability, anticipate that a long-term curriculum plan most likely will be expected. A long-term curriculum plan is the overview of design and intentions of experiences. The type of program will influence the long-term plan. A long-term curriculum plan offers an outline or a blueprint for a year and describes the direction you think likely for the curriculum. Establishing long-range plans allows you and the teaching team to schedule appropriate staff ratios, to order equipment and supplies, and to invite guests and volunteers.

The process of making long-term plans can take different routes. First, the analysis of the existing program is important. The assessment of the children's needs and interests will provide the foundation for curriculum analysis and long-term planning. Identification of the curriculum approach, or combination of approaches, will be a step in the process of long-term planning. You will need to reference the school calendar and attendance pattern. The schedules for the day, week, and, for some schools, the month become essential considerations when you are developing your

---

Figure 6–13 Steps for Long-Term Curriculum Planning

Program guidelines and standards

Assessment of children's interests and needs

Curriculum approach

Curriculum plan

Program schedule

Activities

---

long-term plans. Building a meaningful and intentional long-term curriculum plan can begin with sequential steps (Figure 6–13). Utilizing the steps will lead you to the tangible features of your curriculum—the activities you offer to the children. naeyc 1a, 1b, 1c, 3a, 3b, 4a, 4b ,4c, 4d, 5b, 5c

Building a Schedule

Schedules are intended to focus on the children's needs. Changes in the children's behavior and needs, special occasions, unexpected circumstances and events, and staffing considerations will modify the proposed schedule. Readiness to modify intended schedules is an important teaching skill. Always have back-up or contingency plans. For instance, what meaningful experience will you substitute for the carpentry activity when you are told that the two volunteers, who were scheduled, had to cancel? How will you arrange activities to help the children and staff cope with a neighborhood crisis or tragedy?

Most scheduled activities can be easily rotated or postponed to another time or day, especially under unexpected circumstances. A winter of heavy rainfall would encourage you to temporarily replace the dinosaurs in the sand table with props that are related to rescue or flooding losses. The props might include cars, trees, houses, and people figures that will allow children to express themselves during and after unfamiliar and possibly frightening experiences.

Activities can be organized within a daily schedule with specific activities and experiences. Although this framework is somewhat structured, you can preserve flexibility and spontaneity when implementing the flow of activities. Some programs schedule free-choice blocks of time within the schedule that provide children with spontaneous curriculum opportunities within a framework. This framework could identify blocks of time for child-initiated activities, group time, and perhaps snack and lunch. Activities within blocks of time provide children with choices in a framework that can respect their changing needs and interests.

Take care to allow time for the children to transition from one activity to another. Allow time, as well, for routine activities such as handwashing and cleanup. Arrival and departure times vary with each program. Additionally, some children and their families will benefit from the extra time for unhurried goodbyes. Routine experiences, such as meals and rest, influence the schedule. The environment, especially the proximity of the outdoor area, will also affect the schedule. A free-flow between the indoor and outdoor spaces requires fewer scheduled transitions because, for example, the proximity would allow the children safe access to the outdoors and to the inside bathrooms.

A daily schedule provides a framework to guide interactions and experiences from the time of the children's arrival to departure. The interactions and experiences, including those that are child-initiated and teacher-guided, occur during the daily schedule. The intent of a schedule is to guide young children's successful engagement with the available opportunities arranged throughout the indoor and outdoor settings. Those opportunities are most effective when blocks of time allow the children to explore and discover a range of experiences. The time you might allot for an activity is a projection. For this reason, activities and experiences might overlap. Children take varying amounts of time to enjoy a snack, participate in group time, wash their hands, and prepare for departure. You might also consider the impact of school-related services, such as bus routes and outsourced food delivery. Children need stretches of uninterrupted time to sustain their play. Your daily schedule needs to support this and validate the individual differences of the children and unique aspects of the group.

School demands vary. Children's needs vary. Guidelines for schools vary. Many Montessori Schools, for instance, offer larger blocks of time that allow longer activity periods without interruption. Children snack when they are hungry, eating individually or with a friend (Humphryes 1998). Differences in school goals result in differences in daily and weekly schedules (Figures 6–14 and 6–15). You will achieve best practices by arranging a schedule that meets the varied energy levels of children, equalizes child-initiated and teacher-guided experiences, and balances time and frequency of experiences. The quality and occurrence of experiences initiated by the children are driven by program philosophy and goals.

Figure 6-14 Program Schedule—Full Day

Full Day—Multi-Age Group (3–5 Year Olds)

7:30–8:30	Arrival/Interest and Activity Centers
8:30–8:45	Group time to plan day
8:45–10:00	Interest and Activity Centers
10:00–10:15	Transition: clean up, toileting, hand washing
10:15–10:30	Snack
10:30–10:40	Group time
10:45–11:45	Interest and Activity Centers (indoor and outdoors)
11:45–12:00	Transition: cleanup, toileting, handwashing
12:00–12:30	Lunch
12:30–2:00	Rest/nap/quiet-time Activity Centers
2:00–3:15	Interest and Activity Centers (indoor and outdoor)
3:15–3:30	Transition: cleanup, toileting, handwashing
3:30–3:45	Snack
3:45–4:00	Group time—review the day
4:00–5:30	Interest and Activity Centers (indoor and outdoor)
5:30–6:00	Transition: cleanup, snack available, prepare to welcome arriving families, departure.

Figure 6-15 Program Schedule—Half Day

Half-Day—Multi-Age Group (3–5 Year Olds)

8:30–9:00	Arrival: greeting, quiet time activities
9:00–9:15	Group time to plan day
9:15–10:00	Interest and Activity Centers
10:00–10:15	Transition: cleanup, toileting, handwashing
10:15–10:30	Snack
10:30–10:45	Group time
10:45–11:45	Interest and Activity Centers (indoor and outdoor)
11:45–12:00	Transition: cleanup, prepare to welcome arriving families, departure.

Children benefit when teachers capitalize on spontaneous teaching opportunities, particularly when individual needs of a child are addressed.

Maximizing the Spontaneous Teaching Moments

Allow for ample flexibility when planning your curriculum. This way you will be able to capitalize on spontaneous teaching opportunities that encourage and extend children's interests (Epstein 2007). The unexpected learning opportunities can occur when something happens such as a child mentions that his cat just had kittens or a child arrives with new boots. An interesting bug discovered on the playground can lead to valuable learning about insects and nature. This kind of learning is interesting, meaningful, and relevant to the children. Using teachable moments as one of your teaching strategies can ensure that your teaching remains authentic and intentional.

naeyc 1a, 1b, 1c, 4a, 4b ,4c, 4d, 5a, 5b, 5c

 Video Case

Preschool Daily Schedules and Program Planning

Visit the Early Childhood Education Media Library, and watch the TeachSource Video Case on www.cengagebrain.com

1. How does consistent scheduling help children in the classroom?

2. Should all programs offer a rest time for the children? If not, what alternative options might be scheduled?

Documenting Curriculum Plans

The analysis of your existing curriculum and a conceptualized flexible schedule readies you to decide about a plan for your curriculum. Your curriculum plan will both document what you propose to do and offer a record of what you actually do. The use of lesson plan books or copied pages with designated blank boxes were the conventional way teachers tracked classroom work and assignments. Combining the Curriculum Activity Guides (CAGs) within a curriculum plan offers you a more efficient and accountable option.

Use your time wisely and establish accountability with a curriculum plan that meets your program vision and goals. Curriculum plans in some written form satisfy agency and licensing requirements for many programs. Readily available and visually displayed curriculum plans help the families and volunteers appreciate the way the program fosters children's development and guides their learning. When you disclose what you do, a sense of trust prospers in your school.

Your curriculum plan will depend on the curriculum approach your school has selected. The curriculum plan will also be affected by the daily schedule. Intentional and meaningful curriculum for young children ought to offer activities in all developmental areas and integrate activities across curriculum areas. Intentional and meaningful curriculum also needs to support children culturally and linguistically (Copple and Bredekamp 2009).

There are different ways to document curriculum plans. Some plans list the suggested activities next to the blocks of time on the daily schedule. Other plans list activities for the interest centers and identify a particular experience for group time. Yet other programs develop a plan that combines the day of the week and the time with activities. Basic, identifying information for the curriculum plan ideally includes the date, name of teacher(s), classroom or grouping of children, and goals for the week or day. A section for review and comment is helpful. Schools that use the thematic approach list a theme and the related activities on the curriculum planning form. Utilize the Curriculum Activity Guide (Appendix B) as a basic model for developing your own method. Review the format provided in Figure 6–16 for a way to document a plan using the developmental focus area approach. See Figure 6–17 for documenting experiences organized by curriculum area approach. Figure 6–18 can be utilized to document the experiences you provide in an interest

© Cengage Learning 2013

Figure 6–16 Curriculum Plan—Developmental Focus Area Approach

Date: xx/xx/xx   **Teacher:** Caroline   **Group/Classroom:** *3- to 5-year-olds*

Curricular Guidelines: *To expose children to ecological ways to preserve earth's resources.*

	Physical	**Affective and Aesthetic** **(social-emotional understanding)**	**Cognitive**
Monday	*Body bowling*	*Begin junk art group structure*	*Make "Keep Our School Clean" signs*
Tuesday	*Bath scrubber toss*	*Continue junk art*	*Plastic, wood, metal sorting and gluing*
Wednesday	*Stringing Cheerios*	*Continue junk art*	*Make bird feeders with paper rolls*
Thursday	*Digging up bed for planting*	*Paint junk art sculpture Hang bird feeders*	*Six-pack holder bubble blowing*
Friday	*Clean earth parade on park path*	*Litter patrol in neighborhood Wrap junk art to take home*	*Planting lettuce and radish seeds in raised beds*

Figure 6–17 Curriculum Plan—Curriculum Area Approach

Curriculum Area Approach

Week: xx/xx/xx   **Teacher:** *Janet*   **Group/Classroom:** *3- to 5-year-olds*

Curricular Guidelines: *To introduce children to life on a farm.*

Art	**Creative Dramatics**	**Health, Safety, Nutrition**
Group farm mural *Watercolor farm animals.*	*Set up horse corral outside with stick horses, tack, straw bales, other props*	*Tasting and comparing cow's and goat's milk, yogurt, or soy products* *Cooking Activity: butter* *Cooking Activity: bread*

Communication and Literacy	**Mathematics**	**Movement**
Farm stencil books *Farm sticker dictation* *Farm animal books* *Farm word cards*	*Farm animal sort* *Matching mothers/babies* *Sensorial table: measuring* *bird seed, grain*	*Riding stick horses* *Plowing* *Climbing on hay bales*

Music and Rhythm	**Science**	**Social Understanding**
Old MacDonald *Square dance* *Western music with scarves*	*Eggs—incubator* *Sheep/Wool* *Computer: reference farm*	*Farmers and Tools* *Add tractors to block area* *Farm animals and fences* *Farms helping (co-op, bureau)*

Grouptime *Books: Little Red Hen, Life on the Farm, I Want to be a Farmer*
Guest brings chicken, set up egg incubator.

Theme *Farm Life*

Standards Met

Date   **Comments and Reflections**

Figure 6–18 Curriculum Plan Interest Center Guide

Interest Center Guide

Interest Center *Science*   **Theme** *Spring*

Art	Cooking	Literacy	Quiet Reading	Outside Art	Outside Large Motor
Block	Computer	Manipulatives	Science	Outside Circle	Outside Sand/Water
Circle	Dramatic Play	Music/Rhythm	Sensorial	Outside Garden	Trike Path

Interest Center Guidelines   **Approximate Age Range** *3–5*

Children and families will be invited to contribute signs of spring such as flowers and tree blossoms. Special requests will be made for mulberry leaves for the silk worms.

Developmental Focus   **Physical**   **Affective and Aesthetic**   **Cognitive**

Curriculum Area *Science*

Interest Center Materials

   Constant   *Reference books, plants, flowers, spring flower lotto activity tray, window thermometer and chart, magnifying glasses.*

   Featured   *Silk worms*
                   Worm farm
                   "Signs of spring" flowers and branches

Preparation/Set Up

1. *Set up silk worm farm for viewing (plexiglass)—label.*

2. *Prepare signs inviting parent contributions.*

Teaching Strategies

1. *Teacher will invite children's questions as they observe the worms during a group time.*

2. *Children will feed and monitor worms.*

3. *Teacher and children will check and record temperature.*

Possible Outcomes for the Child or Children

   Concepts   *Flowers bloom in spring.*
                   Birds build nests in spring.
                   The weather warms up during spring.
                   Silk worms eat mulberry leaves.
   Skills   *Observation and prediction*
   Vocabulary *Spring, blossom, silk worm, temperature, mulberry leaves*

Standards Met

Comments and Reflections

Date

center. Figure 6–19 illustrates how you can document curriculum by integrating activities within a theme, unit, or project and additionally categorize the activities by curriculum area.

The sample curriculum plans (Figures 6–16, 6–17, 6–18, and 6–19) document activities suitable for the children who attended the Shasta College Early Childhood Education Center. The center is a teacher preparation facility and a program of learning and care for children of college students and the families in a northern California community. The completed forms illustrate planning for that particular program.

Figure 6–19 Curriculum Plan-Integrating Approaches within a Theme/Unit/Project

_____ Curriculum Plan _____

Week: xx/xx/xx   **Teacher:** *Regina*   **Group/Classroom:** *3- to 5-year-olds*

Curricular Guidelines: *To provide experiences for children to feel special about themselves and their families with positive emphasis on cultural identity.*

Theme/Unit/Project: *I'm Me, I'm Special*

_____ Developmental Focus _____

Physical   (P)   Affective (social-emotional understanding) and Aesthetic (A)   Cognitive (C)

_____ Activities in Curriculum Areas _____

Art	Creative Dramatics	Health, Safety, Nutrition
Body tracing (A)	*Domestic play* (A)	*Cooking individual snack* (P)
Pasting magazine pictures of houses (A)	*Dramatizing* (A)	*Family holiday food* (P)
Mural of copied baby photographs (A)	<u>*Are You My Mother*</u>?	*Cooking: Puree fruits* (P)

Communication & Literacy	Mathematics	Movement
Dictation "I like" (C)	*Baby to adult sequence* (C)	*Shadow dancing* (P)
Book about Me (C)	*Height strips* (C)	*Following footprints* (P)
Recording/listening (C)	*Weighing* (C)	*Digging a hole* (P)

Music and Rhythm	Science	Social Understanding
"I'm very special" (P & C)	*Listening to heartbeat* (P)	*Mirror—Alike/different* (A)
Instrument guessing game (C)	*Thumbprints and magnifying glass* (C)	*What my parents do* (A)
Different smells (C)		*The sound of names* (C)

Group time   *Parent and an infant introduced during group time. Share photos of infant as a newborn.*

Interest Centers

Standards Met

Comments and Reflections

Date

The samples also illustrate that curriculum plans can be modified as needed. Curriculum plans serve as a guide and allow modification for spontaneous learning and the children's changing needs.

Plan for Developmental Focus Area Approach

Activities can be organized in writing in numerous ways. Whatever way you decide, you realize how

important the recordkeeping is for managing quality curriculum planning. Organizing activities by developmental focus area is one approach to consider. An example is provided in Figure 6–16. This form allows you to list activities that contribute to children's growing abilities within three developmental areas, which are often referred to as developmental domains. Experiences for young children

© Cengage Learning 2013

When a Interest Center Guide is provided in each area, it allows teachers, family members, and volunteers to quickly gather information about the possible opportunities for the children participating in that area.

offered throughout the week and month should be balanced among the development focus areas. You can do this by offering some activities to facilitate physical development, some for affective (social-emotional understanding) and aesthetic development, and some for cognitive development.

Plan for Curriculum Area Approach
A plan for managing the curriculum area approach is provided in Figure 6–17. Activities planned for each curriculum area can be documented in this form. You will be able to track that the activities allow children's spontaneous discovery and exploration throughout the week's planned experiences. Maintaining balance among the curriculum areas is important. Look at the week's plan to determine whether children have been given opportunities to participate in the different curriculum areas and if the experiences have relevance to them and their families.

Plan for Interest Centers
The third design provides a way to document the experiences planned within an interest center, also referred to as an activity area. The form for interest centers, Interest Center Guide, may be displayed on a bulletin board, filed in a teacher notebook, or placed in the related center. Protect the form with a plastic cover and mount it to the top of an adult-height shelf in the related interest center (Figure 6–18). When an Interest Center Guide is provided in each center, it allows teachers, family members,

and volunteers to quickly gather information about the possible opportunities for the children participating in that area. The form describes the materials that remain constant in the interest center and the activity or activities that are changed to accommodate the topic or theme featured for a specific period of time. The featured materials relate to a topic, project, or theme that is a consequence of assessment and documentation of the children's evolving interests. Replace the guides when new materials or added activities need to be documented.

Plan for Integrating Curriculum Approaches
The fourth curriculum plan proposes a design for integrating the curriculum approaches. Approaches that can be integrated include the developmental focus area, the curriculum area, and interest centers within a theme, unit, or project (Figure 6–19). Create a large display for this plan. It is difficult to show all the activities on an 8 ½ x 11 size paper. Balancing activities among the developmental focus areas is a priority. You can do this by marking a *P* for physical, *A* for affective (social-emotional understanding) and aesthetic, and *C* for cognitive. Use of the three letters allows you to quickly identify the developmental area and determine if planned activities are sufficiently balanced in all three developmental areas. When you identify a theme or project, more activities may occur in one area than another. Think about the activities you want to propose for one week. Are the activities balanced across areas, and does the plan safeguard flexibility and spontaneous learning?

The plan for integrating curriculum approaches provides room for only the title of the proposed activities. Titles generally do not indicate the purpose and value of the activity. Completed Curriculum Activity Guides for each proposed activity will thoroughly describe the experiences. Completed Interest Center Guides will document how the activity areas will enhance the integrated curriculum arranged for the children, throughout the indoor and outdoor environment.

Adapting Plans for Extended-Day Experiences

There is an advantage for planning experiences for the school-age children attending your extended-day program. The behaviors, characteristics, and needs of school-age children need to be taken into account as you adapt curriculum plans to meet their needs. The primary-age children (kindergarten through third grade) are closer developmentally to preschool children than to older school-age students. Early childhood care and learning programs with flexible and individualized experiences are particularly beneficial to primary-age children who attend extended-day programs.

School-age children have more developed motor skills, yet they still need chances for large and small movement activities. School-age children are more independent than young children. Interaction with their peers is increasingly important as children mature. School-age children have increased attention spans. Nonetheless, relevant and meaningful opportunities are essential to maintain their curiosity, creativity, and joy in learning. Programs for extended-day experiences should offer a caring and supportive environment. School-age children will have already spent six hours in a classroom, too often with reduced play and time outdoors. Familiarize yourself with the elementary school teachers and their assignments for the students from many different schools who attend your extended-day program. In this way you and your teaching team can support continuity and the transition from the school to the extended-day program (Figure 6–20).

The curriculum plan may be completed with appropriate extended-day experiences to meet the needs of the group. Projects are particularly valuable for school-age children. Projects may evolve from their elementary school assigned homework or emerge from the students' interests. Homework help may be given at this time for the school-age children's own assignments or for mentoring the younger children. The extended-day planning form may be the least comprehensive. Documentation of planned activities for the extended day further substantiates your intentional and committed teaching practices. **naeyc** 1a, 1b, 1c, 4a, 4b, 4c, 4d, 5a, 5b, 5c

---

Figure 6–20 Curriculum Plan – Extended Day

Curriculum Plan – Extended Day

Week: xx/xx/xx   **Group/Classroom**: 4th, 5th, 6th   **Staff:** Ricardo

Curricular Guidelines: *To recognize and adapt to seasonal changes that cause allergies for some people.*

Homework Help:
Review correspondence from classroom, grade level teachers.
Post weekly assignments and due dates.
Schedule computer time.

Project: *Blossoms and Allergies*

Activities: **Physical**
                  Healthy sneezing (tissues, elbow)
                  Indoor exercise
                  Healthy snack planning and preparation (noting food allergies)

   Affective (social-emotional understanding) and Aesthetic
                  The allergist
                  Soothing and relaxing poems
                  Helping friends with allergies

   Cognitive
                  Search the Internet for causes of allergies
                  Blossoms beware
                  Charting allergies by person and season

Date: **Review:**

Thinking about What You Have Learned

✔   Write activity titles and goals for the following two activities:

A. Activity Description: Washing tricycles in the outside area with sponges, soap, and water.

Title: _____

Goal: _____

B. Activity Description: Matching shapes found in the outdoor environment with photographs.

Title: _____

Goal: _____

✔   Complete the Curriculum Activity Guide form for a science activity appropriate for preschool children. You have observed the children and found that they need more large movement activities.

✔   Identify three activities that will introduce the concepts of hard and soft. Refer to the section in this chapter titled "Clustering Activities."

✔   Collect and review activity planning forms from other textbooks or online sources. Which portions of those forms would you adapt for your own curriculum planning.

Chapter References

Antonietti, Alessandro. 1997. Unlocking creativity. *Educational Leadership* 54(6), 73–75.

Arends, Richard. I. 1991. *Learning to teach.* 2nd ed. New York: McGraw Hill.

Barnhart, Clarence. L., and Robert. K. Barnhart, eds. 1990. *The world book dictionary.* Chicago: World Book.

Bloom, Benjamin. S. 1981. *All our children learning: Primer for parents, teachers, and other educators.* New York: McGraw-Hill.

Bodrova, Elena, and Deborah J. Leong. 2004. Chopsticks and counting chips. In *Spotlight on Young Children and PLAY.* Derry Koralek, ed. Washington, D.C: National Association for the Education of Young Children.

Bosse, Sherrie, Gera Jacobs, and Tara Lynn Anderson. 2009. Science in the air. *Young Children.* http://www.naeyc.org/files/yc/file/200911/BosseWeb1109.pdf

Bredekamp, Sue. 2011. *Effective practices in early childhood education: Building a foundation.* Upper Saddle River, NJ: Pearson.

Bruner, Jerome. S. 1960. *The process of education.* New York: Vintage.

Burts, D. C., and T. K. Buchanan. 1998. Preparing teachers in developmentally appropriate ways to teach in developmentally appropriate classrooms. In Carol Seefeldt and A. Galper, eds. *Continuing issues in early childhood education.* 2nd ed. Upper Saddle River, NJ: Merrill.

Caples, S. E. 1996. Some guidelines for preschool design. *Young Children* 51(4), 14–21.

Charlesworth, Rosalind. 2011. *Understanding child development.* 11th ed. Belmont, CA: Wadsworth, Cengage Learning.

Christie, J. F., and F. Wardle. "How much time is needed for play?" *Young Children* 47(3), 28–31.

Cohen, Dorothy H. 1972. *The learning child.* New York: Pantheon.

Copple, Carol, and Sue Bredekamp. 2009. *Developmentally appropriate practice in early childhood programs serving children from birth through age 8.* 3rd ed. Washington, DC: National Association for the Education of Young Children.

Craig, Grace J. and Don Baucum. *Human development.* 9th ed. Upper Saddle River, NJ: Prentice Hall.

Dodge, Diane. T., Judy Jablon, and Tony S. Bickart. 1995. *Constructing curriculum for the primary grades.* Washington, DC: Teaching Strategies.

Elkind, David. 2004. "Thanks for the memory: The lasting value of true play" in *Spotlight on Young Children and PLAY.* Derry Koralek, ed. Washington, DC: National Association for the Education of Young Children.

Epstein, Ann S. 2007. *The intentional teacher: Choosing the best strategies for young children's learning.* Derry Koralek, ed. Washington, DC: National Association for the Education of Young Children.

Essa, Eva. L., and Penelope R. Rogers. 1992. *An early childhood curriculum: From developmental model to application.* Albany, NY: Delmar.

Feeney, Stephanie, Doris Christensen, and Eva Moravick. 2009. *Who Am I in the Lives of Children?* 8th ed. New Jersey: Pearson.

Gestwicki, Carol. 2002. *Developmentally appropriate practice: Curriculum and development in early education.* 4th ed. Albany, NY: Delmar.

Greenberg, Polly. 1998. Thinking about goals for grownups and young children while we teach reading, writing, and spelling, and a few thoughts about the "J" word. *Young Children* 53(6), 31–42.

Greenman, Jim. 1988. *Caring spaces, learning places: Children's environments that work.* Redman, WA: Exchange Press.

Hartley, R. E. 1973. Play, the essential ingredient. In Joe K. Frost. *Revising early childhood education – Readings.* New York: Holt, Rinehart, & Winston.

Holt, John. 1967. *How children learn.* New York: Pitman.

Howard, S., A. Shaughnessy, D. Sanger, and K. Hux. 1998. Let's talk! Facilitating language in early elementary classrooms. *Young Children* 53(3), 34–39.

Humphryes, Janet. 1998. The developmental appropriateness of high-quality Montessori programs. *Young Children* 53(4), 4–16.

Hymes, James. L. 1981. *Teaching the child under six.* 3rd ed. Columbus, OH: Merrill.

Jones, Elizabeth. 2004. Playing to get smart. In *Spotlight on Young Children and PLAY.* Derry Koralek, ed. Washington, DC: National Association for the Education of Young Children.

Kostelnik, Marjorie J., Anne K. Soderman, Alice Whiren, and Alice Phipps. 2011. *Developmentally appropriate curriculum: Best practices in early childhood education.* 5th ed. Upper Saddle River, NJ: Pearson.

Landreth, Catherine. 1972. *Preschool learning and teaching.* New York: Harper & Row.

Lionni, Leo. 1994. *Little blue and little yellow.* New York: Mulberry.

Loughlin, Caroline. E., and Joseph. H. Suina, J. H. 1982. *The learning environment: An instructional strategy.* New York: Teachers College Press.

Mayesky, Mary. 2009. *Creative activities for young children.* 10th ed. Albany, NY: Delmar.

Montessori, Maria. 1966. *The secret of childhood.* New York: Fides.

Neugebauer, Roger. 1998, March/April. Guide to early childhood curriculum products. *Child Care Information Exchange* 126, 67–71.

Nourot, Patricia M. and Judith L. Van Hoorn. 1991. Symbolic play in preschool and primary settings. *Young Children* 46(6), 40–50.

Pika, Rae. 2004. *Experiences in Movement, Birth to Age 8.* Albany, New York: Delmar.

Read, Katherine. H. 1976. *The nursery school: Human relationships and learning.* Philadelphia: W. B. Saunders.

Salk, Lee. 1983. *The complete Dr. Salk: An a-to-z guide to raising your child.* New York: World Almanac.

Smilansky, Sara. 1968. The *effects of sociodramatic play on disadvantaged preschool children.* New York: John Wiley and Sons.

Todd, Virginia E., and Helen Heffernan. 1977. *The years before school: Guiding preschool children* 3rd ed. New York: Macmillan.

Vance, Barbara. 1973. *Teaching the prekindergarten child: Instructional design and curriculum.* Monterey, CA: Brooks/Cole Publishing Company.

Activities for Physical Development: Health, Safety, and Nutrition, Movement, Music, and Rhythm

© Cengage Learning 2013

Picture This . . .

Koula hops through the door and hands Teacher Sal a picture. She says, "This is me when I was a baby. I was just a little baby and trying to walk."

Koula unzips her jacket, hangs it on a hook in her cubby. Then she places her snack box on the counter. She looks around the room. She walks to the circular art table. She pulls one of the aprons, hanging on a chair in the art area, over her head. She sits down at the table, cuts with the scissors, squeezes the glue bottle, and places fabric and buttons on her paper. She tries to write her name and then asks the student teacher for help. Before the hour is over, she has moved from the art table to a table where manipulatives are set. She works the puzzle pieces and then stacks shapes. Later, she moves to the sensory table where she sifts sand and pours water.

Koula returns to the art area and works with the lavender-colored playing dough the teachers had newly prepared. Koula pinches and pounds the dough. As the sun warmed the outdoor classroom, the sliding doors are opened. This signaled to Koula that she could play in both the indoor and outdoor spaces. She walks outside, climbs the steps on the slide, slides down, and then runs toward the wagon. She pulls the empty wagon around the path. She stops and invites Jane to climb into the wagon for a ride. She pushes the wagon for a few minutes and then skips over to the outside listening center. The center provides opportunities for her to turn knobs on the DVD player. Finishing with the DVD player, Koula walks back inside the classroom and into the bathroom. She washes her hands after toileting. She joins the cooking experience set up on one of the science center tables. She mixes cream cheese and spreads it on cut-up celery. The sounds from the small group of children in the group time circle invite Koula to participate. She moves her fingers and hands rhythmically to the songs she hears. She finds an empty carpet square, sits down, and listens to the group time discussion about crossing streets safely.

GUIDE TO READING CHAPTER 7

Chapter Outline

Learning Objectives

After reading this chapter, you will be able to

1. Identify large and small physical development movements.
2. Integrate activities to facilitate movement experiences for young children.
3. Design strategies that contribute to the children's understanding of health, nutrition, and safety.
4. Discuss safety topics that have relevancy for young children.
5. Recognize topics and skills important for children's nutritional awareness.
6. Recognize perceptual motor development skills and activities that will facilitate growth in that category of movement.
7. Identify concepts, topics, and activities related to music and rhythm activities for young children.

Key Terms

National Association for the Education of Young Children (NAEYC) Standards for Initial Early Childhood Professional Preparation Programs met by this chapter:

Standard 1: Promoting Child Development and Learning

1a: Knowing and understanding young children's characteristics and needs.

1b: Knowing and understanding the multiple influences on development and learning.

1c: Using developmental knowledge to create healthy, respectful, supportive, and challenging learning environments.

Standard 2: Building Family and Community Relationships

2a: Knowing about and understanding diverse family and community characteristics.

2b: Supporting and engaging families and communities through respectful, reciprocal relationships.

Standard 4: Using Developmentally Effective Approaches

4a: Understanding positive relationships and supportive interactions as the foundation of their work with young children.

4b: Knowing and understanding effective strategies and tools for early education, including appropriate uses of technology.

4c: Using a broad repertoire of developmentally appropriate teaching/learning approaches.

Standard 5: Using Content Knowledge to Build Meaningful Curriculum

5a: Understanding content knowledge and resources in academic disciplines: language and literacy; the arts – music, creative movement, dance, drama, visual arts; mathematics; science; physical activity, physical education, health and safety; and social studies.

5b: Knowing and using the central concepts, inquiry tools, and structures of content areas or academic disciplines.

5c: Using own knowledge, appropriate early learning standards, and other resources to design, implement, and evaluate developmentally meaningful and challenging curriculum for each child.

Standard 6: Becoming a Professional

6c: Engaging in continuous, collaborative learning to inform practice; using technology effectively with young children, with peers, and as a professional resource.

6d: Integrating knowledgeable, reflective, and critical perspectives on early education.

6e: Engaging in informed advocacy for young children and the early childhood profession.

Physical Development

Development comes about when a child's brain and body mature. Development initiates changes, notably increasing a child's abilities and skills. Children's physical development refers to the basic physiological changes that occur in their bodies and motor skills. The acquisition of skills and changes in the body are unique for each child. Individuality in skill acquisition results from a child's heredity and environment.

Children acquire skills sequentially; that is, they acquire skills in a certain order. For instance, a baby sits up independently before he walks. A child balances a three-wheel trike, before she rides a two-wheel bike. A toddler will dump a bucket of sand before pouring the contents of a bucket into another container. As children acquire basic motor skills during the early childhood years, they gain more control and confidence to try new tasks. The

experiences and activities offered to young children in quality early childhood programs help them develop their capabilities.

In the chapter opener, *Picture This* . . . Koula illustrated numerous physical movements as she participated in different experiences. A variety of experiences promote children's physical development. Active involvement is beneficial for young children because it provides them with chances to develop physical skills and behaviors (Figure 7–1).

Large Movement—Possible Outcomes and Activities

Two-, three-, and four-year-olds generally are in motion, whenever they are given the opportunities and as their bodies allow. Motion is what makes young children so observable. They develop rapidly during the preschool years and exhibit an array of physical abilities, competence, and potential.

Figure 7–1 Physical Development Experiences Develop Children's Skills and Behaviors	
agility	fitness
balance	flexibility
cooperation	involvement
confidence	motivation
creativity	participation
endurance	relaxation
expression	strength

Figure 7–2 Children Develop Skills and Behaviors with Large Movement Experiences		
crawling	pulling	galloping
walking	throwing	skipping
jumping	kicking	tossing
hopping	hanging	wiggling
running	sliding	climbing
carrying	balancing	swinging
pushing	lifting	rolling
pedaling	stretching	leaping
swaying	catching	bouncing

Physical motion requires muscular activity. When the large body muscles are in motion, it is called **large movement.** This is also referred to as gross motor skills and gross motor development. Children use large movements for walking, running, climbing, pedaling, and throwing. When they participate in active experiences, they are developing their dexterity, or skillfulness. When they move energetically and vigorously, they are developing skills in more advanced body movements. As the children's coordination, balance, and control mature, their participation in large movement activities increases. Appropriate environments for young children offer indoor spaces and outdoor spaces for climbing structures, building with large blocks, constructing with carpentry materials, pumping on swings, and for pushing and pulling wheel toys. Quality environments for young children have space for them to move, run, and dance.

Skills and Possible Outcomes

Children acquire specific motor skills by actively engaging in physical movement. Motion permits them to feel their bodies move. Motion allows children to become acquainted with their bodies' capabilities. A variety of large movement activities helps children to develop self-confidence. These activities are necessary for healthy physical development. Large movement experiences give children opportunities to release large muscle energy, relieve stress and tension, achieve relaxation, and further enhance the development of their large motor skills (Figure 7–2). naeyc 1a, 1b, 1c

Large Movement Activities

The outdoor environment will offer many opportunities for you to expand the experiences that are commonly included, such as wheel toys and climbing structures. When you add an obstacle course to the outdoor space, the children

will develop large muscles while they are developing problem solving skills. A bean bag toss requires children to stretch, throw, and toss **(Curriculum Activity Guide 40)**. You will be able to schedule large movement activities indoors by modifying an experience, such as the obstacle course or bean bag toss, to the space available.

Creativity offers an advantage for arranging large movement experiences, especially because large pieces of equipment are not always necessary. Children will enjoy lifting and placing unit blocks, running and waving long streamers, skipping to music, and scrubbing down the outside riding toys.

Children profit from programs where individual needs are met and capabilities are developed. The school environment may require modifications for children's special needs. You will be able to enhance inclusion of children by, for example, placing building blocks on raised platforms. The raised and movable block surface accommodates children in wheelchairs. You might also prepare a rectangular board with casters for children to lie on their stomachs and propel themselves with their hands or elbows. This could allow the children to use blocks or manipulative toys that are available on the carpeted floor areas (Spodek and Saracho 1994). Physical and occupational therapists can assist in suggesting simple ways to modify specific activities and the environment (Feeney et al. 2011). naeyc 1a, 1b, 1c, 4a, 4b, 4c, 5a, 5c, 6c

Small Movement Possible Outcomes and Activities

When infants first grasp an object or their parent's finger, their motions trigger their natural exploratory behaviors. Curiosity is what stimulates an infant, a toddler, or a preschooler to investigate every item in their surroundings. They use the small

Large movement experiences give children opportunities to release energy, relieve stress and tension, achieve relaxation, and enhance their skills.

© Cengage Learning 2013

muscles in their arms, hands, fingers, and faces to explore, interact, and respond to whatever is close by. Motor behavior, beginning with touching and grasping, involves the small muscles and is called **small movement** or fine motor development.

Skills and Possible Outcomes

You will have many chances throughout the daily school program to facilitate small movement development of the children. Children engage their small muscles when they manipulate puzzles by interlocking the pieces. Preschoolers will use their small muscles when they stack unit blocks and dip paint brushes at the art easel. Young children expand their self-help skills as they use their maturing small movement skills. They acquire the abilities to zip zippers, button shirts, and pull up their pants.

There will be many opportunities in the indoor and outdoor environments to encourage children's participation in experiences that develop their small movement skills. You will enhance their opportunities by placing props, such as toy

people and animals, in the sand area. Creative interactions with other children and growth of small movement skills are available for children who join experiences at the manipulative tables. The manipulative tables can be filled with various materials, such as puzzles and linking blocks. An interest center for discovery invites children to examine bugs, leaves, and dirt, especially with magnifying glasses. Small motor activities tend to offer more relaxing, slower-paced choices for children. Small motor activities are important in both the indoor and outdoor classroom spaces. Too often large movement activities dominate the outdoor places. Inviting children to pour, dig, place, hold, stack, reach, and assemble objects and materials helps them develop their small muscles and improves their small movement skills (Figure 7–3).

Preschool children vary widely in their abilities to perform small movement skills. Modifications to equipment and materials may be required for children with special needs. Modifications will increase their participation and maximize their potential for developing small motor abilities. Adaptations to the activities, individualized for the child with special needs, will also offer benefit to children without special needs. Most likely, the children who may benefit would be those functioning lower than the expected typical range. You will be able to adapt the presentation of activities by:

- ensuring that a child can see your face and gestures if he is hearing impaired
- using physical prompts until the verbal prompts can be followed for the visually impaired child
- encouraging another child to assist a motor-impaired child
- giving directions slowly and one at a time for a learning or developmentally delayed child (Cook et al. 2000).

Figure 7–3 Children Develop Skills and Behaviors with Small Movement Experiences

holding	plucking	squeezing
fitting	zipping	pinching
placing	painting	keyboarding
clapping	washing	tracing
coloring	smiling	steering
pouring	chewing	writing
cutting	shaking	typing
buttoning	steering	whistling

Small Movement Activities

Small movement activities are important experiences in an early childhood education program because they influence the other areas of development. As children develop physically, they become more aware of their own body movements and the consequences of those motions. Letting go at the top of a slide helps them to acquire concepts of movement and speed. Turning the water faucet many ways before the water flows allows them to enjoy discovery and practice a skill. Moving a computer mouse provides experiences to help a child learn cause and effect and the particular functioning of the computer screen. Placing puzzle shapes into the correct spaces requires a child to make judgments and practice by trial and error.

Small movement will likely unfold when children have opportunities to experience activities that build on their naturally developing skills. An environment is best for young children when it offers them possibilities throughout the day to experience movements such as letting go, turning a faucet, pressing a button, and placing pieces of a puzzle. *Eyedroppers and Soap Suction* and *Tweezers and Ice Cube Trays* are two distinct activities that will develop children's small motor development **(Curriculum Activity Guide 41 and 42** ____**)**.

Connecting Curriculum for Physical Development

Physical development experiences that are incorporated throughout the curriculum will complement the children's natural need for movement. Activities that foster physical development are essential for supporting the children's physiological needs for activity. Large movement activities routinely offered outdoors will fulfill the children's needs for sensory stimulation, fresh air, rest, and nourishment (Copple and Bredekamp 2009). Physical activity promotes brain function and increases the capacity for learning. It improves fitness, muscle strength, and balance. It contributes to social adjustment and skills gained in playing games with others (Pica 2006). naeyc 1a, 1b, 1c, 4b, 4c, 5b, 5c

Integrating Activities

Activity is fundamental for development of children's movement skills and their physical growth. As you have already read in Chapters 5 and 6, some early care and learning programs organize the children's activities by developmental focus area. Others organize activities by curriculum area or theme. Programs meet the children's needs in many ways with a variety of planning approaches. Your decision to **integrate activities** will contribute to your creating an emergent curriculum. As you continue to observe and assess the children, you will think of meaningful ideas for activities. These will be suitable for meeting the children's needs in the developmental focus and curriculum areas. The activities may also correspond with projects and themes (Figure 7–4).

Springtime brings an increasing awareness of growing and planting. During a storytime, Jodie leans toward Teacher Tomas and whispers, "My papa has a big garden." During the weekly staff meeting Teacher Tomas shares Jodie's comment about her papa's garden. A student teacher

A small movement activity such as cutting with a scissors is an important experience that can have positive effects on all areas of development.

© Cengage Learning 2013

Figure 7–4 Activities Integrate Developmental Focus Area, Curriculum Areas, and Themes

Developmental Focus Area	Physical
Curriculum Areas	*Health, Safety, Nutrition Activity:* Cooking fresh carrots
	Movement Activity: Preparing outdoor garden area
	Science Activity: Planting and observing plants grow
Theme	Gardening

Figure 7–5 Curriculum Themes Encouraging Physical Development

Large Movement	Small Movement
Sports for Everyone	Carpentry
Exercising	Tools and Small Machines
Hiking	Stitching and Sewing
All About Me: My Body	My Senses: Touch
Summer Safety	Plants

comments that she has also heard several children in the sand area referring to plants and seeds during the week. The teaching team organizes experiences for the children, translating their interests into large movement activities. Skills develop when children rake, dig, and hoe a garden. A gardening theme or project offers health benefits. Children and all the adults participating in the program learn to cultivate the garden. Appreciation of plants—water, soil, sunshine—can direct the children's attention toward the curriculum area of science, while they are developing their large movement skills.

Teachers who manage activities thematically, the theme approach, may find that certain themes facilitate physical development activities. The theme *Sports for Everyone*, for example, will acquaint the children with amateur, community, and professional sports. *Sports for Everyone* could also introduce the children to the Special Olympics sponsored by many communities for children with special needs. The number and complexity of sports introduced should depend on the children's developmental level and interest. A theme such as *Exercising to Stay Healthy* complements activities that introduce children to occupations related to physical fitness (Figure 7–5).

Teaching Strategies

Children's continuous movements create natural opportunities to facilitate their physical development. Your role as a teacher is to ensure safety

while supporting their motivation. The children will need sufficient time for active participation to develop and expand their physical abilities. Knowing the sequence of physical skills and appreciation of each child's unique timetable allows you to remain flexible and appropriate for the group. Movement contributes to growth in all areas of development. The guidelines for physical education, from preschool through high school, were established in 1990 and updated in 2008 by the National Association for Sport and Physical Education. Physical participation for a healthy lifestyle is highlighted. Teachers are warned to avoid many of the traditional games in which children are singled out, eliminated with no chance to re-enter the activity, and required to perform predetermined moves. Teachers are encouraged to promote positive attitudes to guide discovery and exploration and to de-emphasize competition (Pica 2006).

You will create a child-centered, playful atmosphere by gently guiding and modeling physical movement skills. Helping children feel competent about themselves has lifetime value. Beneficial lifelong experiences include active participation and appreciation of walking, climbing, gardening, and sports. The positive effects are immediately apparent in elementary school. The children who will particularly benefit will have acquired the fundamental motor skills, such as balancing, throwing, and skipping. Your positive, verbal reinforcement helps children feel successful. When you make positive remarks such as, "That was a fine try," or "You did it," or "That was a super way to slide down," you reassure children. Activities that are slightly ahead of the children's developmental reach bring new ideas and challenges as they practice and gain movement skills (Copple and Bredekamp 2009).

Physical Development with Health, Safety, and Nutrition

Healthy Habits for Young Children

Experiencing activities related to the curriculum area of Health, Safety, and Nutrition facilitates young children's potential for physical well-being and fitness. Children benefit when programs offer activities introducing concepts that encourage healthy and safe practices. Learning about good **health**, safety, and nutrition establishes healthy habits for life. Appropriate and meaningful experiences help children to understand more about themselves and their relationships with others. Begin by arranging safe environments and modeling healthy practices. Keep accident prevention a priority.

Give careful attention to accident control because accidents are the leading cause of death during the preschool years. By modeling healthful and safe behaviors, teachers demonstrate beneficial practices that children and parents can use outside the school. Children need to learn about and appreciate their own body functions and needs. This results in a good sense of self and mental health. Miles realizes that his mouth is dry and that his body needs water. He becomes aware that he is sweating and may need to move toward a shady spot in the sand area. He learns that washing his hands before eating a snack helps eliminate germs and the possibility of avoiding illness. Miles is rewarded when you smile approvingly at him when he waits patiently at the drinking fountain for his turn.

Healthy Habits and Possible Outcomes

Children benefit from schedules that allow flexibility and accommodate routine practices. Scheduling everyday practices contributes to healthful habits. Washing hands before mealtimes and cooking experiences is positive and establishes healthy outcomes. Some schools schedule health-related routines. Children learn that brushing their teeth, drinking water, going to the bathroom, and resting their bodies are important ways to stay healthy. Early learning experiences should be planned to encourage positive outcomes, including the introduction to concepts related to healthful habits (Figure 7–6).

You will contribute to the children's understanding about health by using appropriate

Figure 7–6 Concepts Related to Healthful Habits and Possible Outcomes

Activity Title	Concept
Charting Growth	Babies are little.
	Baby photographs of the children in your program demonstrate growth.
Illness Control	Washing hands is a healthy habit.
	Using nose tissues may help to prevent illness.
	Washing tables keeps them clean.
	Resting gives me energy.
Regular Checkups	A visit to the doctor for a checkup.
	Regular checkups contribute to wellness.

Figure 7–7 Vocabulary Related to Healthful Habits—Possible Outcomes

Activity Title	Good Posture and Position	
Vocabulary	posture	stretch
	straight	body functions
	align	body needs: food, water
	spine	
	exercise	fatigue
	elimination	rest

vocabulary related to the activities. Every activity you plan for young children will have vocabulary related to that experience. The vocabulary list should recommend words that may be used by the teacher and other adults participating with the children in the activity. Vocabulary is an element on the Curriculum Activity Guide. You will find many words are useable for more than one activity, whereas some relate to a specific experience (Figure 7–7). The vocabulary can be printed in parent newsletters and displayed on bulletin boards as a way to expand awareness and reinforce the outcome of activities. naeyc 1a, 1b, 1c, 4b, 4c, 5b, 5c, 6d

© Cengage Learning 2013

Children learn that brushing their teeth, drinking water, going to the bathroom, and resting their bodies are important ways to stay healthy.

Figure 7–8 Healthy Habit Topics for Young Children	
Charting Growth	Measuring, weighing, and charting growth
	Displaying baby and toddler photographs
Illness Control	Washing hands
	Identifying and discussing allergies
	Using tissues
	Washing tables
	Scrubbing tricycles, equipment, materials
	Resting
	Going to the doctor
Regular Checkups	Medical—visitor or trip
	Dental—visitor or trip

Healthy Habits Topics and Activities

The topics for healthy habits will be determined by the children's responses to the initial activities that you schedule. These experiences will have been based on observation and assessment of the children. Additionally, events and occurrences in the children's lives will influence curriculum planning. Begin with topics most familiar to the children, such as washing hands and using tissues to wipe noses (Figure 7–8).

A child's absence from school, resulting from a long-term illness, may stimulate an activity or theme. A child welcoming a pet could also generate interest in a topic related to care of family animals. An activity about height and weight will help children become more aware of their own bodies, **(Curriculum Activity Guide 28)** and an experience learning about exercise and heartbeats supports movement and health curriculum areas. **(Curriculum Activity Guide 39)**.

Safety for Self and Others

A safe environment, designed for young children, establishes a sound foundation for **safety awareness**. For instance, you can position paper towels near the sink and within reach of the children to decrease some of the dripping water that makes floors slippery and unsafe. Place rubberized floor mats in the area where children will use water to further increase safety. Model safe practices within all areas of the school environment that focus on the developmental needs of the children enrolled in your center.

Safety and Possible Outcomes

The activities that you plan related to safety will be influenced by your curricular guidelines and the curriculum approach adapted by your school. The planned activities and spontaneous experiences will integrate opportunities for children to gain knowledge and skills related specifically to safety and integrate with other experiences across the curriculum.

Safety topics for young learners should be reviewed by the program administrator and teaching team. Although you review all activities, a more purposeful review may be needed because some health topics are more sensitive. Health topics could be considered outside acceptability to fit with some families' convictions. It may be essential to obtain input and approval from families. Safety topics offer opportunities for the children to expand their understanding of related concepts, skills, and vocabulary. The possible outcomes could include simple concepts related to the topics.

Figure 7–9 Concepts Related to Safety—Possible Outcomes

Activity Titles	Concepts
Floor Safety	Floors can be slippery. Water on the floors makes them slippery.
Locking Gates	The gate is locked to keep me inside and safe.
	Keys unlock certain gates.
Emergency Help	911 number is used when no one can help.
	Looking for an adult first is important.
Fire Engine Siren	The fire engine siren sounds loudly because it is rushing to help.
	Cars stop when the siren is sounding.

Figure 7–10 Vocabulary Related to Safety—Possible Outcomes

Observed Behavior	Wide-eyed Hyung rushes into the center and says, "The car door almost closed on my hand."
Title	Clap and Close
Goal	To practice clapping and relate to a way to increase safe practices while loading into a car.
Vocabulary	clap, car, door, loud, wait, sound, safe, close

Figure 7–11 Safety Topics for Young Children

Environmental	indoor outdoor
Ecological	pollution
Emergencies	first aid 911 calls
Fire	exit plans fire fighters prevention
Food	containers/labels discoloring
Lost/Found	locate appropriate adult hug a tree OK to talk to police officer
Neighborhood	neighborhood watch play area
Pedestrian	walking paths (ramps, light) right of way parking lot safety
Poison	plants cleaning products unmarked containers
Transportation	seat belts signs bike helmets
Weather	appropriate clothing weather reports warnings shelter

Once considered, concepts can be documented in the Curriculum Activity Guides for reference during the specific activities (Figure 7–9).

The vocabulary related to safety activities assists teachers and adults guiding the experiences for the children to expand their learning opportunities. Watching and listening to the children will give you insight about the children's use of words and provide ideas to encourage their vocabulary in relation to specific activities (Figure 7–10).

Safety Topics and Activities

There are many factors that will influence the safety topics you identify for activities. Program standards and guidelines, your curriculum plan, the children's needs, and influences of the local community affect the selection of activity topics related to safety. Safety education topics can be divided into several categories with regional emphasis deciding what you choose to select. For instance, if you live in Maryland, the presence of shipyards and boating activity will direct the type of safety activities planned. Children who live in northern California are familiar with forestry service and rodeo events. Topics about safety that have relevance for children can be found in most regions (Figure 7–11).

Preplanning activities will help you to manage a curriculum to include safety and will maximize your time. Teachers who listen to children's conversations and elicit parental input find that activities will be more emergent. The curriculum plan should allow flexibility to incorporate activities that respond to the current needs of the group. An example of a teacher-directed experience is Dial 911 (**Curriculum Activity Guide 37**). Once introduced by the teachers in a group time, the materials may be provided in an interest center to allow children to initiate their own participation and choice of experiences.

A school's procedure for safety helps manage activities and experiences offered in interest centers. The environment can signal safety messages to children. For example, you are signaling a safety procedure when you specify the number of children who are allowed to participate in an activity. A sign secured to the side of the ladder to the loft area, where children look at books in a quiet cushioned space, shows that three friends can be in the loft at one time. The laminated sign shows three children sitting in the loft.

Cooking activities can also incorporate safety messages. These may be documented in the Curriculum Activity Guides with specific notations in the *Teaching Strategies*. Specific precautions that list handwashing, number of participants, and caution with electrical appliances and cooking utensils are examples. Another way to communicate safety concepts is to provide messages throughout the indoor and outdoor spaces. Hang a photo on the guinea pig's cage, illustrating the safe way to feed and hold the classroom pet. Your reinforcement about safety with materials and equipment throughout the day is a worthwhile practice for children. naeyc 1a, 1b, 1c, 2a, 2b, 4b, 4c, 5b, 5c

Nutritional Awareness: Preparing and Eating Healthy Snacks and Meals

"It's a watermelon inside," Catherine shouted excitedly when the large, green, round watermelon was cut in half by the teacher. Four other children gathered around the table, waiting for a small wedge to be placed in their bowls. The children washed their hands before joining the snack table activity. Catherine shouted out that she has eaten watermelon before and that she was not supposed to eat the black seeds. This was Catherine's first time watching a whole watermelon cut into pieces. When children, just like Catherine, participate in snack preparation with whole foods, they learn about nutrition. Activities like this one help children expand their knowledge about food: where it grows, what it does for their bodies, and how to make healthy choices.

Nutrition education includes activities that help children enjoy food preparation, snacks, and meals. Children will learn to appreciate different foods and identify cultures and ethnicities with their favorite foods. Experiences emphasizing nutrition education introduce concepts such as trying new foods and learning when our bodies tell us we have eaten enough. **Nutritional awareness**

© Cengage Learning 2013

Cooking experiences introduce children to healthy foods and new ways to prepare familiar foods.

extends to families. Include families in the initial planning stages of nutritional awareness. Invite family members to volunteer at school during cooking activities. They provide the needed extra adults and, more importantly, share foods familiar to their families and cultures.

Nutritional Awareness and Possible Outcomes

Becoming familiar with a variety of foods confirms that the children are participating in emergent learning. Food is a relevant and familiar focus. Nutrition education broadens snacks, mealtime, and cooking activities to help children understand often stated comments such as, "Eat your food, it is good for you." You will offer a relevant and meaningful nutrition experience for young children by encouraging pleasurable mealtimes. Pleasurable mealtimes incorporate conversations among the children and adults who are sitting at the table with them. Use this opportunity to model appropriate table behaviors. A word of caution: you and the program administrator need to carefully monitor for food allergies.

Cooking experiences can involve the children in preparation of their own snacks and some of the foods offered for other mealtimes. When cooking experiences are provided during open activity time, children participate in activities that they choose. Food preparation designed for young children should offer items that are pleasurable to their senses. Children can squeeze floured dough, taste the fresh pineapple, stir and watch the pudding thicken, smell the strawberries boil, and crunch the coconut texture in the banana bread. Cooking experiences offer an optimum way to introduce new foods and new ways to prepare familiar foods. Children's appetites and preferences change. They may say they do not like a particular food because they have never tried it. The same food prepared differently or at another time may be more appealing to them. Artichokes are more fun to eat after watching an adult snip off the thorny tips and check the clock while they steam. Cherry tomatoes are tastier when picked from the school's raised garden beds.

Food preparation activities integrate several curriculum areas while meeting children's developmental needs. Children develop small motor skills when they use cooking utensils. They follow directions when they read the picture recipes. Mathematical awareness is enhanced when children measure, count, and monitor time during cooking experiences. Food preparation activities require safe and sanitary conditions that add benefits related to health and safety (Figure 7–12). **naeyc** 1a, 1b, 1c, 2a, 2b, 4b, 4c, 5b, 5c

Nutritional Awareness Topics and Activities

The children's full participation in nutritional awareness activities will occur when the

> ▶❚❚ **Video Case**
>
> Child Care in Action—Preschool: Cooking Activities
>
> Visit the Early Childhood Education Media Library, and watch the TeachSource Video Case on www.cengagebrain.com
>
> 1. Discuss the instructional strategies the teacher demonstrated in the cooking experiences.
>
> 2. What skills did the children acquire by participating in the cooking activities?

experience offers hands-on opportunities. Your preparation for the experiences will establish procedures to facilitate positive outcomes for the children. Children will enjoy preparing foods in activities that relate to a curriculum theme and interest center. Initially, offer activities that include basic foods. This will encourage children to learn about and enjoy nutrition. You will be able to plan and add spontaneous activities related to nutrition; these will also expand children's knowledge about food sources. Different topics related to nutritional awareness and eating healthy snacks and meals can be developed into meaningful activities. Experiences that fit within curriculum areas also will help facilitate skills in the developmental areas. The experiences may also be organized around a theme or project (Figure 7–13).

Figure 7–12 Skills Related to Nutritional Awareness and Preparation of Healthy Snacks and Meals

Skills	Nutrition and Cooking Activities
baking	scones
comparing	Italian gnocchi, latkes, and American dumplings
counting	number of cherry tomatoes for an individual salad
cooperating	at cooking center with other children
cutting	soft strawberries and hard apples
harvesting	fresh squash from school garden
mixing	tofu burgers
observing	flour mixing with the egg and milk
following	recipe directions
shelling	fresh, whole peanuts
squeezing	grapefruit and oranges for juice
spreading	cream cheese on bagels
stirring	fresh peaches and shaved ice for peach freezes

Figure 7–13 Nutritional Awareness and Preparation of Healthy Snacks and Meals—Topics

Nutrition Education	Cooking Activities
Observing others eat	Growing fruits and vegetables
Eating and enjoying meals	Planning meals and menus
Exploring origins of food	Presenting appealing food
Appreciating cultural preferences	Recognizing food allergies
Experiencing healthy foods	Selecting appropriate ingredients
Becoming an aware consumer	Balancing food selections
Storing food safely	Placing leftover pancakes in bags

Children will enjoy preparing nutritious snacks and will gain additional skills by engaging in activities such as *Food Collage* that **(Curriculum Activity Guide ⟋⟍ 36)** offers children activities within the curriculum area of Health, Safety, and Nutrition. naeyc 4b, 4c, 5b, 5c

Physical Development with Movement

Children keep their bodies in motion and, as they do, they begin to feel themselves in relationship to their surroundings. Movement directs children's interactions with others. Movement also directs much of their thinking behaviors during the early childhood years. The basic fundamental movements that develop first, such as throwing, stacking, running, and squeezing, establish a base for the more complex movements. Children's movement patterns develop progressively, beginning with simple actions and advancing to more complex behaviors. The more complex behaviors combine one or two of the basic motions to achieve a new, more complex task. In the *Picture This . . .* at the beginning of the chapter, Koula exhibited many active behaviors. She achieved movement skills through maturation and experience. She climbed, sat, balanced, and pushed. After accomplishing these primary skills, she was able to combine several of these basic movements into the ability to climb up the rungs of the slide and glide down.

Planning appropriate movement activities requires that you consider experiences that are inclusive of the children participating in your program. When children are asked to move from one area to another, additional space is needed to allow the preschooler who walks with the aid of braces. A ringing bell signals to a child who is visually impaired which direction he needs to move. **(Curriculum Activity Guide 47 ⟋⟍).**

Movement and Perceptual Motor Development

The common denominator in each age group of children is movement (Cherry 2001). When a child moves her body to change places or positions, she completes a movement. Physical fitness for everyone is important. You can validate the importance of physical fitness by planning movement and perceptual motor development activities. You will further validate physical fitness by ensuring that the children experience movement and **perceptual**

motor development activities on a daily basis. Activities planned with the young children's capabilities and needs in focus, will foster the children's confidence and competence.

A child changes his place of location and body position in distinctive ways. Austin moves to another place by walking. He stretches his legs while remaining in the same position. He lifts a heavy block from the grass. Austin completed the movements as he walked, stretched, and lifted. Austin's actions illustrate the three types of basic movement: **locomotor**, non-locomotor, and **manipulative** (Pica 2006; Flinchum, 1975) (Figure 7–14). Plan movement experiences for children in many different ways. Plan for them to:

- move from one place to another (walk, roll, jump forward, backward, sideways)
- move body parts while staying in the same place (twist, stretch, rise up on tiptoes)
- aim for close targets (toss bean bags, bat a plastic ball hanging from a string)
- use their hands and feet to touch and control different objects (place pegs in specific holes, move the computer mouse, turn water hose faucets).

Children will experience movement in their own unique ways. As each child acts and interacts throughout the day, he or she does so with the senses. What the child senses—sees, hears, touches, tastes, smells—depends on previous experiences and current needs. Three-year-old Roxanna approaches a popcorn stringing activity slowly. Four-year-old Whit approaches the same activity in a different way. Whit approaches the table with confidence, having experienced popcorn stringing on numerous occasions during his two-year enrollment. Roxanna's perception of this activity is different. She is newly enrolled at the school and does not have the prior experience with stringing popcorn.

Perceptual abilities determine how well children distinguish people and objects with their eyes and hands. The opportunities children have to experience as much as possible during early childhood are most important. When children experience other people, objects, and materials, they develop

Figure 7–14 Basic Movement Categories	
Locomotor	Body moves to another place.
Non-locomotor	Body moves while remaining in the same place.
Manipulative	Hands and feet move to operate and control objects.

their capabilities to sense, judge, and coordinate messages coming in through their senses. The experiences you thoughtfully plan will give children advantages for discriminating size, shape, distance, and depth. Appropriate activities help children integrate the stimuli coming in through their senses so they will be able to make adjustments to their movements in response to their surroundings (Flinchum 1975). As children engage in movement, they improve their abilities to judge the signals and to anticipate a particular movement or action. As children gain these skills, they feel a sense of mastery. Much of the pleasure children find in large and small motor activities comes from the enjoyment of growing agility (Feeney et al. 2006).

Experiences such as jumping over a tire and maneuvering a tricycle on a path contribute to the children's awareness of the space around them. They will also become mindful of their bodies fitting into a space. This concept is called **spatial awareness**. Throwing a balloon up into the air may give a child information about the quality of force. Touching hidden objects in a bucket of sand may give a child information about shapes, textures, and structures. Selecting specific sizes of beads for stringing may give a three-year-old, such as Rosanna, opportunities to develop her eye–hand coordination. A wide range of perceptual experiences contributes to a child's reaching new, more complex, and purposeful movement.

Movement and Possible Outcomes

Teachers who support children's creative and self-directed movements allow them to express their feelings and enjoy locomotor, non-locomotor, and manipulative motion. Guidelines for movement activity recommend starting the young, inexperienced children with chances to build confidence in a comfortable setting (Cherry 2001). A curriculum plan should include activities to balance fast–slow and loud–quiet experiences. The balance will support children's movements and their perceptual motor skills (Figures 7–15 and 7–16).

Movement Topics and Activities

Body movement is essential to everyone's ability to handle everyday activities. Body movement stimulates thinking, yet the goal of movement development is competence. Movement development activities will contribute to basic movement skills. Activities that will build the basic movement skills may be offered naturally throughout the day in an early care and learning program. Many different types of experiences motivate young children. The

Figure 7–15 Perceptual Motor Skills—Possible Outcomes

Skill	Developing Perceptual Awareness
choosing	Choosing pieces for an art wood sculpture.
matching	Matching sizes, shapes.
moving	Moving in response to judged distance on an obstacle course.
stacking	Stacking blocks by shape and size.
touching	Touching and describing objects with touch.
turning	Turning pages while listening to a story.

experiences that will motivate should challenge their abilities and provide opportunities for them to discover their maturing capabilities. Activities are well suited to young children when they minimize frustration and de-emphasize competition. This will help children enjoy movement and gain basic movement skills (Gerhardt 1973).

Watch children in an open carpeted area. They move under, over, and around the large foam sculptured shapes. As they do, they begin to sense feelings about their own capabilities, about others around them, and the space provided. For example, Austin is in the box. He feels the box is around him. Koula jumps into the box with him. They get out of the box, then move behind the box and begin to become aware of location. They can adjust their bodies to assume a different shape when they crawl through a tunnel. Finally, Koula rolls the ball a short distance to Austin.

You will continue to support the children's spontaneous motions with appropriate planned activities. The children's movements will provide you with additional clues about their interests and needs and will help you to balance locomotor, non-locomotor, and manipulative movement experiences (Pica 2006).

When children use more than one of their senses during movement activities, they have opportunities to advance their perceptual motor skills. *Name of the Animal* is a teacher-directed activity inviting one child at a time to reach into a bucket of dried, unpopped popcorn to locate a plastic animal figurine. The teacher makes the sound that the animal figurine would make. As the child listens to the sound of the hidden animal, he or she can recreate the sound and then name the animal. Four-and-a-half-year-old Song

Figure 7–16 Movement Skills—Possible Outcomes

Movement Category	Movement Skills
Locomotor (Large motor)	crawling walking running jumping rolling climbing hopping leaping galloping sliding skipping
Non-locomotor (Large and small motor)	stretching bending clicking with fingers sitting shaking swaying falling pointing pulling pushing swinging turning twisting
Manipulative (Small motor)	lifting pushing pulling throwing kicking catching ball rolling bouncing
Balance	Balancing small box on head.
Time	Sprinkling the water hose quickly over the flowers.
Direction	Hopping over the tires.
Size	Tiptoeing tiny steps.
Shape	Wiggling like a worm.
Distance	Rolling the ball one foot.
Area	Sitting inside a box.
Volume	Filling the wagon with blocks.

Figure 7–17 Discovering Spatial Awareness with Movement

Balance	Balancing small box on head.
Time	Sprinkling the water hose quickly over the flowers.
Direction	Hopping over the tires.
Size	Tiptoeing tiny steps.
Shape	Wiggling like a worm.
Distance	Rolling the ball one foot.
Area	Sitting inside a box.
Volume	Filling the wagon with blocks.

participated in the activity. She named the animal, then pulled the plastic figurine out of the bucket and visually examined it. This activity required Song's coordination of three of her senses. She needed to gather clues through her sense of touch, hear the teacher imitate the animal's sound through her sense of hearing, and confirm what she saw with her eyes, the sense of sight. Besides using her senses, Song developed her spatial awareness by arranging and touching the figures of animals that she could not see initially. Activities that encourage children to use their large and small movements with discovery will facilitate their growth in the developmental areas and further mature their spatial awareness (Figure 7–17).

Children also develop concepts about space, direction, and size as they move. Their movements help them gain the confidence that allows them to continue exploring and discovering. Your support for the children's spontaneous motions is important. As well, you can complement intentionality with appropriately planned activities that are carefully based on your assessments of the children's abilities. Careful observation results in activities that are meaningful to the children and offer a balance of locomotor, non-locomotor, and manipulative movements. naeyc 1a, 1b, 1c, 4b, 4c, 5b, 5c

Physical Development with Music and Rhythm Activities

Music is the common thread that links different languages, cultures, and ages. Quality programs for young children traditionally and consistently include **music and rhythm** activities for young children. Young learners generally respond to melodies, instruments, songs, fingerplays, and rhythmic motion.

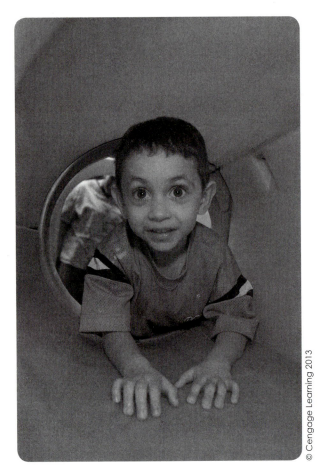

© Cengage Learning 2013

Children naturally express rhythmic sounds and patterns while they move and play.

Figure 7–18 Music and Rhythm Experiences Meet Developmental Needs and Goals

Developmental Focus	Goals
Affective (social-emotional understanding) and Aesthetic	To experience dancing near a partner
	To participate in a group activity
	To express feelings through body movements
Cognitive	To have an opportunity to change sounds into action
	To experience new movements
Physical	To become aware of control of body
	To appreciate feeling of body in space

Music and Rhythm

You will enjoy music and rhythm by creating an environment that allows children to explore, express, and create. Music, singing, and fingerplays can be used to signal transitions in the daily schedule and between activities. Music, singing, and fingerplays help children settle down and relax. Musical and rhythmic experiences can be established to meet developmental needs and help young children enjoy the day and other activities. The creative and enriching activities meet development needs of the children and goals of the program (Figure 7–18). Playing soothing music when welcoming families and children at their early morning arrival will set the tone of the day with a relaxing climate. You can enhance appreciation by showing photographs of pianos when playing keyboard recordings and pictures of mariachi bands when playing Latin ballads.

Children naturally express rhythmic sounds and patterns while they play. You will hear children's expression because you and other members of the teaching team welcome and encourage musical experiences. Music and rhythmic activities will accommodate the curricular planning approach you select. There are numerous resources providing songs to develop children's music awareness and appreciation related to curriculum areas. Creative expression will be promoted with an art activity set up for children to paint a mural together while listening to the music of the *Grand Canyon Suite* (Grofé). Children who participate in a fingerplay called *Five Juicy Apples* will experience mathematical skills in counting and sequencing. A story with actions, *Going on a Picnic*, engages children's listening and rhyming interests. The story with actions will also develop skills in communication and literacy. Invite children to add movements to the songs and fingerplays. You will support their creativeness and appreciation of musical sounds (Figure 7–19 and Figure 7–20).

Music and Rhythm and Possible Outcomes

The benefits of music and rhythm experiences contribute to a tradition welcomed in early care and learning programs. "Music not only provides pleasure and comfort; it also helps improve a child's ability to concentrate and discriminate" (Croft 1990, 68).

Figure 7–19 Going On a Picnic

Tune: *She'll Be Comin' Round the Mountain*

We'll be going on a picnic, that's today, yeah, yeah.

We'll be going on a picnic, that's today, yeah, yeah.

We'll be going on a picnic, we'll be going on a picnic, we'll be going on a picnic, that's today.

We'll be taking six big lunches when we go, yum, yum.

We'll be taking six big lunches when we go, yum, yum.

We'll be taking six big lunches, we'll be taking six big lunches, we'll be taking six big lunches when we go.

We'll be eating all our lunches way out there, chomp, chomp.

We'll be eating all our lunches way out there, chomp, chomp.

We'll be eating all our lunches, we'll be eating all our lunches, we'll be eating all our lunches way out there.

Figure 7–20 Four Juicy Apples

Four juicy apples hanging on a tree
Four juicy apples smiling at me
I shook that tree as hard as I could
Down came one apple. Mum, was it good.

Three juicy apples hanging on a tree.
Three juicy apples smiling at me.
I shook that tree as hard as I could,
Down came one apple. Mum, was it good.

Two juicy apples hanging on a tree.
Two juicy apples smiling at me.
I shook that tree as hard as I could,
Down came one apple. Mum, was it good.

One juicy apple hanging on a tree.
One juicy apple smiling at me.
I shook that tree as hard as I could,
Down came no apples just for me.

When you listen and watch young children, you learn about their reactions and needs. Some children need time to observe the activities before joining the group. Some children react quickly to a new sound or instruments. Others take time to listen. Music and rhythm activities will contribute to the development of skills in various developmental areas. Children will develop abilities including concentrating, discriminating, exploring, and listening (Figure 7–21). Appropriate teacher guidance respects the young children who need to observe the activity for a while. You welcome them when they are ready.

Younger preschoolers will move their hands and fingers while quietly watching the teacher and listening to the words of the songs and fingerplays. Days and weeks may pass before children coordinate hand movements to the music and words. You will increase the likelihood of all the children's participation by providing appropriate props to the music and rhythm experiences. You

Figure 7–21 Music and Rhythm Skills—Possible Outcomes

Concentrating	on number of drum beats to the words of the song
Creating	a new fingerplay to a familiar chant
	words to a familiar tune
Discriminating	sounds from tambourine and cymbals
	high-pitched tones and lowpitched tones
Exploring	fast and slow movements musical instruments
Expressing	feelings in rhythmic movements mood changes
Listening	to words and timing in a song
	to pitch and tone of songs
Relaxing	to flute music
	to tunes and melodies sung in different languages
Respecting	songs and dances from many cultures
	creative musical expression
Rhyming	stories and fingerplays with action

will create a welcoming atmosphere with your positive attitudes toward singing and creative movement. You will model, suggest, and describe movements that respond to the children's developmental levels. Describing and suggesting a movement such as hopping like a popping corn kernel and jumping like a quick bunny are successful strategies for encouraging children's participation. Add comments like these to your actions. Also, an activity that invites children to dance with scarves will support their creative expression while encouraging responsiveness to music and rhythm **(Curriculum Activity Guide 48 ⌐⌐).**

The children's enthusiasm for movement and related experiences will be supported with interest centers. These centers can be arranged to create interest and appreciation for physical development, health, safety, nutrition, perceptual motor development, and music and rhythm.

Music and Rhythm Topics and Activities

Music and rhythm activities provide occasions for children to appreciate the music that their families enjoy. Activities will also introduce children to the music played and enjoyed by other families. As young learners enjoy songs and rhythmic movements from many other cultures, they acquire knowledge about the world outside their immediate community. The pleasurable use of basic instruments, such as drums, gives hands-on experience with music. Comments about the historical and cultural origin add pleasure and information about drums and music exploration. While exploring topics related to the wider world of music, the primary focus should be the enjoyment of these experiences to the participating children (Figure 7–22).

Instruments add to children's knowledge. They learn that a triangle makes one sound that lasts for a long time. A tambourine makes two sounds because it is a little drum with jingles on the side. Drums produce many sounds, quiet when the fingers tap and louder if hit with a stick. Instruments integrate well with creative movement activities to extend children's awareness of their body rhythms. Curriculum integration occurs as themes and curriculum areas blend with the provisions for activities that meet the developmental needs of children **(Curriculum Activity Guide 49 ⌐⌐). naeyc** 1a, 1b, 1c, 2a, 2b, 4b, 4c, 5a, 5b, 5c, 6d

---

Figure 7–22 Music and Rhythm Activity Topics

Fingerplays	Simple hand, finger, and arm movements. Gestures dramatize words to music and songs such as *Open, Shut Them.*
Instruments	Instruments such as drums, bells, rhythm sticks, cymbals, tambourines, and triangles may be purchased. Staff and volunteers can make clappers, drums, and shakers. Teachers use autoharp or guitar to accompany children's songs. Guests invited to introduce instruments such as harp, piano, guitar, flute, and saxophone.
Records, Tapes, CDs, DVDs	Recorded music (record albums, tapes, CDs and DVDs) played for a specific musical experience, as a child-directed individual activity, or for background music. Selection variety should range from international folk songs to classical and instrumental.
Rhythmic Activities	Beats in patterns provide rhythmic experiences. Rhythmic patterns found throughout Indoor and outdoor classrooms: rainwater dripping down pipes and bubbling aquarium. Child can clap hands and stomp feet to copy rhythmic pattern.
Songs	Simple, repetitious words using familiar words and objects. Spontaneous singing, initiated by children and teachers, of traditional and creative songs planned for group time, transition, and special activities.

Thinking about What You Have Learned

✔ List three activity topics for small movement and three for large movement. The activities need to be suitable for supporting the physical development of children ages three to five. Remember to consider assessment of the children as you select the activity topics.

✔ Make three copies of the Curriculum Activity Guide template (appendix B) or download the template from the companion website. Complete the forms by developing activities with a fitness theme. Prepare one health activity, one nutritional awareness activity, and one safety activity.

✔ Review Figure 7–17 (p. 143) "Discovering Spatial Awareness with Movement." Prepare an activity using an idea from the list. Complete a Curriculum Activity Guide for this idea.

✔ Describe in a paragraph the resources available on the websites listed below:

   Center for Disease Control and Prevention
   http://www.cdc.gov/
   KidsHealth. Org
   http://www.kidshealth.org/
   PE Central
   http://pe.central.vt.edu/

✔ PE Central is designed for elementary school-age children. Survey the ideas provided and modify three of the activity ideas to suit preschool-age children. Modify one of the selected activities to accommodate children with limited visual ability.

Chapter References

Cherry, Claire, and Dianne M. Nielsen. 2001. *Creative movement for the developing child: An early childhood handbook for non-musicians.* 3rd. ed. Torrance, CA: Fearon Teacher Aids.

Cook, Ruth E., Annette Tessier, and M. Diane Klein. 2000. *Adapting early childhood curricula for children in inclusive settings.* 5th ed. Englewood Cliffs, NJ: Merrill.

Copple, Carole, and Sue Bredekamp. eds. 2009. *Developmentally appropriate practice in early childhood programs serving children from birth through age 8.* 3rd ed. Washington, DC: National Association for the Education of Young Children.

Croft, Doreen. J. 1990. *An activities handbook for teachers of young children.* 5th ed. Boston: Houghton Mifflin.

Feeney, Stephanie, Doris Christensen, and Eva Moravcik. 2009. *Who am i in the lives of children?* 8th ed. Upper Saddle River, NJ: Prentice Hall.

Flinchum, Betty M. 1975. *Motor development in early childhood: A guide for movement education with ages 2 to 6.* St. Louis, MO: Mosby.

Gerhardt, Lydia A. 1973. *Moving and knowing: The young child orients himself in space.* Englewood Cliffs, NJ: Prentice Hall.

Pica, Rae. 2000. *Experiences in movement: With music, activities and theory.* 2nd ed. Albany, New York: Delmar.

Pica, Rae. 2006. Physical fitness and the early childhood curriculum. *Young Children,* 64(2), 66–67.

Spodek, Bernard, and Olivia N. Saracho. 1994. *Dealing with individual differences in the early childhood classroom.* White Plains, NY: Longman.

Affective (Social-Emotional Understanding) and Aesthetic Development: Art, Creative Dramatics, and Social Understanding Activities

© Cengage Learning 2013

Picture This . . .

Tierney, a second-semester student teacher, arrived at the practicum seminar class without her usual beaming smile. She remained quiet during the opening discussion. Hearing the predictable question, "Did you experience a situation during your field experience that made you uncomfortable?" Tierney shifted her position, leaned forward, and said, "Yes, now I understand that poem you read in class about the little boy."

Tierney's field assignment for the college seminar class takes her into the community twice a week. At the site this morning, she said that a craft activity was arranged by a substitute teacher. Tierney related the following incident:

"The children gathered around the craft table. They shaped and twisted crepe paper. The substitute teacher directed the children to glue the crepe paper shapes onto a small, wooden stick. She then told the children to push the stick into the glob of modeling dough. The substitute teacher took each child's glob of dough with the crepe paper-shaped 'flower' and placed it inside a small, plastic container."

Tierney sighed and continued, "It is not that the activity idea was so off . . . it is how the sub directed the children and what happened at the end of the day. I was assigned to help the children collect their work just before their parents arrived. When I handed Ryan his flowerpot, he immediately shook his head saying, 'That's not mine, that's not mine.' I turned over the flowerpot and pointed to his name written on the bottom. Ryan stood very still, shaking his head, and repeating, 'That's not the one I did!' His eyes watered when he saw his dad walk through the door. Not knowing what to do, I handed the pot to Ryan's father. Ryan walked away, ignoring the flowerpot. When I went to the workroom, I thought about Ryan and began to understand why Ryan was so upset. The substitute teacher was in the workroom continuing to reshape and to rearrange the children's efforts. So, the flowerpot I tried to hand to Ryan was not his . . . it was an adult's finished product. Ryan didn't recognize the flowerpot because it was different from the one that he created."

GUIDE TO READING CHAPTER 8

Chapter Outline

Affective Development
  Social-Emotional Understanding is Affective
    Development
  Social-Emotional Understanding—Harmony, Equity,
    and Respect
  Emotional Development Skills and Possible
    Outcomes
  Emotional Development Activities
  Social Development Skills and Possible
    Outcomes
  Social Development Activities
Aesthetic Development
Aesthetic Development Skills and Possible
  Outcomes
  Aesthetic Development Activities
Connecting Curriculum for Affective and Aesthetic
  Development
  Integrating Activities
  Teaching Strategies
Aesthetic Development with Art
  Art
  Art Possible Outcomes
  Art Topics and Activities
Aesthetic Development with Creative Dramatics
  Creative Dramatics
  Creative Dramatics Possible Outcomes
  Creative Dramatics Topics and Activities
    Dramatic Play
    Guided Drama

  Puppetry
  Sociodramatics
Affective and Aesthetic Development with Social
  Understanding
  Social Understanding
  Social Understanding Possible Outcomes
  Social Understanding Topics and Activities
    Experiences to Strengthen Connections and
      Relationships
Thinking About What You Have Learned

Learning Objectives

After reading this chapter, you will be able to

1. Define affective and aesthetic development.
2. Analyze possible outcomes for emotional and social development.
3. Evaluate the children's skills while they participate in art activities.
4. Recognize the benefits of creative dramatics, dramatic play, guided drama, puppetry, and sociodramatics.
5. Discuss social understanding as a valuable curriculum area.

Key Terms

National Association for the Education of Young Children (NAEYC) Standards for Initial Early Childhood Professional Preparation Programs met by this chapter:

Standard 1: Promoting Child Development and Learning

1a: Knowing and understanding young children's characteristics and needs, from birth through age 8.

1b: Knowing and understanding the multiple influences on development and learning.

1c: Using developmental knowledge to create healthy, respectful, supportive, and challenging learning environments for young children.

Standard 3: Observing, Documenting, and Assessing to Support Young Children and Families

3a: Understanding the goals, benefits, and uses of assessment – including its use in development of appropriate goals, curriculum, and teaching strategies for young children.

3b: Knowing about and using observation, documentation, and other appropriate assessment tools and approaches including the use of *technology* in documentation, assessment and data collection.

Standard 4: Using Developmentally Effective Approaches

4a: Understanding positive relationships and supportive interactions as the foundation of their work with young children.

4b: Knowing and understanding effective strategies and tools for early education, including appropriate uses of technology.

4c: Using a broad repertoire of developmentally appropriate teaching/learning approaches.

4d: Reflecting on own practice to promote positive outcomes for each child.

Standard 5: Using Content Knowledge to Build Meaningful Curriculum

5a: Understanding content knowledge and resources in academic disciplines: language and literacy; the arts—music, creative movement, dance, drama, visual arts; mathematics; science; physical activity, physical education, health and safety; and social studies.

5b: Knowing and using the central concepts, inquiry tools, and structures of content areas or academic disciplines.

5c: Using own knowledge, appropriate early learning standards, and other resources to design, implement, and evaluate meaningful, challenging curricula for each child.

Affective Development

In *Picture This*, Ryan rejected the flowerpot that was handed to him. Ryan was capable of expressing his feelings. He was unhappy and refused the work because it was not the one he created. Ryan's behavior was influenced by the interaction with his family. Ryan began attending preschool at three and half with capabilities to adjust to new people and to express his feelings. Ryan's affective development, his social-emotional understanding, was healthy and mature for a four-year-old preschooler. Programs for young children generally offer experiences that respond to the children's needs and contribute to their maturation in all the developmental areas. Programs may not always be able to guarantee that all volunteers and all substitutes will follow appropriate practices. The experiences at Ryan's preschool no doubt offered affirming activities and interactions on a regular basis. Appropriately planned experiences that encourage positive interactions and relationships allow affective (social-emotional

understanding) and aesthetic development to flourish.

Most of the activities planned in the curriculum areas can be designed to also promote emotional and social development. The affective (social-emotional understanding) and aesthetic areas in this chapter are particularly relevant to three curriculum areas. The developmental focus area of affective (social-emotional understanding) and aesthetic development are particularly relevant to the curriculum areas of art, creative dramatics, and social understanding.

As you begin focusing on affective (**social-emotional understanding**) and aesthetic development, you will contemplate experiences for the children that add to their psychological, social, emotional, and creative growth. The responsive experiences you plan will address the children's needs and contribute to their healthy personalities, positive relationships, and creative abilities.

Play remains one of the most favorable ways to encourage children's affective and aesthetic development. When children play, they can express their own feelings and begin to recognize the feelings of others. When they play, they interact with other children and adults. Children can be free during play to make decisions, imagine, and create. Relaxing materials calm children. Your support and understanding during play and other experiences at your school will ensure that the children's unique identities emerge. naeyc 1a, 1b, 1c, 4a

Social-Emotional Understanding Is Affective Development

After an initial adjustment period, most children are excited about attending preschool. However, some children are distressed and cry when their parents depart. Crying is one way that children express their feelings to family members and teachers. Some children will suck their thumb for comfort when distressed; some will frown; and others will hide behind their parent or caregiver who is bringing them into the school. Children also express their feelings differently in reaction to anger, fear, surprise, and pleasure. You will gain insight into children's emotions as you watch them respond to people, events, and the environment. Emotionally healthy children will learn early to express themselves with the guidance of adults who model acceptable behaviors. Rodney's comment, "I'm sad I can't take the fish to my home today," is an acceptable reaction. Rodney is able to communicate his feelings to Teacher Ellie in a positive and communicative manner.

The foundation for healthy emotional behavior begins in infancy with the development of a sense of trust. The stages of social development and emotional development describe tasks and achievements specific to each stage of development (Erickson 1996). Parents have dreams that their children will experience life positively. Positive behaviors more likely lead to inner confidence, a sense of purpose and involvement, and meaningful, constructive relationships with others. Life experiences considered important include successful school and work experiences, and, primarily, happiness. Children who have high self-esteem are more likely to be happy (Briggs 1975).

Self-esteem is an important healthy characteristic that tends to lead to positive life experiences. Self-esteem is an outlook associated with a sense of self-respect and a feeling of self-worth. Children's self-esteem, how they feel about themselves, and their emotional reactions influence the kinds of friends they will choose. Self-esteem affects how children get along with others.

Self-worth forms the core of children's personalities and determines what they make of their abilities (Briggs 1975). Daniel Goleman (2006) discusses that the environment and the people around children contribute to their feelings of self-worth. Feelings of comfort, confidence, and competence help children begin to handle their emotions such as happiness, sadness, anger, distress, and joy.

Children have an increasing need for independence, which is regulated by their temperament and the adults in their environment. During the early childhood years, children begin handling their feelings, including happiness, sadness, anger, distress, and joy. How we handle our feelings will be influenced by the cultural context of our families and community. naeyc 1a, 1b, 1c

Social-Emotional Understanding— Harmony, Equity, and Respect

Social-emotional understanding extends to acknowledging others. Children will interact with others outside of their family when they begin attending an early childhood program. Some children will meet children who are different from themselves. The other children and teachers may speak a different language. The differences generate ideal opportunities to initiate understanding about harmony, equity, and respect. Children will be familiar with their family customs and rituals. The prospect is good for creating favorable feelings about differences. Children can begin to appreciate distinctions in appearances, language, and behaviors during the preschool years. Activities offered to encourage social-emotional understanding for others can also build children's knowledge, concept, and pride of their own family identity. Quality early childhood programs will foster positive views about our multicultural and multilingual society. Teachers can encourage understanding with statements such as "Everyone's looks are unique and different." Culturally appropriate activities can respond to the diversity of the children's cultures and languages. They assist all children in experiencing and valuing diversity (Derman-Sparks and Edwards 2010). Linguistic and cultural continuity between children's homes and early childhood programs and early childhood are important. Include family pictures and drawings of children with family members in the classroom environment. Have audio recordings of family member's voices, as well as music, books and other materials that reflect cultural identity in a positive way (Derman-Sparks and Edwards 2010). naeyc 1a, 1b, 1c, 4a, 4b, 4c

Emotional Development Skills and Possible Outcomes

Early childhood is a valuable time for children to achieve a growing sense of self. This is also the time for them to develop an appreciation for other people in their surroundings. Affective (social-emotional understanding) and aesthetic experiences help children adjust to separation from home, gain self-confidence, and achieve competence. The respect and value you have for children will affect their feeling about themselves. "Ronnie, thanks for scrubbing the snack table; it looks really great, doesn't it?" Children will become aware of religions and cultures and respect the differences when you do so. For instance, when you say "Jana, we are so glad you brought your great-grandfather's hat from Bolivia," you confirm what is important to her family. You will support opportunities for children to make choices and resolve conflicts by setting limits and accepting their feelings, such as "I can see, Bonnie, that it makes you unhappy to have to wait. But, there is only room for four friends to play in this block area. Let's put your name on the wait list."

Emotional development of children is encouraged by your nurturing behaviors and the activities you organize for them. It is important to respond to the children as individuals, as members of families, and as members of groups interacting within your program. Your positive responses will enhance possible outcomes related to emotional skills (Figure 8–1).

Emotional Development Activities

Children who sense that they are valued develop positive concepts about themselves. Their experiences in school settings can enhance their self-concepts. The experiences offered at early care and learning programs can facilitate children's emotional development. Children are more likely to develop emotionally when teachers are responsive

to them. Interacting caringly with children begins by accepting their feelings and emotions. Your kindness and considerate interactions with young children help them gain skills. The skills will enable them to express their feelings in appropriate ways. One way to establish a responsive and caring school setting is to arrange a predictable routine for the children. When children know what to expect, they respond more effectively both to routine activities and to unexpected changes. Certain activities, such as water play and fingerpainting are particularly effective at reducing tension. Activities like these tend to relieve anxiety while creating a calming space.

Activities can be arranged to allow children to make choices about their participation in experiences. Stretching exercises contribute to the development of self-esteem and offer an alternative for children who do not want to participate in "messy activities." You will be able to enhance children's self-esteem by modeling specific behaviors. You will have opportunities throughout each day to encourage care, sharing, empathy, and sympathy. You will have chances to model respect and cooperation and acknowledge those behaviors in the children. You have multiple chances each day to illustrate problem-solving skills, especially as you positively communicate ideas and welcome the children's comments. Plenty of ideas for activities related to emotional development will emerge. While moving through the daily schedule, make note of the children's actions and needs; from those notes specific activities will emerge for you to create an integrated curriculum **(Curriculum Activity Guide 9 and 10** ___). naeyc 1a, 1b, 1c, 4a, 4b, 4c, 4d

Social Development Skills and Possible Outcomes

Early care and learning programs are generally the first group situation outside the family and home that children encounter. These programs offer opportunities for children to cooperate and become part of a group. In a welcoming group situation, children become aware of other's behaviors and thinking. They learn that there are different ways to do something and that not everyone shares the thinking or language or food of their own family. Young children function best in small groups that are suitable for their social development. The definition of a small group, however, is often determined by the age of the children and the type of activity. A group of four could be considered small if the children were four-year-olds. Yet, if eight ten-year-olds

> **Figure 8–1** Emotional Development Skills—
> Possible Outcomes
>
> Accepting limits
>
> Appreciating pleasurable experiences
>
> Establishing self-regulating behaviors
>
> Expanding or achieving a sense of trust
>
> Expressing and clarifying feelings positively
>
> Recognizing personal abilities

participated in an activity, their group could be considered small as well.

Early childhood programs provide smaller versions of communities and societies. In their small society, the preschool, children can gain social competence as they interact with others. Specific activities planned for social development enable children to develop skills that will prepare them to interact in social situations in the larger community and society. In social contexts, children will need to listen, consider what was said, and, most likely, make decisions.

Activities planned for **social development** can be offered to help children develop a sense of community. Developing a positive sense of community may shield children from societal changes that negatively affect their social health and that of their families (Garbarino 1999). You will reduce children's vulnerability to societal negatives by supporting worthwhile interactions among adults and children in your program. You can contribute to healthy social development by acknowledging children's considerate and caring behaviors. For example, Vincent tells Georgia to take one of his freshly baked biscuits from the basket he is holding. Later in the morning, Georgia runs over to help Vincent when he falls off a tricycle. Your approving smile encourages Georgia and Vincent to continue their nurturing behaviors toward one another.

Children will acquire social skills as they mature. They will become less centered on their own needs and thoughts. With supportive and caring adults guiding them, children will develop prosocial skills. These are the abilities to cooperate, give, share, and care. Prosocial skills allow us to show empathy and sympathy for others. While children are in the preschool years, their prosocial skills are developing. You will model prosocial skills in your care for the children and interaction with their parents and other adults. Prosocial skills might also be considered an aspect of altruism. Altruistic behaviors or altruism is our unselfish interest in helping others. Prosocial skills and altruism require that we understand others' point of view. For this reason, young children have varying capacities for prosocial skills. Children will be further motivated in an environment that is suitably organized and supervised. Prosocial skills prepare children for responsible group participation while they are in school and throughout their lives.

Teachers who reinforce desirable behaviors find that young children capably demonstrate empathy, sensitivity, and negotiating skills. For example, Caroline handed Ralph her large house-painting brush when his brush fell on the ground. She said, "You can use mine, and I'll get another from Teacher Jane." Caroline showed concern and empathy for Ralph. Desirable social skills are more likely to emerge when children watch cooperating behaviors, interact with caring adults, participate in positive family activities, and receive appropriate guidance to control natural impulses (Figure 8–2). **naeyc** 1a, 1b, 1c, 4a, 4b, 4c, 4d

---

▶❚❚　Video Case

Preschool: Social Development, Cooperative Learning and Play

Visit the Early Childhood Education Media Library, and watch the TeachSource Video Case on www.cengagebrain.com

1. Discuss the advantages for children who are offered opportunities for problem solving with others in a group.

2. What would be your role as a teacher facilitating preschool children's problem solving in a group?

Social Development Activities

Benjamin, Christian, and John rapidly move large flannel shapes of firefighting equipment on a board secured to the outside of the wheel-toy shed. The boys laugh and talk as they work together to recreate a firefighting station. The activity meets several social development goals. The boys acquire decision-making skills. They decide whose turn it is to move one of the flannel pieces. They also cooperate about the placement of the flannel

---

Figure 8–2 Social Development Skills—Possible Outcomes

Caring

Cooperating

Empathizing

Giving

Learning about their community

Making appropriate choices

Participating with others and in small groups

Respecting differences

Sharing

Sympathizing

Using empathetic words and gestures

shapes. The experience allows them to cooperate because there is ample space for them to move freely in front of the flannel board. In addition, this activity is appropriately supervised by adults. The teacher's aide stands close enough to answer questions without interfering in the boys' play. In this way, she supports the small group interaction. An activity such as, *When I Was a Baby*, might increase children's awareness of themselves. They would also acquire information about their own growth. When children learn more about themselves, it builds their confidence and personal image.

(Curriculum Activity Guide 11). This activity, like many of the other teacher-guided experiences, could be converted to a child-initiated one. The experience could also be offered in an interest center where the *When I Was a Baby* focus expands in the dramatic play area with special baby props and mini-albums of the children when they were babies (Figure 8–3). The activity *Litter Patrol* gives the children chances to interact in a group while developing a sense of pride and responsibility for their community. **(Curriculum Activity Guide 12)**. naeyc 1a, 1b, 1c, 4a, 4b, 4c, 4d

---

Figure 8–3 Interest Center Guide – Domestic Scene – Baby Nurturing

Interest Center   *Domestic Scene-Baby Nurturing*   **Theme**   *I'm Me, I'm Special*

Art	Cooking	Literacy	Quiet Reading	Outside Art	Outside Large Motor
Block	Computer	Manipulatives	Science	Outside Circle	Outside and/Water
Circle	Dramatic Play	Music/Rhythm	Sensorial	Outside Garden	Trike Path

Interest Center Guidelines   **Approximate Age Range**   *3–5*

Baby props to be introduced during group time then added to dramatic play interest center area.

Developmental Focus   **Physical**   Affective and Aesthetic   **Cognitive and Language**

Curriculum Area   *Social Understanding*

Interest Center Materials

Constant   *Play food and dishes*
                   Adult dress-up clothing

Featured   *Baby props, dolls*
                   Non-bias photos of families nurturing babies
                   Baby bed, rocker, books

Preparation/Set Up

1. *Locate and laminate pictures/photos*
2. *Locate baby props; prepare labels for shelves*
3. *Add baby props to Dramatic Play Interest Center*

Teaching Strategies

1. *Introduce baby props during group time.*
2. *Teacher helps children set up props in area.*
3. *Teacher facilitates children's understanding of baby nurturing with appreciation of diverse ways to hold and carry babies.*

Possible Outcomes for the Child or Children

Concepts   *All babies need special care.*
                   Families including mothers, fathers, and relatives care for babies.

Skills   *Social understanding and caring*
                   Social interaction

Vocabulary   *family, mother, father, baby, care, relatives, hold, soothe*

Child Participation   **Date**

Aesthetic Development

Aesthetic expression is natural and spontaneous for some children. Children can create sounds, move their fingers through the sand, and draw on frosty windows. They can decide that an egg carton is a perfect oven for donuts made of playing dough. Quality early childhood settings nurture children's natural drive to imagine. Teachers who understand development support children's creativity. You will enrich the program you provide for young children by giving them choices of materials. They will be receptive to materials that are pleasing to, and involve, their senses.

Aesthetics is an essential part of the early childhood curriculum. If you plan to include aesthetics, you will enjoy watching children discovering nature, beauty, and art. In particular, you will see them experience the world with their senses. This is possible by surrounding children with many opportunities to appreciate and to explore their world. Enjoy, with the children, a spider web, the design of a poster, a cloud formation, the feel of a seashell, and the sounds of a violin.

Aesthetic Development Skills Possible Outcomes

Appreciation of nature and beauty is a beneficial outcome to activities planned to develop aesthetic skills. Children could potentially develop favorable emotional behaviors. When they enjoy arranging flowers in a vase, they could experience the pleasures of scents and color. They would also develop their observational skills and could illustrate their originality. Certain activities would give children pleasure in music sounds and rhythm and recognition of musical variations (Figure 8–4).

Figure 8–4 Aesthetic Development Skills—
Possible Outcomes

Appreciating nature and beauty

Enjoying sounds, music, and rhythm

Illustrating originality

Observing color, shape, and form

Releasing and expressing feelings

Recognizing musical variations

Responding empathetically to others' feelings and behaviors

Aesthetic Development Activities

The potential for children to develop aesthetic awareness increases when programs for them support exploration of natural objects and surroundings. Children will increase their aesthetic skills when they are encouraged to respond to the beauty in nature and art. Child-initiated and teacher-guided activities foster enjoyment and a sense of wonder. (**Curriculum Activity Guide 50**).

Connecting Curriculum for Affective and Aesthetic Development

One of the means for achieving affective and aesthetic development is to focus on the process of the activities rather than on the product. Four-year-olds, such as Benjamin, Christian, and John, in the previous example, (page 154), enjoyed placing flannel figures of fire engines on the board. In doing so, they gained skills in cooperation. The experience also contributed to their developing prosocial skills. Open-ended and flexible activities allow children to make choices. You will be most supportive of their developing skills by redirecting their behavior as needed. As well, you will enhance their experiences by providing props and equipment that will augment their play. As you do so, you will be communicating by using appropriate language. You will soon recognize the preschoolers who are gaining prosocial behaviors with this support. In addition, you will admire how children begin to express their sense of wonder about nature and beauty. naeyc 1a, 1b, 1c, 4a, 4b, 4c, 4d

Integrating Activities

The observations and assessments of the children in your program will direct the types of activities for affective and aesthetic development. Comprehensive curriculum planning suggests that you balance activities among the curriculum areas as you meet the developmental needs of the children. As you integrate activities by balancing the experiences across the curriculum areas, the experiences will align with the goals of your program. For example, a teacher's observation of three-year-old Lew indicated that he walked up to the flannel board activity three times. Each time Lew watched Benjamin, Christian, and John move around the flannel figures of the fire engines. Lew watched the four-year-old boys from his perch on a tricycle. An additional activity might emerge from the Lew's interest. It suggests that you plan additional activities related to fire engines and flannel boards. The additional activities could be planned to integrate curriculum areas, such as math and science, and one of the developmental focus areas; for example, cognitive. An activity such as designing a trike path detour, might meet Lew's interest since he has been observed riding a trike throughout the week. Designing a trike path detour is the type of activity that will help Lew and other children with skills in one or more of the developmental focus areas work as well with activities in more than one curriculum area; it could tie in with a theme like Transportation (Figure 8–5). Lew's social participation in the new experience may remain minimal, yet the activity allows him to experience a group interaction that fits his stage of development. The three older preschoolers model social skills such as problem solving, negotiating, and cooperation as they join in the added activity.

Listening and observing the children will offer ways for you to enhance the curriculum. Curriculum themes can be proposed in long-term curriculum planning that will specifically relate to developing children's social and emotional needs. There are particular themes that

© Cengage Learning 2013

Children gain an appreciation of nature and beauty when they experience specific activities planned for nurturing aesthetic skills.

could help children with what might be strange and fearful to them. Other themes that will support affective (social-emotional understanding) and aesthetic development include topics about family, celebrations, emotions, and character building. (Figure 8–6). naeyc 1a, 1b, 1c, 3a, 3b, 4a, 4b, 4c, 4d, 5d

---

Figure 8–5 Activities Integrate Developmental Focus Area, Curriculum Areas, and Theme

Developmental Focus Area	Affective (social-emotional understanding) and Aesthetic
Curriculum Areas	*Health, Safety, and Nutrition* Activity: Safety on the path
	Social Understanding Activity: Sharing rides with friends
	Mathematics Activity: Counting passengers in vehicles
Theme	Transportation

Figure 8–6 Themes Encouraging Affective (Social-Emotional Understanding) and Aesthetic Development

Social	Emotional	Aesthetic
Helping My Community	Rain, Wind, Thunder	Colors Everywhere
Friends	Family Traditions	Art in Our Museum
Celebrations	Feelings	Music We Like
We Are Alike and Different	Family Members	Sculptures in Our Park

Teaching Strategies

As an early childhood professional, you are second only to the children's families. You definitely and directly influence the development of children's identity and their social behaviors. Your attitude and values affect the flow of the daily schedule and the successful pace of activities. Teachers who enjoy and understand the curiosity of young children will respond to them by creating supportive, safe environments. When children feel secure, they gain the confidence to explore new objects and spaces. Teachers who address the goals of affective and aesthetic development will anticipate the needs of children and then respond with experiences that are relevant to their experiences. Children who know what to expect will adjust more readily to the rules needed for group interaction. When you are flexible, you meet the changing needs of children and maintain a consistent yet relaxed atmosphere for care and learning.

Aesthetic Development with Art

Art

Appropriate **art** activities encourage relaxation, exploration, and pleasure. Children benefit from art experiences when the activities are soothing and developmentally focused on their needs. Children who engage in art develop

Appropriate art activities for preschoolers encourage them to relax, explore, and enjoy creating.

© Cengage Learning 2013

concepts in other curriculum areas while they aesthetically enjoy such activities as finger-painting, paper sculpting, molding clay, and making playing dough. Mural painting is another art activity and one that children will take pleasure in doing together. Mural painting involves and exposes the children to many different tasks. First, they must observe and help measure a long piece of butcher paper to fit across a fence or other space open for securing the paper. This task introduces children to beginning mathematical concepts. When the children paint on the expansive piece of butcher paper, they may become aware of science-related ideas. They may observe changes in colors as they mix tempera paint. When children paint a mural they may express feelings about themselves. They may also talk about others as they interact and together spread paint on the same stretch of paper.

The front of home refrigerators are testament to the priority that families give to art work. You will, like other teachers who favor best practices, support the process of art work rather than the end product. The value of art is in the unlimited ways children express themselves. They can explore the paste, move the paintbrush across the mural paper, and look at each other's work. During the process of art, children will be squeezing, pulling, patting, pounding, and rolling clay. They will be hanging, collecting, and water painting on different surfaces. The "doing" is more important to the children's development than the way it's done or what the final product might be or look like. Teachers who value the artistic process will avoid materials that coerce children to copy the samples provided by the adult. You will delight in seeing children manipulate, explore, and express.

Art Possible Outcomes

Art activities promote fine-motor coordination and sensorial discovery. Cold earth clay smells different and feels good to children who squeeze, pinch, and pull a damp ball of it. Art activities encourage the development of affective and aesthetic skills including appreciating nature, coordinating small movement, expressing feelings, and making choices (Figure 8–7).

As you prepare art activities, remember that younger preschoolers may approach new activities hesitantly. They might first experiment by

Figure 8–7 Skills Related to Art – Possible Outcomes

Activity Title	Skills
Taking Photographs of Flowers	Appreciating nature
Mixing Modeling or Playing Dough	Coordinating small movement
Painting with Foaming Soap	Expressing feelings
Creating Seashell Collage	Making choices

Figure 8–8 Basic Art Materials

Material	Activity Use
Clay	Manipulating and molding
Collage	Miscellaneous items such as buttons, golf tees, magazine pictures
Crayons	Drawing and rubbing
Chalk	Drawing Dip in starch and draw
Pencils/Markers	Drawing Tracing Writing
Glue	Constructing
Paint	Fingerpainting Roller painting Sponge painting String painting Cotton swab painting
Paper	Collage Cut Paste Paint
Prints	Shaped sponges Wood blocks Rubber stamps Objects
Modeling Dough	Mold prepared modeling dough Make modeling dough
Scissors	Cutting

touching, dipping, and spreading the fingerpaint or adhesive paste. The skills of young children continue to develop as they work with the same types of materials repeatedly. A specific type of art activity can be varied by providing different surfaces for the paint, chalk, clay, and felt-tip pens. When burlap is substituted for paper, children enjoy watching the paint absorb and adhere differently than it does to paper.

The strength of your indoor and outdoor environments influences the way art activities progress. The art interest center should have low tables, easels, sinks with running water, and open-organized shelves. These shelves can be stocked with materials for the children's creative expression. The shelves allow children to select and use the materials throughout the day when activity centers are made available. The materials can include various types and sizes of paper, scissors, hole punches, rulers, markers, crayons, paste, glue, and items for collage. Using found items from nature contributes texture, color, and additional variety. Smocks and aprons protect children as they attempt art activities that tend to be messy. Water buckets and sponges, placed near the art activities, encourage children to take responsibility to independently wipe up spills. To avoid some spills, purchase paintbrushes with shorter handles or cut and sand the ends. The shorter handles are easier for the children to manipulate. The environment, materials, and activities can be adapted for children with special needs to encourage everyone's participation.

The children's reactions to art materials depend on their previous experiences with paper, pencils, glue, clay, playing dough, and paint. In a suitably arranged and supervised art area, children will discover many ways to use the materials provided. Creating collages with paste is different from creating with glue. Building a paper sculpture out of egg cartons and straws gives children a three-dimensional experience with materials. When you allow space and time to explore, you will like the results; children will begin to master art materials (Figure 8–8).

Art Topics and Activities

When you arrange activities that allow children to make choices, they develop confidence. This also supports their creativity. Damian smiles and shows you that he is really proud of the plastic shapes he pasted on a piece of wood. You will encourage children to find their own creative inner self. Your interactive questioning will also support their creativity and confidence, especially with suggestions such as, "What do you think will happen when you try that?" or "Try wiping the brush on the side of the container if you want less paint." Remain sensitive to the cultural needs of the children and families. Many families would not approve of using food for art or sensory activity material. The culture, traditions, and religions of families might believe this to be wasteful and disrespectful.

Art, as a curriculum area, does not need to be limited to art materials. Children will benefit from exposure to various art forms, such as appreciation of art, which helps them use their senses. They can react to what they see, what they hear, and what they feel in their surroundings. Aesthetic awareness is a fundamental aspect of art appreciation. You will help children see beauty in nature, in their communities, and within their cultures. You can find art in the design of buildings, gardens, trucks, cars, and textiles. Children also learn to appreciate each other's artwork. Display the work of noted artists and designers famous for different forms of creativity. Rotate famous art work and the work of the children to create aesthetically pleasing spaces.

Art and works of art define our cultures and lifestyles. Therefore, they have an important place in the curriculum. Drawings of animals and children have been found on ancient pottery. The drawings offer interesting visual illustration for children, even though their concept of time and ancient relics is beyond their comprehension. Media, the Internet, and travel expose children to many more experiences than before. You may be surprised at the interest and reaction from the children. So, listening to the children may reveal their curiosity in ancient art work and international art. Assessment gives you direction as your curriculum plan unfolds with a balance of stimulating and suitable art activity topics (Figure 8–9).

In settings where teachers respect the children's work, enthusiasm to explore continues as use of other art media expands. Art experiences

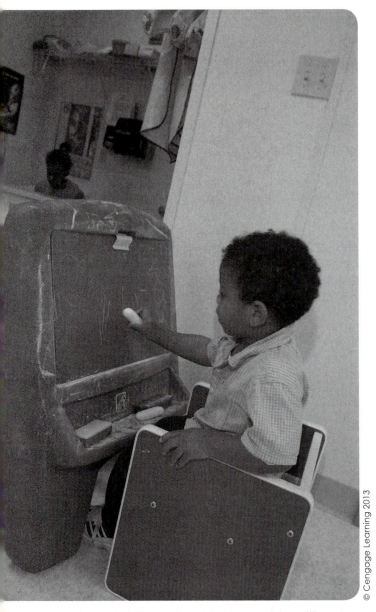

© Cengage Learning 2013

An art activity can be varied by providing different surfaces. Chalk for example, can be used on an easel, on paper, and outside on the cement.

Figure 8–9 Art Experiences for Young Children

Enlarged reproductions of noted artists

Children's art display

Collage

Cutting and tearing

Drawing—chalk, crayons, felt pens, pencils

Gluing and pasting

Mobiles—paper chain and natural objects like driftwood and seashells

Molding—clay, modeling dough, playing dough

Painting—fingerpainting, object, roller, sand, soap, tempera

Printmaking—stamps, rollers, objects

Sculptures—objects, clay, modeling dough, paper, wood, buttons,

Taking photographs—digital, cell phones, and disposable cameras may relate to a curriculum theme that was generated from your direct observation of the children. Art experiences will also be offered within one or more interest centers. The center would accommodate activities such as *Tire Track Art* **(Curriculum Activity Guide 46 ___)**. You will encourage art expression by planning meaningful activities that are integrated across the curriculum areas. An activity such as a nature collage is one example of integrating the curriculum. The materials needed for this activity give children the opportunity to creatively express themselves (curriculum area is art) while exploring items from nature (curriculum area is science). naeyc 1a, 1b, 1c, 4a, 4b, 4c, 4d, 5a, 5b, 5c, 5d

Aesthetic Development with Creative Dramatics

Creative Dramatics

Creative dramatics can be defined in various ways. The definitions and guidelines for the implementation of the related activities will be determined by each school. The age of the children who will be participating in creative dramatics will also influence what is presented and how it is done. Nonetheless, you will find that the words *pretend, imagine,* and *play* appear frequently in the description of creative dramatics, which is adapted in this textbook as a general term to organize four categories of activities. The four organizing categories significantly contribute to affective and aesthetic development of young children. The creative dramatics categories are dramatic play, guided drama, puppetry, and sociodramatics.

The terminology used to describe creative dramatics, as with so many other early childhood program descriptions, varies from one professional to another and from one program to another. The content of creative dramatics tends to remain stable and focused on pretending, playing, creating, and imagining. Categories also tend to overlap in curriculum areas; for this reason you can locate ideas for creative dramatics activities indexed under the subjects of movement, literature, social studies, and play.

Creative Dramatics Possible Outcomes

Creative dramatics allows a child to playfully pretend to be someone or something else. Children are able to act out and pretend to be like people

Figure 8–10 Skills Related to Creative Dramatics—Possible Outcomes

Collaboration

Cooperation

Combine ideas

Concentration

Creativity

Flexibility

Imagination

Interpersonal relations

Language and vocabulary

Pretending

Problem solving

Satisfaction

they know or have encountered. Children also can imagine being an animal or an object. While children playfully pretend, they are gaining valuable skills, and in this way, creative dramatics becomes an essential and powerful approach to learning (Johnson 1998; Smilansky 1968) (Figure 8–10).

Creative Dramatics Topics and Activities

Dramatic play, guided drama, puppetry, and sociodramatics are organized activities that prepare children for life experiences. The play activities contribute to their development with opportunities to develop collaboration and cooperation skills. Dramatic play, guided drama, puppetry, and sociodramatics activities can be flexible and stimulating. These activities will promote children's imagination while encouraging their language and vocabulary skills. Children can practice problem solving with critical thinking as they engage in guided drama and sociodramatics during interaction with other children. naeyc 4a, 4b, 4c, 4d

Dramatic Play

Children can find satisfaction through **dramatic play** as they develop and use their creativity and imagination. Children will imagine as they replicate the roles of their family members, teachers, and friends. Young children will also satisfy their own wishes as they pretend. This allows them to participate, observe, and perform (Smilansky 1968). In addition, dramatic play gives young children chances to learn about concepts. They can discover how people and objects function. They can practice roles. You will observe children pretending and imagining most often in the interest center that is delegated for dramatic play. Children imitate voices and gestures of adults and television and movie characters. Children dress up in clothing and use the props that you provide in the dramatic play area. Teachers become aware early in their careers to avoid overwhelming children with too many props that might distract and confuse them (Croft 1990). It is recommended that teachers introduce simple props first, and then add new props to keep the play interesting (Schickedanz 1999) or reflect a current theme.

Guided Drama

Guided drama, another category of creative dramatics, is the pantomiming and acting out of a poem, short story, or rhyme. This type of active experience encourages children to dramatically and creatively act with guidance from the teacher or another adult. The children's ages will direct the way a guided drama moves forward. With younger preschoolers, you might begin by suggesting that they "wiggle like a worm." Older preschoolers might be ready for you to guide them through acting out a few pages of a favorite story, such as *Bears Make Rock Soup*. The stories in this book, written by Lise Erdrich and illustrated in paintings by Lisa Fifield, offer opportunities for the children to act out the behavior of animals and objects in nature (2002).

Guidelines are recommended for implementing creative dramatics for older preschoolers and school-age children. These include providing some

Puppetry continues to excite children's imagination and creativity.

© Cengage Learning 2013

structure that may include modeling or demonstrating actions and sounds. The creative dramatics activities should remain open ended to encourage exploration and alternative variations. A safe environment is suggested, with time set aside for children to reflect on their experiences (Johnson 1998).

Guided drama experiences are often centered on one idea or topic. This gives children chances to experiment and originate images by pretending. Experiences for younger children need to be simple and familiar. Stories and books, walks through the neighborhood, and visitors to the school stimulate the children's imaginations. Open participation is ideal so that no child is forced to participate (Edwards 1990). A walk to the local bakery might stimulate a guided drama: "Pretend you are a muffin in the oven and you are baking." After a book is read, you can suggest to the children, "Pretend you are the bears in the story. Show us how they curled up to sleep."

Puppetry

Puppetry, which has a long history as a method of entertainment for adults in many cultures, continues to excite children's imagination and creativity. There are many types of puppets: some you will purchase, many you will design, and some you will spontaneously create. Puppets have many uses. They may introduce a concept and expand an idea. Puppets can be introduced in three stages by modeling the use of puppets, creating and using puppets together, and arranging for children to make and use the puppets (Jackman 2005). Puppets will contribute to young children's growing skills in the developmental focus areas (Figure 8–11).

Sociodramatics

Children pretend to be moms, teachers, dads, bakers, babies, dump truck drivers, dancers, and firefighters during sociodramatics. They participate voluntarily in a social play activity by taking on a role. Sociodramatic play guides children's pretend actions with the props and imaginary objects (Smilansky 1968). The children's social play relates to the roles present and familiar to them in their community and regional locations. Playing forest ranger is relevant to some children, driving a taxi to another, while becoming a beach lifeguard is more familiar to others.

Sociodramatics (Figure 8–12) helps children clarify concepts and contributes to their understanding of their community and community workers: Where does Bobby's mother work? Elaine's father takes a bus to work to manufacture jackets. The newspaper editor came to school to take our pictures. You might invite the lead firefighter,

Figure 8–11 Puppets Enhancing Developmental Focus Areas

Puppets hold a unique fascination for young children, a fact that insightful teachers will use to good advantage. Puppets provide a nonthreatening avenue for children to consider ideas, express creativity, explore emotions, and participate in problem solving.

Teachers routinely use puppets to focus group times, introduce concepts, and facilitate transitions, and may have specific puppets designated for these purposes. Initially, it is helpful to identify a group time puppet, complete with a name and personality (don't forget them, as the children won't!). Examples of how a group time puppet can facilitate and enhance developmental focus areas are:

Affective: A "shy" puppet learns the names of all the children and leads a name song.

Cognitive: A puppet encourages communication and enhances language acquisition by engaging children in conversation.

Physical: A puppet can be used to lead children in large motor exercises. In addition, fine motor development is increased by the child's own manipulation of a hand or finger puppet.

Teachers are sometimes self-conscious about using puppets and altering their voices. Remember that young children provide a very forgiving audience. For those who remain apprehensive, try a "shy" puppet who only whispers in the teacher's ear. You'll gain the children's rapt attention as you build your own confidence.

Kathy Barry, MA

Principal, Shasta County Office of Education

Figure 8–12 Sociodramatic Role-Play Prop Boxes

Social Role	Role-Play Props
Auto service/ mechanic	Tools, mechanic skate, credit cards, hoses, pumps, tires, patches, empty oil cans, work clothes, rags, window cleaner, (safe for child-use) buckets, signs, hats, money, cash registers, charge cards.
Baker	Toastmaster (without electrical cords), baking pans, utensils, muffin tins, cash register, bags, display case, aprons, signs.
Forest ranger	Shovels, flashlights, hats, maps, badges, boots, tents, signs, jackets, brochures, photographs.
Gardener	Wheelbarrow, buckets, gloves, blunt clippers, branches, flowers, potting soil, rake, hoe, watering cans, seed packets, hoses, hats, tools, nozzles, sunscreen, planters.
Grocer	Signs, folding shelves, empty food and can samples, bags, cash registers, grocery cart, play money, markers, signs, stickers for pricing, plastic produce and food.
Librarian	Books, shelves, tables, rug, counter, posters, stamps, paper, library cards, rolling cart.
Veterinarian	Stuffed toy animals, linen, bandages, pet food samples, posters, cages, flashlights, medical jacket, collars, leash, appointment book, telephone, index cards for records.

whose name is Sharon, to bring her coat, boots, and helmet to try on at school. Your curriculum plans can include highlighting the work of both men and women. Children will learn that work and jobs require specific training, not specific genders. In sociodramatics children will also acquire negotiating skills when they interact with the other children. Sociodramatics helps them to acquire concepts about the many roles and occupations available to them in their communities and outside their immediate area. **naeyc** 1a, 1b, 1c, 4a, 4b, 4c, 4d

Affective and Aesthetic Development with Social Understanding

Social Understanding

The curriculum area of **social understanding** ideally supports affective and aesthetic development. Social understanding helps children understand themselves, their families, and their communities. Early childhood is the appropriate time for children to begin to acquire prosocial skills. Acquisition of prosocial skills is the link to becoming responsible citizens who are capable of predicting, and reacting appropriately in, social situations.

Families, communities, and the larger society establish social practices. Early childhood curriculum that promotes healthy socialization features goals to recognize the importance of families, communities, and cultures. This balance prepares children for our pluralistic society, one that has many customs, traditions, languages, and histories. Because children's primary experiences are in their homes, they bring the perspectives of their families to the preschool and care and learning programs. Children adjust to new people, routines, and food. We can make the transition easier by bringing more of the children's home values and practices into the school setting. The Montessori Method arranges practical life exercises for children. These tasks help teach the children about themselves—grooming, dressing, shining shoes—and care of their indoor and outdoor environments. This is accomplished by fostering an environment in which children can practice washing, sweeping, table setting, and weeding and raking (Orem 1974). We can expand understanding by including the diverse practices representative of the children's families and others outside of their immediate neighborhoods.

The conventional reference to this curriculum area, social understanding, is social studies. Lessons about people in society can be arranged into subcategories such as society and communities, geography, history, political science, economy, and languages. Preschool children have limited comprehension of historical events and distant places. You will, nonetheless, be able to introduce the initial concepts with specific activities. Initial activities can include experiences that help children understand themselves, their families, and the people in close community proximity. Helping children to understand themselves and others facilitates their affective and aesthetic development.

Social Understanding Possible Outcomes

Consider the curriculum area of social understanding and the way it can be applied appropriately for young children. Children need to become more aware of themselves, their families, and their communities. You can facilitate this awareness by broadening the traditional social studies unit with subcategories. You can plan activities to benefit children as they learn to accept new routines (self-understanding). For example, at home Marty can sit wherever she wants. At school she will learn to accept the chair that is empty and available. Marty is the youngest child in her family. Her older siblings respond to her desires without her verbal requests. At the center, Marty needs to express her wishes verbally to let the teachers or other children know what she wants (social understanding). The guidance Marty receives from the teachers will positively promote Marty's personal awareness and interpersonal skills. Marty may choose to sit in the grouptime where a guest, Firefighter Sharon, is talking about her uniform (community understanding) (Figure 8–13).

The children's communication and literacy skills will also improve as you add meaningful vocabulary to the social understanding–related activities (Figure 8–14). naeyc 1a, 1b, 1c, 4a, 4b, 4c, 4d

Figure 8–13 Skills Related to Social Understanding – Possible Outcomes

Self-Understanding	Social Understanding	Community Understanding
Accepting	Appreciating differences	Accepting others
Comforting	Collaborating	Cooperating in community
Expressing	Distinguishing right/wrong	Developing responsibility
Initiating	Empathizing	Expanding viewpoint
Making choices	Interacting with others	Helping
Motivating	Predicting consequences	Locating community places
Nurturing	Problem solving	Participating
Separating	Respecting differences	Visiting

Figure 8–14 Vocabulary Related to a Social Understanding Activity

Activity Title	When I Am Afraid	
Vocabulary	feelings	scared
	afraid	reaction
	alarmed	response
	fearful	solution
	frightened	well-being

Social Understanding Topics and Activities

Although the study of people in society covers a broad range of topics, you will maintain an emergent curriculum by keeping focused on meaningful activities for young children. These integrate different curriculum areas while focusing on the children in your program, their families, and their communities (Figure 8–15).

Topics that will enhance social understanding can be related to sensitive issues. This will require that you work with the program administrator to establish guidelines. School pets die. Family members become ill and may die. Children experience trauma and violence. Thoughtful consideration should include the developmental ages of the children in the program and their cultural and religious backgrounds.

Another area associated with social understanding relates to gender and social roles in society. During early childhood, children begin to clarify gender roles as they relate to their families' values and societal standards. Early childhood programs can provide experiences that are bias free and encourage equity. Arrange for all of the children to have access to real tools such as hammers and nails. Have both gender specific and gender neutral materials in the dramatic play areas. Promote all of the materials and activities in the indoor and outdoor spaces with boys and girls alike. Teachers can encourage positive self-esteem of the children by respecting the dynamics and practices of their homes. Teachers can support community awareness and responsibility to reject stereotypic actions and negative conduct against alternative lifestyles.

Social understanding topics and activities allow children to develop collaborative behaviors. They will emulate your respect for others. Some schools disallow weapons and other related war toys altogether. Other programs limit adventure and media-induced toys. Whatever guidelines your school establishes, the goal is to help children develop sensitive and empathic behaviors while learning to understand consequences of their actions (Wichert 1989). Children can be included in decision making. For instance, invite their ideas to encourage democratic voting. Bobby came up with several ideas, but agreed with Elaine's choice to move the rabbit's cage under the shady tree.

Children are affected by the violence in society. The primary response of teachers must be to provide safe and secure environments in school programs. Children need emotional stability in places that create unhurried time. The number of teachers should exceed minimum standards whenever possible for the needs of individual children to be met. Children can work together with the teacher to develop meaningful safety and kindness rules for their own group. While we advocate nonviolence in the lives of children, teachers can promote their children's critical thinking and evaluation about what is presented or available. We can do this by extending their interests, even if some of these interests include role models and action figures that typically may not be acceptable in an early childhood program. We can reinforce the children's positive comments by reflecting on what they say and showing pleasure that they shared their thoughts. Respond encouragingly to the children's comments that are nonviolent. Give children substitute words for "language filled with violent allusions . . . such

Figure 8–15 Activities Promoting Community Responsibility and Meeting Developmental Needs of Children

Developmental Focus	Activity Title	Activity Description
Physical	Helping Families	Place collected food in bags for families after a disaster (fire, flood, twister, or earthquake).
Affective (social-emotional understanding) and Aesthetic	Snack with Friends	Visit senior citizens for snack time or meals together.
Cognitive	Helping Too!	Visit toddler area to put away sand toys and rake the sand.

as 'break a leg' or 'I'm gonna knock 'em dead' . . . moving [them] away from our violent idioms," recommends Wilma Gold, who chaired the Non-Violence in the Lives of Children Project for the California Association for the Education of Young Children (1999, 4–5). Become involved in the children's play. Ask them questions that encourage empathy. Help children think beyond stereotypes by making comments such as, "How does the bad guy feel?" "What does Superman do on his birthday?" (Feeney et al. 2006).

Continue to formulate new ways to promote cooperation. Themes, topics, and activities can expand children's views and their prosocial abilities. The theme *Learning about My Friends* introduces children to concepts that identify both similarities and differences: "Once we were all babies; we have different hair; Lettie sees with glasses; Manuel has one brother like me." Some themes and topics emerge from observation of the children, while other relevant topics remain popular and consistent in programs for young children (Figure 8–16). **naeyc** 1a, 1b, 1c, 4a, 4b, 4c, 4d

© Cengage Learning 2013

Programs build strong values for children when a positive regard for families is promoted and encouraged.

Figure 8–16 Social Understanding Topics for Young Children

Topic	Conventional Description
When I Was a Baby	History or Biology
Plans for Tomorrow	History or Civics
Finding Home and School	Geography
Responsible to My Community	Civics and Citizenship
Friend Photo Match	Civics and Citizenship
Workers at My School	Social Studies
Jobs in My Community	Social Studies
Visitors Share Their Work	Social Studies
Together We Decide	Political Science
Family Celebrations	Anthropology
Where Do Babies Sleep	Social Studies
Families Have Favorite Foods	Social Studies
Family Day Visit	Anthropology
Earning and Spending Money	Economics
We Are in the News	Journalism or Literature
Only Special TV Programs	Journalism or Literature

Experiences to Strengthen Connections and Relationships

Social understanding is a sound curriculum area for supporting multicultural values. Families directly influence the way the child views the world. School is the place where children learn to appreciate the differences and similarities among other children, adults, and families.

You will be able to strengthen your curriculum and the relationships among the children and adults at your school with a solid curriculum design. Your curriculum can respond to the diversity of families and communities with authentic inclusion. This action recognizes children and families with positive regard for their identity and identities, language and languages, and values and principles. Nonbiased, nonstereotyping activities may require that you and other members of your teaching team research new resources for appropriate and meaningful activities to help you achieve harmony in your program, equity in opportunities for the children, and respect for differences.

As you discover the resources, adapt the suggestions to fit your local community. While we can respect and appreciate differences of the children's families, it is also valuable to emphasize similarities as human beings. We are more alike than we are different. Essentially, there is great variation among people of the same racial, cultural, or ethnic group. Learn as much as possible about families, cultures, languages, and religions, and avoid holding any fixed descriptions of a group or a child from that ethnicity. Many factors influence who you are and with which culture you identify. These include, but are not limited to, your education and the availability of education to your parents. Socioeconomic status, regional location, and the changes that occur each generation also impact cultural, racial, and ethnic identity. Cultural framework and identity influence the way teachers create routines and plan curriculum (Gonzalez-Mena 2008). Everyone has a culture with meaningful and rich customs for all to appreciate (Figure 8–17).

Creative activity ideas that will encourage children to recognize similarities and differences include a variety of experiences. Activities such as matching pictures of traditional holiday dress, hair beading on wigs representing diverse backgrounds, and books in Braille are suggested (Hall 1999). Plan activities to promote community awareness and responsibility **(Curriculum Activity Guide 13 ___\)**. Design experiences to encourage cooperative behaviors and a positive sense of self. Arrange opportunities for children to resolve conflict in communicative ways and encourage opportunities for friendship **Curriculum Activity Guide 14 ___\)**. **naeyc** 1a, 1b, 1c, 3a, 3b, 4a, 4b, 4c, 4d, 5a, 5b, 5c

Thinking About What You Have Learned

✔ Visit an art museum, in person or on an Internet site. Identify the programs the museum offers for young children and their families. Inquire about art appreciation. Does the museum loan prints of national and international artwork? If the museum does not have a lending program for the prints, check with the educational outreach department in an elementary school district.

✔ Research the topic of puppetry. Prepare a two-page report to be utilized for teacher workshops at your school.

✔ Access the websites listed below. Collect appropriate activity ideas and resources for authentic curriculum activities. Multicultural resources need to represent families and their celebrations without bias and stereotypes.

Multicultural Awareness Activities
http://curry.edschool.Virginia.EDU/gomulticultural/activityarch.html
Multicultural Calendar
http://www.kidlink.org/KIDPROJ/MCC/
New Zealand Perspective to Early Childhood Education Curriculum
http://members.xoom.com/koaroha/index.htm

Chapter References

Briggs, Dorothy. C. 1975. *Your child's self-esteem.* New York: Doubleday Dolphin Books.

Croft, Doreen. 1990. *An activities handbook for teachers of young children.* 5th ed. Boston: Houghton Mifflin.

Derman-Sparks, Louise, and Julie O. Edwards. 2010. *Anti-bias curriculum: Empowering our children and ourselves.* Washington, DC: National Association for the Education of Young Children.

Edwards, Linda. C. 1990. *Affective development and the creative arts.* Columbus, OH: Merrill Publishing.

Erdrich, Lise, and Lisa Fifield. 2002. *Bears make rock soup: And other stories.* San Francisco: Children's Book Press.

Erickson, Erik. H. 1996. A healthy personality for every child. In *Sources: Notable selections in early childhood education.* Guilford, CT: Dushkin Publishing Group.

Feeney, Stephanie, Doris Christensen, and Eva Moravcik. 2009. *Who am i in the lives of children?* 8th ed. Upper Saddle River, NJ: Prentice Hall.

Garbarino, James. 1999. *Raising children in a socially toxic environment.* San Francisco: Jossey-Bass.

Figure 8–17 Curriculum Topics Celebrating Children and Families

We Are All People	What We All Need	What We All Can Do
Skin Colors	Food and Water	Communicate
Hair	Homes	Celebrate
Thumb Prints	Families	Work
Names	Love	Believe

Goleman, Daniel. 2006. *Social intelligence: The new science of human relationships*. New York: Bantam Dell.

Gonzalez-Mena, Janet. 2008. *Diversity in early care and education*. 5th ed. New York: McGraw Hill.

Hall, Nadia. S. 1999. *Creative resources for the anti-bias classroom*. Albany, NY: Delmar.

Johnson, Andrew P. 1998. How to use creative dramatics in the classroom. *Childhood Education*, 75(1), 2–6.

Jackman, Hilda. L. 2005. *Early childhood curriculum: A child's connection to the world*. 3rd ed. Albany, NY: Thomson Delmar.

Orem, Reginald C. 1974. *Montessori: Her method and the movement*. New York: Capricorn.

Schickedanz, Judith A. 1999. *Much more than the abc's: The early stages of reading and writing*. Washington, DC: National Association for the Education of Young Children.

Smilansky, Sara. 1968. *The effects of sociodramatic play on disadvantaged preschool children*. New York: John Wiley & Sons.

Wichert, Susanne. 1989. *Keeping the peace: Practicing cooperation and conflict resolution with preschoolers*. Santa Cruz, CA: New Society Publishers.

chapter 9

Cognitive Development: Communication and Literacy, Mathematics, and Science Activities

© Cengage Learning 2013

Picture This . . .

"How will I know she is learning?" This is a common question from families who enroll their children in early care and learning. Mothers, fathers, grandparents, and guardians will often ask, "What should I do to make sure that he will talk?" "When should he be reading?" The family members are really asking, "When, how, and what should I be *teaching* my child?" Over time, the questions and especially the anxieties about learning have not varied significantly. Parents want the best for their children. They want them to do well in school and succeed in life. Early childhood educators support families by helping them to have reasonable expectations for their children. With your guidance, family members will grasp the connection between the curriculum you plan and their children's development. In the end, the entire program benefits.

The task of reassuring family members is not easy or instant. You will need to have patience. You will need to be informed and ready to explain the basic ideas regarding the learning process for young children. An 18-month old's pleasure in placing a wet washcloth on a chair shows her natural motivation to accomplish a task. You appreciate that moment because you know that every sight, sound, and movement is affecting her brain development. Brooke is careful as she places the washcloth, after opening the folds, on the top part of the wooden chair. She watches the washcloth slip down, smiles, and picks it up again and begins to drape it on the chair another time. Over and over, over and over, Brooke seemingly enjoys the task with her whole body, taking pleasure in the repetition, not yet knowing or caring that she is learning. As she matures, her parents will read books to her. Eventually, Brooke's demands will include, that her parents "read it again" and it will not be just her attempt to avoid going to bed. Her interest in books will contribute to her understanding of herself, her family, her pets, and her surroundings even before she begins attending an early education program. Brooke will begin to show preferences for certain books. Will she like *Are You My Mother?, Goodnight Moon,* or *Little Blue and Little Yellow?* Brooke will listen to her parents read, not concerned that the activity will positively affect all her development. Encouraged to explore and rewarded for her curiosity, Brooke is happy and eager for more stories—that is what learning is about.

GUIDE TO READING CHAPTER 9

Chapter Outline

Cognitive Development
    Cognitive Development Skills and Possible Outcomes
    Cognitive Development Activities
Connecting Curriculum for Cognitive Development
    Integrating Activities
    Teaching Strategies—Mindful of Children's Needs and Interests
    Blending Technology into the Curriculum
Cognitive Development and Language Development
Cognitive Development with Communication and Literacy
    Communication Skills and Possible Outcomes
    Communication Activities
    Literacy Skills and Possible Outcomes
    Literacy Activities
Cognitive Development with Mathematics
    Mathematics Skills and Possible Outcomes
    Mathematics Activities
Cognitive Development with Science
    Science Skills and Possible Outcomes
    Science Activities
Thinking About What You Have Learned

Learning Objectives

After reading this chapter, you will be able to

1. Recognize the value of cognitive experiences during the early childhood years.
2. Write age-appropriate skills and concepts for cognitive development activities.
3. Evaluate the inclusion of appropriate technology in early childhood programs.
4. Identify experiences to support language development including communication and literacy.
5. Recognize curriculum activities that will promote mathematical skills of young children.
6. Design experiences to promote and sustain children's natural curiosity about science.

Key Terms

National Association for the Education of Young Children (NAEYC) Standards for Initial Early Childhood Professional Preparation Programs Met by this chapter:

Standard 1: Promoting Child Development and Learning

1a: Knowing and understanding young children's characteristics and needs, from birth through age 8.

1b: Knowing and understanding the multiple influences on development and learning.

1c: Using developmental knowledge to create healthy, respectful, supportive, and challenging learning environments for young children.

Standard 3: Observing, Documenting, and Assessing to Support Young Children and Families

3b: Knowing about and using observation, documentation, and other appropriate assessment tools and approaches including the use of *technology* in documentation, assessment and data collection.

Standard 4: Using Developmentally Effective Approaches

4a: Understanding positive relationships and supportive interactions as the foundation of their work with young children.

4b: Knowing and understanding effective strategies and tools for early education, including appropriate uses of technology.

4c: Using a broad repertoire of developmentally appropriate teaching/learning approaches.

4d: Reflecting on own practice to promote positive outcomes for each child.

Standard 5: Using Content Knowledge to Build Meaningful Curriculum

5a: Understanding content knowledge and resources in academic disciplines: language and literacy; the arts – music, creative movement, dance, drama, visual arts; mathematics; science; physical activity, physical education, health and safety; and social studies.

5b: Knowing and using the central concepts, inquiry tools, and structures of content areas or academic disciplines.

5c: Using own knowledge, appropriate early learning standards, and other resources to design, implement, and evaluate meaningful, challenging curricula for each child.

Cognitive Development

The noise level and busy behavior of children should be obvious when you walk into a quality early care and learning program. Children actively engage in experiences when the environment is specifically planned to meet their needs. Children's abilities to communicate their ideas and to reason about how objects function and people act expand rapidly during the early childhood years. **Cognitive development** is about knowing and thinking. It relates to knowledge and how that knowledge is acquired. As you begin to plan for children in the developmental focus area, consider the children's ages and maturity. Cognitive development is about their mental abilities, critical thinking, problem solving, memory, comprehension, conceptualization, creativity, language development, and communication. Experiences that provide engaging and relevant opportunities for children enhance cognitive development.

Researchers continually confirm that the brain during the early childhood years is active and amazingly capable of self-organizing information. Because the immature brain is more flexible and adaptive, it is capable of integrating more experiences than when children are older. Evidence shows that the experiences that promote development are the ones that cause the brain's activity. Two implications are apparent for early childhood curriculum. Children's growing brains need developmentally provocative experiences, and children need to interact with appropriately responsive adults (Thompson 2008). Prepare your school curriculum and environment for young children with creative and varied experiences. They can be provocatively stimulating and adjusted to the children's readiness for new learning to occur. Some of the activities you plan can be specific to a curriculum area; for example, matching toy horses with numbers offers a mathematical experience. You will be able to integrate curriculum areas with the activities you offer for the children. Planting and charting the growth of carrot seeds provides a science experience that also exposes children to mathematics. Encourage children to communicate about exploratory and manipulative materials throughout the day. Cognitive growth progresses as children engage in more and more experiences. They acquire skills and their abilities increase in memory, problem solving, critical thinking, and language. You will support children in their cognitive development by helping them to recognize their original ideas and by reinforcing their creativeness. **naeyc** 1a, 1b, 1c

Cognitive Development Skills and Possible Outcomes

The activities you provide will offer ample time for the children to play. Play allows children to think critically—to see, to explore, and to reason. Children's natural curiosity directs their eagerness to solve problems and to think critically about a task. For instance, Bri enjoys matching and sorting gardening tools. Mo investigates bird nests on the science table. When Bri and Mo explore real objects, they naturally discover, inquire, remember, classify, label, compare, and begin to see cause and effect. Critical thinking skills emerge, and children make meaningful choices when they are allowed to explore during play.

Emma's discovery of ice in the water table outside begins a conversation: Emma asks, "Who put the ice outside?" Discussion about temperature and water leads Teacher Corinne to suggest to Emma that she take some of the ice inside the classroom. The ice is placed on a sturdy paper plate and taken inside. Although other children excitedly make predictions, Teacher Corinne encourages Emma to watch her ice on her own paper plate. Emma places ice cubes taken from the kitchen freezer on another paper plate. Teacher Corinne is ready to facilitate Emma's learning in the classroom that has been designed to expand and enrich the children's learning opportunities. In this way, Emma and the other children will improve critical thinking skills in a nurturing environment. You might check that your own environment facilitates emerging capacities for cognitive development. Are the children curious about new people and materials? How do they explore and experiment? Do they stay with a particular activity and concentrate on it? What do they remember about the day's experiences? (Cohen et al. 2008).

Figure 9–1 Cognitive Development Skills— Possible Outcomes

seeing	labeling
hearing	observing
touching	organizing
tasting	problem-solving
smelling	remembering
classifying	reasoning
comparing	seeing cause and effect
discovering	exploring
exploring	inquiring

You already know that appropriate curriculum for young children supports their cognitive development. The curriculum provides concrete child-initiated and teacher-directed experiences that are relevant. Children will begin to understand number concepts, spatial awareness, and ideas about time when activities are planned with individually appropriate and age-appropriate experiences. You will clarify concepts for children with your words: "The trike is next to the path" (spatial concept); "We need one chair for each friend" (number concept); and "Your dad will pick you up after snack" (temporal concept) (Figure 9–1). The children will develop skills as their become familiar with concepts.

Cognitive Development Activities

Children repeat certain activities over and over. As they work through the tasks associated with activities, they are learning and improving their thinking. You will encourage children to work through experiences, with concentrated pleasure, by organizing ample objects that allow discovery. Several wicker baskets filled with round objects will help children distinguish similarities and differences. You can help them see cause and effect and to gain a sense of space. Certain materials will acquaint them with sequencing. A tray of clocks and watches with matching pictures provides children with experiences about time. Offer children chances to see colors, shapes, sizes, and patterns (Cohen and Stern 1983). An activity such as *Fix-It Shop* introduces concepts about repair and tools **(Curriculum Activity Guide 15 ⬚)**. Participation by children may stimulate the need to create a project about repair in an interest center (Figure 9–2).

Figure 9–2 Interest Center Guide – *Construction/Fix-It*

Interest Center *Construction/Fix-It*　　　　　　　　**Theme** *Community Workers*

Art	Cooking	Literacy	Quiet Reading	Outside Art	⬚ Outside Large Motor
Block	Computer	Manipulatives	Science	Outside Circle	Outside and/Water
Circle	Dramatic Play	Music/Rhythm	Sensorial	Outside Garden	Trike Path

Interest Center Guidelines　　　　　　　　　　　**Approximate Age Range** *3–5*

Set up special Interest Center for construction in outside large motor area to give children opportunities to repair.

Developmental Focus　　　　**Physical**　　　⬚ **Affective and Aesthetic**　　　**Cognitive and Language**

Curriculum Area *Social Understanding*
Movement

Interest Center Materials

Constant *Obstacle course, table, chairs, grassy area*

Featured *Prepare and place Fix-It Shop sign on rearranged obstacle course ladders to replicate a shop. Add tools, broken (but safe) small appliances, short pieces of wood, wire, glue.*

Preparation/Setup

1. *Prepare Fix-It Shop sign.*
2. *Prepare appliances—remove cords, loosen screws.*
3. *Outline tools on trays.*
4. *Arrange shop.*

Teaching Strategies

1. *Introduce safe use of tools in Interest Center as children select to participate.*
2. *Supervise, interactive questioning as children take apart and "repair" appliances. (How would you tighten that screw?)*

Possible Outcomes for the Child or Children

Concepts *Tools can take apart appliances*
Construction workers and repair persons use tools.

Skills *Fine motor development, social understanding, role playing, problem solving, confidence.*

Vocabulary *tools, repair, construction, fix-it*

Child Participation　　　　　　　　　　　　　　**Date**

The activity *Growth Sequence* acquaints the children with sequence and ordering **(Curriculum Activity Guide 16** **).** naeyc 1a, 1b, 1c, 4a, 4b, 4c, 4d, 5a, 5b, 5c

---

▶❚❚ **Video Case**

2–5 Years: Piaget's Preoperational Stage
Visit the Early Childhood Education Media Library, and watch the TeachSource Video Case on www.cengagebrain.com

1. How do children's egocentric behaviors affect their play?

2. Describe how Piaget's theory of preoperational thinking helps you to be more effective as a teacher of young children.

Connecting Curriculum for Cognitive Development

The "Guidelines for Decisions about Developmentally Appropriate Practice," in the revised edition of *Developmentally Appropriate Practice in Early Childhood Programs,* provide direction for appropriate experiences to enhance cognitive development. Curriculum will meet the children's needs when teachers respect the intelligence of the enrolled children and build on what they already know. The activities should be based on the children's interests and respect their familial and linguistic diversity. Teachers will more likely achieve developmentally appropriate practice when they offer young children choices and time to explore relevant, purposeful activities. The experiences you offer will further their cognitive development and support enjoyment of learning. Children's development is further enhanced when you involve them in the planning and review of their work (Copple and Bredekamp 2009).

Integrating Activities

Guidelines for age-appropriate and meaningful experiences for young children emphasize that curriculum plans focus on children—who they are and where they live. Activities planned with cognitive development in mind integrate across curriculum areas. For instance, activities about the

post office will provide children with opportunities to think and communicate about a community service. The children will also gain information about social roles (curriculum area—social understanding). Activities about the post office will include exposure to counting letters, reading zip codes, and collecting money for stamps (mathematics) as well as introduce the children to postage stamp designs (art appreciation). Play experiences related to the post office facilitate children's abilities in communication. Activities related to the post office and postal clerks are often included in the list of themes commonly offered at schools. Your introduction will purposefully stimulate the children's interest, especially for those who have never walked into a post office. The curriculum focus on the post office may be initiated when a child shows interest in writing and mailing a letter. The post office activity or theme offers children benefits in language development. A specific activity (letter writing) features literacy readiness. Activities can focus on a developmental focus area as well as curriculum areas and connect with a theme (Figure 9–3).

Projects, themes, and interest centers support the development of cognition and language in different ways. A theme that features a specific curriculum area, such as day and night may be more relevant to the development of critical thinking (cognition). Another theme, celebrations, favors experiences related to language development. Most themes will provide an integrated curriculum plan with beneficial activities related to many curriculum areas and themes (Figure 9–4). naeyc 1a, 1b, 1c, 4a, 4b, 4c, 4d, 5a, 5b, 5c

Figure 9–3 Activities Integrate Developmental Focus Area, Curriculum Areas, and Theme

Developmental Focus Area	Cognitive
Curriculum Areas	*Communication and Literacy* Activity: Writing Letters
	Movement Activity: Walking to the Post Office
	Social Understanding Activity: Sociodramatic Play—Mail Carrier
Theme	Community Helpers— Mail Carrier

Figure 9–4 Themes Encouraging Cognitive and Language Development

Cognitive	Language
Water Safety	Celebrations
We Are Alike/Different	Adventures—Outdoors
Make Believe	Drama/Fine Arts
Day and Night	Family Gathering

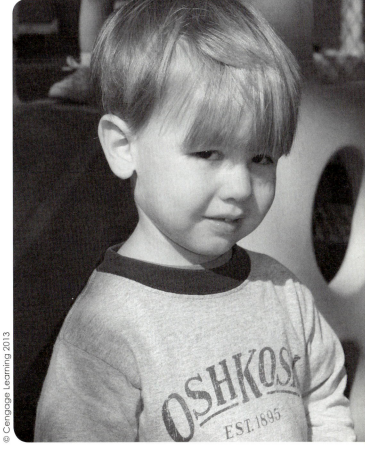

© Cengage Learning 2013

Teachers of young children will encourage curiosity and confidence by first knowing each child's individual needs.

Teaching Strategies—Mindful of Children's Needs and Interests

Parents ask what they can do to ensure that their children will do well in school. This inquiry is often about intellectual functioning because society places great emphasis on academic achievement. To enhance cognitive development you will need to first know each child's needs and encourage each child's curiosity and confidence. Validate the process of acquiring a skill, rather than expecting a finished product from an activity. Look at inventive ways to enhance the children's critical thinking, communication, and literacy. Design activities to encourage children to observe, listen, speak, and write. Avoid structuring unrelated experiences that push children to acquire meaningless facts, such as memorizing isolated facts, letters, and numbers. Practices that ignore exploration put the children's motivation at risk. The developmentally appropriate practice guidelines describe giving children choices, providing activities that cover concepts based on prior knowledge, problem solving, and plans for children to review and work as the suitable way to enhance cognitive activities.

Blending Technology into the Curriculum

Changes occur everywhere and influence children's lives. Changing family patterns, the urbanization of society, and technological advances affect children. **Technology** is altering children's routines. Early childhood professionals have taken steps to determine how to best use technology with young children.

As the information age increasingly influences education, children will be faced with increasing choices about that information. You will participate in selecting appropriate technology and software for your program. Early educators can access the National Association for the Education of Young Children (NAEYC) Position Statement related to technology. The paper states that technology is appropriately utilized as a tool to support children's activities and maintain equitable access. The teacher's role is critical in making certain that decisions regarding the use of technology are in children's best interest. Teachers must support children in their use of technology to ensure that potential benefits are achieved (1996).

Teachers and program administrators should start by reviewing software and packaged applications to run learning programs on a computer, with consideration of two points. First, look at the content and match it to the developmental age of the children enrolled in your program. Is the content presented for a variety of levels? Secondly, the software for young children should hold their attention by attracting and sustaining their involvement for about ten minutes per session. Consider this by posing the following questions. Does the software program give children feedback indicating progress and completion of goals for the computer activities? Does the software avoid bias and violence? Will the software ensure safeguards for appropriate Internet sites? Will the software offer computer-friendly-use and value for the price (Hohmann 1998)? Does the software program offer something important for young children, or is the experience something that simply looks good? (Tsantis et al. 2003).

Technological tools provide a supplement for education and learning. Technology does not replace the teacher (Pool 1997). Understanding technology and using it requires that you to understand and evaluate information accessed with technology. What is the feasibility of multimedia projects? Yet, you will need to interpret the children's abilities and readiness to comprehend what flashes through the computer and PowerPoint onto the screen (Elkind 1996).

Joey brings his envelope to a student teacher whose name is Shelly. He asks for help with the label of his name printed on the computer. As they walk back, Joey says, "This picture is for my grandpa, he's in the hospital and needs it." The student teacher suggests that they ask to use the scanner in the prep room. Joey's eyes widen and he says, "Yes," excitedly. When the task of scanning and sending the picture is complete, the student teacher gives Joey his drawing and an extra copy to place in his cubby. Later, during activity time, Joey approaches Shelly again because the printer has run out of paper. Once again, Shelly is available to assist Joey with the technological equipment.

Technology is about machines, tools, products, and devices. Technology is a huge part of local and global communications. Technology assists children and their families in daily life activities. Technology also contributes to the functioning of schools and communities. Technology is constantly changing. The changes affect everyone. In just one day, a child receives assistance to scan his drawing into the computer and send an e-mail; observes the grocery clerk electronically debit food at checkout; and watches the numbers on the digital gas station pump that can print a receipt. Technology enhances children with special needs, to access

and participate in programs. **Assistive technology** improves the operation of wheelchairs, hearing aids, and on-screen keyboards specially designed for children who are unable to use their hands and fingers.

Experiences and activities with technology can integrate into every curriculum area. Technology, particularly the microcomputer, helps us to access information about new books, about science, about community events, and about other children. The microcomputer also allows schools to post information for parents about the curriculum. Most children have significant and direct experiences with technology on a daily basis. Technological inventions extend our abilities to see (batteries and lights); to communicate (cell and smart phones, iPads and iPads); to remember (digital camera, camcorders, webcams); to medically heal (lasers); to cook (microwaves); and to travel (airplanes and rapid transit).

Technology includes and expands the curriculum areas of mathematics and science. Children develop a positive working relationship with technology when they use devices to plan, predict, and participate in activities. A walk to the library begins with a planning session with discussion about the number of books, the return walk, and a stop at the cafeteria to pick up a snack. Predicting that the books and snack may be heavy, children suggest bringing the wagon to carry the books and snack. Children are introduced to two concepts about technology: a wagon is a tool to help us carry heavy items, and a wagon has wheels that allow the wagon to move when we walk. Planning for a subsequent walk leads the children to "discover" and "invent" another device. After the teacher records the children's comments in her laptop, the projected image of the information leads children to discuss what is needed. They discover that they need a device to prevent the books from sliding around in the wagon. The teacher leads the small group discussion and the outcome is that the children decide to place empty, plastic tubs around the wagon to hold the books in place. Smart phone photographs of the wagon with the plastic tubs are placed in the discovery center and labeled with a sign prepared and printed by the computer—"Invention." Children continually develop awareness of technological concepts as they interact in an enriched environment (Figure 9–5). **naeyc** 1a, 1b, 1c, 4a, 4b, 4c, 4d, 5a, 5b, 5c

Figure 9–5 Activities with Technology Enhance Cognitive Development

Skill	Teaching Activity
Planning	Walks to the fire department; auto repair shop
Predicting	Which wheel turns faster
Participating	Lifting objects with a pulley
Creating	Pictures of the pets with computer graphics
Comparing	Whipping cream with hand and electric beaters
Exploring	Tools that drive nails into wood
Inquiring	About water available in homes
Investigating	Adding machines and calculators
Observing	Products of telecommunications

Cognitive Development and Language Development

Language development begins with infant's cries. That is how babies communicate their needs. The language or languages an infant acquires are important milestones. When the infant produces language, it is evidence that cognition is developing. Thinking about an idea and then communicating that idea in words is a significant cognitive achievement. Language is the foundation of a child's interaction with his or her family. During play, infants, toddlers, and preschoolers reveal their needs, feelings, and their curiosity. Language is tied to how children think. The acquisition of language has lasting influences. The influences are apparent in regional accents and the use of words that are learned from family members including parents, siblings, grandparents, and extended family members. Children's language is further affected by the television and media they watch and by others in their community (Weiner and Elkind 1972). When children learn their primary language, they acquire a set of beliefs. Children also become acquainted with the expectations and practices of their families. They bring the values and experiences of their homes to their school. It is up to teachers to respectively bind their diverse ways and languages into one setting (Fillmore 1993). naeyc 1a, 1b, 1c

A language-rich environment stimulates children's formation of communication skills. Adults model language. Adults, especially teachers in the early childhood setting, accept the children's language and regularly expand on their communication.

You will embrace opportunities to enhance children's language abilities. As the children become interested in the printed word, you will enhance language development by enhancing their attempts at symbolic representation. You will achieve responsive communication with the children in numerous ways. Teachers answer the children's requests and questions. Teachers invite discussion and conversation. Teachers express ideas and words. Teachers accept the child's expressions. Teachers listen to every child and encourage every child to listen. Teachers provide names for objects, people, and events. All actions that teachers take to facilitate language also stimulate the children's thinking. You will help children remember what they said or saw. You will enrich their day with rhyming words. You will also model language when you communicate with their families, other teachers, program administrators, volunteers, and guests.

An early childhood environment is an interest center for language development. You will create print-rich settings, indoors and outdoors, by featuring printed labels and signs of words placed within the children's view. Teacher-guided memory games will enhance the children's critical thinking skills. Large charts and books will allow children to see big print, record reflective ideas about activities and move felt shapes to match with words in the story. Laminating and binding dictation of the children's words and drawings allows routine publishing of their work. Teacher-guided activities and related communication support the development of important cognitive development skills (Figure 9–6).

Figure 9–6 Teacher's Communication Facilitates Language Development Skills

Answering	"Yes, Sally Jo, hang your jacket in this cubby hole."
Expressing	"I see you have a cap. Is it new?"
Listening	"You can hear the hummingbird's wings."
Naming	"That is a marigold. This flower is called a poppy."
Observing	"You are riding the tricycle smoothly."
Questioning	"Do you prefer the orange juice or the cranberry juice?"
Recalling	"Yesterday, the bus driver enjoyed eating a snack with us."
Rhyming	"Yes, the cat sat on the mat."
Speaking	"It will be clean-up time in five minutes."

Appropriately planned activities encourage a child's verbal fluency. Verbal fluency is his ability to speak. When a teacher writes down what the child says about an activity or experience, it is called dictation. Dictation, included with an art activity such as fingerpainting, records what the child says about their fingerpainting experience. You will ask a child to tell you about her work. Ask if she wants her comments written down. *Smart Telephone Partners* invites children to manipulative the telephones. You can add interactive questions such as: "What do you think the person will say when they answer the phone?" "Was there a busy signal?" "Did the icons on the phone tell you who was calling?" **(Curriculum Activity Guide 17 ▬▬).**

Cognitive Development with Communication and Literacy

Communication and literacy are significant parts of cognitive and language development. As you organize your curriculum plans, you may choose to identify communication and literacy as one of the curriculum areas. You can review the organization of curriculum areas by returning to the section, curriculum areas in Chapter 5.

You were likely introduced to literacy as a series of subjects in grade school that may have included spelling, reading, and writing. Or, you may have attended a school where whole language was emphasized with "writing across the curriculum." Early childhood programs integrate learning across the curriculum and encourage emergent experiences in the children's curriculum plan. You might hear other teachers refer to communication and literacy as language arts. **naeyc** 1a, 1b, 1c, 4a, 4b, 4c, 4d, 5a, 5b, 5c

Communication Skills and Possible Outcomes

Children first begin to communicate with their family members. The way children communicate sounds and words with particular tempos and pitches is a consequence of listening to their family members. The first two years are important for language learning. Children's innate temperament also influences their **communication** with the home language exerting tremendous influence on what and when sounds take shape. Your support and respect for linguistic diversity creates optimal learning opportunities for the children enrolled in your program. Language diversity in early childhood programs is an advantage. This brings the entire group of children into experiences where they will hear and learn to appreciate other languages than their own. Language diversity in the school also validates and preserves the children's home languages while supporting their acquisition of English as their second language.

Language and languages are tied to our personal identities. When children hear other languages they learn that there are many forms of expression (Figure 9–7). A dynamic for an inclusive community becomes the expected norm (Seefeldt and Galper 1998). Children are learning language through countless interactions with others across varied sociocultural contexts (Genishi and Dyson 2009). **naeyc** 1a, 1b, 1c

Developing communication skills involves more than just speaking. When children develop

Figure 9–7 Experiences Expand Multilingual Communication	
My Name in Many Colors	Prepare name tags with the children's names written (manuscript or DeNealian) in several different languages. Color code each language in a specific color or colors. Introduce name tags during a group time.
	Demonstrate the teacher's name tag first and then the children's in multiple languages. Allow children choices to select name tags in language preference.
Same Tune, Different Words	Sing familiar songs in primary language spoken by the majority of children. Sing the same songs in another language helping children to recognize that the tunes are the same.
Signing the Song	Guide the children in learning to sign a familiar song in American Sign Language, Signing Essential English, or Signing Exact English.
What do you call Your grandmother?	Display pictures of grandmothers.
	During a group time present photos of grandmothers representing diverse ethnicities. Provide the word for grandmother in many languages. Ask children what they call their grandmother. Follow-up activities may include grandfather, aunt, uncle, etc.

communication skills, they answer questions, discuss ideas, and express their feelings. Communication also involves listening, naming, observing, questioning, recalling or remembering, and rhyming. You will plan activities that offer children varied linguistic experiences. The varied linguistic experiences allow communicative interaction that is meaningful for the children in the program, for their families, and other adults participating in the program. You will enhance conversations by using simple sentences and speaking slowly and clearly. You will also foster encouraging behaviors for positive conversations by varying your tone of voice and choosing appropriate and meaningful words. Be sure to pause between sentences and use concrete vocabulary. Avoid using the word *that* to describe objects that have a name or label. Watchful, active teachers understand that children need time to learn and develop language skills. They create a flexible curriculum that allows for both verbal and non-verbal communication (Genishi and Dyson 2009).

When you are communicating with multiple-birth children, twins and supertwins (triplets and more in the group), try to speak to each child individually. Twins and supertwins are accustomed to sharing parental time for language learning. This is the reason they will benefit from individualized and direct conversations, in itself, with you. Engaging twins and supertwins in conversations does not ever justify separating the children into different classrooms (Arce 2010). As you will with the singleborn children, accept the twins and supertwins' language as they communicate to you and build on each of their own phrases and sentences.

Interactive questioning continues to be an important responsibility. You can pose comments that challenge the children to think, wonder, and discover by asking questions such as: "Imagine what it might look like if ten butterflies landed on our picnic table?" "How do you think we should walk into the library," "What might happen if we did not mix the water into the bowls with the flour?"

Children are aware of people speaking different languages. Children notice that some children communicate with their hands. Children will watch when you write down words that they say. Communication also involves listening and observing. Young children remember ideas and images they saw on television, in stores and restaurants, and in books. Their memory or remembering is referred to as recall.

There are many opportunities to enrich the communication skills of young children. You will

Books gives young children many pleasurable opportunities to build their communication and literacy skills.

© Cengage Learning 2013

Figure 9–8 Experiences Supporting Communication

Creative Dramatics	Role playing—acting like a cat, moving like the wind.
Interactive software	Computer software invites child's verbal response.
Dictating stories	Adult records in writing child's words and stories.
Discriminating	Perceiving and responding to different sounds and letters.
Discussing	Teacher-guided discussion during mealtime and group time.
Feeling box	Feeling and describing objects concealed in a special box.
Large movement	Walk up and down; crawl in and out; hop front and back.
Memory games	Show three items. Hide in basket. Can you remember?
Puppets	Speak, listen, and tell a story, poem, or teach a song.
Sequence stories	Tell part of familiar story. Child continues or completes.
Telephones	Dramatic play props (batteries removed for safety) dramatic prop.
Recorders	Records a child's messages; available for interactive stories.

have many chances to offer an extensive variety of linguistic experiences as you interact and converse with the children throughout their preschool years (Figure 9–8). naeyc 1a, 1b, 1c, 4a, 4b, 4c, 4d, 5a, 5b, 5c

Communication Activities

Observe and listen to the children. You will be able to identify their needs and interests for developing appropriate activities that support communication. The options are the same for planning activities. You can organize the curriculum from a thematic approach, developmental focus area approach, curriculum area approach, or within interest centers. Validating the children's emerging abilities with assessments that will establish credibility for your curriculum. Nate cuts a piece of paper in half. He walks to Charlotte and hands her the paper. Nate says, "This is your ticket to the fair, we gonna go to the fair." The teacher hears Nate's comment and is provided with a clue to Nathan's interest and prior experience with his family. Nate's developing communication skills will be supported with activities created around a project, theme, or interest center (Figures 9–9). A specific activity that utilizes a flannel board offers visual objects to help children tell a story. (**Curriculum Activity Guide 18**). **naeyc** 1a, 1b, 1c, 4a, 4b, 4c

---

Figure 9–9 Activities Contribute to Communication Skills

Observed Behavior: Nate cuts a piece of paper in half. He walks to Charlotte, hands the paper to her, and says, "This is your ticket to the fair, we gonna go to the fair."

Theme or Interest Center: County Fair

Activity	Skills
1. Ticket booth	Asking for ticket
Large box for ticket booth; rubber stamp; fair brochures; play money; music; money and ticket collection box; maps; employee hats.	Discussing maps Listening to ticket requests
2. Amusement Games	
Bean bags and cardboard target; ping pong balls and metal bucket; hidden treasure; pictures of prizes; tickets; ticket box; large boxes and tables.	Observing target Recalling hidden items Listening—balls in bucket

Literacy Skills and Possible Outcomes

"That's my letter." "I wanta write my name." "That says, stop."

Children become aware of the printed word everyday in a literate society. There are expectations for reading and writing performances. **Literacy** is important for learning in and out of school, for careers, and lifelong enjoyment.

Pre-Literacy skills during early childhood are connected with skills needed later, such as reading, fluency, comprehension, writing, and spelling. There appears to be certain skills that are consistently related to success. The National Early Literacy Panel suggested that teachers take a more purposeful approach in guiding young children. The panel cited research evidence showing the following foundational skills provide a thorough beginning to reading (2009).

- knowing the names of printed letters
- knowing the sounds associated with printed letters
- being able to manipulate the sounds of spoken language
- being able to rapidly name a sequence of letters, numbers, objects, or colors
- being able to write one's own name or even isolated letters
- being able to remember the content of spoken language for a short time

A challenge for early childhood educators committed to the value of play and discovery learning, is adapting research-evidenced recommendations to the activities that will engage the children age-appropriately. Activities that are incorporated into every day play times will reinforce these skills in a natural way. Another challenge is to help family members understand ways to encourage and support children's readiness for literacy. Family members are anxious for the children to do well in school. Too often this concern is translated into rushing the children's developing skills. You will be able to enhance children's competence without inappropriately pushing elementary school tasks into the preschool. Appropriate introduction to literacy will encourage a strong educational foundation of basic academic skills for children when best practices are honored.

The International Reading Association (IRA) and the National Association for the Education of Young Children (NAEYC) adopted a joint position paper. This statement points out to teachers and families that reading aloud to children is the most important activity. Reading aloud to children will develop their skills. Reading aloud

Figure 9–10 Concept Learning Contributes to Literacy Readiness

Concept:	Fruit		
Label	**Description**	**Features**	**Similarities/Differences**
Orange	Round	To eat	Round like an apple
	Smells	Squeeze for juice	Smells a little like a lemon

Concept:	Animal		
Label	**Description**	**Features**	**Similarities/Differences**
Guinea pig	Furry	Squeals	Looks like a cat
	No ears	Wiggles nose	Is not a rabbit

Figure 9–11 Related Vocabulary for an Activity

Activity Title	Cooking Pasta, Fideo, and Noodles	
Vocabulary	noodles	heat
	pasta	stir
	fideo (Spanish—a type of noodle)	sieve
		drain
	boil	soft
	sautée	long

supports children's comprehension of ideas and concepts. **(Curriculum Activity Guide 20 📖).** Focus on the rewards and pleasures of reading, writing, and labeling the spaces with words. Look at literacy as another way to communicate feelings, needs, and plans. As you help children along the pathway to literacy competence, accept their words and introduce them to new ideas and concepts. A concept is actually just an idea about an object, person, or event that children encounter or experience. Children explore their world with their senses, gaining distinct information about each item. As children begin to discriminate the features of objects they also make associations among them. You can help the children to organize and classify generalizations and relationships about objects and ideas. When children see how objects relate, they learn concepts.

You will enjoy supporting concept learning by emphasizing verbal and written language. Begin by labeling objects in the environment: "This is a gate." "Gus is our guinea pig." "Our guest today is a postal clerk. Her name is Ella." Provide descriptions of objects, such as, "The gate is metal," "The gate surrounds our play area," "The gate is gray." Add descriptions with fun and interesting adjectives, such as "The guinea pig is furry," "The guinea pig likes really fresh, green celery." The children will learn more ideas and begin to group these ideas into categories. Children also need to understand

how objects work and what animals do. Continue to communicate ideas verbally and by labeling the objects with written words and phrases. The guinea pig wiggles her nose. "Stacy fed the guinea pig today; see your name on the chart." Then, you can identify similarities and differences of the idea or object (Read 1976). In these ways you expand children's comprehension of concepts and you support literacy (Figure 9–10).

Early childhood programs can also be arranged to facilitate literacy by adding lists of the activity-related vocabulary in the weekly and monthly family newsletters. The lists can also be posted on the school's Websites and on bulletin boards (Figure 9–11). Parents becoming aware of the vocabulary will be able to reinforce the use of words and labels, thereby contribute to their children's literacy development.

Literacy Activities

Literacy activities for young children can begin with familiar topics and activities. Build on the children's previous experiences. Children's literacy skills will develop in settings where they hear and use language throughout the day. Literacy experiences relate to everything and everyone—to routines, materials, resources, and the children themselves. Teachers who enjoy reading books and other literature model a positive attitude about literacy to the children and their families. The children who are regularly provided with books and ample time for adults to read to them will develop reading abilities earlier and more successfully for both pleasure and information (Lay-Dopyera and Dopyera 1982). Research studies have indicated that many types of experiences give children a verbal advantage. These increase their readiness to read. The activities you plan to endorse literacy development ought to be concrete experiences. For the children who are unable to visit a zoo, pictures of zoo animals in books and on Websites will replace the genuine face-to-face encounter. The value of literature crosses over into many areas of the curriculum. For example, art activities extend children's oral language because they can express their feelings and ideas to others while developing skills in creative expression. Cooking

---

Figure 9–12 Young Children's Books Relate to Cooking Activities

Blueberries for Sal by Robert McCloskey. 1948. New York: Viking.

Bread and Jam for Frances by Russell and Lillian Hoban. 1964. New York: Harper & Row.

Chachaji's Cup. Written by Uma Krishnaswami and Illustrated by Soumya Sitaraman. 2003. San Francisco: Children's Book Press.

Chicken Soup with Rice by Maurice Sendak. 1962. New York: Harper & Row.

Stone Soup by Marcia Brown. 1947. New York: Charles Scribner's Sons.

---

activities are versatile and compatible with literacy learning. Award-winning books for young children (Figure 9–12) will augment cooking activities and contribute to literacy development.

There are numerous meaningful and instructive ways for you to advance the development of children's literacy skills (Figure 9–13). You will get great pleasure in reading books, telling stories, using puppets and flannel boards to support the children's emerging literacy skills. Children will learn that ideas and words can be represented symbolically in many ways including books, charts, and signs. **(Curriculum Activity Guides 27 and 21).** naeyc 1a, 1b, 1c, 4a, 4b, 4c, 4d, 5a, 5b, 5c

Cognitive Development with Mathematics

Asking children to place one napkin by each chair helps them to understand one-on-one correspondence. Setting up an activity for children to walk up and down steps helps them become aware of

---

Figure 9–13 Experiences Support Literacy

Bulletin board	Children place photographs or drawings of their pets under the words dog and cat.
Dictation	Adult writes down child's words, story.
Dramatic play props	Food orders, catalog orders, debit and charge receipts.
Labels	Meaningful word labels throughout indoor and outdoor environment.
Literature	Child listens to stories and books read by adult (picture books or Big Picture Books). Asks questions before, review story after.
Matching games	Purchased or prepared games allow matching similar pictures.
Microcomputer	Software for child or small group.
Object hunt	Searching for identified and labeled items familiar to children.
Observing adults	Writing, pointing to words in Big Books during story; writing child's name on work; writing messages from left to right, top to bottom.
Puppets	Manufactured and created, used to tell story or have children use to relate a story to be dictated. Can introduce an idea or open a group time.
Sign-in	Clipboard with children's names in large print for optional check off upon arrival and departure when parents sign in.
Storytelling	With small groups; use flannel board or props (optional). Children need to see and be able to listen to storyteller.
Backpack/briefcase	Writing materials, rubber stamps, rulers, books.
Visual charts	Charts for activities, such as cooking, that have pictures and words. Experience charts with children's descriptions of an activity.
Waiting lists	Waiting lists of children interested in participating in popular activities are maintained.
Writing center	Desk with variety of writing tools to include templates, magnetic letters, index boxes of each child's favorite letters or words.

their own body in relation to objects in a given space. Providing measuring tapes helps them to become aware of the length of their legs. What you plan and how you arrange the indoor and outdoor spaces will establish important beginnings for children to construct mathematical awareness. Early experiences are beneficial for building a foundation for later, more formal mathematical operations. **Mathematics** is a curriculum area that can be enjoyable to you and the children. This is possible because you and the teaching team will arrange experiences for exploration and discovery. You will encourage children to be inventive as they discover numbers, sizes, weights, lengths, time, sequence, and spatial relationships throughout the day. Mathematical experiences will enhance children's critical thinking, reasoning, and problem solving skills.

© Cengage Learning 2013

Appropriately arranged spaces for children allow them to begin establishing important beginnings for mathematical awareness.

Mathematics Skills and Possible Outcomes

Numbers are everywhere. Children are exposed early to ideas about numbers, size, and amounts through everyday experiences. Numbers are on television sets, smart phones, ovens, watches, price tags, money, and clocks. Numbers describe a child's age, older brother's size, how long it takes to get to school and the cost of a yogurt cone. Children learn early what *more* means and the significance of *big*. Discovering the relationships among objects in the home and school environments is a basic process of mathematics. Discovering the order or sequence of objects is also a basic process of mathematics. As you encourage curiosity, you will find that young children continue to investigate and find out about the objects and substances you provide throughout the day.

During their investigations, children become aware of mathematical concepts. They begin to realize that some objects sink and some float (weight); that the number two comes before the number three and three objects are more than two (sequence and quantity). Preschoolers discover concepts by manipulating real objects and materials in self-directed activities and teacher-guided activities. Interest centers can offer many experiences with mathematical concepts. The experiences will add to the children's maturing mathematical skills. Mathematical activities that will enhance skills include experiences

such as arranging buckets, ordering tricycles, and patterning or sequencing the drum beats (Figure 9–14).

Experiences with mathematical concepts should emerge from the children's interests and needs. Your overall plan will guide your activities as you introduce concepts and skills in appropriate sequence. The children will uncover their own areas of competence and areas needing opportunities for growth. Plan experiences that contribute to their developing mathematical skills (Figure 9–15). **naeyc** 1a, 1b, 1c, 3b, 4a, 4b, 4c, 4d, 5a, 5b, 5c

The mathematics program for children ages three to five years requires hands-on resources. Hand-on materials allow children to explore informally, in planned experiences, and in interest centers. Children need to be able to use, store, distribute, and replace the materials and other manipulatives when they have finished using them. Selection of appropriate mathematical materials for young children should meet recommended criteria. Recommendations suggest that materials are sturdy and versatile, fit the program guidelines and children's developmental stages, are safe, easily supervised, and bias-free (Charlesworth 2004).

Figure 9–14 Interest Centers Offer Mathematical Experiences

Interest Center	Recommended Materials for Rotation
Manipulative	Pegboard, geoboard, nesting blocks, puzzles, cubes, rods, stringing beads, mazes, linking blocks, magnet shapes, sorting-grouping-matching games, clocks, scales, measuring tapes and cups, spoons, timers, play money, calculator, shapes, tiles
Unit blocks	Unit blocks and storage shelf in carpeted area, play people, block size vehicles, signs, tracks
Cooking	Cooking utensils to include bowls and pans in various sizes, measuring spoons, scale
Large motor outside	Obstacle course, rebounder (counting and sequencing jumps), stop watch, ladder and steps (going up and down)
Dramatic play	Play money, calculators, receipts, checkbooks, maps, address books, compass, odometer, scale, stop watch, calculator, adding machine, credit cards, stamps
Sensorial area	Sand, water, textures, jars (to explore color, size, shape, size), and items from nature such as rocks and shells.

Figure 9–15 Mathematical Skills—Possible Outcomes

Arranging	Sand buckets from smallest to biggest
Ordering	Grouping, sorting, classifying objects that look alike; all tricycles to the wheel-toy garage.
Pairing	One space for each tricycle; one-to-one correspondence.
Patterning	Repeating sequence of drum beats.
Comparing	There are four flowers on that plant, two on this one.
Measuring	Amount of flour needed to make modeling dough.
Reversing	Following the path back to the preschool.
Analyzing	Whose plant is taller?
Graphing	Visually graphing children who drink juice or milk.

Mathematics is a curriculum area that is easily integrated throughout the children's day and planned experiences. Teacher Betsy remarks, "I see four children in the block area; check the sign and see if there is room for you." Later in the day, during snack time, Teacher Betsy comments, "You can cut this apple in half so that there is one piece for you, Michael, and one for Megan." In doing so, Teacher Betsy is guiding the children and enhancing their awareness of mathematical concepts. Activities in interest centers encourage sensory experiences and create numerous chances for the children to measure rice, shift sand, and pour cups of cornmeal. Materials placed in a mathematics interest center, or the manipulative center, need to be organized in containers and displayed on low, accessible shelving. Teachers should rotate the mathematical manipulatives periodically as the children's interests and development change or to relate the mathematical materials to a theme or project. Starting with topics that are familiar are more likely to be accepted by the children, especially concepts that relate directly to them (Figure 9–16). Routine classroom experiences also promote awareness

Figure 9–16 Interest Center Guide—Mathematics Measuring and Monitoring Growth

Interest Center *Mathematics*   **Theme** *I'm Growing*

Art	Cooking	Literacy	Quiet Reading	Outside Art	Outside Large Motor
Block	Computer	Manipulatives	Science	Outside Circle	Outside and/Water
Circle	Dramatic Play	Music/Rhythm	Sensorial	Outside Garden	Trike Path

Interest Center Guidelines   **Approximate Age Range** *4–5*

To provide experiences for children to measure and monitor their growth.

Developmental Focus   **Physical**   **Affective and Aesthetic**   **Cognitive and Language**

Curriculum Area Interest Center Materials

    Constant *Puzzles, cylinders, Legos, matching cards, unit rods, cubes, patterning and matching lottos.*

    Featured *Trays with mirrors, measuring tapes, cotton string, envelopes, scissors, index cards, felt pens, bath scale, pictures of hands, legs, heads.*

Preparation/Setup

1. *Add materials to trays.*
2. *Set trays on shelves in manipulative or sensorial area.*

Teaching Strategies

1. *Introduce new materials during Grouptime. Show pictures, measuring tape. Measure finger with tape and string.*
2. *Provide guidance and assistance for children as they request when measuring and cutting string the size of their foot, leg, or fingers.*

Possible Outcomes for the Child or Children

    Concepts *Fingers, legs, and arms are different sizes. A measuring tape tells the amount of inches or feet.*

    Skills *measuring, comparing*

    Vocabulary *measure, length, inch*

Child Participation   **Date**

Experiences will support children's mathematical concept and skill development when the activities remain suitable to their developmental stages.

© Cengage Learning 2013

of mathematics and provide enjoyment for children, "Chae, the goldfish needs just one ounce of food."

Mathematics Activities

Everly Jane seems very excited that Teacher Naomi has planned a visit the neighborhood medical clinic. She has talked about her grandpa often and said that she's going to visit him in the hospital. The school's visit to the neighborhood medical clinic is a purposeful activity planned to respond to Everly Jane and other children's needs to know more about hospitals. There are opportunities to expand their mathematical awareness and specific mathematical skills with a medical clinic focus. Mathematical concepts need to remain suitable for the children's developmental stages. To make these possible, activities need to remain simple with concrete, hands-on experiences (Figure 9–17).

The entire school spaces, indoors and outdoors, will become places for mathematical learning. You will be able to plan informal, unstructured, or teacher-guided interest centers for individual or small groups of children (Figure 9–18).

Manipulative experiences that encourage and support children's mathematical concept and skill development engage them as they handle, store, distribute, and replace the material. Activities in an early childhood setting will contribute to the children's mathematical awareness and concept building (Figure 9–19). **(Curriculum Activity Guide 30 📖).** naeyc 1a, 1b, 1c, 4a, 4b, 4c, 4d, 5a, 5b, 5c.

Figure 9–17 Mathematical Concepts for an Activity—Possible Outcomes	
Observed Behavior:	Everly Jane, using the telephone in the dramatic play area, says, "I'm going to visit my grandpa in the hospital."
Activity Title	Walking to the Neighborhood Clinic
Mathematical Skills	**Mathematical Concepts**
Pairing	Everyone walks with one friend.
Seriating	First we pair into twos, then we walk to the clinic. Next we look at the items, then we walk back.
Classifying	There are four waiting room chairs and two examining rooms.
Predicting	Will the bus have room to park?

Figure 9–18 Introducing Mathematical Concepts

Classification. Grouping objects with similar characteristics and features. Putting child-size shoes into one category or box and adult size shoes into another category or box.

Conservation. Understanding the amount does not change even though it may appear that way. Manipulating materials provides foundation for the skill to understanding that when five buckets are spread out across the sand box or next to each other, there are still only five buckets.

Seriation. Ordering or sequencing objects or events. Each day when the child arrives she checks off her name when her parent signs-in, then puts away her jacket into her cubbyhole, then enters the indoor activity area.

Concepts About Time. Also called temporal concept. "When will my daddy pick me up?" "It is clean-up time in five minutes, the big hand will be on the 12."

Concepts About Numbers. Stand with one friend for the walk. There were four large beds.

Concepts About Space. The lab for nurses is next to Jan's mother's classroom. The stethoscope was around the teacher's neck. Each preschooler sat on top of the hospital bed.

Figure 9–19 Activities Contribute to Mathematical Awareness

Activity	Skills
Big, Small, Medium Envelopes	sorting
	arranging
	ordering
Organizing Mail for Delivery	analyzing
	comparing

Cognitive Development with Science

Children learn about science whenever they actively experience natural phenomena in their immediate surroundings. Hands-on activities favor children's way of learning in the science curriculum area. Science is happening all around. You can support children's natural curiosity of nature by taking pleasure in the way they see their surroundings. You will have chances every day, some unexpected opportunities, to answer their many "Why's?" and "How come questions?" You will benefit from the valuable time you allow the children to enjoy the spring blossoms, touch wet sand, scoop fresh fallen snow, and feel the sun rays.

The study of science systematically organizes information about the world. Science is divided into two broad fields, biological science and physical science. The biological sciences include study about growing and living elements of the world. Physical science studies the causes and effects of matter, energy, and space.

Experiences remain child-focused if they are simple and real. Listen to what children are really saying and asking. Remain well acquainted with the children's homes because their comments are based on their prior experiences. Guide the children's discovery and investigations. Meaningful discovery is possible when relevant activities take children beyond simple observation of objects. Introduce children to experiences that allow them to mix, pour, stir, float, dissolve, and monitor what they see. Watch their reactions. Listen to their comments. Ask the children questions that allow them to "see" connections and consequences. For instance, do you acknowledge the children's reactions to the experience? Do you reflect on their comments and behaviors? Comment on and help children to think about the wet sand that feels and moves differently than the dry sand. Clarify misconceptions—"The sand does feel different. How does sand pile become wet? What happened when we were indoors?" Suggest caution to the children about their exploration of science materials. If you do not know the animal, you should approach carefully. Some plants may not be all right to touch and eat. Check with teachers or family members before smelling the contents of unknown containers. You will be able to integrate concepts of health and safety with science to help children become aware of hazards in their surroundings. Rapidly moving water is not safe. Food that is discolored may not be healthy to eat.

FiguRe 9–20 Safety Guides Children's Science Investigations

Guide	Introduce
Watch	Listen
Ask	Clarify
Alert	Integrate

Your role is to safely and thoughtfully guide the children's science exploration and investigations (Figure 9–20).

Science Skills and Possible Outcomes

Observing, classifying, quantifying, and communicating are skills that three-, four-, and five-year olds will use as they explore and investigate during science activities. The processes that help children gather information include inquiry. They need to know what and how to ask questions. Children also need to know it is acceptable to investigate because that is the way they will find out about objects and nature. Observation is the very basic to science investigation. Guide the children in their developing science skills by helping them to look, hear, smell, taste, and feel. Then help them to use the information gathered from their observations to make connections, see cause and effect and talk about what they observed. As they talk about their observations, you can point and add specific vocabulary and ideas. They begin to classify these concepts, finding similarities and differences.

Classification is another important skill in the science curriculum area. Classification helps children make sense out of objects. Children need opportunities to handle materials to develop and use their understanding of relationships between items (Prairie 2005). They can group objects according to the observable characteristics. Science involves abilities to compare, count, and measure. How much space did we need for the butcher paper? Was it hotter yesterday than today? Quantifying relates to the children's skills at observing, classifying, and describing objects more precisely (Neuman 1978). Inferring (thinking and talking about what might happen) and applying information are more abstract tasks reserved for older preschoolers and school-age children. Place the emphasis of science activities on emergent experiences, rather than isolated tasks and preconceived, commercially packaged experiments. Acceptable science topics for young children need to be useful for them. The topics should build basic science knowledge, promote useful skills, and be able to be explored through a variety of activities; and permit the children to discover by actively engaging with materials (Conezio and French 2003) (Figure 9–21).

Relevant, well-planned science activities contribute to the development of children's concepts while advancing their cognition. Conceptual awareness increases as children become increasingly perceptive of their surroundings. The activities you planned and the activities that spontaneously emerge, introduce children to the biological and the physical sciences. The children will acquire concepts about their bodies, pets, food, plants, and environment as they participate in biological science activities. They will acquire

Science activities contribute to the development of concepts and promote cognition.

© Cengage Learning 2013

Figure 9–21 Science Skills—Possible Outcomes

Exploring	sounds created by tapping on metal, plastic, wood.
Observing	the guinea pig eat lettuce.
Communicating	labeling, questioning, and talking about flowers in window box garden.
Organizing	rock collection.
Applying	experiences about healthy eating.
Relating	frozen bird bath to very cold weather/temperature.
Inferring	the wood block will sink and the feather will float.

concepts about physics and the elements like water and wind when you plan physical science activities (Figure 9–22).

Your approach to science will encourage children's positive attitude about natural and physical phenomena. Five-year-old Raymond brings photographs his family took on a vacation to his uncle's ranch. He points to sheep in the photograph that are corralled in a field. Raymond is excited about the wire that created a temporary corral. He shouts loudly, "we can't go near because the wire will hit us." The children who are nearby hear Raymond and begin gathering around Raymond to see the photograph and hear about the ranch, the sheep, and especially the hot wire. During the afternoon group time the children began talking about the sheep. It was agreed, Raymond's uncle would be invited to visit the school to talk about his ranch and the wire, ". . . maybe, said Raymond, he'll bring some sheep" (Figure 9–23).

Science Activities

Children's natural curiosity initiates ideas for incredible and numerous science activities. Your curriculum approach will identify strategies for presenting science experiences to the children in your program. Plan activities for children with familiar and natural materials. Keep the concepts and vocabulary simple: "Lambs are baby sheep," "A mommy sheep is called a ewe." Concrete, hands-on experiences build the children's knowledge. Scientific inquiry is fun and exciting when children observe cause and effect. With your guidance, they will experience natural events (cloud formation) and arrange materials in their environment (smelling different fruit). Children develop science skills and begin developing positive attitudes during their preschool years. Interest centers create places for science experiences. Science materials overlap and integrate with other curriculum areas and interest centers (Figure 9–24). As

Figure 9–22 Science Concepts—Possible Outcomes

Biological Science	Physical Science
Our bodies grow	The sun heats up metal tricycles
Pets need food, water, care	Blowing on a pinwheel makes it move
Some plants can be eaten	Warmed juice dissolves gelatin
Trees provide shade	The moon looks different at night
Creek water comes from snow	A wood block falls faster than a feather

Figure 9–23 An Activity Includes Science Concepts and Vocabulary

Activity Title	Visit From a Community Helper: Sheep Rancher Brings Lamb
Concepts	Sheep ranching is a job and business
Vocabulary	rancher corral grazing sheep hot wire wool lamb electricity shear barn section weave livestock

Figure 9–24 Interest Centers Support Science

Interest Center	Recommended Materials for Rotation
Manipulative	Color paddles, prisms, weights, scales, lenses, sundial, sponges, magnets, puzzles, microscope, flashlights, compass, magnifiers
Discovery/ Sensory	Weights, collections (shells, rocks, soil, textures), microscope, water (coloring, sponges, eyedroppers, straws), objects (touching, seeing, tasting, smelling, hearing), ant colony, aquarium, ant and silkworm farms, terrarium (plant and worm)
Cooking	Cooking utensils and appliances
Pets	Staff preference and commitment to pet care and available space determines selection. May include guinea pigs, birds, and fish—indoors
Gardening	Indoor safe plants throughout center; herbs; outdoor garden area—shovels, trowels, rakes, watering cans, hose, signs, sun hats, soil, seedling containers, gloves
Dramatic Play	Clothing and props for science-related occupations: gardener, horticulturist, botanist, meteorologist, geologist, astronomer, chemist, chef, veterinarian, engineer

children explore ideas (where does rain go), their critical thinking and language develops (timing and changes of stop lights). You and your teaching team will plan science activities that will enhance possibilities for cognitive development. **(Curriculum Activity Guides 31 and 32 📖).**

naeyc 1a, 1b, 1c, 4a, 4b, 4c, 4d, 5a, 5b, 5c

Thinking About What You Have Learned

✔ Observe two preschool children to assess their interest in books and the printed words. Prepare one activity for each child that supports their literacy development. Complete a Curriculum Activity Guide for each activity.

✔ Plan two mathematics activities that will help family members understand the value of hands-on, manipulative materials for young children. Complete Curriculum Activity Guides to document each activity. Be prepared to present the activities to your peers.

✔ Access one of the following Web sites. List three science activities that could be suitably adapted to meet young children's needs. If these sites are not active, locate another Web site that lists science or mathematics activity ideas.

> http://www.exploratorium.edu/
> science_explorer/
> http://www.geocities.com/wyllz
> http://www.magnasystems.org
> http://pbskids.org/zoom/activities/preschool/

Chapter References

Charlesworth, Rosalind. 2004. *Experiences in math for young children.* 5th ed. Albany, NY: Delmar Learning.

Cohen, Dorothy H., Virginia Stern, and Nancy Balaban. 2008. *Observing and recording the behavior of young children.* 5th ed. New York: Teachers College Press.

Conezio, Kathleen and Lucia French. 2003. *Science in the preschool classroom: Capitalizing on children's fascination with the everyday world to foster language and literacy development.* In Derry G. Koralek, ed. *Spotlight in Young Children and Play.* Washington, DC: National Association for the Education of Young Children.

Copple, Carol, and Sue Bredekamp. 2009. *Developmentally appropriate practice in early childhood programs serving children from birth through age 8.* 3rd ed. Washington, DC: National Association for the Education of Young Children.

Elkind, David. 1976. *Child development and education: A piagetian perspective.* New York: Oxford University Press.

Fillmore, Lily. W. 1993 Summer. Educating citizens for a multicultural 21st century. *Multicultural Education,* 10–12, 37.

Genishi, Celia and Ann Hass Dyson. 2009. *Children, language and literacy: Diverse learners in diverse times.* NY: Teachers College Press.

Hohmann, Charles. 1998. Evaluating and selecting software for children. *Child Care Information Exchange,* 123, 60–62.

Lay-Dopyera, Margaret, and John E. Dopyera. 1982. *Becoming a teacher of young children.* 2nd ed. Lexington, MA: DC: Heath.

National Association for the Education of Young Children. 1998. Learning to read and write: Developmentally appropriate practices for young children. A joint position statement of the International Reading Association (IRA) and the National Association for the Education of Young Children (NAEYC). *Young Children* 53(4), 30–45.

Neuman, Donald B. 1978. *Experiences in science for young children.* Albany, NY: Delmar.

Pool, C. R. 1997. A safe and caring place. *Education Leadership* 55(4), 43–77.

Prarie, Arlene P. 2005. *Inquiry into math, science, and technology for teaching young children. Clifton Park,* NY: Thompson Delmar Learning.

Read, Katherine H. 1976. *The nursery school: Human relationships and learning.* 6th ed. Philadelphia: W. B. Saunders.

Seefeldt, Carol and Alice Galper. 1998. *Continuing issues in early childhood education.* 2nd ed. Upper Saddle River, NJ: Merrill.

Thompson, Ross A. 2008. Connecting neurons, concepts, and people – Brain development and its implications. In *Preschool Policy Brief.* Ellen C. Frede and W. Steven Barnett, eds. New Brunswick, NJ: National Institute for Early Education.

Tsantis, Linda A., Cynthia J. Bewick, and Suzanne Thouvenelle. 2003. *Examining some common myths about computer use in the early years. Beyond the Journal.* http://journal.naeyc.org/btj/200311/CommonTechnoMyths.pdf

Professional Growth: Success with Curriculum Management

chapter

10

© Cengage Learning 2013

Picture This . . .

The college students who ask questions during course lectures and discussions generally introduce important issues. It is sincerely rewarding to acknowledge students as they progress successfully through a course. The terms and concepts that were introduced to them at the beginning of each semester become an integral part of their vocabulary. As you begin to use the language of early childhood education, do so with a commitment to the profession. Your commitment to improving the quality of care and learning for young children has lasting benefits. You improve the lives of children and their families. You participate in a professional process with integral educational benefits for yourself as well. Throughout your continuing professional development you will be able to refer to your textbooks to reinforce the knowledge you acquired during your coursework. You can return to sections for answers to some of the questions that appear during your initial teacher preparation. The continuing access to applicable knowledge strengthens your advancement as an early childhood professional.

Assessing Knowledge for Continued Professional Development

Common Question	Chapter	Chapter Section
"How do you make curriculum fun and keep the children's interest?"	Chapter 1	Understanding Curriculum and Early Childhood Education
	Chapter 2	What You Need to Know About Meeting the Needs of Young Children
	Chapter 6	Promoting Playful Experiences during Early Childhood
"Are there regulations that must be followed related to curriculum?"	Chapter 1	Types of Programs Fundamental Principles Shape Early Childhood Education
	Chapter 5	Guidelines and Standards
"I think that I have been doing the right activity, I just don't know why I plan the activities that I do?"	Chapter 2	Supporting the Young Child's Development
	Chapter 3	Observation and Assessment: Using the Cues from Children for Curriculum Planning
	Chapter 4	Authentic Curriculum: Environments and Learning for All
"How can I convey to the children that they might not always have choices?"	Chapter 4	Partnering with Families for Meaningful Program Experiences
	Chapter 5	Guidelines and Standards
	Chapter 6	Establishing a Curriculum Schedule
"How can I provide meaningful activities for children with special needs?"	Chapter 1	Strengthening Connections: Harmony, Equity, Respect in Children's Programs
	Chapter 2	Each Child is an Individual
	Chapter 3	Becoming Part of an IEP Team
	Chapter 6	Maximizing the Spontaneous Teaching Moments
"What is the right way to teach children in a group who are different ages?"	Chapter 2	Influences on Young Children's Growth and Development Individualizing Curriculum Experiences
	Chapter 5	Individualizing Curriculum Experiences Multi-Age Groups

GUIDE TO READING CHAPTER 10

Chapter Outline

Advantages of Planning Early Childhood Curriculum
    Value for Children, Families, and Teachers
    Satisfy Children's Needs and Program Guidelines
    Curriculum Planning Takes a Team Effort
Professional Preparation and Growth
    Professional Commitment
    Evolving Trends for Early Childhood Professionals
Thinking About What You Have Learned

Learning Objectives

After reading this chapter, you will be able to

1. Explain the advantages of planning early childhood curriculum.
2. Discuss how curriculum plans meet school and program guidelines.
3. Document three ways that a team effort in curriculum planning are beneficial.
4. Identify the significance of professional commitment for a successful early educator.
5. Recognize suitable professional growth and educational opportunities.

Key Terms

National Association for the Education of Young Children (NAEYC) Standards for Initial Early Childhood Professional Preparation Programs Met by this chapter:

Standard 4: Using Developmentally Effective Approaches

4a: Understanding positive relationships and supportive interactions as the foundation of their work with young children.

Standard 6: Becoming a Professional

6a: Identifying and involving oneself with the early childhood field.

6b: Knowing about and upholding ethical standards and other professional guidelines.

6c: Engaging in continuous, collaborative learning to inform practice; using technology effectively with young children, with peers, and as a professional resource.

6d: Integrating knowledgeable, reflective, and critical perspectives on early education.

6e: Engaging in informed advocacy for young children and the early childhood profession.

Standard 7: Early Childhood Field Experiences

7a: Opportunities to observe and practice in at least two of the three early childhood age groups (birth–age 3, 3-5, 5-8).

7b: Opportunities to observe and practice in at least two of the three main types of early education settings (early school grades, childcare centers and homes, Head Start and other programs).

Advantages of Planning Early Childhood Curriculum

Ideally, curriculum planning becomes a natural and customary practice for you as an early childhood professional. Planning with a specific educational vision will guide your adoption of a curriculum approach and the related teaching strategies. Building your curriculum around a curriculum approach and meaningful strategies will contribute to predictability and confidence in your work with young children. As your knowledge of early childhood education builds, so will the probability that your program for your children will be one of quality.

Planning curriculum with the children's needs and interests foremost allows you to create a responsive program for them. Planning curriculum also allows time to bring together teachers that will ensure a stable environment for care and learning. When you thoughtfully and purposefully design curriculum, you maximize your time

and program resources. This will increase opportunities for additional quality interaction with the children and among your teaching team. You will also find that you have more individualized time for the children.

Value for Children, Families, and Teachers

Creating and managing a curriculum requires rechecking children's assessments. Planning requires that you meet regularly with the teaching team to review and modify the plan. Have the activities evolved from the assessments? Do the activities meet the children's needs appropriately? **Team planning** enables you and the other teachers to determine whether activities are balanced among the curriculum areas. Working together to review the schedule will help pinpoint whether activities are distributed among the developmental focus areas. Continuous review is valuable because modifying activities is a strong indication that you are adapting to the children's changing needs. A particularly important benefit for the program is the improved utilization of the facility and resources. When the teachers know what is expected, they are able to concentrate on supporting the children. When parents know what to expect, they will be able to prepare and offer their time more suitably. Planning also helps establish a common attitude among teachers. Collaborating and cooperating creates a common sense of purpose (Hearron and Hildebrand 2006).

You will help family members appreciate their children's work. Display curriculum plans so that they are accessible to parents and other family members. Be available to explain and answer questions about the schedule and planned activities. Parents will develop respect for the way young children learn. They will also respect you, a professional who is committed to offering well-planned and validated activities (Hearron and Hildebrand 2006).

Satisfy Children's Needs and Program Guidelines

The **program guidelines** your school has adopted will directly affect your curriculum planning. Standards, guidelines, and policies influence the schedule and activities. To a large extent, standards, guidelines, and policies also determine the way you interact with the children and their families. Research has not suggested that one curriculum planning approach is necessarily superior.

A team effort has positive implications for children and families in early care and learning programs.

© Cengage Learning 2013

Rather, curriculum is best when it recognizes the fundamental principles of early childhood education and when it suits the children's needs. It is best when the practices are validated with research-based knowledge about child development and learning during early childhood.

Curriculum Planning Takes a Team Effort

A team effort has positive implications for the entire program. A dynamic, well-functioning team has benefits for you, other teachers, children, and the families. Strong interpersonal relations, respect for personal characteristics, and mutual outlook regarding your work with young children are vital factors for successful curriculum planning. Because you are a teacher, you are part of an organization. This requires you and the others on your teaching team to work together as colleagues (Arends 2007).

Your program administrator or site supervisor should be a resource for you to develop your own style of teaching and interpersonal relations with other teachers. Welcome suggestions from the program administrator, site supervisor, or other mentor. They should have insight regarding children's needs and how you might adjust the curriculum for optimum outcomes for the children. Hopefully, the feedback from supervisors and mentors is positive and contributes to your activity planning. Supportive staff will make it easier for you to become a successful professional. Periodic review of long-range curriculum plans is productive when teachers participating in the evaluation know what to expect and what they are required to contribute. Teachers need to believe that time given to review is well spent. A prepared agenda, e-mailed or posted in advance, is one way to establish the value of the meeting. Early distribution of an agenda also allows teachers to add topics and elicits their support in a collaborative planning process.

Professional Preparation and Growth

You keep hearing that the more you learn about children, the more you will want to learn. As a teacher of young children you have already committed to learning as much as possible about children, how they develop and learn. Have you thought about the way you learn? What motivates you to continue seeking knowledge? What else do you think you need to know, as you further your professional preparation? You can energize your own motivation for inquiry or more information by collaborating with your peers in study sessions, participating in special staff meetings away from the school, and networking with colleagues and former classmates for curriculum resource exchange. The children will motivate you with their curiosity and enthusiasm about discovery. They will compel you to seek more answers and find better ways to meet their needs.

Professional Commitment

The two words, *professional* and *commitment,* go together. A professional is an individual who is in some way related to an occupation or line of work. A professional is engaged in a career. An occupation, as well as most careers, requires special preparation and education, unlike a hobby or casual volunteering. In this role, you are dedicated to a career requiring college coursework, in-service training, and in most states some form of certification that documents work experience. Your commitment to acquiring knowledge affirms learning as a continuous adventure with lifelong benefits.

Professional commitment begins with you and your perception of your career. The field of early childhood education needs teachers of young children to *want* to be in their position. Curriculum for young children is as valuable and as much fun as you make it! Yet, it also will be necessary to continually clarify what is important for children.

An early childhood educator's responsibilities remain focused on the children. You will form partnerships with their families as well. Teachers of young children are also parent and family educators. You are responsible for creating a seamless transition between your program and the children's homes. The links you establish between the school and the children's homes have advantages for everyone, including children, families, and teachers. You will be competent as a professional when you help families enjoy parenthood and grandparenthood. Your compassionate guidance will help families feel competent about their actions and interactions with their children.

Early childhood education needs to become increasingly sensitive to gender equity within the profession. Studies suggest that fathers become more involved with their children when appropriate opportunities are provided. One strategy is to offer opportunities to men to participate in activities that may lead to early childhood care and learning

© Cengage Learning 2013

Children are able to continuously engage teachers to seek more answers and find better ways to meet their needs.

employment (Cunningham and Watson 2002). Hiring and retraining men in early childhood education programs require that professionals in the field recognize the value and importance of male teachers in the schools for young children. The probability that male teachers will remain in programs is related to how they feel in the setting. Are there posters of children with men? Do the children's books depict men? Are the shirts and aprons modified to accommodate a variety of styles, including fabric prints and sizes? Do the in-service topics refer to fathers and men? (Cunningham and Watson 2002).

Professional commitment is all about your dedication to continue learning. You will be able to achieve a sense of professional satisfaction when your work with children is acknowledged. You will feel gratification as a member of a teaching team that works collaboratively and cooperatively. You will contribute to a respectful setting by sharing resources and information with staff members (Katz and Ward 1989). Another way to achieve professional satisfaction is to support entry-level staff. Mentor the volunteers and student teachers. Demonstrate your commitment to the profession with ongoing advocacy for quality care and education and appropriate compensation for teachers of young children.

Child advocacy became prominent in 1990 (Hymes 1991) as a movement to connect knowledge about children and early education. Membership in one or more professional organizations will connect you with other professionals in the field (Figure 10–1). **naeyc** 4a, 6c, 6e

Figure 10–1 Early Childhood Professional Organizations—Partial Listing

ACEI	Association for Childhood Education International
	www.acei.org/
AMS	American Montessori Society
	http://www.amshq.org/
AMI	Association Montessori Internationale
	www.montessori-ami.org/
CEC	Council for Exceptional Children
	http://www.cec.sped.org/
CDA	Council for Professional Recognition
	www.cdacouncil.org/res_org.htm
NAEYC	National Association for the Education of Young Children
	http://www.naeyc.org
NBCDI	National Black Child Development Institute
	http://nbcdi.org/
NFCA	National Family Caregivers Association
	http://nfcacares.org/
NCCA	National Child Care Association 1016 Rosser Street Conyers, GA 30012
	www.nccanet.org/

Professional organizations also offer conferences, training, and peer-reviewed journals. Larger organizations research and formulate positions regarding public policy. Additional resources distributed by professional organizations offer information for you to share with families and local community groups. Membership in a professional organization profiles you as a professional and an advocate for improving the care and learning for young children.

Professional preparation for a career requires some form of preparedness, training, and experience in the occupational area. Training of early care and education professionals is essential to the provision of high-quality services for young children. Access to educational preparation and employment requirements vary by state. Field experiences and clinical practice are usually planned and sequenced so that students and teachers develop the knowledge, skills, and professional dispositions that are necessary to promote the development and learning of young children across the entire developmental period of early childhood (NAEYC 2010). Research has confirmed that the quality of early childhood care experiences is largely determined by the presence of well-trained and responsive caregivers (Child Development Policy Institute Education Fund 2003). Effective training can be informal and occur within the center or school. Frequently this type of professional preparation is enhanced with the assistance of a mentor or group of supportive colleagues. In early childhood education, preparation includes experience, training, and knowledge. Knowledge includes courses in child development, teaching and curriculum, health and safety, guidance, family relationships, diversity, and management. Access to educational preparation and training varies widely by state. Employment qualifications and requirements also vary by state (NCCIC 2010). **naeyc** 6a, 6b, 6c, 6d, 7a, 7b

There are many points of entry into the early childhood profession. The ways jobs, positions, and roles are designated are diverse. You will also find that in the different types of early childhood programs, the description and responsibilities of the teachers, teacher assistants, and teacher aides differ. For instance, a teacher assistant might be called an associate teacher in one program and an entry-level teacher in another. Training and education for a career working with young children also have distinctive features and requirements. The Child Development

Associate Credential (CDA) provides competency-based training and evaluation. The CDA is administered by the Council for Early Childhood Professional Recognition. CDAs are awarded to candidates who meet the six core competency areas of the credential (Sciarra and Dorsey 2003). Two-year colleges offer coursework leading to certificates and associate degrees. Four-year colleges and universities also offer certificates and bachelor degrees. These institutions of higher education require varied sequences of coursework, including core content about child development, family and community, curriculum, guidance, diversity, and inclusion.

Professional growth is an important and ongoing commitment in an early childhood education career. Professional growth generally requires teachers and program administrators to continue accessing knowledge about child development and early care and learning. Professional growth may be an employment requirement or may be necessary for renewal of certification and credentials. You may decide to take professional growth classes or attend workshops because of a particular interest or to acquire information about a child or children in your group. Professional growth offers opportunities for you to gather new curriculum ideas, acquire knowledge about current research, and collaborate with others in your profession.

The outcome of well-planned professional growth is the sense of fresh energy. Workshops, conferences, in-service training, and formal courses allow teachers to review and evaluate the process of lifelong learning. Professional development is an ongoing practice. Professional commitment encourages relationships with other teachers. Professional growth sets in motion time for you to reflect about your teaching and your curriculum. Professional growth urges teachers to receive new information and contemplate ways to appropriately apply the new research and ideas in your professional work. Professional growth encourages involvement and membership in professional organizations. Groups such as the National Association for the Education of Young Children (NAEYC), Association for Childhood Education International (ACEI), and the National Family Child Care Association (NFCCA) have national, state, and local affiliations or chapters and regularly hold conferences. These organizations offer support, education, connections with other professionals, and updates on the latest research in the field.

Evolving Trends for the Early Childhood Professionals

Early Childhood teachers who strive for quality programs for young children, their families, and communities face challenges. Creating inclusive and caring programs requires that you have ongoing opportunities for continuing education. Creating quality programs invites you to honor staff collaboration. Teachers who are given these opportunities are more likely to plan curriculum that will meet the children's needs appropriately.

Preparation for this profession requires some form of preparedness, including experience and academic study. Research indicates that staff with formal college coursework and credentials provide higher quality care and education of young children. Professional growth, in the form of in-service workshops, conferences, and formal course work, allows teachers to review and evaluate in order to continue advocating for curriculum that is meaningful for young children.

For now, you are concentrating on your college coursework and the application of that knowledge in your practicum work with young children. There are challenges facing education and challenges facing teachers of young children. How can a stronger connection be built to bridge families and programs? Which policies are most beneficial for children? Can policies benefit the school and remain responsive to families? Have the educational requirements for career preparation become more accessible? Is public policy moving forward for equitable compensation?

Translate the challenges into a list of commitments. As a teacher, you will continuously model the value of learning to children, their families, and the community. You will remain knowledgeable with your membership in professional organizations. Seek out information about curriculum and activity planning. Appreciate the diversity of our cultures. Deliver curriculum to young children with a variety of teaching strategies that meet their needs and interests. Continue your commitment to the profession and advocate for curriculum that is meaningful for young children.

Thinking About What You Have Learned

✔ Meet with a member of an early childhood professional organization. Discuss the benefits that the organization provides to members. Accompany, if possible, the member to a local meeting.

✔ Make a list of your experiences and academic preparation related to early childhood curriculum. What workshops and/or coursework have you completed?

✔ What negative remarks have you heard from persons outside the field of early childhood about the early care and learning field? List the remarks and prepare a thoughtful, written response to one of the remarks.

✔ Log on to the following two websites. Provide the name, address, and contact phone number of the organization. Also list the name of the president for each professional organization.

http://www.naeyc.org
http://www.nccanet.org/

Chapter References

Arends, Richard I. 2007. *Learning to teach.* 7th ed. New York: McGraw-Hill.

Child Development Policy Institute Education Fund. 2003. Promoting School Success: Closing the Gap between Research and Practice. http://www.thechildrenscollabrium.com/Promotingschoolsuccess.pdf

Cunningham, Bruce. 1999. Hiring and retaining male staff. *Child Care Information Exchange,* 125, 66–69.

Cunningham, Bruce, and Lemuel W. Watson. 2002. Recruiting male teachers. *Young Children* 56(6): 10–15.

Hearron, Patricia F., and Vera Hildebrand. 2006. *Management of child development centers.* 6th ed. Upper Saddle River, NJ: Merrill.

Hymes, James L. 1991. *Early childhood education: Twenty years in review, a look at 1971–1990.* Washington, DC: National Association for the Education of Young Children.

Katz, Lillian G., and Evangeline H. Ward. 1989. *Ethical behavior in early childhood education.* Washington, DC: National Association for the Education of Young Children.

National Child Care Information and Technical Assistance Center (NCCIC). 2010. State Core Knowledge and/or Competencies. http://nccic.acf.hhs.gov/pubs/goodstart/corekc.html

Sciarra, Dorothy J., and Ann G. Dorsey. 2003. *Developing and administering a child care center.* 5th ed. Albany, NY: DelmarThomson Learning.

appendix

A

Making Early Learning Standards Work for You

Early learning standards provide a shared framework for teachers and program administrators to develop and offer meaningful curriculum planning. Standards are not intended to become the curriculum or an assessment tool. Rather, standards have been designed to help teachers and program administrators communicate expectations regarding children's development. The framework can assist early childhood professionals to meet their own state early learning standards in their curriculum, environments, and interactions with children (Riley et al. 2008). To find your state's standards and quality rating assessment methodologies, you can visit http://nccic.acf.hhs.gov/resource/state-early-learning-guidelines.

The Curriculum Activity Guide (CAG) template (appendix B) provides an area for *standards met*. The examples provided below illustrate the inclusion of standards and demonstrate how you will be able to utilize the format and include relevant standards that apply in your state and that may be required by your program.

Meaningful activities planned for your children potentially meet their needs in more than one developmental focus area. An activity could meet their cognitive needs and at the same time satisfy and promote their physical development. An activity might meet children's needs in all three developmental focus areas: physical, affective (social-emotional understanding) and aesthetic, and cognitive. The standards listed below in the sample Curriculum Activity Guides (CAGs) provide reference to curriculum areas as they were presented in Chapter 5. Curriculum areas merge and overlap in practice. An activity might relate to two or more curriculum areas, such as mathematics and social understanding. Similarly, a single activity may contribute to many performance standards. For instance, an activity designed to provide children with measuring experiences using the water table promotes their mathematical skills and at the same time advances fine motor skills, science knowledge, cognitive-processing skills, social skills, self-regulation skills, and language development (Riley et al. 2008).

The following three Curriculum Activity Guides offer examples of how to list standards met by some of the experiences and activities offered in early care and learning programs. Standards from various states are listed according to the curriculum area and developmental focus listed for the activity.

(Riley, Dave, Robert R. San Juan, Joan Klinkner, and Ann Ramminger. 2008. *Social and emotional development: connecting science and practice in early childhood settings.* St. Paul, MN: Redleaf Press.)

CURRICULUM ACTIVITY GUIDE 6

The Three Bears: Creative Dramatics

Goal: To give children an opportunity to dramatize a familiar story

Curriculum Area	Developmental Focus	Location/Interest Center
Creative Dramatics	Affective—Social	Inside Dramatic Play

Participants	Time	Age Range
1 to 4 children	10 to 20 minutes	3 to 4 years old

Materials

A "Three Bears" storybook, three chairs, three plastic bowls and spoons, three mats, or blankets to serve as beds

Preparation/Setup

Locate props. Set up dramatic play area as for the bear's house.

Teaching Strategies

Teacher reads a "The Three Bears" storybook at group time. Teacher explains that props are available in dramatic play area to act out the story. Children use props to freely act out story.

Possible Outcomes

Concepts
We can act out stories.
We can take turns playing parts.

Skills
Social interaction, cooperation, opportunity for affective development

Vocabulary
actor, drama

Date

Standards Met
Connecticut State Department of Education
Educational experiences will assure that preschool children will assume the role of someone or something else and talk in the language/tone appropriate for that person or thing.

Comments and Reflection

CURRICULUM ACTIVITY GUIDE 29

Sorting Seashells

Goal: To give the children opportunities to explore and sort seashells

Curriculum Area	Developmental Focus	Location/Interest Center
Mathematics	Cognitive—Critical Thinking	Inside Manipulative

Participants	Time	Age Range
Individual child	5 minutes	3 to 4 years olds

Materials

Sorting tray with numerous compartments (muffin baking tin), assortment of seashells

Preparation/Setup

Locate all materials. Set up sorting tray and collection of shells in large container.

Teaching Strategies

Child takes activity from shelf and sorts shells by type and/or size. Teacher can facilitate child's experience by discussing attributes of shells. Child replaces all materials, returns activity to shelf. Other materials from nature can be used such as leaves, rocks, sticks, etc. Science items such as magnifying glasses can be added.

Possible Outcomes

Concepts
I can sort shells. Sorting means to match the shells that look the same.

Skills
Differentiation skills, mathematical development

Vocabulary
Alike, different, shells, sort, match, same

Date

Standards Met

Massachusetts Department of Education Program Standards
D. Activities, materials, and equipment promote EDUCATIONAL GOALS through concrete learning

1. Learning experiences support problem solving, critical thinking, communication, and social skills within a meaningful context for the child.
2. Play experiences foster development and organization of knowledge about the world around them.

Comments and Reflection

CURRICULUM ACTIVITY GUIDE 38

Jumping Frog Obstacle Course

Goal: To give children the opportunity to jump

Curriculum Area	Developmental Focus	Location/Interest Center
Movement	Physical—Large Motor	Outside Large Motor

Participants	Time	Age Range
5 to 8 children	10 to 20 minutes	Appropriate for all ages

Materials

Bicycle tires or hula hoops, large mats (blue mats could simulate frog ponds), signs, arrows or carpets to indicate starting point and direction

Preparation/Setup

Set up a "jumping frog" obstacle course with tires or hoops to jump into, mats to serve as "ponds" to jump into. Make signs with drawings or photos of frogs. Signs can indicate: "Jumping Frog Obstacle Course," "Frog Pond," "This Way," and "Jump In!" Select and prepare music that inspires jumping.

Teaching Strategies

Discuss how frogs like to jump. Model jumping actions to the children. Invite children to try the "Jumping Frog Obstacle Course." Children jump through the course like frogs. Encourage children verbally, "Look at this frog jump!"

Possible Outcomes

Concepts
Frogs jump. Children can jump like frogs. Leap is another way to jump and move forward.

Skills
Large motor development, following directions, dramatic play opportunity, moving to music

Vocabulary
Jump, frog, obstacle course, leap, pond

Date

Standards Met

Connecticut State Department of Education
Educational experiences will assure that preschool children will demonstrate competence in a variety of activities that require coordinated movement using large muscles. Examples: Climbing stairs and ladders, jumping, hopping, dancing, creative movement

Wyoming Early Childhood Readiness Standards

VII. Physical Health and Development Domain/Content Area (A) Gross Motor Skills Standard: The child demonstrates control, balance, strength, and coordination in gross motor tasks.

Comments and Reflection

Curriculum Activity Guide (Template)

Curriculum Activity Guide

Title

Goal:

Curriculum Area   **Developmental Focus**   **Location/Interest Center**

Participants   Time   **Age Range**

Materials

Preparation/Setup

Teaching Strategies

Possible Outcomes

Concepts

Skills

Vocabulary

Date

Standards Met

Comments and Reflection

appendix
C

Curriculum Activity Guides Listed by Curriculum Areas

appendix
D

Curriculum Activity Guides (CAGs) 1–50

CURRICULUM ACTIVITY GUIDE 1 — Sociodramatic Play: Domestic Scene

Goal: To give children the opportunity to role play families

Curriculum Area	Developmental Focus	Location/Interest Center
Social Understanding	Affective—Social	Inside Dramatic Play

Participants	Time	Age Range
1 to 4 children	20 to 30 minutes	Appropriate for all ages

Materials

Housekeeping props, gender-specific and non-specific clothing, baby clothes, blankets, dolls, and related props, photos of families emphasizing diversity, inclusiveness, relationships, and nurturing, storage for materials

Preparation/Setup

Display photos of domesticated scenes showing diverse families and family structures in dramatic play area. Locate clothing and display in area.

Teaching Strategies

Introduce clothing to the children during group time. Include clothing commonly worn by both men and women and clothing worn exclusively by men or by women. Encourage questions as selected clothing pieces are displayed and circulated during group time. Children freely explore materials in dramatic play area. Assist children trying on clothing. Interact and answer questions.

Possible Outcomes

Concepts
Boys and girls can pretend to be adults, mommies and daddies, by trying on a variety of clothing. Some clothing is worn by both men and women (mommies and daddies). Some clothing is worn by only women (mommies). Some clothing is worn by only men (daddies).

Skills
Exposure to clothing differences. Accepting attitude toward differences.
Practice domestic roles.

Vocabulary
Clothing, men, women, adult, mommy, mommies, daddy, daddies, parents, children

Date

Standards Met

Comments and Reflection

CURRICULUM ACTIVITY GUIDE 2 — Sociodramatic Play: Becoming a Bus Driver

Goal: To give children the opportunity to explore the role of bus driver

Curriculum Area	Developmental Focus	Location/Interest Center
Social Understanding	Affective—Social	Inside or Outside Dramatic Play

Participants	Time	Age Range
5 to 8 children	10 to 20 minutes	3 to 4 years old

Materials

Child-size chairs (5 to 8), battery operated radio (optional), hand-held radio or walkie-talkie (optional), pennies, tokens, and tickets, cardboard box or plastic container for pennies, tokens, and tickets, sign

Preparation/Setup

Set up chairs to replicate the inside of a bus—One chair in front for a driver and two to four rows behind the driver.
Set up radio and walkie-talkies for "driver."
1. Prepare fare receptacle to accommodate pennies, tokens, and tickets.
2. Prepare signs: "Ride the Bus," "Take Rapid Transit," "Use Public Transportation."

Teaching Strategies

Encourage children's role-play riding and bus driving, using pennies, tokens, and tickets as fare.
Facilitate children's enactment of bus driving with interactive questioning and modeling.

Possible Outcomes

Concepts
Bus drivers have an important job. Boys or girls can become bus drivers. Bus riders must pay a bus fare (money, tokens, or tickets) to ride the bus. Public transportation is available in most towns and cities and accessible for everyone. Buses have regular routes, ways that they follow each day.

Skills
Role and dramatic play, social interaction

Vocabulary
Bus driver, riders, fare, tokens, tickets, public transportation, public transit, route

Date

Standards Met

Comments and Reflection

CURRICULUM ACTIVITY GUIDE 3 — Free-Play (Problem Solving)

Goal: To allow children to make individual play choices

Curriculum Area	Developmental Focus	Location/Interest Center
Social Understanding	Cognitive—Critical Thinking	Inside Circle

Participants	Time	Age Range
More than 8 children	30 to 45 minutes	Appropriate for all ages

Materials
Carpets for group time

Preparation/Setup
Set up group time area with carpets.

Teaching Strategies

Discuss activity-time choices with children at group time ("In the art area we have marble painting"). Ask each child where they are going to play. Ask open-ended questions to further focus free-play choices of activities. Children verbalize their choice and leave to go and play. Assist children in problem solving regarding play choice if they are undecided. Teacher can observe and document children's choices and activities during free-play.

Possible Outcomes

Concepts
I have many choices. I can make a decision about the kind of play I want to do. I can play alone or with other children.

Skills
Decision making, socialization, opportunity for autonomy (being alone)

Vocabulary
Choice, free-choice, alone, together, play, outside, inside, interest center names

Date

Standards Met

Comments and Reflection

CURRICULUM ACTIVITY GUIDE 4 — Cultural Pattern Match

Goal: To give children the opportunity to explore cultural patterns

Curriculum Area	Developmental Focus	Location/Interest Center
Social Understanding	Cognitive—Critical Thinking	Inside Manipulative

Participants	Time	Age Range
Individual child	10 minutes	3 to 4 years old

Materials
Trays, small containers for fabric swatches, fabrics with distinct patterns representative of diverse cultures. Books showing different cultural heritage dress and other items using fabric and textiles

Preparation/Setup
Locate and cut fabrics with distinct patterns and textures into uniform size. Outline and laminate a mat for the activity tray. Set up tray with containers and fabrics.

Teaching Strategies

Set out activity tray on shelf. Encourage children to explore the properties of the fabric, matching and comparing. Facilitate children's exploration by asking open-ended questions.
Reinforce learning by explaining origin of the fabrics and textiles.

Possible Outcomes

Concepts
Fabrics are used culturally and internationally. Fabrics and textiles are unique.
Fabrics have patterns and texture, density (thick-thin, heavy-light, course-smooth). Fabrics are related to the climate and needs of the families.

Skills
Differentiation, discrimination, awareness of cultural diversity, relate cultural need and climate to fabric used

Vocabulary
Pattern, fabric, texture, density, culture,

Date

Standards Met

Comments and Reflection

207

CURRICULUM ACTIVITY GUIDE 5 — Parent Visit

Goal: To give children the opportunity to explore family roles

Curriculum Area	Developmental Focus	Location/Interest Center
Social Understanding	Affective—Social	Inside Dramatic Play

Participants	Time	Age Range
1 to 4 children	20 to 30 minutes	Appropriate for all ages

Materials
Survey the interests and talents of parents and other family members. E-mail, letter or note inviting families to visit classroom (may ask them to bring in items representing their family culture and heritage).

Preparation/Setup
Call, e-mail, or write note to all parent(s) and family members requesting their visit and participation to share their cultural heritage with the preschoolers. Review parent surveys and/or children's files identifying families with diverse languages and cultural diversity to ensure they receive and understand the invitation.

Teaching Strategies
Welcome parent and other family members into classroom, inviting them to join or observe the classroom activities. Introduce the parent(s) and other family members to the children informally. Invite the parent(s) and child to share the familial and cultural items representing their families during group time.

Possible Outcomes
Concepts
Every family has a cultural identity. Cultures have particular relics, clothing, food, and customs. Every family is not alike. Children belong to families. Families are special—in some ways they are alike and in some ways they are different.
Skills
Awareness of new cultural information, accepting attitude toward cultural differences, developing sense of community
Vocabulary
Culture, ethnicity, custom, heritage, visitor, specific cultural terms related to families participating

Date

Standards Met

Comments and Reflections

CURRICULUM ACTIVITY GUIDE 6 — The Three Bears: Creative Dramatics

Goal: To give children the opportunity to dramatize a familiar story

Curriculum Area	Developmental Focus	Location/Interest Center
Creative Dramatics	Affective—Social	Inside Dramatic Play

Participants	Time	Age Range
1 to 4 children	10 to 20 minutes	3 to 4 years old

Materials
A "Three Bears" storybook, three chairs, three plastic bowls and spoons, three mats, or blankets to serve as beds

Preparation/Setup
Locate props. Set up dramatic play area as for the bear's house.

Teaching Strategies
Teacher reads a "The Three Bears" storybook at group time. Teacher explains that props are available in dramatic play area to act out the story. Children use props to freely act out story.

Possible Outcomes
Concepts
We can act out stories. We can take turns playing parts.
Skills
Social interaction, cooperation, opportunity for affective development
Vocabulary
actor, drama

Date

Standards Met

Comments and Reflection

CURRICULUM ACTIVITY GUIDE 7 — We All Have Families

Goal: To give children the opportunity to explore the concept of family

Curriculum Area	Developmental Focus	Location/Interest Center
Social Understanding	Affective—Social	Inside Circle

Participants	Time	Age Range
5 to 8 children	10 to 20 minutes	Appropriate for all ages

Materials
Books, pictures, and photographs of variety of families (authentically inclusive, representing diverse and mixed groups); lined paper for dictation; plain paper for drawing, marking pens

Preparation/Setup
Locate books, pictures, and photographs. Set up materials for extension of group time at art table.

Teaching Strategies
Teacher introduces concept that "we all have a family" at group time, shares book and/or pictures and photographs. Discuss the children's family makeup, similarities, and differences. Extend group time at art table, with opportunity to draw family. Take child's dictation about their drawing.

Possible Outcomes
Concepts
We all have families. Families are alike and different too.
Skills
Exposure to concept of the family, development of self-identity, acceptance of differences
Vocabulary Family,
family names, same, different

Date

Standards Met

Comments and Reflection

CURRICULUM ACTIVITY GUIDE 8 — Neighborhood Field Trip

Goal: To give children the opportunity to explore their neighborhood

Curriculum Area	Developmental Focus	Location/Interest Center
Social Understanding	Affective—Social	Unselected

Participants	Time	Age Range
More than 8 children	20 to 30 minutes	Appropriate for all ages

Materials
Field trip backpack (emergency cards, first aid kit, tissues, 2-way radio, or cell or smart phone, etc.)

Preparation/Setup
Make prior arrangements with neighborhood business. Arrange for maximum staffing and parent help. Secure all necessary signed permission slips. Set up for group time to discuss trip a few days before and the day of the field trip.

Teaching Strategies
Teacher discusses field trip with children about expected behaviors and actions; what they will see on the walk and at the neighborhood business or place. Discuss staying close together; holding hands, being safe. One teacher facilitates and leads discussion. Trip follow-up—children cooperatively prepare group thank-you dictation project.

Possible Outcomes
Concepts
There are businesses in our neighborhood. We can walk safely together.
Skills
Social understanding, social interaction, exercise
Vocabulary
Neighborhood, business, walk

Date

Standards Met

Comments and Reflection

To Access Downloadable Versions of the Curriculum Activity Guides Log on to www.cengagebrain.com

---

CURRICULUM ACTIVITY GUIDE 9   Exploring Feelings

Goal: To give children the opportunity to identify and explore feelings

Curriculum Area	Developmental Focus	Location/Interest Center
Social Understanding	Affective—Emotional	Inside Circle

Participants	Time	Age Range
5 to 8 children	10 to 20 minutes	Appropriate for all ages

Materials
Pictures of various adults and children depicting different emotions, small unbreakable mirrors, group time small carpets

Preparation/Setup
Laminate pictures and photographs. Locate mirrors—one per child. Set up carpets for group time.

Teaching Strategies
Teacher settles down group with active songs and fingerplay(s). Teacher assesses children's understanding of emotions—discusses pictures and photographs. Teacher engages children in interactive questioning (What do you think is happening here?). Teacher and children model same emotion while looking in their mirrors.

Possible Outcomes
Concepts
Everyone has feelings. It is okay to feel mad or sad sometimes.
Skills
Language opportunity, emotional development, socialization
Vocabulary
Happy, sad, angry, mad, worried, feelings, emotions

Date

Standards Met

Comments and Reflection

CURRICULUM ACTIVITY GUIDE 10   Puppetry (Making Friends)

Goal: To give children the opportunity to experience puppets discussing friendship

Curriculum Area Center	Developmental Focus	Location/Interest
Creative Dramatics	Affective—Emotional	Inside Circle

Participants	Time	Age Range
5 to 8 children	10 to 20 minutes	Appropriate for all ages

Materials
Puppets—two (preferably a boy and a girl puppet), pillowcase or bag, group time carpet squares

Preparation/Setup
Locate puppets and place in pillowcase. Set up carpets for group time.

Teaching Strategies
Teacher settles down children with active songs and fingerplay(s). Teacher tells children she/he has some special friends that came to group time today. Teacher introduces each puppet (one has difficulty making friends). Involve the children in problem-solving, how he/she could make friends. Teacher puts puppets in the reading area after group time for the children to use.

Possible Outcomes
Concepts
Puppets look like animals and sometimes people. The puppet wants a friend. There are special ways to make friends.
Skills
Social interaction, concept of social skills, emotional development
Vocabulary
Friends, share, join, puppets

Date

Standards Met

Comments and Reflection

CURRICULUM ACTIVITY GUIDE 11   When I Was a Baby

Goal: To give children the opportunity to consider their growth

Curriculum Area	Developmental Focus	Location/Interest Center
Social Understanding	Cognitive—Critical Thinking	Inside Circle

Participants	Time	Age Range
5 to 8 children	10 to 20 minutes	3 to 4 years old

Materials
Baby items—bottles, bibs, diapers, baby food containers, etc., baby doll, pictures of babies, families nurturing babies. Optional: Book about growing up. Large paper, teacher marker

Preparation/Setup
Set up carpets for group time. Locate all materials.

Teaching Strategies
Teacher settles down children with active songs, fingerplay(s). Teacher brings out baby props, discusses their use. Teacher elicits discussion of growing bigger, writes children's responses on paper. Teacher hangs paper "All by Myself" with responses. Teacher puts baby props in the dramatic play area after group time for children to use.

Possible Outcomes
Concepts
I am getting bigger. I was very small when I was a baby. I used to be a baby. We take care of babies.
Skills
Social understanding, sense of identity, sense of nurturing
Vocabulary
Baby, grow, family

Date

Standards Met

Comments and Reflection

CURRICULUM ACTIVITY GUIDE 12   Litter Patrol

Goal: To give children the opportunity to beautify the area around their school

Curriculum Area	Developmental Focus	Location/Interest Center
Social Understanding	Affective—Social	Unselected

Participants	Time	Age Range
More than 8 children	20 to 30 minutes	3 to 4 years old

Materials
Recycled bags with handles, waterless sanitizing hand wash.

Preparation/Setup
Set up carpets for group time. Locate bags and hand wash, gloves for adults to pick up litter and place in a separate bag.

Teaching Strategies
Teacher prepares children for a field trip at group time. Teacher discusses litter and "litter patrol." Teacher discusses safety issues—no cigarettes, glass, gum, etc. During field trip, children are supervised carefully.

Possible Outcomes
Concepts
I can help clean up my neighborhood. Litter hurts our environment.
Skills
Exposure to concept of environment, social responsibility, social interaction
Vocabulary
Litter, environment, clean

Date

Standards Met

Comments and Reflection

To Access Downloadable Versions of the Curriculum Activity Guides Log on to www.cengagebrain.com

CURRICULUM ACTIVITY GUIDE 13   Community Awareness: Grocery Store

Goal: To give children the opportunity to interact in a grocery store interest center

Curriculum Area	Developmental Focus	Location/Interest Center
Social Understanding	Affective—Social	Inside Dramatic Play
Participants	**Time**	**Age Range**
1 to 4 children	10 to 20 minutes	3 to 4 years old

Materials

Plastic food, empty food containers, grocery bags, sacks, toy cash register and/or small calculators, paper and pencils, scale for weighing food. Optional: shower curtain backdrop.

Preparation/Setup

Collect empty food containers from parents, staff. Set up dramatic play area with all props.
Optional: Using a white shower curtain liner, draw a grocery store scene with permanent markers.

Teaching Strategies

Children interact in familiar grocery store setting, buying and selling food. Teacher can facilitate children's writing of signs and labels for foods. Children use paper and pencil to write up grocery lists and receipts.

Possible Outcomes

Concepts
I know about grocery stores. Grocery stores are also called markets.
Skills
Social understanding, social interaction, literacy and mathematics skill development
Vocabulary
Grocery, buy, sell, cash register, scale

Date

Standards Met

Comments and Reflection

CURRICULUM ACTIVITY GUIDE 14   Making New Friends ("I'm Thinking of a Friend")

Goal: To give children the opportunity to consider their uniqueness

Curriculum Area	Developmental Focus	Location/Interest Center
Social Understanding	Affective—Social	Inside Circle
Participants	**Time**	**Age Range**
5 to 8 children	10 to 20 minutes	3 to 4 years old

Materials

Carpets for group time

Preparation/Setup

Set up area for group time.

Teaching Strategies

Teacher readies children for group time with songs, fingerplays. Children initiate activity "I'm thinking of a friend . . ." (who likes to build, who likes to sing, who likes to climb in the loft)—emphasizing traits shared by many. Teacher facilitates children's discovery that they share many traits. Teacher ultimately describes a trait unique to one child.

Possible Outcomes

Concepts
We are all alike in some ways and different in others. Children can have many different friends.
Skills
Listening skills, prediction skills, social interaction
Vocabulary
Friend, same, different, trait

Date

Standards Met

Comments and Reflection

CURRICULUM ACTIVITY GUIDE 15   Fix-It Shop

Goal: To give children the opportunity to role play a repair shop

Curriculum Area	Developmental Focus	Location/Interest Center
Social Understanding	Affective—Social	Inside Dramatic Play
Participants	**Time**	**Age Range**
1 to 4 children	10 to 20 minutes	3 to 4 year olds

Materials

Broken small appliances (cords removed)—check for sharp edges, safety, small tools, primarily screwdrivers with short handles, sign: "Fix-It Shop"

Preparation/Setup

Locate small appliances like a toaster or hand mixer (note request in parent newsletter). Set up table with tools and appliances. Loosen screws throughout to facilitate children's success. Remove electric cord and tape for safety.

Teaching Strategies

Teacher discusses repair, Fix-It Shop. Children work on taking apart and putting together appliances. Parts may be saved for a group junk sculpture later on.

Possible Outcomes

Concepts
I can take things apart. I can pretend to be a repair person.
Skills
Hand–eye coordination, fine motor development, social understanding
Vocabulary:
Repair, Fix-It Shop, tool names

Date

Standards Met

Comments and Reflection

CURRICULUM ACTIVITY GUIDE 16   Growth Sequence

Goal: To give children the opportunity to use an activity focusing on growth sequence

Curriculum Area Center	Developmental Focus	Location/Interest
Social Understanding/ Science	Cognitive— Critical Thinking	Inside Manipulative
Participants	**Time**	**Age Range**
Individual child	5 to 10 minutes	3 to 4 years old

Materials

Uniform-size pictures of growth sequence from baby to old age, placemat for tray, container to hold pictures

Preparation/Setup

Locate and laminate picture cards, sequence of 3 to 5. Outline placemat with place for cards in sequence and container. Place activity tray on shelf.

Teaching Strategies

Child takes activity tray from shelf and puts pictures in order of growth sequence. Teacher can facilitate language development, discussing "baby," "teenager," etc. Child replaces pictures in container and replaces tray on shelf.

Possible Outcomes

Concepts
There is a sequence to growth. Babies grow up. Children get bigger.
Skills
Ordering skills, social understanding
Vocabulary
Growth, baby, child, teenager, adult, older adult

Date

Standards Met

Comments and Reflection

To Access Downloadable Versions of the Curriculum Activity Guides Log on to www.cengagebrain.com

---

CURRICULUM ACTIVITY GUIDE 17   Smart Telephone Partners

Goal: To give children the opportunity to interact with each other by "telephone"

Curriculum Area	Developmental Focus	Location/Interest Center
Communication/ Literacy	Cognitive—Language	Inside Dramatic Play

Participants	Time	Age Range
1 to 4 children	5 to 10 minutes	Appropriate for all ages

Materials

Two landline telephones or cell phones without batteries, small table and two chairs, pictures and photographs of people talking on phones, materials to make a sign

Preparation/Setup

Set up small table with two phones so that children will be facing each other. Locate pictures and laminate. Make a sign: "Let's Talk on the Phone!"

Teaching Strategies

Children can freely choose to use the phones to talk to one another. Teacher can enhance conversation and language development by asking interactive questions, "Did you tell him about . . .?", "I wonder if you asked about . . .?"

Possible Outcomes

Concepts
I can pretend to talk on a telephone. Telephones help people communicate when they are not close to each other. Some telephones can take photos and some can access the Internet.
Skills
Language development, social interaction
Vocabulary:
Telephone, cell and smart phones, talk, conversation, greeting

Date

Standards Met

Comments and Reflection

CURRICULUM ACTIVITY GUIDE 18   Flannel Board Story Retelling

Goal: To give children the opportunity to retell a story with a flannel board

Curriculum Area	Developmental Focus	Location/Interest Center
Communication and Literacy	Cognitive—Language	Inside Circle

Participants	Time	Age Range
1 to 4 children	5 to 10 minutes	3 to 4 years old

Materials

Storybook, corresponding flannel board story pieces, flannel board

Preparation/Setup

Set up area for small group storytelling opportunity. Locate all materials.

Teaching Strategies

Teacher reads story to small group of children. Teacher introduces flannel pieces, involving children in identifying them. Children have opportunity to retell the story, using flannel pieces. Place flannel board and flannel board pieces in the reading area for further use.

Possible Outcomes

Concepts
I can remember a story. I can use flannel board pieces to tell a story.
Skills
Memory skills, social interaction, literacy development
Vocabulary
Story, flannel board, remember

Date

Standards Met

Comments and Reflection

CURRICULUM ACTIVITY GUIDE 19   Storybook Reading

Goal: To encourage literacy awareness with storybooks

Curriculum Area	Developmental Focus	Location/Interest Center
Literacy Social Social Understanding	Affective—Social	Library or Book Corner

Participants	Time	Age Range
1 to 4 children	20 to 30 minutes	Appropriate for all ages

Materials

Appropriate children's literature (consider illustrations, text, non-bias concerns)

Preparation/Setup

Set up area for storybook reading. Select one or two books that are appropriate for specific age and group participants and emergent curriculum focus.

Teaching Strategies

Introduce the book by discussing the cover. Ask, "What do you think this book will be about?" Discuss title page, identifying author and illustrator's name. Discuss art medium used in illustration (if known). Read storybook and encourage feedback from the children.

Possible Outcomes

Concepts
Book covers can tell us something about the story. Books have an author and an illustrator. Books are considered part of literature. Books have a beginning, a middle, and an ending.
Skills
Increased attention span, exposure to language, literacy opportunity, aesthetic appreciation for books
Vocabulary
Author, illustrator, artist, cover, read, literature

Date

Standards Met

Comments and Reflection

CURRICULUM ACTIVITY GUIDE 20   Story Sequence

Goal: To give children the opportunity to explore story sequence

Curriculum Area	Developmental Focus	Location/Interest Center
Communication and Literacy	Cognitive—Language	Inside Quiet Reading

Participants	Time	Age Range
Individual child	5 to10 minutes	3 to 4 years old

Materials

Story sequence cards with beginning, middle, end (familiar stories work best at first) Placemat with outline for each section, tray

Preparation/Setup

Outline placemat and place on tray with story sequence cards. Set activity tray on shelf.

Teaching Strategies

Child uses activity tray, placing cards in order of sequence of a story. Teacher facilitates child's understanding by asking questions, "Which one do you think is the beginning?" Child replaces all materials and returns tray to shelf.

Possible Outcomes

Concepts
Stories have a beginning, a middle, and an ending.
Skills
Sequence development, literacy development
Vocabulary
Beginning, middle, ending, order, one after another

Date

Standards Met

Comments and Reflection

To Access Downloadable Versions of the Curriculum Activity Guides Log on to www.cengagebrain.com

CURRICULUM ACTIVITY GUIDE 21   Picture Word Card Match

Goal: To give children the opportunity to explore letters and words

Curriculum Area	Developmental Focus	Location/Interest Center
Communication and Literacy	Cognitive—Critical Thinking	Literacy

Participants	Time	Age Range
Individual child	5 to 10 minutes	3 to 4 years old

Materials

Stickers, pictures, or photographs of simple familiar words (cat, dog, ball, house, etc.) card stock, container for picture cards

Preparation/Setup

Cut cards in a uniform size. Place a sticker, picture, or photograph on a card. Write the word for each object on separate card.

Teaching Strategies

Child chooses cards with stickers, pictures, or photographs to match with words written the separate cards. Teacher facilitates child's literacy development by identifying letters, reading words, and responding to the child's questions. Child replaces activity on shelf. Teacher rotates cards and words appropriately to coordinate with curriculum and children's interests.

Possible Outcomes

Concepts
I can match the pictures to these words. Words are made of letters.
Skills
Picture recognition, letter recognition, literacy development
Vocabulary
Pictures, words, letters, alphabet, match

Date

Standards Met

Comments and Reflection

CURRICULUM ACTIVITY GUIDE 22   What's Our Favorite Apple?

Goal: To give children the opportunity to graph apple preferences

Curriculum Area	Developmental Focus	Location/Interest Center
Mathematics	Cognitive—Critical Thinking	Inside Circle

Participants	Time	Age Range
5 to 8 children	10 minutes	3 to 4 years old

Materials

Apples (green, red, yellow), cutting board, knife, napkins, large paper divided in three, red, yellow, green markers

Preparation/Setup

Locate all materials. Set up area for group time.

Teaching Strategies

Children and teachers wash hands. Teacher discusses apples, differences, similarities. Teacher draws green, red, and yellow apples on large paper. Teacher cuts apples and lets each child eat a slice of each color apple. Teacher and/or children graph their favorite apple on chart.

Possible Outcomes

Concepts
We all like different apples. We can tell which apple is the favorite by looking at our chart. Apples are different colors and can have different shapes.
Skills
Mathematical concepts, social interaction
Vocabulary
Apples, favorite, taste, chart, graph

Date

Standards Met

Comments and Reflection

CURRICULUM ACTIVITY GUIDE 23   Planting Seeds

Goal: To give children the opportunity to observe the process of plant growth

Curriculum Area	Developmental Focus	Location/Interest Center
Science	Cognitive—Discovery	Outside Garden

Participants	Time	Age Range
1 to 4 children	10 minutes	Appropriate for all ages

Materials

Seeds (bean seeds work well), potting soil, individual flower pots, water, spoons or small spades, permanent marker

Preparation/Setup

Presoak beans for 2 to 3 hours (for quickest growth). Gather materials, set up table outside.

Teaching Strategies

Talk to children about seeds. Discuss growing. Children use spoons or small spades to place potting soil in pots. Children place 1 to 2 seeds in the pot, cover with soil. Teacher writes children's names on pots. Children water pot and place it in sunny location. Children watch growth over time.

Possible Outcomes

Concepts
Plants grow from seeds. Seeds need soil, water, time, and sun to grow.
Skills
Exposure to science concept of plant growth.
Vocabulary
Seed, roots, plant, grow, soil

Date

Standards Met

Comments and Reflection

CURRICULUM ACTIVITY GUIDE 24   Colors in Nature

Goal: To give children the opportunity to experience observing the colors in nature

Curriculum Area	Developmental Focus	Location/Interest Center
Science	Cognitive—Discovery	Outside Area Neighborhood walk

Participants	Time	Age Range
5 to 8 children	10 to 20 minutes	Appropriate for all ages

Materials

Pictures or photographs of colors in nature (animals, plants, ground covers, etc.)

Preparation/Setup

Locate and laminate pictures or photographs. Set up for group time. Repeat the activity during different seasons

Teaching Strategies

Discuss colors in nature at group time, show pictures. Divide group into 3 to 4 children per adult—suggest color to observe. Children take nature walk with teachers and other adults, observing for "their" color. Teachers facilitate discussion of colors in nature and where colors can be found.

Possible Outcomes

Concepts
Bright colors stand out in nature. Colors can be observed in many different shades. Some animals and insects change color to camouflage or hide in nature.
Skills
Observation skills, differentiation skills, appreciating nature
Vocabulary
Color, nature, camouflage, hide, color names

Date

Standards Met

Comments and Reflection

To Access Downloadable Versions of the Curriculum Activity Guides Log on to www.cengagebrain.com

CURRICULUM ACTIVITY GUIDE 25 — Let's Feed the Birds!

Goal: To give children the opportunity to create feeders for birds

Curriculum Area	Developmental Focus	Location/Interest Center
Science	Cognitive—Discovery	Outside Garden

Participants	Time	Age Range
1 to 4 children	10 to 15 minutes	Appropriate for all ages

Materials

Pine cones, peanut butter, bird or grass seed, spreaders, plastic knives, small containers for the peanut butter, bird or grass seed, ribbon or yarn

Preparation/Setup

Place bird seed and peanut butter each in small containers. Place pine cones next to containers for children to choose. Cut yarn or ribbon in small lengths to tie onto the top of the pine cones.

Teaching Strategies

Discuss birds and bird feeders, show examples. Explain that birds look for food. Child spreads peanut butter on pine cone. Child sprinkles bird or grass seed on pine cone. Child ties or is assisted to tie yarn, or ribbon around top of their pine cone, leaving ends dangling free. Teacher assists children in hanging feeders outside from trees or bushes. Children observe bird feeders and birds.

Possible Outcomes

Concepts
Birds eat bird seed or grass seed. We can help the birds.

Skills
Fine motor skills placing peanut butter and bird seed on pine cones, observation, and appreciation for nature

Vocabulary
Bird, bird seed, trees, bushes, hungry, pine cone

Date

Standards Met

Comments and Reflection

CURRICULUM ACTIVITY GUIDE 26 — Hands, Eyes, and Nose Tell Me

Goal: To give children the opportunity to use their senses

Curriculum Area	Developmental Focus	Location/Interest Center
Science	Cognitive—Discovery	Unselected

Participants	Time	Age Range
1 to 4 children	10 to 15 minutes	3 to 4 years old

Materials

Sensory table, fresh herbs (basil, mint, dill, rosemary, cilantro). Add and vary herbs as activity is reintroduced or expanded over a period of time, blindfold, and large bowls (5) for herbs, small bowls for children to individually smell and touch herbs

Preparation/Setup

Obtain herbs (purchase or gather from school garden). Prepare sensory table with herbs separated into five bowls. Collect photos identifying herbs in plant form and use of herbs. Laminate photographs of herb plants and herbs used for seasoning.

Teaching Strategies

Invite children to the sensory table to visually explore and sort herbs. Offer children the use of the blindfold to identify and sort herbs by touch and smell. Facilitate children's exploration with discussion about the herbs and their use of senses.

Possible Outcomes

Concepts
Herbs have different scents (smell), appearance (look), and touch (feel). Herbs can be distinguished by their appearance, feel, and scent. Herbs are used for cooking; and they distinguish the taste of the food. Adding herbs changes the smell of food, candles, soap, perfume, and other products.

Skills
Sensory exploration, differentiation, mathematical development including comparing and sorting

Vocabulary
Herb, herbs, basil, mint, dill, rosemary, cilantro, scent, smell, touch, feel, see

Date

Standards Met

Comments and Reflection

CURRICULUM ACTIVITY GUIDE 27 — Labeling Science Share Items

Goal: To give children the opportunity to communicate about science share items

Curriculum Area	Developmental Focus	Location/Interest Center
Science	Cognitive—Language	Science

Participants	Time	Age Range
Individual child	5 to 10 minutes	Appropriate for all ages

Materials

Trays, paper, marking pens

Preparation/Setup

Welcoming teacher is ready to check and accept appropriate share item when child arrives.

Teaching Strategies

Child brings in science item from home for science shelf at school. Teacher facilitates communication about item. Teacher writes down child's words about item, where it was found, etc. When possible, add science reference materials, and magnifying glasses, etc. to trays to expand information.

Possible Outcomes

Concepts
I can talk about my science share item. My teacher will help me learn more about it.

Skills
Communication/language development, science concepts, sense of discovery

Vocabulary
Science, share, look up

Date

Standards Met

Comments and Reflection

CURRICULUM ACTIVITY GUIDE 28 — Height Strips

Goal: To give children the opportunity to experience the concepts of height and measurement

Curriculum Area	Developmental Focus	Location/Interest Center
Health, Safety, Nutrition	Cognitive—Discovery	Inside Art

Participants	Time	Age Range
1 to 4 children	10 to 20 minutes	Appropriate for all ages

Materials

Cash register paper rolls, children's marking pens, scissors, adult permanent marker. Optional: tape measure

Preparation/Setup

Clear a long table and set out marking pens. Locate paper rolls, scissors.

Teaching Strategies

Teacher holds up paper roll to child, informally measuring height. Teacher draws a line across to designate height, writes child's name above. Child draws on his/her strip with markers. Hang on a bulletin board to compare heights. Introduce measuring tape to children who show interest.

Possible Outcomes

Concepts
I am getting taller. I am taller than some children and shorter than others. The length of the paper shows my height. There are many ways to measure.

Skills
Mathematical concepts, creative expression

Vocabulary
Height, tall, measure

Date

Standards Met

Comments and Reflection

To Access Downloadable Versions of the Curriculum Activity Guides Log on to www.cengagebrain.com

CURRICULUM ACTIVITY GUIDE 29 — Sorting Seashells

Goal: To give children the opportunity to explore and sort seashells

Curriculum Area	Developmental Focus	Location/Interest Center
Mathematics	Cognitive—Critical Thinking	Inside Manipulative

Participants	Time	Age Range
Individual child	5 minutes	3 to 4 years old

Materials
Sorting tray with numerous compartments (muffin baking tin), assortment of seashells

Preparation/Setup
Locate all materials. Set up sorting tray and collection of shells in large container.

Teaching Strategies
Child takes activity from shelf and sorts shells by type and/or size. Teacher can facilitate child's experience by discussing attributes of shells. Child replaces all materials, returns activity to shelf. Other materials from nature can be used such as leaves, rocks, sticks, etc. Science items such as magnifying glasses can be added.

Possible Outcomes
Concepts
I can sort shells. Sorting means to match the shells that look the same.
Skills
Differentiation skills, mathematical development
Vocabulary
Alike, different, shells, sort, match, same

Date

Standards Met

Comments and Reflection

CURRICULUM ACTIVITY GUIDE 30 — Measuring/Pouring Bird Seed

Goal: To give children the opportunity to explore measuring and pouring

Curriculum Area	Developmental Focus	Location/Interest Center
Mathematics	Cognitive—Discovery	Sensorial

Participants	Time	Age Range
1 to 4 children	10 minutes	3 to 4 years old

Materials
Sand and water table, set up with three tubs, bird seed, measuring cups, spoons

Preparation/Setup
Locate bird seed. Set up sand and water table with bird seed in three tubs, measuring cups and spoons in each.

Teaching Strategies
Children explore the bird seed by measuring and pouring. Children discover mathematical concepts by experiential use of materials. Teacher may facilitate experience by communicating with child.

Possible Outcomes
Concepts
I can measure and pour.
Skills
Mathematical concept development, tactile experience, social interaction
Vocabulary
Bird seed, measure, pour

Date

Standards Met

Comments and Reflection

CURRICULUM ACTIVITY GUIDE 31 — Grass Seed Growing on a Sponge

Goal: To give children the opportunity to observe grass growing on a sponge

Curriculum Area	Developmental Focus	Location/Interest Center
Science	Cognitive—Discovery	Science

Participants	Time	Age Range
5 to 8 children	10 minutes	3 to 4 years old

Materials
Tray, grass or bird seed, sponges, squirt bottle with water

Preparation/Setup
Assemble all materials on tray.

Teaching Strategies
Teacher works with small group to discuss growing grass seeds. Children wet sponge with squirt bottle. Children sprinkle ample grass seeds on top of sponge and water again. Children observe grass seed over time on science shelf as they begin to grow. Children can use children's scissors to cut grass after seeds grow.

Possible Outcomes
Concepts
Grass grows from seeds. Grass needs water to grow. Grass needs time to grow.
Skills
Science concept development, prediction skills, social interaction
Vocabulary
Grass, sponge, water, grow

Date

Standards Met

Comments and Reflection

CURRICULUM ACTIVITY GUIDE 32 — Ice Melt

Goal: To give children the opportunity to explore properties of ice

Curriculum Area	Developmental Focus	Location/Interest Center
Science	Cognitive—Discovery	Science

Participants	Time	Age Range
1 to 4 children	10 minutes	3 to 4 years old

Materials
Large blocks of ice in tubs or water table, rock salt in small containers, eyedroppers, water dyed with food coloring in small containers (at least two primary colors)

Preparation/Setup
Freeze water in large blocks, or purchase. Locate and set out all materials.

Teaching Strategies
Child sprinkles rock salt on ice and uses eyedropper to squirt water. Child observes ice melting and colors mixing. Teacher facilitates experience by discussing observations. Teacher can encourage children to draw pictures of the sequence of the ice melting.

Possible Outcomes
Concepts
Ice melts. Salt makes ice melt faster. Colors mix to make new colors.
Skills
Science concept development, color-mixing opportunity, observation skills
Vocabulary
Ice, melt, salt, colors

Date

Standards Met

Comments and Reflection

To Access Downloadable Versions of the Curriculum Activity Guides Log on to www.cengagebrain.com

CURRICULUM ACTIVITY GUIDE 33 — Let's Look It Up!

Goal: To give children the opportunity to research information about a question and expand information about an interest

Curriculum Area	Developmental Focus	Location/Interest Center
Science	Cognitive—Discovery	Reading or Computer

Participants	Time	Age Range
1 to 4 children	10 to 15 minutes	Appropriate for all ages

Materials
Science reference books, computer, variety of insect/bug visiting containers

Preparation/Setup
Prepare for spontaneous questions from the children. Maintain appropriate reference materials, books, and supervised use of computer to research information on the Internet.

Teaching Strategies
Respond to children's questions with, "Let's look it up" together, especially when they bring in items, such as insects and butterflies. Work with child and other interested children looking up information together in reference books and on the Internet. Print out or copy information. Post copies by items or give copies to child to place in his or her cubby. Teacher and child cooperate to make signs. As appropriate, release insect safely.

Possible Outcomes

Concepts
Answers to questions can be found in books and on the Internet about my interest.
Insects can be returned to their natural habitat.

Skills
Researching and finding answers to questions, continue stimulating curiosity

Vocabulary
Reference book, research, Internet, look up, discover, investigate, release

Date

Standards Met

Comments and Reflection

CURRICULUM ACTIVITY GUIDE 34 — What Kind of Muffin?

Goal: To give children the opportunity to make a choice about a muffin

Curriculum Area	Developmental Focus	Location/Interest Center
Health, Safety, Nutrition	Affective—Social	Unselected

Participants	Time	Age Range
More than 8 children	10 to 20 minutes	Appropriate for all ages

Materials
Recipe, ingredients, and baking utensils, and paper muffin/cupcake cups for plain muffins, bowls of seeds, nuts, dried fruit such as apricots and peaches, wheat germ, and chopped fresh fruit

Preparation/Setup
Set up for a cooking activity. Assemble recipe, ingredients, and baking utensils. Prepare pictograph of an individual portion muffin recipe.

Teaching Strategies
Wash hands (teacher and children). Prepare plain muffins providing children with their small, individual bowls. Encourage each child to choose two to three additional ingredients to add to their muffins. Options include: seeds, nuts, dried apricots and peaches, raisins, wheat germ, chopped fresh fruit. Consult current list of identified allergies to nuts. Label child's muffin paper cup on the outside bottom before baking. Enjoy muffins at snack time. Encourage conversation about additional ingredients. Facilitate older children to document their additional ingredient choices, for example how many and types.

Possible Outcomes

Concepts
Muffins can be changed by adding different ingredients. I can make choices for myself. I can prepare a healthy snack.

Skills
Decision making, changing outcomes by altering a recipe, nutritional awareness

Vocabulary
Muffin, choice, change, recipe, ingredients, nuts, seeds, dried fruit, fresh fruit

Date

Standards Met

Comments and Reflection

CURRICULUM ACTIVITY GUIDE 35 — Bumps on a Log (Individual Snack)

Goal: To give children the opportunity to make their own healthy snack

Curriculum Area	Developmental Focus	Location/Interest Center
Health, Safety, Nutrition	Cognitive—Critical Thinking	Unselected

Participants	Time	Age Range
Individual child	5 to 10 minutes	Appropriate for all ages

Materials
Snack items for each child (peanut butter and celery, crackers with cream cheese, etc.)
Cooking smocks, utensils for spreading, cutting, etc., cooking chart, paper plates

Preparation/Setup
Prepare a visual cooking chart with pictures of each step. Sanitize a table to prepare for cooking activity. Set out cooking smocks—one for each child at activity.

Teaching Strategies
Children and teacher wash hands and come to cooking table. Each child prepares his or her snack and places on plate for snack time. Teacher uses opportunity to discuss healthy eating habits.

Possible Outcomes

Concepts
I can make my own snack. Healthy foods help us grow.

Skills
Fine motor development, perceptual–motor development, exposure to nutrition concepts

Vocabulary
Snack, spread, prepare, healthy

Date

Standards Met

Comments and Reflection

CURRICULUM ACTIVITY GUIDE 36 — Food Collage

Goal: To give children the opportunity to make collages of their favorite healthy foods

Curriculum Area	Developmental Focus	Location/Interest Center
Health, Safety, Nutrition	Cognitive—Critical Thinking	Inside Art

Participants	Time	Age Range
5 to 8 children	10 to 20 minutes	3 to 4 years old

Materials
Magazine pictures of food (can be precut—older children can cut their own), scissors, glue and glue applicators, paper plates

Preparation/Setup
Cover table and set out art smocks. Arrange all magazine pictures on a tray. Set out glue, scissors, etc. for each child.

Teaching Strategies
Children can look through magazine pictures, cut out food pictures. Children glue pictures of favorite healthy foods on recyclable paper plates. Teacher facilitates discussion of healthy foods.

Possible Outcomes

Concepts
Healthy foods help us grow. Healthy foods are fresh fruits and vegetables. Healthy foods can be grown in gardens.

Skills
Decision-making opportunity, differentiation, fine motor development

Vocabulary
Healthy foods, vegetable, fruit, grow, gardens, balanced diet

Date

Standards Met

Comments and Reflection

To Access Downloadable Versions of the Curriculum Activity Guides Log on to www.cengagebrain.com

CURRICULUM ACTIVITY GUIDE 37 — Dial 911

Goal: To give children the opportunity to be exposed to the concept of 911 Emergency

Curriculum Area	Developmental Focus	Location/Interest Center
Health, Safety, Nutrition	Cognitive— Critical Thinking	Inside Circle

Participants	Time	Age Range
5 to 8 children	10 to 20 minutes	4 to 5 years old

Materials

A variety of phones including cell phones, smart phones, dramatic play cell phones, small red circle stickers, bulletin board with a phone enlarged

Preparation/Setup

Make a bulletin board with 911 and phone face enlarged. Locate unconnected phones. Set up for group time.

Teaching Strategies

Teacher will introduce concept of an "emergency" at group time. Teacher will discuss calling 911. Teacher will discuss possible scenarios and model them for group. Children will practice dialing 911, teacher acts as operator. Phones can be placed in dramatic play area for continued practice.

Possible Outcomes

Concepts
I know about emergencies. I can use the phone in an emergency. There are special people who can help me in an emergency.

Skills
Exposure to important safety concept, role-playing opportunity

Vocabulary
911, emergency, dial

Date

Standards Met

Comments and Reflection

CURRICULUM ACTIVITY GUIDE 38 — Jumping Frog Obstacle Course

Goal: To give children the opportunity to jump

Curriculum Area	Developmental Focus	Location/Interest Center
Movement	Physical—Large Motor	Outside Large Motor

Participants	Time	Age Range
5 to 8 children	10 to 20 minutes	Appropriate for all ages

Materials

Bicycle tires or hula hoops, large mats (blue mats could simulate frog ponds), signs, arrows or carpets to indicate starting point and direction

Preparation/Setup

Set up a "jumping frog" obstacle course with tires or hoops to jump into, mats to serve as "ponds" to jump into. Make signs with drawings or photos of frogs. Signs can indicate: "Jumping Frog Obstacle Course," "Frog Pond," "This Way," and "Jump In!" Select and prepare music that inspires jumping.

Teaching Strategies

Discuss how frogs like to jump. Model jumping actions to the children. Invite children to try the "Jumping Frog Obstacle Course." Children jump through the course like frogs. Encourage children verbally, "Look at this frog jump!"

Possible Outcomes

Concepts
Frogs jump. Children can jump like frogs. Leap is another way to jump and move forward.

Skills
Large motor development, following directions, dramatic play opportunity, moving to music

Vocabulary
Jump, frog, obstacle course, leap, pond

Date

Standards Met

Comments and Reflection

CURRICULUM ACTIVITY GUIDE 39 — Trampoline and Stethoscope

Goal: To give children the opportunity to explore heartbeat and exercise

Curriculum Area	Developmental Focus	Location/Interest Center
Health, Safety, Nutrition	Physical—Large Motor	Outside Large Motor

Participants	Time	Age Range
1 to 4 children	10 to 20 minutes	3 to 4 years old

Materials

Small trampoline, carpets for waiting children, working stethoscope

Preparation/Setup

Set up trampoline in safe area outside, away from climbing and riding equipment. Locate stethoscope.

Teaching Strategies

Teacher sits children down for exercise activity, explains how to jump safely. Teacher helps children to feel their heartbeat and listen with the stethoscope before exercise. Children jump on trampoline, and then listen again. Teacher talks about the relationship between movement, especially exercise, and heartbeat.

Possible Outcomes

Concepts
My heart beats faster when I exercise. Jumping is an exercise that makes my heart beat faster. A stethoscope monitors heartbeat.

Skills
Large motor development, concept of health exercise

Vocabulary
Heartbeat, movement, rapid, exercise, trampoline, stethoscope

Date

Standards Met

Comments and Reflection

CURRICULUM ACTIVITY GUIDE 40 — Bean Bag Toss

Goal: To give children the opportunity to toss a bean bag through a target

Curriculum Area	Developmental Focus	Location/Interest Center
Movement	Physical—Large Motor	Outside Large Motor

Participants	Time	Age Range
1 to 4 children	10 minutes	Appropriate for all ages

Materials

Approximately 12 bean bags, boxes, baskets, or pre-made target (bucket or box), carpet squares

Preparation/Setup

Set up an area outside with targets and carpets for child to stand on while throwing (can be done inside in rainy weather). Set at least three bean bags on each carpet for each child.

Teaching Strategies

Invite children to try throwing bean bags at the target (bucket or box). Carpets can be moved closer or farther from the target to accommodate developmental levels of children.

Possible Outcomes

Concepts
I can throw. I can aim.

Skills
Hand–eye coordination, perceptual motor skill

Vocabulary
Bean bag, toss, throw, aim

Date

Standards Met

Comments and Reflection

To Access Downloadable Versions of the Curriculum Activity Guides Log on to www.cengagebrain.com

---

CURRICULUM ACTIVITY GUIDE 41 — Eyedroppers and Soap Suction

Goal: To give children the opportunity to use an eyedropper

Curriculum Area	Developmental Focus	Location/Interest Center
Movement	Physical—Small Motor	Inside Manipulative

Participants	Time	Age Range
Individual child	5 to 10 minutes	3 to 4 years old

Materials
Plastic eyedroppers, water with food coloring added in small container, plastic soap suction holders, small sponge, and tray

Preparation/Setup
Prepare a placemat for tray, outlining all materials. Place materials on tray, place tray on shelf or table.

Teaching Strategies
Teacher may need to introduce use of eyedropper. Child squeezes water into eyedropper, placing one drop on each suction cup of the soap holder. When finished, child uses sponge to wipe up water and get it ready for the next child.

Possible Outcomes

Concepts
I can use an eyedropper. Squeezing the top of an eyedropper pulls the water up.

Skills
Fine motor development, increased attention span, concentration

Vocabulary
Eyedropper, squeeze, pull

Date

Standards Met

Comments and Reflection

CURRICULUM ACTIVITY GUIDE 42 — Tweezers and Ice Cube Trays

Goal: To give children the opportunity to use tweezers

Curriculum Area	Developmental Focus	Location/Interest Center
Movement	Physical—Small Motor	Inside Manipulative

Participants	Time	Age Range
Individual child	5 to 10 minutes	3 to 4 years old

Materials
Tray, plastic ice cube tray, tweezers, items to pick up (beans, plastic spiders, pom poms, etc.) in container

Preparation/Setup
Make a placemat for tray, outlining materials.
Set up all materials on tray.
Items to pick up can change with curriculum focus or theme.

Teaching Strategies
Encourage child to use tweezers to pick up items and place in compartments of ice cube tray.
Child uses tweezers to return items to container when finished.

Possible Outcomes

Concepts
I can use tweezers. Tweezers are a tool used to pick up very small items. We need to be careful with tweezers.

Skills
Fine motor development, perceptual motor development, concentration

Vocabulary
Tweezers, squeeze, small

Date

Standards Met

Comments and Reflection

CURRICULUM ACTIVITY GUIDE 43 — Marble Painting

Goal: To give children the opportunity to experience painting with marbles

Curriculum Area	Developmental Focus	Location/Interest Center
Art	Affective—Aesthetic	Inside Art

Participants	Time	Age Range
1 to 4 children	10 minutes	3 to 4 years old

Materials
Marbles (large and small), box lids, tempera paint(mixed medium thin), in open containers, paper cut to fit box lid, spoons, and permanent marking pen

Preparation/Setup
Cut paper to fit box lids. Mix paint to desired consistency. Place one large and one small marble in each container with spoon.

Teaching Strategies
Write child's name on paper prior (or lid) to activity. Child uses spoon to place two marbles in lid. Child rolls marbles on paper by tilting lid.

Possible Outcomes

Concepts
You can paint in different ways. Marbles are round. Marbles roll.

Skills
Aesthetic pleasure. Introduction to new art medium

Vocabulary
Marble, roll, paint

Date

Standards Met

Comments and Reflection

CURRICULUM ACTIVITY GUIDE 44 — Body Tracing

Goal: To give children the opportunity to experience body parts through a new medium

Curriculum Area	Developmental Focus	Location/Interest Center
Art	Affective—Emotional	Outside Art

Participants	Time	Age Range
Individual child	10 to 15 minutes	Appropriate for all ages

Materials
Butcher paper, crayons or non-toxic felt pens, masking tape

Preparation/Setup
Locate butcher paper, crayons, tape. Use clear area indoors or outdoors in a space appropriate for tracing.

Teaching Strategies
Invite individual child to lie down on a piece of butcher paper. Draw around child's body outline and name parts (e.g. foot, leg, etc.) Invite child to use color crayons or paint to fill the traced outline. Tracings can be taped on fence or building for child to complete. Children can take turns tracing one another's bodies.

Possible Outcomes

Concepts:
My body has different parts. My body is my own. My body parts together "make me."
No one else has my body.

Skills
Awareness of the names of body parts. Sense of self as an individual

Vocabulary
Body, head, neck, arms, legs, trunk, myself, tracing

Date

Standards Met

Comments and Reflection

To Access Downloadable Versions of the Curriculum Activity Guides Log on to www.cengagebrain.com

CURRICULUM ACTIVITY GUIDE 45 — Art Appreciation

Goal: To give children the opportunity to develop aesthetic appreciation of art

Curriculum Area	Developmental Focus	Location/Interest Center
Art	Affective—Aesthetic	Inside Art

Participants	Time	Age Range
1 to 4 children	10 to 20 minutes	Appropriate for all ages

Materials

Art reproduction posters, calendar art, or art books, corresponding art medium (water color, chalk, collage, tempera paint, etc., paint smocks, table cover

Preparation/Setup

Familiarize yourself with art medium used in example. Locate and set up appropriate art materials. Cover table, provide paint smocks.

Teaching Strategies

Teacher introduces artist's work, describes medium used. Children examine artist's work, and discuss. Children explore art medium in their own work. Display children's work and artist's work together.

Possible Outcomes

Concepts
I am an artist. I enjoy the work of artists. Different art mediums create different looks.

Skills
Exposure to quality artwork, decision making skills, aesthetic appreciation

Vocabulary
Artist, medium, appreciation

Date

Standards Met

Comments and Reflection

CURRICULUM ACTIVITY GUIDE 46 — Tire Track Art

Goal: To give children the opportunity to paint with toy cars

Curriculum Area	Developmental Focus	Location/Interest Center
Art	Affective—Aesthetic	Inside Art

Participants	Time	Age Range
Individual child	5 to 10 minutes	3 to 4 years old

Materials

Tempera paint (mixed medium thin), paper—large is best, aluminum pie pans, small cars, trucks with interesting tire tracks

Preparation/Setup

Locate all materials, cover table, set out art smocks. Pour small amount of tempera into pie pan to cover bottom. Set out large pieces of paper in front of each chair at art table. Place two to three small cars/trucks in each tempera-filled pie pan.

Teaching Strategies

Children use cars/trucks to drive across and paint their paper. Teacher can facilitate discussion of different tracks. Hang tire track artwork to dry—Teacher may write "Tire Track Art" to inform parents.

Possible Outcomes

Concepts:
There are different ways to paint. Car tires can make tracks.

Skills
Creativity, aesthetic pleasure, small motor development

Vocabulary
Tire, tracks, art, imprints

Date

Standards Met

Comments and Reflection

CURRICULUM ACTIVITY GUIDE 47 — Coloring to Music

Goal: To give children the opportunity to experience music combined with art

Curriculum Area	Developmental Focus	Location/Interest Center
Music and Rhythm	Affective—Social	Inside Art

Participants	Time	Age Range
1 to 4 children	5 to 10 minutes	4 to 5 years old

Materials

Butcher paper to cover table (round is preferable), felt pens/markers, DVDs of instrumental music with varying tempo/rhythms, DVD player

Preparation/Setup

Cover table with paper and set out markers in center—use no chairs. Set up DVD and DVD player nearby.

Teaching Strategies

Teacher turns on music, invites children draw to the rhythm. Children freely walk around table, drawing to the music. Teacher can facilitate discussion of tempo—fast/slow, etc. Group art project can be displayed for all to enjoy.

Possible Outcomes

Concepts:
Music has different tempos. Tempos change, and change makes me feel different. I can draw with the music's rhythm and tempo.

Skills
Music appreciation, aesthetic enjoyment, social interaction

Vocabulary
Music, art, tempo, rhythm

Date

Standards Met

Comments and Reflection

CURRICULUM ACTIVITY GUIDE 48 — Hopping Like a Popcorn Kernel

Goal: To give children the opportunity to pretend to be popcorn

Curriculum Area	Developmental Focus	Location/Interest Center
Creative Dramatics	Affective—Social	Inside Circle

Participants	Time	Age Range
5 to 8 children	10 to 20 minutes	Appropriate for all ages

Materials

Air popcorn popper, popcorn kernels, clean white sheet, carpets for group time

Preparation/Setup

Set up area for group time. Locate popcorn popper, popcorn, take to group time. Locate sheet.

Teaching Strategies

Teacher readies children for group time with songs, fingerplays, etc. Teacher introduces popcorn popper—asks the children what they think will happen. Teacher spreads out sheet, discusses that the popper's hot and what to expect, talks about safety, staying on the edge of the sheet, waiting until popcorn is cooled off before eating. Children observe and taste cooled popcorn, discussing the experience. Sheet is put away, and children pretend to be small and pop like popcorn kernels.

Possible Outcomes

Concepts
Popcorn pops open from the kernel. Popcorn makes a sound when it pops open. Popcorn has a distinct smell. Children can pretend to pop like popping popcorn.

Skills
Sensory experience, role-playing opportunity, social interaction

Vocabulary
Popcorn, kernel, pop, popper, hop

Date

Standards Met

Comments and Reflection

To Access Downloadable Versions of the Curriculum Activity Guides Log on to www.cengagebrain.com

CURRICULUM ACTIVITY GUIDE 49	Oatmeal Box Drums

Goal: To give children the opportunity to beat a rhythm on a drum

Curriculum Area	Developmental Focus	Location/Interest Center
Music and Rhythm	Physical—Large Motor	Outside Large Motor
Participants	Time	Age Range
1 to 4 children	10 to 20 minutes	Appropriate for all ages

Materials

Oatmeal boxes (children can pre-decorate with paint, markers), instrumental DVD and DVD player

Preparation/Setup

Set up an area outside for four children to experience drums. Locate an appropriate DVD with rhythmic tempo.

Teaching Strategies

Teacher invites children to experiment with "drums." Teacher facilitates the children's experience by joining and modeling. Teacher can vary the instrumental selection (DVDs) to provide different tempos.

Possible Outcomes

Concepts
I can beat a drum. Music has a rhythm. I can match my drum sound with the music tempo.

Skills
Following directions, music appreciation

Vocabulary
Drum, beat, rhythm, tempo

Date

Standards Met

Comments and Reflection

CURRICULUM ACTIVITY GUIDE 50	Comparing Children's Illustrators

Goal: To give children the opportunity to examine and compare illustrators

Curriculum Area	Developmental Focus	Location/Interest Center
Art	Affective—Aesthetic	Inside Circle
Participants	Time	Age Range
5 to 8 children	10 to 20 minutes	3 to 5 years old

Materials

A variety of children's books; including at least two that include illustrations by the same illustrator; small carpet squares for group time.

Preparation/Setup

Locate and familiarize yourself with books. Set up carpets for group time.

Teaching Strategies

Teacher settles down children at group time with songs and fingerplay(s). Teacher discusses illustrations and shows books. Teacher discusses different mediums used by illustrators. Teacher guides children to examine and compare the work of book illustrations. Optional: Set up art activity to include art medium used by illustrations of books reviewed.

Possible Outcomes

Concepts
Illustrators are artists. Artists use different mediums. Pictures help tell the story.

Skills
Aesthetic development, art appreciation, differentiation

Vocabulary
Artist, illustrator, paint, draw

Date

Standards Met

Comments and Reflection

To Access Downloadable Versions of the Curriculum Activity Guides Log on to www.cengagebrain.com

Glossary

A

activity. Enriching experience planned and offered for children in an early childhood setting.

activity goal. Statement that describes the purpose of an activity. The goal describes the information that the teachers would like the children to experience.

aesthetic development. Developing awareness and responsiveness to beauty in nature and surroundings.

affective development. Growth and changes in young children's social and emotional behaviors.

age-appropriate. Experiences in early childhood settings that are suitable for the participating children.

age range. Chronological age span of the children as a reference for their participation in the activities that are planned.

art. Curriculum area encouraging relaxation, exploration, and aesthetic pleasure with varied experiences ranging from art appreciation to painting and molding.

assessment. Ongoing observation and documentation of children. Assessment provides information about the children's needs and interests while contributing to curriculum planning decisions.

assessment methods. Data about children collected informally (notes, conversation, participation) and formally (checklists, logs, time sampling).

authentic inclusion. Activities fully integrated throughout the curriculum that respect and value the children's cultures, families, languages, and abilities.

B

best practices. Teaching strategies, experiences, and settings suitable to meet the developmental age, individual, cultural, and linguistic needs of the young children participating in an early childhood program.

C

child advocacy. Promotion of positive issues affecting young children and their well-being, education, and families.

child-initiated. Curriculum that is focused on meeting the needs of young children by encouraging their active learning with opportunities for choices within a planned environment.

clustering. Activities for young children organized to pattern the experiences to progress from the simple to the more complex.

cognitive. Relates to knowledge and how knowledge is acquired. Cognitive is identified as one of the three developmental focus areas.

cognitive development. Growth of knowledge and understanding, including mental and intellectual abilities. Language acquisition is categorized with cognitive development.

communication. Ability to relate feelings and ideas. Communication and Literacy form a curriculum area for young children.

concepts. Single ideas about an object or subject written and spoken simply for a child's understanding. One of the elements of a Curriculum Activity Guide.

cooking. Part of the curriculum area of Nutrition that helps children to appreciate different foods and experience pleasure in food preparation.

constructivism. Approach that promotes learning that encourages children to create and discover by actively interacting with the environment.

creative dramatics. Adapted as a general term to organize four categories of activities that contribute to affective and aesthetic development of young children: dramatic play, guided drama, puppetry, and sociodramatics.

creativity. Process of developing and expressing abilities such as originality, imagination with encouragement; appreciation of new views, ways, and ideas.

culturally and linguistically appropriate. Programs and practices that are sensitive and responsive to each child's family culture and languages; experiences that would build children's confidence and tolerance for diversity.

curiosity. Self-motivated interest and inquiry about surroundings, people, and events. Teachers encourage natural curiosity of young children within flexible settings.

curricular guideline. Idea or plan that defines an intended direction that a program expects to provide for the children, staff, and parents. Educational beliefs, commitment to children, and goals of a center influence guidelines.

curriculum. Broadly refers to all the school or program-related experiences that affect the children. Specifically, the organized experiences and activities planned to meet the children's developmental needs and interests.

Curriculum Activity Guide. Form, or template, to document activities and guide the direction of experiences in a program of care and learning for young children.

curriculum area. Subject or content area that organizes experiences by discipline including art, language, mathematics, music, physical education, science, and social studies.

curriculum plan. Written guide documenting the proposed long and short-term plans for experiences and activities designed to meet the needs and interests of the enrolled children.

curriculum resources. Materials, supplies, and volunteer time provided by family and community members; relate to cultural enrichment, occupational information, equipment, and special events offered to enhance the learning opportunities for the children.

daily schedule. Framework of suggested time and activities that includes free-choice blocks of time, transition, and routines. Provides a guide, carries out program goals, and meets children's needs.

development. Individualized sequence of changes and patterns of growth within physical, affective (social understanding) and aesthetic, and cognitive areas.

developmental age. Each child's individual patterns of growth influenced by their unique heredity and life experiences.

developmentally appropriate practices (DAP). Activities designed to respond to the unique needs and interests of the enrolled children, emphasizing each child's age, developmental level, interests and needs.

developmental focus approach. Approach to curriculum planning emphasizing the development of the whole child with consideration of each one's developing skills.

developmental focus areas. Areas of growth and behavior categorized by professionals for the study and understanding of children; referenced in this book as three domains: physical, affective (social and emotional understanding) and aesthetic, and cognitive.

discovery. Occurrence of a behavior resulting from a child's natural interest to try out unstructured and flexible materials; allows the child to arrive at a new level of understanding.

dramatic play. Voluntarily observing, participating, and playing in creative activity using imaginary objects and imitating people and surroundings.

early childhood education. Study and instruction of young children from infancy though the primary grades; includes programs, experiences, and services and strategies to facilitate their development.

elements. Parts of an activity planned for young children; elements include title, goal, materials, standards, etc.

emergent. Curriculum offering activities and experiences that naturally flow from the children's interests and needs.

emotional development. Growth and expression of feelings, self-worth, and preferences influenced by heredity, culture, language, region, and era.

environment. Surroundings, conditions, and locations where care and learning for young children may take place; the indoor and outdoor spaces.

equity. Fair access to programs, facilities, and educational opportunities with respect to diversity and differences.

expectation. Anticipated behavior of children within an age range.

experiences. Planned and unplanned developmentally appropriate activities creating the core of the curriculum and meeting program goals.

exploration. Curiosity and self-motivated activity to investigate an object or idea; leads to discovery and learning.

extended-day activities. Before-and after-school programs offered for primary and school-age children.

families as resources. Family members contribute their time and input to sharing their cultures, hobbies, and occupations; enriches the curriculum learning experiences.

fundamentals. Basic ideas that organize curriculum concepts throughout this book; offer a general guide and a conceptual framework for work with children.

group time. Teacher-guided activity bringing children together in circle time with a specific goal, such as introduction of a new idea or to enjoy social interaction.

guidelines. Beliefs and values of the program staff that influence everyday interaction with children, daily experiences, and the curriculum.

guided drama. Pantomime or acting out of a poem, short story, or rhyme.

harmony. Peaceful understanding and appreciation of differences and diversity.

health. Wellness, physical well-being, and fitness.

healthy habits. Behaviors and actions that contribute to well-being and fitness.

I

inclusive.   Actions and Programs for young children that promote non-bias behaviors with experiences and opportunities for children with different abilities and from diverse cultural backgrounds.

inclusive settings.   Environments prepared to respond to the great diversity of children, cultures, languages, and abilities.

individually appropriate.   Experiences suitable for a child's ability, temperament, patterns of growth, family culture, and current needs and interests.

individualizing curriculum.   Process of adapting experiences to the changing needs and interests of a child as growth and behavior change.

indoor places.   Flexible child-centered space and equipment arranged indoors.

integrated.   Curriculum that offers activities and experiences that are balanced among the developmental focus areas.

integrating activities.   Balancing and blending experiences and activities for children among the developmental focus areas and across the curriculum areas.

intentional teaching.   Teaching with a purpose towards developmentally appropriate practice and providing rationale about the purpose of experiences and activities.

interactive questioning.   Teacher's behavior that encourages and expands children's language through appropriate and sensitive questions, body movements, and verbal responses.

interest centers.   Delineated areas for specialized activity within an indoor or outdoor environment.

Interest Center Guide.   A method of documenting the experiences within an interest center.

L

language.   Communication, including gestures, movements, and words; tied to thinking, beliefs, and emotions.

language development.   Acquisition of communication skills; influences thinking, a cognitive achievement.

large movement.   Activity or motion propelled by the gross (large) body muscles.

learning centers.   Designated areas of activity; also referred to as interest centers.

literacy.   Reading and writing skills; early exposure to print and word awareness; benefits young children when experiences are appropriate and positive.

location/interest center.   Area for a specific activity; one of the elements listed on the Curriculum Activity Guide.

locomotor.   Moving oneself from one location to another.

M

manipulative.   Material or an object encouraging activity and small motor development; a puzzle is a manipulative.

materials.   Supplies needed to prepare curriculum activities, or those used by the children during curriculum experiences.

mathematics.   Curriculum area of learning about numbers, size, sequence, quantity, etc.; encourages exploration and discovery about arranging, comparing, ordering, and measuring.

Montessori Method.   Environments typically meeting the individual needs of young children; appreciation for children's sensitive periods of development; planned environment emphasizes learning through senses.

movement.   Use of muscles to allow a range of small or large activity to change the position or place of the body or body parts; also refers to a curriculum area.

movement and perceptual motor development. Acquisition of specific motor skills through active participation in physical activity encouraging coordination, balance, and control of large and small muscles; promotes sensorial and discriminating skills.

movement skills.   Sequential development of large and small muscles allowing capabilities in walking, running, climbing (large motor), and holding, pouring, and reaching (small motor).

multi-age grouping.   Grouping or placement of children of different ages in settings where they participate for either partial or full-day scheduling in the same classroom and area.

multiple intelligences theory.   Howard Gardner's theory identifying seven-plus different capacities of intelligence. Appropriate experiences encourage children to think about objects and ideas in many different ways.

music and rhythm skills.   Participation and appreciation of songs, instruments, rhymes, fingerplays, and dancing.

N

non-bias curriculum.   Program and experiences promoting positive understanding of diversity, cultures, languages, genders, differing abilities, faiths, and economic statuses.

nutrition.   Healthy awareness of food and meal preparation. A component of the curriculum area of Health, Safety, and Nutrition; emphasizes healthy living habits and wellness behaviors.

nutritional awareness.   Education outlining activities that help children enjoy food preparation and mealtime while emphasizing lifelong healthy habits.

O

observe/review/plan. Individualizing curriculum with collection of data about each child; identifying behavioral changes and preparing activities and experiences to meet the identified needs.

outdoor places. Natural surroundings and places for activity providing opportunities for learning; especially accommodating for large movement and gardening.

P

participants. One of the elements of an activity listed on a Curriculum Activity Guide; provides the recommended number of children to engage in an activity.

physical development. Dimension of growth that relates to basic physiological changes and growth.

play. Spontaneous, unrestricted, and joyful response to the environment; helps children learn about their world, acquire competencies, and resolve challenges and conflict.

possible outcomes. Description of the behavior that a child may be expected to achieve after participating in the specific activity; includes concepts, skills, and vocabulary as Curriculum Activity Guide elements.

preparation/setup. Arranging materials needed for an activity; includes the suggested steps and is an element on the Curriculum Activity Guide.

professional accountability. Continuous professional development experiences to ensure that program goals support early childhood education principles and maintain balance of activities to meet the needs of enrolled children.

professional commitment. Perception and dedication to career, including responsibility to children and families, and dedication to continued learning.

professional growth. Acquiring new information related to child development, curriculum, and research; collaborating with professional colleagues.

professional preparation. Education, training, and experiences in an occupational field. Early childhood education preparation includes experience, training, and learning about child development, teaching and curriculum, health and safety, guidance, family relationships, diversity, and program management.

project approach. Curriculum that evolves around a theme or topic, such as gardening, and integrates learning experiences across content areas over a period of time.

puppetry. Use of a figure resembling a person or animal used by teachers to present new ideas, encourage creativity, explore emotions, and enjoy movement.

R

reflective practice. Reviewing experiences and activities planned and presented to children to determine if, how, and why their needs are being met and identifying necessary modifications to curriculum and teaching strategies.

S

safety. Component of the curriculum area of Health, Safety, and Nutrition; encourages safe practices and accident prevention.

science. Information about the world divided into two fields (biological and physical); includes study about growing and living elements and causes and effects of matter, energy, and space.

sensorial. Discovery and exploration of materials using one's senses in concrete experiences. Sensory education is a major aspect of the Montessori Method.

settings. Surroundings, conditions, and locations where care and education of children take place; includes the buildings and play spaces.

shelving. Flexible, low storage throughout indoor and outdoor spaces; can store selected curriculum materials accessible to children.

skills. Developed abilities in body movement, thinking, and social and emotional behaviors.

small motor abilities. Children's innate fine movement capacities that develop with maturation.

small movement. Pouring, placing, holding, stacking, reaching, and assembling; engages children's fine (small) muscles.

social development. Acquisition of skills that enable children to react and interact with others as they mature and begin to understand the point of view of others.

social understanding. Appropriately planned activities help children develop self-awareness and skills to react and interact positively with others.

sociodramatics. Children voluntarily engage in activity by pretending to be someone or something, while acquiring negotiation skills during interaction.

standards. Early learning guidelines; outline expectations for what preschool-age children should know or be able to do.

storage. Places to keep materials, supplies, and equipment that are essential to the operation of programs for young children.

T

teacher-guided. Activities and experiences that are facilitated by a teacher to introduce new ideas and materials and interact directly with children.

teaching strategies. Recommended actions for the teacher who is guiding an activity; may suggest sequence or procedures for guiding the child's participation; an element of the Curriculum Activity Guide.

team planning. Collaborative efforts among the staff working together to arrange and facilitate the curriculum and program.

technology. Tools such as computers, iPhones, and digital cameras that provide access to information and enable production of multimedia projects.

thematic approach. Curriculum activities organized around a theme, such as My Family; balances experiences and activities among the curriculum areas.

theme. Unit of study around a topic such as "pets"; sets a general framework allowing children to explore and enjoy theme-related experiences balanced among the curriculum areas.

theoretical perspectives. Ideology explaining and predicting behavior of children developed by educators and psychologists; includes behavioral, cognitive, developmental, ecological, maturational, and psychodynamic categories.

title. First element of the Curriculum Activity Guide naming and describing the activity.

type of program. Determines whether early childhood programs offer care and learning to infants and toddlers, preschoolers, or school-age children. Program categories include cooperative, employer-supported, child care, enrichment/ compensatory, family child care, preschool/ nursery, training/lab, and faith-based.

V

value of play. Benefits of active learning by doing, practicing, and pretending; play develops children's abilities in all developmental areas and enhances children's skills including discovery, communication, curiosity, commitment, self-acceptance, optimism, gaiety, cooperation, and emotional maturity.

vocabulary. Possible outcome listed on the Curriculum Activity Guide; words related to an activity to be used appropriately in conversation with the children participating in the activity.

W

webbing. Creating and recording the ideas suggested by children during "brainstorming" session; contributes to activity planning related to a project topic or theme.

whole child. Concept of supporting the development of each child in all areas of growth, including physical, affective (social and emotional) and aesthetic, cognitive, while respecting each one's individuality.

Index